THE NEW WAVE

THE NEW WAVE

Truffaut, Godard, Chabrol, Rohmer, Rivette

James Monaco

New York
OXFORD UNIVERSITY PRESS
1976

Library of Congress Catalogue Card Number: 75-38099

Printed in the United States of America

for my parents
a book about generations

PREFACE

What is "The New Wave"? Like most such critical labels it resists easy definition. Coined by Françoise Giroud in the pages of *L'Express* in 1958, it originally referred to a new, youthful spirit then making itself felt in French film. It quickly gained currency and became a versatile catchphrase applied not only to film, but to any cultural phenomenon that was seen to be new or rebellious or hip. Colloquially, "New Wave" soon degenerated into a synonym for "Avant Garde," although it had a connotation that was perhaps less stodgy.

For the purposes of this book, however, "New Wave" means simply "Truffaut, Godard, Chabrol, Rohmer, Rivette," five French filmmakers who, despite evident differences manifest in the more than one hundred films they have completed in the last twenty years, nevertheless share, I believe, a basic attitude towards the art of film which unites them as a group and separates them from the majority of their predecessors. Having shared apprenticeships as critics, all of them see film essentially as a phenomenon of intelligence. This is not to suggest that their films are devoid of feeling; on the contrary, they are often invested with profound emotional significance. But always we are led back to a basic structure of ideas. There is an underlying logic, no matter how passionately it is developed. Film is, for them, a fascinating way to discover the world and to develop an understanding of its politics, its psychology, its structure, its language.

As a result, the New Wave became an integral part of the intellectual structure of French life in the 1960s and 1970s. The urgent curiosity these five artists display is, I think, their main contribution to cinema, and I hope the pages that follow reflect that attitude faithfully. My aim has been not to judge the cinema of the New Wave but to participate in the vital dialogue the films invite. I hope the present effort communicates a sense of both the logic and the passion of the New Wave (what Godard called "Method and Sentiment") and that it gives some idea of the development of this significant dialectic.

Although Alain Resnais did not share the experience of *Cahiers du Cinéma* with Truffaut, Godard, Chabrol, Rohmer, and Rivette, an understanding of his separate but parallel development of many of the same concepts is important, and indeed he is often considered a New Wave director. An article on Resnais will be published elsewhere, as will a detailed filmography of the New Wave.

The English-language titles of the films are often different in Britain and the U.S. Wherever a title first appears, the American title is given first in parentheses, followed by the British title and any other variants. (It should be remembered also that these various English-language titles are not always direct translations from the French.) All English-language titles will be found in the index. All quotations of dialogue are from the soundtracks of the films themselves and all translations are my own, unless otherwise noted. In cases where it is clear that consecutive citations are from the same source, only the first has been footnoted. The illustrations are, in most cases, publicity stills. Although I have chosen those photographs which most closely approximate the actual shots of the film, there are a number of cases in which the angle or the framing is slightly off. In several instances, illustrations are actual frame enlargements, a fact which is always noted in the captions.

I owe a very real debt to a number of people who have helped in various ways. This book is, in a certain sense, a collaborative effort. I want first to thank my students at the New School for Social Research. My conversations with them in seminars devoted to the films of the New Wave were invaluable. I want also to thank Dean Allen Austill for affording me the opportunity to teach those courses and, especially, Wallis Osterholz of the Dean's Office for her stanch encouragement and vital support.

Bea Hermann of Audio-Brandon Films, Kent Carroll of Grove Press

Films, Ben Barenholtz of Libra Films and Dan Talbot and Jose Lopez of New Yorker Films kindly lent me prints and arranged screenings. Marion Billings, the French Film Office, Grove Press Films, *L'Avant-Scène du Cinéma*, Kent Paul of Janus Films, the Museum of Modern Art/Film Stills Archive, Sarah Risher of New Line Cinema, Sandra Kohlenberg of New Yorker Films, and the New York Film Festival were all helpful in providing stills used for illustration. Charles Silver of the Museum of Modern Art Study Center provided facilities for the selection of frames and Harvey Zucker made the enlargements.

Sreekumar Menon, Catherine Plumb, Paul Hillery, Chuck Kleinhans, and Edward Perry each read sections of the manuscript. Their suggestions and corrections were both welcome and valuable. I'm also grateful to Philip Rosenberg not only for his comments on the manuscript but also for twelve years of valued conversation.

Pamela Cleveland, Nelly Dosogne of the French Cultural Services, Penelope Houston, Tom Milne, David Newman, Carol Platt, Richard Roud, and Deborah Vandermar all provided essential facts which I was unable to discover myself. Catherine Verret of the French Film Office was also extraordinarily helpful in this respect. I also owe her sincere thanks for her encouragement.

I have been particularly fortunate at Oxford University Press. James Raimes helped develop an appropriate structure for the book, supported the project fully, and gave freely of his time and energies. His judicious comments helped make *The New Wave* a better book than it might have been. Stephanie Golden hammered a complex manuscript into readable prose. Her insightful suggestions were most welcome. Dana Kasarsky designed the book with care. I should also like to thank my agent, Virginia Barber, without whose efforts the project never would have been realized.

Finally, I owe more than thanks to Susan Schenker who read and criticized the manuscript, who talked out difficulties with me, who supplied the first word, and who is responsible more than she knows for the publication of *The New Wave*.

This book is set in Palatino (10/13), a typeface created in 1948 by the noted designer Hermann Zapf and first published in the *Gutenberg Jahrbuch* of 1950. Classified as a Venetian/Roman face, Palatino, like many Zapf designs, is noted for its balance and readability. It is named after the famous sixteenth-century penman Johannes Baptista Palatinus, author of the influential *Libro nel qual s'insegna a scrivere* (Rome, 1540), the most widely used of all the sixteenth-century Italian copy-books. The display type is 30 pt. Optima. Composition and camera-work: University Graphics, Inc. Printing and binding: Halliday Lithograph Corp.

The photographs on pp. 110, 123, 134, 167, 195, 204, 208, 211, and 301 appear courtesy of *L'Avant-Scène du Cinéma.* The photographs on pp. 18 and 299 appear courtesy of The Museum of Modern Art/Film Stills Archive. Photographs on pp. 45, 58, 83, 111, 144, 147, 182, 271, 328, and 331 appear courtesy of the French Film Office (New York). Photographs on pp. 47, 48 and 51 appear courtesy of Janus Films, Inc. The enlargement on p. 183 was processed by Computer Opticals, Inc., New York.

New York City J. M.
December 1975

CONTENTS

THE NEW WAVE

1

INTRODUCTION
The Camera Writes

If ever a film were made about the early days of the New Wave* certainly the first scene would take place in the small screening room on the Avenue de Messine which housed the Cinémathèque Française in the late forties. The image is coarse-grained black and white. The standard Hollywood aspect ratio recalls the Warner Brothers "biopics" of the late thirties. There are only a handful of people in attendance for the program this raw October day—possibly a screening of a complete Louis Feuillade serial . . . or a collection of five or six eight-reelers from Monogram Pictures on loan from Prague, with Czech titles to translate the English. The audience has dispersed itself carefully throughout the fifty seats in the small room. In the front two rows are three young men, separated from each other by respectful distances of three or four seats. They are impatient for the film to begin.

Cut to a close-up of the boy seated to the left of the others. He is better dressed than they are; he wears tinted glasses, and he passes the dead time before the program starts scribbling furiously in a small notebook, which he then returns to the inside pocket of his suit jacket.

*Possible titles: *Les Quatre Cents Coups de cinéma; Loin de Hollywood; Jacques, Jean-Luc, et François vont en bateau.*

He carries a bagful of books—ethnology textbooks, modern poetry, possibly a weighty volume on the history of art—and when he is not writing, he is reading.

Cut to the second boy, sitting in the second row center. He is a bit younger—barely seventeen—gawky, sallow, awkward in his movements, but with eyes that betray a maturity beyond his years. His ears stick out; he has an unruly shock of black hair; he looks a little like Jean-Pierre Léaud; he wears clothes a little too large for him and a worn leather jacket. He stares directly ahead at the blank screen as if he expected it to respond to his gaze.

Seated in front of him and a little to the right is the third boy, a little older than the other two, although he doesn't look it. He's not as street-wise as the second boy, nor as scholarly as the first. There is a hint of a rather foolish smile on his face, a provincial look that lets us know immediately that he is not from Paris. He passes the time trying to puzzle out a few words of Henry James in English. It does not seem possible, but he is even more gaunt, more diminutive than the others.

The lights dim, the film begins—and just at that moment two more young men rush in: one in his late teens, well-dressed, good-looking, but his face is rather puffy. We can tell already that he is developing a taste for good food and wine. He's clearly the kind of self-assured middle-class kid who plays practical jokes, cuts school, but still succeeds. The second latecomer is a shadowy figure indeed. He does not sit down, preferring to stand in the back aisle. About all we can tell about him is that—unlike the others—he is in his late twenties.

Through a series of long, slow lap-dissolves six or seven or eight hours pass. The lights come up. The two latecomers have left long ago. Only the three boys in the front rows are left. They leave, glassy-eyed, one by one, without speaking to each other. The next day they are back again in the same seats. Again—each of them shyer than the next—they do not speak. This goes on for several weeks until finally (possibly after a screening of Renoir's *Le Crime de M. Lange*) one of them ventures a word with the others. They adjourn to the room of the boy in the leather jacket, who makes a pot of tea, and discover while talking that all three of them desperately want to make movies.

According to Jacques Rivette, this is just about the way he did actually meet Jean-Luc Godard and François Truffaut in 1949 or 1950. Soon they all got to know the latecomers—Claude Chabrol and Eric Rohmer—as well. It was their shared passion for cinema that drew them together, although, as Rivette explains, "Each one had his special thing: Jean-Luc had his anguish, François had his writing, and so forth. . . ."[1] They would never again be so close as they were during the first few years of the fifties, but nevertheless the shared education they received in the Cinémathèque taught all five of them something: to make films which reveal a fascination with the question of how a story is told in the medium of film. Unlike most of the filmmakers who had come before them, they were imbued with the history of their art, and all the films they have made since the salad days of the Cinémathèque in one way or another reveal that shared concern.

But they looked forward as well as back. In 1948, the young novelist, critic, and filmmaker Alexandre Astruc had written a landmark essay in which he called for filmmakers to realize the full power of their art so that it could become "a means of writing just as flexible and subtle as written language." He labeled this approach to film "La Caméra-Stylo" (The Camera-Pen). Astruc was not the first theoretician of film to envision an art so powerful and flexible that it could actually challenge the 7000-year pre-eminence of written language—in the twenties critics Louis Delluc and Ricciotto Canudo had written eloquently about the potential of the new medium, and a decade before Astruc's manifesto Barbaro of the Centro Sperimentale had spoken in similar terms—but his essay touched a responsive chord and it was to become the declaration of independence for a "New Wave" in film.

> To come to the point [he wrote]: the cinema is quite simply becoming a means of expression, just as all the other arts have before it, and in particular painting and the novel. After having been successively a fairground attraction, an amusement analogous to boulevard theatre, or a means of preserving the images of an era, it is gradually becoming a language. By language, I mean a form in which and by which an artist can express his thoughts, however abstract they may be, or translate his obsessions exactly as he does in a contemporary essay or novel. That is why I would like to call this new age of cinema the age of *caméra-stylo*.[2]

It was ten years, however, before the filmmakers of the New Wave were to fulfill Astruc's dream and turn theory into practice. During the fifties they continued their education at the Cinémathèque and the film clubs, took jobs as assistant directors and publicity agents, and—most important—Truffaut, Godard, Chabrol, Rohmer, and Rivette all wrote for *Cahiers du Cinéma*, the militant journal for the new movement in film which André Bazin had founded in 1950 and which he edited until his death at the age of forty in 1958.

The "godfather" of the New Wave was Henri Langlois, founder of the Cinémathèque Française, this "dragon who guards our treasures,"[3] as Cocteau called him. It was Langlois who provided the materials with which the critics of *Cahiers du Cinéma* were to fashion a new esthetic. But the father of the New Wave was André Bazin. As editor of *Cahiers* he exerted a kind of moral force that existed separately from his own writings. For Truffaut, in particular, be became a surrogate father: "From that day in 1948 when he got me my first film job, working alongside him, I became his adopted son," Truffaut has written. "Thereafter, every pleasant thing that happened in my life I owed to him."[4]

More important, perhaps, for our purposes was Bazin's theoretical influence on these filmmaker/critics. Like the best critics in any field, Bazin studied his subject in the broadest of contexts. Film was never for him simply an art or a language, no matter how beautiful or flexible, existing in splendid isolation, but always an active factor in political, philosophical, even religious equations. The breadth and relevance of his approach would later be mirrored in the films of the New Wave. Yet Bazin's commentaries on the specific nature of the medium, the *language* of film, were unmatched for their deep comprehension of the technology of the medium and the psychology which stems from it and, indeed, his work paved the way for the more acutely philosophical study of the phenomenon of film by semiologists like Christian Metz today.

Astruc had noted that "the fundamental problem of cinema is how to express thought. The creation of this language has preoccupied all the theoreticians and writers in the history of cinema."[5] Bazin was no exception. For him the evolution of the language of cinema was a progression away from the tricks of expressionism and montage and towards realism, mise-en-scène, and deep focus (which he saw in opposition to montage). He is, then, a "realist," but the word must be understood in the special way Bazin meant it: as more a matter of ethics and psychology than of esthetics. Like all of his criticism, his theory of mise-en-scène was grounded in an eloquent concern for the human relationship between artist and observer. For him, mise-en-scène and deep focus are not matters of pure style, but "a dialectical step forward in the history of film language," because:

> (1) . . . depth of focus brings the spectator in closer relation with the image . . . [and that implies]
> (2) . . . both a more active mental attitude on the part of the spectator and a more positive contribution on his part to the action in progress. . . .[6]

It is the vitality and honesty of the commitment between artist and observer that concerns Bazin, not vague, abstract esthetic dicta. His realism is a moral and ethical code which is deeply rooted in the psychology of the film medium. He found, in Jean Renoir and Roberto Rossellini, models for this moral realism of mise-en-scène and deep focus, and in such essays as "The Evolution of Film Language," "The Ontology of the Photographic Image," and "In Defense of Mixed Cinema," he began the job of describing the nature of cinema in dialectic and psychological terms which continues today.

Astruc sounded the call; Langlois provided the material; Bazin supplied the basic architectonics. In the pages of *Cahiers du Cinéma* in the 1950s, Truffaut, Godard, Chabrol, Rohmer, and Rivette argued out a new theory of film. It wasn't cool, logical work; it was rather passionate, organic—sometimes wild. It centered on the twin concepts of the *politique des auteurs* and film genres, and, even if Truffaut is usually given credit for having written the statement of the auteur theory, this critical system was nevertheless truly a collective work. Each of the filmmaker/critics worked from a different set of premises—their careers would diverge radically in the sixties—yet they drew from the material they shared (the experience of the Cinémathèque) conclusions which are surprisingly congruent.

The *politique des auteurs* and its accompanying genre theory are simple principles, but with complex reverberations. In 1957, Bazin restated the broad aims of the auteur theory this way:

> [It] consists, in short, of choosing the personal factor in artistic creation as a standard of reference, and then of assuming that it continues and even progresses from one film to the next.[7]

It is a simple idea; in literary theory it would be considered a truism. But it had a special value as a theory of film, just because that art—unlike literature—was still in its infancy and therefore bore a much more direct relationship to myth. It was most often considered a social rather than personal expression. The great Hollywood films of the thirties and forties were made in studio factories, after all. Bazin and his colleagues on *Cahiers* were obsessed with American film, and in this context the theory that a film always has one prime author (and that that author *should* be the director) seemed quite perverse. European films of the early decades of sound may have been identifiable by author (important artists like the poet Cocteau and Jean Renoir, the son of the painter, had chosen film as a natural means of expression), but American films were usually identified with the factories (Warners, Paramount, MGM) that produced them.

In order to judge the "personal factor," then, it was necessary to discuss the work of the auteur in context, and this was the film's genre: that set of conventions and expectations which it shared with other films of its kind—Westerns, Gangster films, Films Noirs. The auteur "standard of reference" was the vertical axis against which a film was plotted; the horizontal axis was the genre.*

Now, there are two corollaries of the auteur theory which have important ramifications for the films these young critics eventually made. First, it insists on a *personal* relationship between filmmaker and film viewer. Movies must no longer be alienated products which are consumed by mass audiences; they are now intimate conversations between the people behind the camera and the people in front of the screen. It is immediately clear that the ethics of the *politique des auteurs* owed a great debt to Bazinian moral realism. Second, auteurism leads naturally to a dialectical view of the film process. A movie becomes the sum of a whole set of oppositions: between auteur and genre; between director and audience; between critic and film; between theory and practice; or between "Method and Sentiment," in Godard's words. It is no longer a product to be consumed but a process to become engaged in. What else could we expect from a group of film*goers* who dearly wanted to become film*makers?* It was natural for them to connect the two activities.

These important corollaries of the auteur theory became controlling factors when the critics turned to filmmaking. But they weren't necessarily clearly expressed in the essays they wrote as young men. Often the practice of the theory was muddled, impetuous. We must raise other significant objections to auteur theory, as well. It often led to absurd conclusions in favor of directors who will remain forever minor artists. It was a righteous theory. It was also of very limited usefulness. It measured only one factor in the equation of the art of film to the exclusion of others, equally important. Yet the auteur theory was a necessary stage of the development of these filmmakers' thought.

Theory was a felt necessity for the critic/filmmakers of the New Wave. If any single characteristic unites these disparate artists it is their concern with making sense of the history of film by understanding how film (and other arts) relates to its "raw material," life: how do we use film, how does it change us, how does it help to explain our existence, how does it function as a language? These questions are raised in their early critical essays; they are answered, in part, in their films.

At about the same time that Alexandre Astruc wrote his essay on the Caméra-Stylo, Roland Barthes, considered by many to be France's most

*Parallel with the *Cahiers* critics' preoccupation with genre and auteur and sometimes overlapping with it is the development of what, for want of a better phrase, we might call the *nouveau roman* film by Alain Resnais and those novelists who wrote screenplays for him (and later turned to directing themselves)—notably Alain Robbe-Grillet and Marguerite Duras.

brilliant contemporary literary critic, was beginning to work out a theory of literature which is not dissimilar to the New Wave vision of film. Barthes suggests a subtle and variegated critical theory that places emphasis not on the historical dimension of literature (what he calls its "language"), nor on the personal dimension (the "style") but on a third thing, the product of the two—what Barthes calls *écriture* ("a mode of writing"). "A language and style are blind forces," he wrote,

> a mode of writing [*écriture*] is an act of historical solidarity. A language and style are objects; a mode of writing is a function: it is the relationship between creation and society, the literary language transformed by its social finality, form considered as a human intention and thus linked to the great crises of History.[8]

There is a difficult density in Barthes's often poetic prose, but notice the presence in this passage of two ideas that were also of vital importance to André Bazin and the *Cahiers* critics: first, the dialectical relationship between the history of the art and the artist's personal action (respectively, "language" and "style" for Barthes, "genre" and the auteur theory for Bazin). Second, that these two forces interact to create a third thing, *écriture*.

I think that this is a useful way to approach the cinema of the New Wave: as a tertium quid—a cinematic *écriture* that combines "language" and "style" and is "written" with a Caméra-Stylo, fulfilling Astruc's wishes and solving Barthes's theorem. The New Wave filmmakers were all—in different but parallel ways—involved in working out the relationship between the historical dimension and the personal dimension. It is this fascination with the forms and structures of the film medium as they used it that sets their films apart from those that preceded them and marks a turning point in film history. Partly this is the result of their shared heritage as critics. More important, however, it is generally a matter of their common experience as French intellectuals in the fifties and sixties. While Barthes was developing a semiology of literature in the late forties and early fifties, Jean-Luc Godard, a sallow teenager, was studying ethnology at the Sorbonne and becoming fascinated with the ideas of linguists like Saussure and Parain. A few years later the five *Cahiers* critics were deeply involved in developing what we might call a "structural anthropology" of film. Like structural ethnographers comparing and analyzing numberless myths in order to divine a "deep structure" that would unite them, the critics of *Cahiers du Cinéma* made forays into the profuse jungle of film history at the Cinémathèque and returned with an understanding of the "deep structure" of cinema. This they expressed in terms of auteurs and genres.

What could possibly connect a comedy like *Twentieth Century* with a Film Noir detective story like *The Big Sleep* or a Western like *Hatari?* One deep structure that the films shared was Howard Hawks, their auteur. Strip off the conventions of the genre in each case and you revealed a core of significance which belonged wholly and exclusively to the director. This was more than a matter of stylistic tics; what counted was the dialectical relationship between author and genre, between "style" and "language" in Barthes's terms.

The *Cahiers* critics never expressed themselves in quite these terms in the fifties. But it is clear they were thinking along these lines. Ironically, their most important characteristic may be not that they were cinéphiles—film buffs—but rather that they were also steeped in the literary and philosophical culture of their time. This is plainly evident with a director like Rohmer, whose films draw on a thorough acquaintance with the French intellectual traditions of three centuries. It is also true of Rivette, whose cinema paradoxically reveals a passionate interest in theatre. Meanwhile, Godard as film "essayist" and Truffaut as film "novelist" both fulfill Astruc's hope for a cinema as flexible and eloquent as literature. If Jean Renoir is a prime source for Truffaut, so is Balzac; and Godard evinces a fascination with the medium of print which easily equals and sometimes surpasses his interest in film.

All five directors also show an easy familiarity with the traditions of the visual arts. Godard quotes painters in his films as often as philosophers. Chabrol's magnificent sense of landscape, Truffaut's impressionistic pleasure in the varieties of light of the city's times and places, and Rohmer's strict observance of the qualities and evocative nature of his carefully chosen locales also evince an assured command of the tropes of the visual arts.

So the New Wave filmmakers brought a varied cultural background to their work, as well as sophisticated theories of film. Yet the phenomenon of the New Wave would still not have been possible were it not for a concurrent revolution in the technology of film. It was, after all, their technical facility with the "Caméra-Stylo," the instrument of their art, that made it possible for them to turn from the practice of theory in the fifties to theory in practice in the sixties and seventies. Fast filmstocks, lightweight cameras, new lighting equipment, and the liberation from the Hollywood set that all this implied, made the Caméra-Stylo a reality in the late fifties and early sixties not only in France but elsewhere as well. The movement towards a freer cinema was building in Sweden (Bergman), in Italy (Fellini and Antonioni), in England (where the Angry Young Men of the theatre were moving into film and the "Free

Cinema" movement was bearing fruit), and even in the U.S., where, with the benefit of hindsight, we can descry the first faint beginnings of the post-Hollywood cinema.

The *annus mirabilis* was 1959 (give or take six months) during which Chabrol, Truffaut, Godard, Rivette, Rohmer, Resnais, Lelouch, Hanoun, and Demy all made their first films. But at the same time came Antonioni's *L'Avventura,* Fellini's *La Dolce Vita,* Bergman's *Virgin Spring,* and even John Cassavetes's *Shadows*—all of which pointed in new directions. There quickly followed the Woodfall films in England and, within a few years, the Czech renaissance. It was truly a period of extraordinary creativity. The French filmmakers were not alone, but they led the way. It was to France that young filmmakers—especially in the Third World—turned in the sixties. After the New Wave came new cinemas in many other countries: *le cinéma nouveau* in Quebec, *Cinema novo* in Brazil, *das Neue Kino* in West Germany; all paid allegiance to their French predecessors—especially to Jean-Luc Godard.

The metaphor of the "New Wave," then, was surprisingly apt: the wave had been building for a long time before it burst on cinematic shores. It was a result of the mutual reinforcement of a variety of wavelets—technological, theoretical, philosophical, critical—and its reverberations are still being felt. The New Wave has left us with a cinema forever changed, enlarged, more powerful, more eloquent, more acute.

Those five young men who first met in the darkened Cinémathèque screening room on the Avenue de Messine nearly thirty years ago were all in one way or another obsessed with the question of how a story is told in the medium of film. They not only wanted to make films, they wanted to understand how they were made. For Godard, this question eventually became a rigorous ethical problem with distinct political implications. Truffaut, more practical than the others, and perhaps more cynical, considering the painful experiences of his childhood, interested himself almost exclusively in the forms of cinema that already existed, the genres. Rohmer turned to a comparison of film with literature; Rivette to a contrast of film with theatre. Chabrol, a little perversely, purposely limited his palette to one genre, even as had his idols of an earlier generation. None of them, I'm sure, suspected at the time not only that they would achieve their personal goals, but that they would reach out past the boundaries of art into life.

In the early winter of 1968, André Malraux, Minister of Culture in the De Gaulle government, came to the decision that Henri Langlois was no longer satisfactorily performing his duties as head of the Cinémathèque

Française. He decided to replace him. Led by Godard, Truffaut, and their colleagues, the French film community took to the streets in support of the orotund, genial packrat. Not a few historical commentators regard those February demonstrations as the first manifestation of the spirit that was to bloom in May and June of that year. A political revolution had begun with an argument over film!

That is another reason why the New Wave is important.

2

TRUFFAUT
The Antoine Doinel Cycle

By the time he was twenty-six years old François Truffaut had developed a not undeserved reputation as an uncompromising, thorough, and sometimes vicious film critic. He was described in *L'Express* as "a hateful *enfant terrible* who put his foot in his mouth with unbearable self-conceit." Claude Autant-Lara had tagged him the "young hoodlum of journalism." (To which Truffaut replied: "'Young Hoodlum' is an outdated expression that leads straight to the Legion of Honor and a house in the country.")[1] In 1958, after railing for years against the very idea of film festivals, Truffaut was finally banned from the Cannes Festival.

A year later he returned, not as critic but as filmmaker. His first feature, *Les Quatre Cents Coups (The 400 Blows),* had been chosen as the official French entry. Truffaut was chosen Best Director. While *Les Quatre Cents Coups* was not the first of the New Wave films, its instant critical and commercial success not only afforded Truffaut considerable artistic independence right from the beginning of his career, but also made it much easier for other *Cahiers* critics turned filmmakers to finance their own projects; at least a modicum of success for the new movement in film was assured. *Hiroshima mon amour* was released the same year (and, incidentally, beat out *Les Quatre Cents Coups* by one vote in the *Conseil des dix* ratings in *Cahiers du Cinéma* in July 1959). With Truffaut's sponsorship Godard was able to complete his first feature, *A bout de souffle,* soon after. Chabrol had already finished his second film, *Les Cousins,* and was busy producing Rohmer's first, *Le Signe du lion.* Jacques Rivette, meanwhile, was still at work on *Paris nous appartient,* shooting when he could, with leftover bits and pieces of film stock; it would take him two years to complete.

For Truffaut, the challenge to graduate from critic to filmmaker was put almost mythically. In 1957 he married Madeleine Morgenstern, the daughter of a well-known film distributor whose films Truffaut often reviewed scathingly—even after the marriage. Eventually, father-in-law Morgenstern put it bluntly to his brash son-in-law: "If you know so much, why don't you make a film?" The result was *Les Quatre Cents Coups,* which was made for less than $100,000, a third contributed by Morgenstern, a third the proceeds from government subsidies for shorts Truffaut had done, and a third raised from friends.

Les Quatre Cents Coups is, above all, a film about childhood, a subject which has continued to fascinate Truffaut and which is part of a worthy French tradition stretching from Jean Vigo's work in the thirties, through Melville and Cocteau's *Les Enfants terribles* (1949) and *Les Quatre Cents Coups,* to Maurice Pialat's fine *L'Enfance nue* (1968) and Truffaut's own *L'Enfant sauvage* (1970). It is a subject about which Truffaut has evidently thought long and hard.

While it is true that our main interest in *Les Quatre Cents Coups* and the succeeding Doinel films has to do with their value as spiritual autobiography, they also bear considerable factual resemblance to Truffaut's life, at least through the middle of *Baisers volés.* Born in Paris on 6 February 1932, Truffaut was immediately handed over to a wet nurse and then sent to live with his grandmother until he was eight. When she died, his parents took him back reluctantly. "They weren't bad people," he says, "just nervous and busy." His experiences at school closely paralleled those of Antoine Doinel. He played hooky often, with his friend Robert Lachenay (now a film critic), offering excuses as outlandish as Antoine's. At the age of eleven he ran away from home and slept in bomb shelters, stealing brass doorknobs and selling them to survive.

> My father found me, put me back in school, and told the school authorities everything I'd done. I was a black sheep. Everything I did was frowned upon, so I didn't go back. I used to go to the municipal library and devour Balzac.[2]

At the age of fourteen Truffaut was pretty much on his own, holding down for varying periods of time jobs as messenger, shop assistant, storekeeper, clerk, and welder in a factory. He lived with Lachenay; together they started a neighborhood film club called "The Film Addicts" with a 16 mm print of *Metropolis* which they had managed to acquire.

But the Film Addicts screenings conflicted with those of another ciné-club so no one came. Truffaut went to visit the director of the other club and ask him to change the days of his screenings. That is how he met André Bazin. A week later his father traced him through the Film Addicts announcements and turned him over to the police. Truffaut was sent to Villejuif, which he describes as "half an insane asylum and half a house of correction." Bazin went to much trouble to get him out, and Truffaut's parents "rather easily gave up the rights that, by law, they had over me."[3]

Working at a succession of jobs, Truffaut became an habitué of the Club de Faubourg where, when there were lectures on movies, he "would kick up a row. People used to laugh at how indignant I got." Eventually he fell in love with a girl who sold yard goods in a shop with her mother. He moved into a hotel opposite the shop and began spying on her every night, "but after awhile I got tired of seeing her go to the movies with other guys, so I enlisted in the army."[4]

He fared even less well in the army than he had in civilian life and went AWOL on leave shortly before his unit was to be dispatched to Indochina. He was ashamed to let Bazin know where he was, but:

> One night I happened to meet Chris Marker in a cafe. He was very surprised and said to me: "I thought you were in Indochina." So I told him the whole story. He telephoned Resnais and the two of them sent me off to Bazin's place in Bry-sur-Marne. Bazin persuaded me to turn myself in and go on sick call.

After another attempted escape Truffaut finally was let out for "instability of character."[5] Here the parallel with the Doinel films stops. Antoine has no Bazin and has to make it, slowly, on his own, whereas André Bazin immediately gave Truffaut (then twenty) the chance to write for *Cahiers du Cinéma.* He produced a major piece which led quickly to a job with *Arts,* and he wrote constantly and successfully for the two magazines until shortly after the release of *Les Quatre Cents Coups.*

Even if we disregard the natural tendency for a beginning artist to turn to autobiographical sources, the childhood world of *Les Quatre Cents*

Coups is no surprise. Truffaut has expressed himself often and at length on the subject:

> Even as a child, I loved children. I have very strong ideas about the world they inhabit. Morally, the child is like a wolf [this many years before *L'Enfant sauvage*]—outside society. In the early life of a child, there is no notion of accident—merely of *délits*—while in the world of the adult everything is allowed.[6]

It is this deeply rooted existential sense of responsibility—the idea that there are no accidents—that makes the childhood world so fascinating for Truffaut and that gives *Les Quatre Cents Coups* its special tension. This tension appears in most of the films that follow, but it is clearest and strongest in this first film, which climaxed a period during which Truffaut himself had artistically "fait les quatre cents coups" (raised hell).

Writing about James Dean in 1956, Truffaut had characterized adolescence as

> modesty of feeling, continual fantasy life, moral purity without relation to everyday morality but all the more rigorous, eternal adolescent love of tests and trials, intoxication, pride, and regret at feeling oneself "outside" society, refusal of and desire to become integrated—and, finally, acceptance—or refusal—of the world as it is.[7]

The parallels with the filmmaker's life Truffaut has led since are evident. The passage nicely describes Truffaut's most important short film, "Les Mistons" ("The Brats"), made in 1958, which is a sketch of the world he was to delineate more precisely in *Les Quatre Cents Coups* a year later.

"Les Mistons," based on a short story by Maurice Pons, is a twenty-five-minute essay on adolescent love. Seen from the point of view of a group of young boys, the film gives us glimpses of what seems an idyllic relationship between Bernadette (Bernadette Lafont) and Gérard (Gérard Blain). The narrator explains that "a virginal heart obeys a childish logic. Too young to love Bernadette we decided to hate her." After a series of pranks, Gérard is seen leaving. Later, the boys discover he has been killed in a mountain-climbing accident. Their jealousy has been crudely satisfied, but months later as they play in the street, Bernadette passes without seeing them. The episode is over. The story is simple, fragile, and not nearly so important as what Truffaut does with it. What is interesting about the children of "Les Mistons" is their coldness, their objectivity. The film rises above the category of sentimental memory because Truffaut's children have a Darwinian talent for survival in a hostile world. They are not sweet, they are "rascals," "brats," and especially in "Les Mistons" they are rather cruel, albeit unthinkingly. This distancing is what enables Truffaut to handle children and adolescents—here and elsewhere—with so little condescension. He knows them as people and accepts them as such. "Most films about children," he has noted, "make the adult serious and the child frivolous. Quite the other way around."[8]

Cinematically, "Les Mistons" is an absorbing and proficient essay in movement. The freedom that the children envy in Bernadette and Gérard is sharply conveyed by the lyrical, swift tracking shots of the girl and her boyfriend on their bicycles as opposed to the stumblings of the children. There is a kind of jealousy here that Truffaut identifies with, for the boys, like Truffaut, are observers, cut off from action. They will grow, with time, into the quiet, relatively passive men of Truffaut's later films.

Truffaut had originally conceived of "Les Mistons" as part of a trilogy on the theme of childhood together with *Les Quatre Cents Coups* and another scenario which was never filmed. The trilogy was never completed (unless we can, after the fact, add *L'Enfant sauvage* to the previous two), but *Les Quatre Cents Coups* became the starting point for a new scheme, this time organized chronologically rather than thematically. As early as 1956 or 1957 Truffaut had completed a short treatment for a film that would show Antoine Doinel several years later, after a couple of reform schools and a stretch in the army. He attempted several times to shoot this scenario himself (first with Jean-Claude Brialy, then with Gérard Blain) but the project was never realized. The scenario later became the outline for Godard's *A bout de souffle;* the development of the story of Antoine Doinel, however, was to take a different track entirely.

After the success of *Les Quatre Cents Coups* Truffaut shied away from following it up with a sequel, lest his audience should think he was milking the subject. But in 1962 an offer to make a 30-minute segment of an anthology film on the subject of "young love" presented Truffaut with an unpretentious opportunity to continue the story of Antoine. This was "Antoine et Colette," from *L'Amour à vingt ans (Love at Twenty).* The Doinel tetralogy was completed with *Baisers volés* (*Stolen Kisses,* 1968) and *Domicile conjugal* (*Bed and Board,* 1970). The four films together form a remarkable work: an extended portrait of the *éducation sentimentale* of a young man portrayed by an actor who is growing,

Jean-Pierre Léaud in a famous publicity still from *Baisers volés,* standing in front of a photograph of himself as he appeared in "Antoine et Colette" standing in front of a painting of himself as he appeared in *Les Quatre Cents Coups.*

physically as well as emotionally and intellectually, during the course of twelve years of intermittent shooting.* Even during the shooting of *Les Quatre Cents Coups,* Truffaut says, his conception of Antoine Doinel began to modify considerably as he became familiar with the personality of Jean-Pierre Léaud. As the series progressed, Léaud became a significant collaborator, and the ultimate portrait we have of Antoine Doinel may owe as much to Léaud as to its ostensible model, Truffaut. As the director learns from the actor, so the teacher learns from the student: Truffaut dedicated *L'Enfant sauvage* to Jean-Pierre Léaud.

Truffaut and Léaud share the obsession with cinema that underlies the Doinel character, even though it is never made explicit. In "Antoine et Colette" Truffaut gives Antoine a fascination with music in place of his own addiction to moviegoing; in *Domicile conjugal* Doinel is a budding novelist, not filmmaker, but always there is the sense that Antoine shares with Truffaut and Léaud the belief that the reality of art is somehow more valid, more enticing than the reality of the street. From Antoine's first adoring obsession with Balzac to his symbolic infatuation with Kyoko in *Domicile conjugal,* literary reality always takes precedence. When he pays homage to Balzac as a schoolboy by paraphrasing—significantly—*La Recherche de l'absolu* in a composition, we are meant to share with him the deep hurt when the teacher prefers to interpret his literary flair as plagiarism. When he falls in love with Fabienne Tabard in *Baisers volés,* it is Balzac's *Le Lys dans la vallée* that draws them together. Throughout the series, Antoine prefers to write letters rather than express his various loves personally. Partly this is because he is shy, of course, but it is also because a written statement will somehow make the declaration of love more real, more permanent. His masterpiece is undoubtedly his reply to Fabienne Tabard's gift of ties; and Truffaut's camera takes the opportunity to pay homage to the *pneumatique* system, reverently following the path of the letter through the tubes in the bowels of Paris to its destination. This concern for art is a major *subject* of Truffaut's films (as for most of the New Wave filmmakers), but, as we shall see, it is also probably the most prominent characteristic of Truffaut's esthetic dialectic.

The series begins with two relatively straightforward realistic films—*Les Quatre Cents Coups* and "Antoine et Colette"; but by the time of *Baisers volés* there is a significant dimension of irony in each of Truffaut's films which must be taken into account when we decide how we

*In the four episodes Doinel is, respectively, 12, 18, 20, and 22 years old; when they were shot, Léaud was, respectively, 14, 18, 24, and 26.

should approach them. That irony is objective and material; in other words, it provides the films with a strict esthetic distance, one which is conveyed through the *material* nature—the objects of the film, its shots and cutting—rather than through strict narrative devices. This distancing irony is more important to a study of Truffaut's genre films, for it is those complex and subtle movies that depend most significantly on our understanding of that irony for their full effect, but it is worth noting here as well, since ignorance of this distancing effect makes both *Baisers volés* and *Domicile conjugal* seem much hollower and more facile than they actually are. In fact, nearly all of Truffaut's films operate on two parallel levels of meaning: there is the obvious *narrative* level—the characters, the story line, the atmosphere—but there is also a very real, if much less easily discerned, *material* level, congruent with the narrative but separate and distinct, which is concerned with purely cinematic esthetic matters. The dialectic between the narrative and material natures of Truffaut's films creates this subtle irony.

Baisers volés is dedicated to Henri Langlois; its first shot gives us the shuttered Cinémathèque. Truffaut thus announces that this film is about his own youth not only as it was measured by the people he knew and the jobs he held, but also as it is described by the films he had seen and grown to love: *Les Films de ma vie,* in his own phrase. The Charles Trenet 1930s *chanson* which recurs on the soundtrack, Doinel's own romantic isolation from his contemporaries, the idealization of both Christine and Fabienne as types of bourgeois womanhood, the comic exaggeration of his various jobs—all these elements should be seen as ironic commentary on the system of values which suffused the movies of the thirties and forties with which Truffaut grew up.

This material irony is even clearer in *Domicile conjugal.* Besides the weight of the references to Truffaut's own previous films, the last chapter of the Doinel saga is redolent with allusions and evocations. The Renoiresque courtyard which now fairly limits Antoine's world becomes quite suffocating, until we realize that the thick layering of art is essential to the idea of the film. It is Antoine's novel, he explains, which has come between him and Christine: art is now antithetical to life. Though the weight of the references and allusions is heavy upon us, it is not precious, as it first seems, but necessary. What started in *Les Quatre Cents Coups* as the jeu d'esprit of a young filmmaker delirious with film history and his ardor for it became during the twelve years that followed a method. In *La Nuit américaine,* Léaud plays the role of Alphonse (the name Antoine gave his son in *Domicile conjugal*), a young cinéaste who is an alter ego for Doinel. The question that recurs like a refrain in this quasi-Doinel film— "Is film more important than life?"—has a special poignancy for Truffaut (and also for Léaud). Luckily they have managed to maintain a balance between the two long enough to forge an evocative cinema out of the dilemma.

The vitality of Truffaut's cinema is somehow more apparent in the Doinel films than in the genre films which were interspersed with them throughout the sixties. They are more straightforward than those complicated essays in cinematic modes of discourse and more concrete. What Truffaut loves best about cinema is its ability to capture the poetry of *la vie quotidienne;* he allows himself free reign in this respect in the Doinel films.

- A gym teacher takes his class out for a jog through Paris streets. Blowing his whistle rhythmically, he loses first one boy, then another, then two, then three, as we watch the quickly shrinking column from high above.
- Antoine steals a bottle of milk and guzzles it quickly for fear of being caught, then disposes of the empty bottle in a nearby sewer, listening for the satisfying crash as it hits bottom.
- Antoine steals a photo of Harriet Andersson from a theatre display case.
- Ferrand dreams *he* steals glossies of Orson Welles.
- Antoine teaches Christine to butter biscottes without breaking them.
- Antoine has a date with a very tall girl. *(Formidable!)*
- Kids take a penmanship lesson, ripping out failed pages one after the other.
- A woman loses her dog in the street and a man tries to help her. He has ulterior motives, of course.
- Fabienne serves coffee and asks if Antoine likes music. "Oui, monsieur!" the scared kid blurts out, to his undying shame.
- Colette writes: "Dear Antoine, Your love letter was nicely phrased; it reflects a man of experience. . . . Thanks for the books. . . . Oh, I forgot to mention that my mother thinks you look romantic, probably because of your long hair."
- Antoine learns how to press a record at the Phillips factory.
- Antoine does a terrible job of wrapping a package at the shoe store.
- Antoine dyes flowers for a living. One of them always refuses to turn color.
- Christine, having nearly fainted at a concert when she looked into the orchestra pit, practices standing on a table.

Antoine and René (Patrick Auffay) steal a still of Harriet Andersson. In *La Nuit américaine* Truffaut dreams he steals stills from Orson Welles movies.

- Antoine steals a kiss from Christine in the wine cellar. Years later, Christine steals a kiss from Antoine.
- Antoine makes an expedition to the bathroom: he carries: a flashlight, a book, a knife to cut the pages with, a newspaper.

Truffaut makes vibrant mosaics out of bits and pieces like this. The production notes he made for the Doinel films reveal long lists of such items—many the result of research and interviews. None of the Doinel films tell a complete story (not even the last); each is a framework for the mosaic. As the Doinel story progresses, so does the complexity of the mosaic. There is far less of it in *Les Quatre Cents Coups* and "Antoine et Colette" than in *Baisers volés* or—especially—*Domicile conjugal.* Indeed, in this last film it almost seems as if Truffaut might well have preferred to dispense with the story altogether in order to use the space and time for even more of the complicated mosaic patterns of short scenes and isolated shots that already do such an efficient job of creating the mood of the film as Antoine and Christine painfully discover each other—and themselves. It is more than a little surprising to find this density of narrative structure in the Doinel films, which give a first impression of simplicity and directness. What could be more straightforward than a series of films about a young man growing up? But Truffaut's real purpose is to capture the *quality* of the life, the *tenor* of the *éducation sentimentale*—not its historical details.

Both the mosaic technique and the dimension of ironic commentary have a common source, which they share with nearly all the innovative methods and techniques the *Cahiers* critics developed: Bazinian realism. Like Godard's "return to zero," Rohmer's para-literary essays, and Rivette's "stretched time," Truffaut's mosaics and material irony are motivated by a deep-rooted desire to increase the quotient of honesty and clarity in film and thereby decrease the distance between author and observer. For those weaned on the general run of popular American action movies, which for the most part are antithetical to the ethics and esthetics of Bazinian realism, Truffaut's films may be vaguely disappointing: his genre films, seemingly recognizable in form, move too slowly; the Doinel films seem sprawling and diffuse.

The difficulty is that although Truffaut's films do share a complex, ironic mode of discourse, they don't announce it clearly (as do Godard's films, or Rivette's). Yet Antoine Doinel's *éducation sentimentale* is not only a matter of learning how to hold a woman or a job; it is also an investigation of the function of art. The question of *La Nuit américaine:* "Are films more important than life?" is central. It can be answered in the affirmative from two separate perspectives. From the point of view of Truffaut and Léaud the film buffs, the phantoms of the cinémathèque, the answer is obviously—and unhappily—yes. But from the point of view of the media theoretician, the student of the sociological and psychological effects of film, the answer may also be a qualified yes; and this "yes" then becomes the major premise for an important discussion of how the media have altered our existence. Godard deserves major credit for pursuing this line of thinking; he has spoken more eloquently about it than anyone else. But Truffaut deserves some credit as well.

More evident (and more engaging) in the Doinel cycle is the continuous search for the answer to Alphonse's second question in *La Nuit américaine:* "Are women magic?" Actually, the question is rhetorical. We never doubt for a moment that Léaud's Doinel believes that women are the quintessence of magic. Throughout the cycle his attachment to jobs is perfunctory, even as the jobs themselves are only sources of comedic material. Even at the end, when it is finally clear that Antoine is an artist, we nevertheless learn nothing about his novel except that it has "neither drums nor trumpets." Yet from the first moment in *Les Quatre Cents Coups* when Antoine stares at his mother's legs, we are aware that his shyness with women will be a major concern of the cycle. He is at once aggressive and passive; he throws himself into situations involving women, but he often seems paralyzed once the relationship has been initiated. It is Fabienne who must come to *him* in his garret near Sacré-Coeur; Christine who finally makes the decision to seduce him; and Mlle Kyoko who consciously draws him into an affair which has loomed large in his fantasies but about which he has done little.

This combination of aggressiveness and passivity is the hallmark of Doinel's personality and reveals itself not only in his relationships with women, but also in his concern for his life's work. It is the peculiar dilemma of the active artist that much of his work consists of passive observation. The *act* of writing a novel is relatively constricted, cramped work when compared with, say, being a stock clerk.

What is true of the manchild is true of the films as well, for the Antoine Doinel cycle is expressed in a whole set of passive-aggressive oppositions: men versus women, adults versus children, films versus life. These form the coordinate structure. An anecdote illustrates Truffaut's own dialectical approach. While he did not have in mind a full cycle of Doinel films while shooting *Les Quatre Cents Coups*, he nevertheless must have felt that there would be at least one sequel, for he refused permission to the labs to destroy the unused footage of the first film (which would have been normal practice). When he later returned to the Doinel story he was able to use these "outtakes" to insert a flashback that had actually been filmed four years earlier when both Léaud and Patrick Auffay (who plays René) were still children. The contrast between Léaud at fourteen and Léaud at eighteen is striking. Truffaut, who considers Léaud to be "the best French actor of his generation,"[9] had, by the time *Les Quatre Cents Coups* was finished shooting, developed an almost dialectical relationship with the actor. Doinel in Truffaut's original conception had been much quieter and more secretive than the character who eventually emerged. Like Doinel, Truffaut explains, "Jean-Pierre was an anti-social loner and on the brink of rebellion; however, he was a more wholesome adolescent and quite often he was downright cocky." It was this tension between the reclusive, objective, flat portrait that Truffaut had conceived and the cocky, vivid, and somehow aggressive personality of Léaud that gave resonance and dimension to the image of Doinel, not only in *Les Quatre Cents Coups* but also in the films that followed, which were much more evidently collaborative efforts.

Truffaut was not alone among his colleagues in this ironic dependence on actors. All the auteurist critics, when they came to make films, developed equally strong relationships with actors and actresses (often marrying them). But Truffaut's relationship with Léaud has lasted longest and has arguably produced the richest artistic results. At first glance it may seem ironic that critics who championed the centrality of the director should offer so many reaffirmations of the importance of the actor in the cinematic process. Yet Bazin had never presented his version of realism as documentary; and in fact—as we shall see with Godard—there is a sophisticated argument to be made in favor of the realism of acting.

Much of the vividness of *Les Quatre Cents Coups* is due to the loose framework Truffaut designed and the numerous opportunities he gave Léaud for improvisation: "He instinctively found the right gestures, his corrections imparted to the dialogue the ring of truth and I encouraged him to use the words of his own vocabulary. . . . When he saw the final cut, Jean-Pierre, who had laughed his way through the shooting, burst into tears: behind this autobiographical chronicle of mine, he recognized the story of his own life."[10]

The specificity which Léaud brought to the film is closely united, however, with an opposite, general relevance which was very much Truffaut's intention and which is equally important to the success of the film. Truffaut has described more than once the clinical syndrome that he felt was the basis of *Les Quatre Cents Coups:*

> I made my film on this crisis that specialists call by the nice name of "juvenile identity crisis," which shows up in the form of four precise disturbances: the onset of puberty, an emotional weaning on the part of the parents, a desire for independence, and an inferiority complex. Each one of these four factors leads to revolt and the discovery that a certain sort of injustice exists.[11]

As he worked it through, the film gradually became not just a chronicle of adolescence but a specific evocation of the difficulties of the age of thirteen. Childhood for Truffaut was a series of "guilt-bearing malfeasances," and he has always distrusted adults' nostalgic reminiscences of their own childhood. The only way to cope with the discovery that a certain sort of injustice exists is "faire les quatre cents coups." The film simply describes that experience.

Once Antoine passes that crisis, his personality and that of the films become much calmer; there is a definite difference of tone between *Les Quatre Cents Coups* and "Antoine et Colette," which succinctly provides the necessary bridge between childhood and adulthood. The anguish of the first film has faded, and Antoine finds himself in a period of relative hope. His painful shyness remains, but at the end of the film, if he hasn't won the girl he has at least won her parents, and this may be more important for the boy who was disowned four years earlier. The pattern has been set for the adult personality; like most of Truffaut's male characters, Antoine is always out of phase with women. When they want to be treated as romantic objects he insists on relating to them realistically and humanly; when they would prefer to dispense with their masks, Antoine perversely romanticizes them. The Antoine of Truffaut is shy and clumsy, but the Antoine of Léaud is tenacious and witty. These are the dimensions of the adult Doinel.

Baisers volés is also situated in the period of relative calm between crises. (In a way, "Antoine et Colette" is a sketch for the film which succeeds it.) Once more Antoine wins the parents, but this time he also wins the girl. In addition, the intervening six years have seen considerable changes in the artistic personalities of both Truffaut and Léaud. Both are much more self-assured by 1968. Truffaut has paid his debt to Hitchcock and genre films; Léaud has proved his worth as an actor outside the character of Doinel. The result is Truffaut's most seductive film. *Baisers volés* is charming, humorous, cleanly executed, and generally affirmative; consequently it has been very popular.

Not surprisingly, there was a critical reaction against that charm. Pauline Kael, for example, found it "charming, certainly, and likeable, but it's too likeable, too easily likeable. . . ."[12] Remembering that Godard had once characterized Truffaut's films as "rigorous and tender," Kael suggests that *Baisers volés* "isn't rigorous, and without the rigor the tenderness is a little flabby." The problem here is that since Truffaut had already covered the calm center of Doinel's *éducation sentimentale* historically in "Antoine et Colette," he was free in *Baisers volés* to indulge himself by concentrating on the commentative, ironic dimension, which received added emphasis from the circumstances of the shooting schedule in the spring of 1968. Truffaut started shooting on 5 February. Four days later he attended the momentous board meeting of the Cinémathèque at which its founder Henri Langlois was ousted. "From that time on," he explains, "I led a double life as a filmmaker and a militant agitator, making phone calls between takes to raise funds, alert public opinion, set up a Defense Committee and frequently missing rushes to attend demonstrations. Throughout the shooting, our slogan was: If *Stolen Kisses* is good, it will be thanks to Langlois. . . ."[13]

Truffaut's consciousness of the filmic dimension, which would have been strong in any event, must have been enhanced greatly by this double life. Just as, nine and a half years earlier, the urgency of *Les Quatre Cents Coups*, a film about parents and children, had been amplified and sharpened by the death of Truffaut's surrogate parent André Bazin the day after shooting began, so his understanding that *Baisers volés* was as much about the films he had grown up with as about the character was heightened by the imminent "death" of Langlois. Truffaut succeeded in l'affaire Langlois; he also succeeded with the film.

Baisers volés is a carpe diem piece about that last moment of the passage from youth to adulthood before responsibilities become unavoidable.

Thus the dramatic focus of the film does not rest with Antoine Doinel, although he remains the emotional focus and the organizing principle, but rather with the gallery of misused, abused, and ragged men with whom Antoine comes into fleeting contact: Georges Tabard, the magician's friend, Monsieur Henri, Julien, the deceived husband, Christine's pursuer, and—not least—Colette's tired husband Albert. Nearly all have been hurt by their relationships with women, and their lives are warnings to Antoine, who is still innocent. In his rocking chair at the hotel, wrapped comfortably in a blanket, Antoine reads a copy of *La Sirène du Mississippi*—Truffaut's subsequent film, which delineates in even greater detail the pain and sorrow that is the currency between men and women in contemporary sexual relationships. Antoine tells Christine, "Even when I thought I loved you, I didn't admire you."

Paul explains to Antoine that "making love after death is like a way of compensating . . . as if you need to prove that you still exist." When Henri dies offscreen, in the midst of the life of the office, Antoine searches out a prostitute. Only after he understands the connection between love and death do things work out all right with Christine. The film is a set of variations on this theme. Only a few of them involve Antoine directly; for most of them he is an observer. The process that began with Antoine's ambiguous freedom at the end of *Les Quatre Cents Coups* ends with *Baisers volés:* he has satisfied his desire for independence; his successes with Fabienne Tabard and then with Christine have marked his new maturity; the discovery that a certain sort of injustice exists has been made. And he has started to learn how to cope with it. Truffaut has noted that "it is precisely because of his anachronism and romanticism that I found Jean-Pierre so appealing."[14] The romantic idealism of *Baisers volés* is tempered, at the end of the film, by an emotional knowledge that love and death are inextricably intertwined.*

Clearly, metaphysics of this sort are open to the charge of sentimen-

*Not surprisingly, Truffaut's own experience as a filmmaker parallels Doinel's new knowledge: "Once a picture is finished I realize it is sadder than I meant it to be. This happens with every picture. I had expected *Stolen Kisses* to be a funny picture. When I started making movies I had the idea that there were things that were funny and others that were sad, so I would put funny things and sad things in my films. Then I tried to switch abruptly from something sad to something comical. In the course of making *Stolen Kisses* I came to feel that the best of all were the kind of situations that were funny and sad at once.[15]

tality; one could easily respond to the moral of Truffaut's film: ah! sweet mystery of life! Yet I think a condemnation of the film as sentimental is wrongheaded. True, there is a dimension of nostalgia, but Truffaut has a complex attitude towards it; he pictures his youthful self as, at times, stupid and unfeeling. (He will do so again in *Domicile conjugal.*) In addition, there is that thin wash of irony which distances us. Nevertheless, the French *sentiment* (as opposed to the English "sentiment") is a strong element of every one of Truffaut's films so far. *Sentiment* encompasses the English senses of affection and feeling, but it also has connotations of perception, sense, consciousness, and sensibility. For years, Truffaut's mentor Jean Renoir suffered from similar charges of sentimentality. Maybe in the latter half of the twentieth century it takes a certain quirky moral courage to make art which intends affirmative statements. (Imagine Fabienne's story of her father's death in an Anglo-Saxon film: "Before he died, my father motioned to his doctor to come closer. He whispered to him: 'People are wonderful' ['Les gens sont formidables'] and died a few minutes later.") Yet it is just this aspect of Truffaut's worldview which is most valuable. If the affirmations sometimes ring hollow for some of us, that is perhaps more our problem than Truffaut's, for, as we shall see, the Truffautesque gesture of affirmation is not baseless, but grounded in distinct and relatively sophisticated politics.

Baisers volés is, on the whole, richer in feeling than any of the other films. It is Truffaut's most personal film, even more intimate than *Les Quatre Cents Coups*. When Antoine first meets Fabienne Tabard (Delphine Seyrig), he is filled with wonder. Surely women are magic! He phones in his report to Ida at the Blady Detective Agency:

IDA What shape face?
ANTOINE *(waxing lyrical):* It's a perfect oval shape . . . I mean a slightly triangular oval. And her complexion is radiant . . . as if illuminated from within!
IDA Look, Antoine. What we want is a report, not a declaration of love![16]

It is this tension between the mode of the report and that of the declaration of love that gives *Baisers volés* its special eloquence. But reportage and commentary gradually win out. When Fabienne goes to visit Antoine in his garret overlooking the Sacré-Coeur she explains to him that *Le Lys dans la vallée* is not a beautiful love story, it's "a pathetic tale. . . . Moreover," she insists, "I'm *not* an apparition, I am a woman . . . which is exactly the opposite!"[17] In the final Doinel film, Delphine Seyrig's "radiant, slightly triangular oval face" will be parodied by the mysterious television comedian, and the demystification will be complete. Women are no more magic than men—but no less, either.

Domicile conjugal is a necessary sequel to *Baisers volés*. The desperate knowledge that women are not magic must be assimilated. The narrative of the first years of Antoine and Christine's marriage is the story of Antoine's grudging acceptance of that fact. The epiphany, if there is one, comes in the penultimate scene of the film. Antoine, despite his best instincts, is prolonging his affair with Kyoko and finds himself having what should be a romantic dinner with her. He is, however, excruciatingly bored and telephones Christine periodically throughout the evening, hoping that she will give him the excuse to return to her. He was never bored with her: this isn't a triangle in the usual sense. He simply was seduced (one last time) by the magic of the Japanese woman. While he sits in bed reading *Les Femmes japonaises,* his wife lies beside him indulging her own fantasies with Nureyev. Doinel is a considerably less attractive character in this last film than he has been heretofore. The charm of youth has faded, and he is ill-equipped to be a functioning adult. He is still very shy—he won't undress in front of his wife. He now has to face responsibilities of parenthood, but he has no noticeable career. If women aren't magic, he doesn't yet know what it is they are. He is self-centered to the point of missing the birth of his own child, and the jokes of his failures are no longer so humorous. In the previous films, Doinel could lose, but he could never be beaten. Now, reality threatens. Like all Truffaut's men, now that he is of age, Antoine is movingly vulnerable, open and wounded.

Our main sense of him in *Domicile conjugal,* as in *Les Quatre Cents Coups,* is deeply colored by his isolation. The film is a collection of lonely images of Antoine: in a telephone booth at night, trying to find someone to tell about the birth of his son; beside a fake lake playing with toy boats; alone on his mattress working on his manuscript in a flat so large that he and Christine have lost each other in it; and picking up his book, his flashlight, his cigarettes, and his newspaper (as if he were a small boy leaving home) for his journey to the bathroom, that citadel of isolation. Their lack of a telephone emphasizes their isolation, as do many of the shots of the pair in bed against cold blue sheets and the architecture of the apartment, which puts the bathroom across an airshaft and causes them several times to hold conversations through open windows.

In *Domicile conjugal* for the first time in the Doinel cycle•we can see clearly that the provenance of a Truffaut film is political. A marriage is the smallest political unit, and domestic politics provide a microcosm

Antoine and Christine (Claude Jade): the marriage ceremony at the breakfast table, marked by an exchange of notes, sealed with a heart-shaped bottle-opener, and sanctified by the ritual buttering of biscottes.

for us. At the end of the film Antoine and Christine mimic the stereotyped comic model of their bourgeois neighbors, the tenor and his wife, which has been a running joke throughout the film: Antoine paces officiously in the corridor waiting for Christine. Women! They're never on time. Yet we shouldn't place undue emphasis on this final joke. Earlier, Antoine and Christine have spoken clearly—almost eloquently—to each other about their situation. Antoine, visiting Christine and the baby, has discovered that she has a date that night. He follows her, a bit plaintively, out into the street, where she turns on him angrily (for the first time):

CHRISTINE	And you're irresponsible! All you know is what you want: I'm supposed to kiss you when you feel like it . . . to leave you alone when you want to think . . . I'm not "yours to command"!
ANTOINE	All right.
CHRISTINE	Not anymore!
ANTOINE	That's enough . . . Look, I'm sorry, I understand how you feel . . .
CHRISTINE	Oh, I know that line: "I understand you . . . I'm a bastard . . . you're much too good for me"!
ANTOINE	I don't pull that.
CHRISTINE	You've done it a hundred times. You can put it all in your novel . . . [18]

It's clear that Christine isn't going to settle for the bourgeois model. Earlier, an old friend of Antoine's, discovering he's now married to a musician, has commented, "A musician, huh? You always did like nice little bourgeois girls!" There's no denying that Antoine has an acute appetite for "nice little bourgeois girls." That has been clear since Colette. Fabienne and Christine are classic models of the type! But the real emphasis in this exchange lies in Antoine's expressed pride at his wife's profession. And an unavoidable aspect of *Domicile conjugal;* as the title suggests sarcastically, is Christine's clear independence. Antoine may have dreams of becoming a novelist, but Christine has already had some success as a violinist. She brings in at least as much money as he does, and is never seen at housewifely chores. She has the baby independently of her husband, and she doesn't turn into a domesticated mother. When her husband leaves her, she raises the child, does her work, and finds time for a social life. She knows a good deal more about their situation than he does.

After the heated exchange in the street, Christine gets into a taxi. She softens a bit; Antoine is, after all, nothing if not forlorn. He kisses her gently and salutes her with one of his best romantic lines (which is continually echoed in Truffaut's films):

> You're my little sister, my daughter, my mother . . .

Christine replies simply:

> I'd hoped to be your wife.[19]

There it is, eloquently phrased: the contrast between the romantic roles we have assigned women and the realistic roles they need and want. The cab pulls off and Antoine walks slowly down the street. Christine has made her point; women will no longer be magic for Antoine.

Baisers volés began with Antoine getting laid for his army buddies (and for us) and ended with him getting married (for us); *Domicile conjugal* completes the circle; its next scene shows Antoine at a bordello in the Place Pigalle. There is one more point to be made and the tall prostitute he chooses will make it. She has specific political opinions and voices them: "Some administration! The minute I saw what they looked like on TV, I knew we'd had it. Aren't you interested in politics?" she asks. It's a question which by now we'd all like to ask Doinel (and Truffaut). He fashions an answer, and Marie continues: " . . . remember: 'if you don't follow politics, politics will get you in the end!'"[20] The scene is a grace note, not very important except to remind us that Truffaut is aware of the political implications of the film. It is a signal in the foreground that we should take a closer look at the background of the film. The narrative of *Domicile conjugal* might seem to avoid political questions, but the material of the film is strongly evocative.

Renoir comes to mind. Just as the bonhomie of the courtyard life is getting to be a bit much, one remembers the courtyard from *Le Crime de M. Lange* and the people who lived and worked together in and around it with such good spirits. (Truffaut had quoted *Lange* the year previously in *La Sirène du Mississippi*.) What Renoir was after in that film, and what Truffaut is intent upon in *Domicile conjugal*, is the delineation of an ideal community. Renoir was much more specific: *Lange* goes to considerable lengths to describe the benefits of cooperative organization and its ramifications. But Truffaut has only to allude to the Renoir film in order to convey much of the same information.

Like *Baisers volés*, *Domicile conjugal* contains a gallery of characters, each of whom reinforces its philosophical aura. But whereas in the earlier film those characters were isolated from each other—separate and alone, if parallel—in the last film of the cycle they have come together, with the courtyard as their focus. There is Césarin, the owner of the cafe; the tenor and his wife; the "strangler" (the only discordant note in the grouping—until they find out he is a comedian and welcome him into the club); Ginette, the love-starved waitress (Truffaut was surprised to remember that the name of Renoir's secretary was Ginette Doynel!); Mme Martin, the concierge; little Christophe; the parking attendant; the sanitation department man; and finally, as counterpoint, the voluntary recluse, M. Desbois, who joins the group only by leaning out of his window.

Doinel spends relatively little time outside the courtyard. When he does go out he invariably runs into the haunting figure of the Moocher, Jacques Robiolles, who skulks continuously through the Paris streets. Originally Truffaut had wanted the office group at the hydraulic plant to echo the communal atmosphere of the courtyard, but little of them remains in the final film, except for the sympathetic figure of Monique.

This adopted family of the courtyard provides a matrix for the developing relationship of Antoine and Christine. As Antoine himself has explained, for him the family is the main attraction of bourgeois life. Truffaut elaborates: "Antoine proceeds in life like an orphan and looks for foster families, but once he has found them, he tends to run away, for he remains by nature an escapist."[21] He has, remember, chosen the profession of novelist, which implies a strict isolation: it is not a communal art, and therefore serves to counterpoint both the domestic politics of Antoine and Christine and the larger politics of the courtyard.

Although we know there are other reasons, Antoine explains to Christine that it's the novel that has separated them:

> It's all I can think about right now. That's why I'm so fouled up. But I'm sure that once it's done, we'll get along better.

But Christine, always a little wiser, replies:

> Don't send me a copy. I won't read it. I don't like the idea of telling all about your youth, of blaming your parents, of washing dirty linen in public. . . . I'm not an intellectual, but I know this: writing a book to settle old scores isn't art![22]

It is as if Truffaut were trying to tell us (and himself) something about his own relationship with the Doinel cycle. Antoine and Truffaut have apparently given up something important for their respective novel and film. Antoine postfigures Truffaut's own failure with marriage, and although we have no way of knowing Truffaut's feelings about his divorce, it seems that Antoine in *Domicile conjugal* is in part his attempt at exorcising his own anxiety about a life in which films have been, by all evidence, more important than people.

There is a devious logic at work here, and it points up the ironic dilemma of Truffaut's world: for him, films may very well be more important than people, but people are undeniably the most important element of films. In his own work, the focus shifts continually back and forth between characters on the one hand and the film medium itself on the other. The result is a richly allusive but quietly subtle conflation of art and reality. For example, images of separation, visual tropes which summarize Truffaut's own feelings about the human condition, punctuate most of his films:

- Jules, Jim, and Catherine look out of separate windows of their shared villa, united and alone;
- an airshaft separates Antoine and Christine in *Domicile conjugal;*
- Antoine often calls to Colette from his window across the street in "Antoine et Colette," while at the concerts they attend they are separated by rows of seats;
- in the Blady office in *Baisers volés* six distinct dramas are being acted out, each separated from the others by walls, desks, empty space;
- finally, Antoine learns about the birth of his son only by focusing through a telephoto lens on a magazine spread a secretary is holding up across the lagoon as she points carefully to the male child in the picture.

Sharing the same bed but not the same fantasies: *Domicile conjugal.* Compare the shot from *2 ou 3 choses . . .* on p. 185.

This last image certainly is a classic example of Truffaut's poignant visual inventiveness. Not only is Antoine separated from his wife at the moment she gives birth, but he is also separated from the woman who brings him news of it. Furthermore, he gets the information only through her allusion to an artistic medium, and he can perceive that allusion only by using an artist's tool, a camera lens—and one which is noted for its distortion of reality, to boot! In each of these images of separation—most definitively in the last—material structure is at the service of narrative, which may lead us to the circular but valid conclusion that films are more important than life because, ironically, they can tell us so much about life. Truffaut, it must be remembered, so confuses life and film that he names his children Laura and Eva—yet it isn't clear whether he is honoring the heroines of the films by Preminger and Losey, or the films themselves.

This elusive tone which characterizes Truffaut's films and which is one of their most intriguing qualities is further complicated by the fact that we must "read" not only the content of a Truffaut shot but also its structure in order to get a complete sense of his meaning, for the two are often dialectically opposed. The images of isolation and separation catalogued above seem to have simple enough meanings, but when we set them in a structural context another dimension becomes apparent. (Again, the "birth announcement" sequence is the most instructive example.)

Building on Bazinian theories of deep focus and the commitment to the humanist rubric that implies, Truffaut has elaborated the effect of the stationary camera. He does want his camera to comment and it does so continually, but quietly. For Truffaut, deep focus is the source of what we might call the "considered pan." The last shot of *Les Quatre Cents Coups* is as good an example as any. As Antoine runs desperately to the sea across the wide beach, Truffaut's camera tracks beside him, just leading. As he reaches the sea, the camera pans quickly to reveal the ambiguous barrier. Then the image freezes, as do Antoine's alternatives. The airshaft shots in *Domicile conjugal* are also useful illustrations of a visual trope that might very well have its source somewhere deep in Truffaut's hero Hitchcock, the master of visual storytelling, but the following courtyard scene from that film is even more instructive: Antoine thinks he has the secret for obtaining absolute red carnations. We watch him as he pours the new dye into the pail of flowers. Then the camera tilts up and over to M. Desbois in his window as Antoine speaks to him, then tilts down following a newspaper Desbois has dropped ("I think you'd better read the want ads," he says), then pans over to the pail which now contains only a few frazzled and still smoldering flowers. This is the kind of economy of style that fascinates Truffaut in Hitchcock's films.

The considered pan comments very quietly on the action, but that isn't it's only attraction for Truffaut. His quiet economy was evident from the very first frames of *Les Quatre Cents Coups,* a film which was much more strikingly advanced technically in 1959 than it seems today, when many of the New Wave innovations have been thoroughly assimilated. It was the freshness of that film—the simplicity of its montage and the freedom Truffaut gave his characters by letting in natural sound and admitting the pauses of natural time—that made it so invigorating. Truffaut often seems to be almost embarrassed to hold a shot too long, and this quiet, quick, unpretentious rhythm is a salient characteristic of his films. Truffaut's montage has a real modesty which stems, I think, from his concern never to exploit his characters simply to entertain his audiences. The people of his films have real lives for him. At the end of *Baisers volés,* for example, Antoine and Christine seal their relationship with a quiet exchange of notes at the breakfast table. We never see the contents. "Tough luck for us," Truffaut remarks in the script. There are some privacies even the camera and the microphone must respect.

Truffaut's colleagues knew precisely what he was up to. As we shall see, the New Wave directors shared an interest in revolutionizing the time frame of films as well as their plastic space. Here is Jacques Rivette describing what Truffaut accomplished with *Les Quatre Cents Coups:*

> . . . the idea of length and shortness that so haunts F. T. seems in the end to have hardly any meaning in his case; or perhaps on the contrary it was necessary to have such an obsession about length, about *temps morts,* such an abundance of cuts, of jerks, of breaks, that eventually he could get rid of the old clockwork time and rediscover real time, that of Mozartian jubilation. . . . [23]

Coupled with that desire to break time back into real time was an equally strong wish to expand the effect of deep focus. So Truffaut shot his first feature film in scope, thinking that he could thereby overcome the depression of the decor. His next three films (including "Antoine et Colette") were also in scope, but he avoided it throughout the sixties and now returns to it only occasionally. It has always seemed significant to me that the first two Doinel films were widescreen, while the last two are regular width. Doinel's story may be seen as a rite of passage from the freedom of the widescreen to the limitations and compromises of the classic aspect ratio. Likewise, Truffaut forced upon himself the limitations of the more "mature" aspect ratio, almost as a test of faith.

The sum effect of Truffaut's idiom may lead us to expect a more precise, cooler, and more objective cinema than we actually get. The concrete mosaic and the combination of widescreen, realtime editing, and the considered pan may not be the most effective language for the romantic lyric essays that the latter Doinel films first appear to be. But in fact it is through the control of his idiom that Truffaut overcomes the potential excesses of his sentiments. It is the dialectic between what he says and how he says it that allows him to make a private film about film language at the same time as he makes a public film about the loves and labors of Antoine Doinel.

Like Ida in *Baisers volés,* we want a report. We get it. But we also get an often painful declaration of love: "Les gens sont formidables!"

3

TRUFFAUT
The Statement of Genres

The Doinel films, regularly punctuating Truffaut's career as they do, provide a paradigm of his growth as a filmmaker. In them we see reflected and distilled the feelings and ideas which he was working out with more precision, and greater difficulty, in the other films he made during that fifteen-year period. The complexity, precision, and subtlety of *Baisers volés,* for example, were the direct result of countless little experiments in the series of genre films of the mid-sixties. Despite such exceptions as *Jules et Jim* or *La Nuit américaine,* most of Truffaut's films during the last fifteen years have been less well received than the Doinel films, which are both more approachable and simpler in conception and organization.

There are good reasons for this critical diffidence, as we shall see, but those reasons do not truly justify the received opinion of Truffaut as a filmmaker whose films are mildly disappointing, too private, too cautious, or—at the other extreme—too facilely "popular." Pauline Kael, for example, has condemned him as "a bastard pretender to the commercial throne of Hitchcock," yet it has been a commonplace of many newspaper reviews of Truffaut's recent films that they are too private, too introverted to be considered commercial entertainment.

It seems to me that Truffaut might derive a certain intellectual pleasure from the dialectical opposition between the two censorious critical positions. The difficulty with Truffaut's films has been precisely that they have a private and intellectual dimension as well as a public, communicative, and entertaining purpose. In addition, Truffaut had the mixed fortune to begin his career with two films—*Les Quatre Cents Coups* and *Jules et Jim*—which were immediate and monumental critical and popular successes. Both spoke intimately and directly to the emotions of their audiences and were exuberant and exciting in their technical virtuosity. They became instant "classics," but they have come to haunt Truffaut during the last ten or twelve years while he has been conscientiously working out problems of film language and logic which have been achingly apparent to him, if not to his popular audiences. In the process, he has exhibited a kind of Bazinian moral courage, bluntly confronting such questions as are raised by the phenomenon of genre films and the encrusted narrative traditions of popular cinema. In this sense, all his films have been experimental, though the experiments have been unannounced, and the films offer themselves at first as *examples* of their various genres rather than as the critiques of them they also are.

Truffaut turned to a direct examination of these esthetic and moral dilemmas in his second film, *Tirez sur le pianiste (Shoot the Pianoplayer, Shoot the Pianist),* which established a mode of inquiry that he was to follow throughout the next decade and laid the foundations for the dialectics of the phenomenon of genres as Truffaut saw them. In the four films of the mid-sixties—from *La Peau douce* through *La Sirène du Mississippi*—he was mainly concerned with working through the questions raised by those dialectics, and this is the main reason those films suffer from relatively poor reputations. They are all ambitious and difficult films and certainly not entirely successful (since ideally it should not be necessary to understand the experimental intentions in order to appreciate the films).

By the autumn of 1959 both Godard and Truffaut had completed their first films and were looking towards their second ones. On the evidence at the time, one would have judged Truffaut to be the more "political" filmmaker. *Les Quatre Cents Coups* seemed to make a minor but effective political point about the treatment of children in contemporary society, while *A bout de souffle* was notably concerned with the panache of its hero and is even now best remembered for its stylistic innovations rather than for its social or political commentary. The knowledge that Truffaut had spent a period in the mid-fifties as assistant to Roberto Rossellini and that Godard had a reputation as a more emotionally responsive and more esthetically inclined reviewer would only have strengthened the feeling that Godard was the less political of the two.

By the time they completed their second films, however, this popular view of them was reversed, for Godard chose as a subject (for *Le Petit Soldat*) the major political issue facing France at that time—the war in Algeria—while Truffaut seemed to retreat into the apolitical world of American genre films with *Tirez sur le pianiste.* As it happens, Godard's politics, as evidenced in *Le Petit Soldat,* were muddy at best, but no one knew that at the time since the film had the good luck to be banned and was not released until France had finally withdrawn from Algeria. Several years later, when Godard's cinema became more overtly political, the cliché was sealed; and it has been the received opinion ever since that Godard is the only political intelligence of the New Wave.

Yet it was Truffaut, not Godard, who spent time in the brig for deserting from the army; Truffaut who in 1960 signed "le Manifeste des 121" organized by Sartre, which urged French soldiers to desert rather than fight against the Algerian people; and Truffaut who in 1968 organized the opposition to the dismissal of Langlois which was a harbinger of the events of May. Truffaut did have political sentiments, even if they were not overtly displayed in his films. He was slowly and carefully constructing—as evidenced in the Doinel films—a politics of intimacy which begins with the smallest political unit—what the French in the late sixties learned to call a "groupuscule" of two or three—and builds from there. Thus in addition to their value as introductions to the esthetic problems Truffaut had committed himself to studying, *Tirez sur le pianiste* and, especially, *Jules et Jim* are important first steps in the development of his political dialectic. Indeed, esthetics and politics, as with Godard, are united.

Truffaut's reaction to the success of *Les Quatre Cents Coups* was ambivalent. For a filmmaker who had been so shy that he made his first film about children rather than adults the adulation that was heaped upon him must have been somewhat disquieting.

A few years later he explained that he saw

> this modest family enterprise suddenly become a great international film that was picked up by all sorts of associations, groups, organizers of galas—how could I know?
>
> The film escaped from my hands and became something academic that I didn't recognize anymore.
>
> It belonged to a public that doesn't like movies, to the spectator who goes to the movies twice a year. . . . With my second film I felt myself being watched, waited for by this public, and I really wanted to send them all packing. . . . This time I wanted to please the real film nuts and them

> alone, while leading astray a large part of those who liked *Les Quatre Cents Coups*. . . .
>
> I refused to be a prisoner of my first success. I discarded the temptation to renew that success by choosing a "great subject." I turned my back on what everyone waited for and I took *my pleasure* as my only rule of conduct. . . .[1]

Thus Truffaut describes on the most elementary level what elsewhere he has called "the desire to contradict" which led to the choice of subject for his second film. Already two of the contradictions of the esthetic dialectic were clear to him: the conflict between author and audience and the dialectical relationship between two successive films.

Truffaut saw immediately the necessity for counterbalancing the effects of the freedom he had given himself by this choice.

> I was free as a breeze. Therefore I chose some limit so that I wouldn't go crazy. I put myself in the position of a filmmaker who had orders imposed on him: a detective novel, American, that was transposed to France.[2]

So *Le Pianiste* became a direct continuation of the work Truffaut had been doing as a critic. *Les Quatre Cents Coups* had been something of a digression, a personal essay rather than a critical one, but from now on Truffaut's films would exist against the matrix of genre films and the curious rules that applied to them. Partly, this choice was a matter of personal preference—Truffaut had always liked the novels of David Goodis and the films that had been made from them—but it was also a matter of artistic necessity. Truffaut was consciously trying to protect himself from the Sartrean nausea he knew would come with absolute freedom of the sort that his colleague Godard was going to impose upon himself eventually with his obsession with "returning to zero." The laws of the Gangster genre would give Truffaut something against which to react and, like most of his characters, he has always preferred to *re*act, rather than act.

Like Hawks or Hitchcock or Walsh, Truffaut was now confronted with a story from another medium which he had to translate into film and which also belonged to a genre and was therefore subject to a set of more or less arbitrary rules. He had in addition the challenge of transposing the story from American into French terms and the problem of fitting Charles Aznavour into the film. The original Goodis hero is much more physically imposing, more active. When Truffaut decided to use Aznavour the whole concept of the film had to change. As *Les Quatre Cents Coups* had been the product of the interaction between Truffaut's original passive conception of Doinel and Léaud's more aggressive personality, so *Tirez sur le pianiste* would now find a source of power in the conflict between Goodis's Eddie and Aznavour's Edouard. Finally, there was yet another opposition to be exploited—the subject matter of the film versus its style. This last contradiction, of course, is the basis for almost all dialectical criticism of film, and it had been an important factor in *Cahiers* criticism in the fifties: the whole idea of genre criticism and the auteur theory depends on an at least implicit view of the art of film as dialectical. The *politique des auteurs* presupposed a dialectical structure: there was a natural opposition between the genre and the author of a film, between films of the past and films of the present, between Hollywood and Paris, between actors and directors. These were all common subjects for the critics of *Cahiers* in the 1950s.

Truffaut described his excursion into genres as "something very precise that I would call a *respectful pastiche* of the Hollywood B-films from which I learned so much." *Tirez sur le pianiste* was certainly not meant to be a parody. ("I detest parody except when it begins to rival the beauty of what it's parodying.") Soon after the film was released, Truffaut made these remarks during a discussion which followed a screening of it at the Federation of Ciné-Clubs:

> I know that the result seems ill-assorted and the film seems to contain four or five films, but that's what I wanted. Above all I was looking for *the explosion of a genre* (the detective film) *by mixing genres* (comedy, drama, melodrama, the psychological film, the thriller, the love film, etc.). I know that the public detests nothing more than changes in tone, but I've always had a passion for changing tone [my italics].[3]

This is the most precise statement of what Truffaut had in mind with *Tirez sur le pianiste:* an explosion of genres by a mixture of them; a contradiction of the unity of tone. There was no doubt that he succeeded. Everyone was aware of the clash of tones, even if they couldn't understand why the nice young man who had made the charming *Les Quatre Cents Coups* would do such a thing. Bosley Crowther put it this way:

> It looks from where we are sitting as though M. Truffaut went haywire in this film. . . . It looks as though he had so many ideas for a movie outpouring in his head, so many odd slants on comedy and drama and sheer clichés that he wanted to express, that he couldn't quite control his material. . . . One finds it hard to see or figure what M. Truffaut is about.[4]

Crowther is right of course; that was the point of the film. What led Truffaut to this position? Genre theory and the politique des auteurs had been so important to him as a critic that it was impossible not to try working out the contradictions in practice, confronting genres himself. Godard, too, felt something of this compulsion, but Godard eventually felt it possible to begin the "return to zero"; Truffaut did not.

The basic structure of *Le Pianiste* comes from David Goodis's novel *Down There* (1956), a standard "gangster" book. It is not a detective story (as Truffaut's comment above implies), but a rather straightforward narrative about a former concert pianist who now bangs an upright in a South Philadelphia gin mill.

Onto the basic Gangster structure Truffaut grafted the love story of Charlie and Léna (Marie Dubois), the flashback love story of Edouard (Charlie) and Thérésa (Nicole Berger), the antagonism between Plyne and Charlie, and the relationship between Charlie and his younger brother Fido (in order to provide a role for Richard Kanayoun). Most of these elements exist in embryo in the novel, but Truffaut has amplified and refined them so that—in the film—they take on greater significance and disrupt the unity of mood that the novel has. While the novel is cold, straightforward, linear, the film is a mélange of cold and warm tones, sometimes deviously elaborate.

Take the first scene. The action of the first shots of the film is parallel to the first paragraphs of the novel: Chico (Albert Rémy) runs into a lamp post and falls down. But the rhetoric contrasts sharply with Goodis's. Truffaut's Chico is helped to his feet by a stranger and the two—without skipping a beat—launch into a pleasant philosophical discussion of marriage. Truffaut has injected an element of community which is quickly followed by some thoughts on relationships between men and women, two themes which will thread their way through the films to come; the spare, cool, tough milieu of Goodis's novel is transformed into a more human atmosphere.

Truffaut's Charlie Kohler is just as isolated as Goodis's Edward Webster Lynn, but whereas Lynn is pictured as a relatively strong, self-confident guy who has chosen his solitude, Truffaut's Charlie Kohler has found his isolation almost inevitably: he was always shy, withdrawn, reclusive. "My characters are on the edge of society," Truffaut has explained many times; "I want them to testify to human fragility because I don't like toughness, I don't like very strong people, or people whose weaknesses don't show."[5]

Charlie's affair with Léna, short though it is, is fraught with ambivalence. He wants her very much, as we know from the early scene in which he walks her home, agonizing over whether and how to make an advance. When he finally gets up the courage, Léna has disappeared. From that point on the affair is controlled by Léna. Indeed, it is she who narrates the flashback in which we learn of Charlie's earlier life as

Edouard Saroyan, concert pianist, and the melodramatic death of his wife Thérésa (which, Truffaut notes, is his homage to Nicholas Ray and Samuel Fuller). Practically, it is necessary for Léna to narrate the flashback since we could never conceive of Charlie revealing so much about his past life, but the effect is also to further distance the life of Edouard Saroyan for us. What Léna tells us (and she tells us more than she could possibly know) is her version of Edouard, someone whom, from the evidence of the posters that plaster her wall, she has studied with a special fixation for quite a while. Charlie has been driven to reject the life of the successful Edouard not out of any particular existential scruples but because that life, or at least the success which colored it, was the literal creation of a woman, Thérésa. If she had not slept with Lars Schmeel there would have been no Edouard Saroyan, famous concert pianist. And, with perfect irony, if she had not told Edouard that she was responsible for his career in this way, she would not have been driven to suicide and Charlie Kohler would not have materialized.

From another perspective, it was the magnitude of Edouard's career that drove the wedge in his marriage to Thérésa, so it was only fitting that that career be sacrificed as a memorial. What Léna sees in this story is further evidence of the romantic ideal which Charlie represents (not only to her but also to the denizens of the cafe for whom he effortlessly grinds out music). But she also should see that she is in the same relationship to Charlie that Thérésa was to Edouard. She doesn't know, however, that she will meet the same end. What is fascinating about these twin love stories is the unusual imbalance of the relationships. Charlie/Edouard truly plays a passive role in each and becomes, therefore, an embodiment of the romantic fantasies of both women. This double triangle is a pattern which will become quite familiar in many of Truffaut's succeeding films—as will the shy, isolated hero.

It should be remembered, however, that Charlie is not entirely alienated: he demonstrates a real concern for his kid brother Fido to whom he is a surrogate father. This makes him rather more interesting than the relatively wooden protagonist of Goodis's novel, or than a classic existential hero like Camus's Meursault. It is Fido's kidnapping that provides the impetus for Charlie's flight, even if it is Charlie's accidental murder of Plyne that finally forces the issue. Léna, as well, has a role to play in this chain of interlocking responsibilities: it is she whom Charlie and Plyne fight over. As so often in Truffaut's films it is the woman who controls the relationship and, thus, the story.

Yet the women are not the focus of *Tirez sur le pianiste* as they are in other films. The film is a portrait of Charlie Kohler. His face dominates the screen as Truffaut tries to capture the weary, thoughtful, introspective, frightened, persistent character he divines in Aznavour. Once again an actor has dominated the film and changed its nature. "Aznavour gives the tone," Truffaut explained. "What hit me about him? His fragility, his vulnerability, and that humble and graceful figure that made me think of St. Francis of Assisi."[6]

As with Léaud, Truffaut was extraordinarily lucky with Aznavour. The great paradox of the New Wave is that the critics who had championed the author of a film—the director—had such tremendous assistance from a broad gallery of talented actors when they began making films themselves. Aznavour, Léaud, Belmondo, Brialy, Moreau, Deneuve, Dorléac, Karina, Blain lead the list of remarkable talents. Strangely, Truffaut never again used Aznavour after *Tirez sur le pianiste*, and the adult male protagonists of his succeeding films never quite catch the full flavor of Aznavour's "fragility, vulnerability, and grace." As the films become narrower in intent, so do their protagonists, it seems, and Truffaut chooses actors more professional than Aznavour (who had been and remains a singer) but less striking, less precise.

In fact, of the succeeding films only *L'Enfant sauvage* and *La Nuit américaine* give so large a space to male heros (we are excepting the Doinel films for the moment) and, significantly, Truffaut chose to play the main roles in both of those films himself. For the rest, from *Jules et Jim* through *L'Histoire d'Adèle H.*, the focus rests more often on the female protagonists. Having caught the substance of the particular kind of male character he finds fascinating in his first two films (especially *Le Pianiste*), Truffaut seems to have turned his attention to women, who remain even today vaguely mysterious. ("Are women magic?")

In a small book, *L'Existentialisme est un humanisme*, published just about the time *Tirez sur le pianiste* was released, Jean-Paul Sartre defended that nebulous philosophy against the charges of pessimism and quietism which were so often leveled against it. The book announces the changes of mood and direction that were taking place at the time in existentialist thought, as the possibility of action became more attractive. Truffaut's Charlie Kohler is an existential hero who seems carefully balanced between the relatively passive philosophy of the fifties and the more active mood of the sixties. He is still unable to take control of his life, yet far more able than existential characters of the past to understand the dimensions of it. He has already made the Camusian choice when we meet him: Edouard Saroyan has rejected his own existence and built another, considerably more isolated. He now exists almost outside of everyday reality and has only one strong connection with another human being—his brother Fido. His life is as close and circular as his theme song. But just as the melody of the song

Charlie at work in the closed, comfortable world of the cafe.

repeats itself, so will the pattern of Charlie's life. A new woman begins the whole intolerable business of feeling all over again; and the tragic conclusion is parallel. It is Charlie's terrible burden that his simple story always ends in someone else's death, not his own. The pattern is Sisyphean. There is no resolution for Charlie's dilemma, but there is some relief in his art. At the end of the film he has retreated once more to the comfort of the piano, as he is introduced to the new waitress and the story begins again.

In a way, Charlie is a surrogate for Truffaut at this point in his career, for both have rejected the world of "serious" bourgeois art in order to make genre art: Charlie for the people in the bistro, Truffaut for the "film nuts." Any conscious genre filmmaker has made a commitment to popular art similar to Charlie's, and we may surmise that some vague, unexpressed political sentiments lie behind Truffaut's decision to devote himself to genre films, just as such sentiments seem to support Charlie's own choice.

Nevertheless, despite the wealth of hints we receive in *Tirez sur le pianiste* as to Truffaut's political worldview, the complex narrative structure of the film makes it difficult to draw conclusions. Charlie abstracted from the film may very well fit these developing theories. But Charlie inside the film is a creature of his women. Our point of view is Léna's (and Thérésa's), strictly speaking, and the subtle narrative tension between the audience's analysis of Charlie and the women's is what makes the film still intriguing. Charlie's is a life overheard, not boldly offered. And it is grudgingly given up to us in fractured pieces. Mirrors play an important part in the narrative: we are introduced to

Charlie through a mirror, we most often observe him at the piano through the overhead mirror, he stares at himself in a fractured mirror at the climax of the film in the little house in the mountains. Posters and paintings of his face are important as well. We get bits of his life in almost random order and have to piece them together. It is the mosaic approach again.

There are notably fewer long and inclusive pans in this film. The wholeness that such pans convey in *Les Quatre Cents Coups* (and the other Doinel films) is not part of the gestalt of *Tirez sur le pianiste* (nor that of most of the other genre films). The technical metaphor that *is* common in Truffaut's second film is what we might call the "edited zoom," a series of three or four quick shots of a detail in which each shot successively magnifies the image. This device is jarring, explicit, and introspective, and it fits Charlie's fractured story well.

In the standard text on editing, Karel Reisz and Gavin Millar describe a classic example of this device. When Charlie goes to Schmeel's office for an audition, he doesn't enter right away. He hears someone playing the violin and, not wanting to interrupt (or simply because he is too timid), he is left standing in the hall, caught in the midst of one of the miniature dilemmas of everyday life which has suddenly become unbearable. At this point Truffaut inserts a quick series of shots of Charlie's finger poised above the doorbell button, each more magnified than the one which preceded it. For Reisz and Millar,

> The shots provoke a whole string of reactions: (1) They are funny. (2) They are menacing, as all moments are when the action slows up, or the cutting begins to go into a great deal of detail. . . . (3) They are psychologically accurate since they represent his timidity. (4) They draw attention to a notorious *temps mort,* that time which we all spend standing outside doors that won't open. . . . (5) Charlie is a protagonist who embodies the philosophy of discontinuity.[7]

A heavy freight of meaning to load upon such a simple metaphor? Perhaps. But the sequence stands as classic Truffaut. It is concrete, evocative, self-effacingly edited, and it speaks volumes. Charlie eventually does ring the bell and enter. But Truffaut, with what will become characteristic reserve, chooses not to follow him into the audition. Instead, we watch the woman who had been playing the violin a bit earlier leave Schmeel's, walk down the long corridor and leave the building, while we hear the stirring strains of Charlie's melodramatic audition on the soundtrack. The sequence emphasizes and respects Charlie's privacy at the same time that it unites him with the violinist—a woman whom he'll never know, but with whom he at least has shared both a moment and a way of life.

Charlie and the doorbell.

This sequence could stand as an emblem for the whole film: it is dialectical (this time in a specifically Eisensteinian sense, through the montage which opposes characters, sentiments, and shots); it gives us two characters alone and isolated—strangers in fact—and manages cinematically to unite them in community; and finally it also carries some of the feeling about art that Truffaut always injects into his films, for it is the music—first the violin, then the piano—that speaks in the scene, not the people. (Is *music* more important than life?)

Jules et Jim is undoubtedly Truffaut's most popular film. It was so soon after it was released; it is still so more than a dozen years later. *Les Quatre Cents Coups* was a film of innocence, *Tirez sur le pianiste* of experience; *Jules et Jim* united the two. Truffaut explains the dialectic:

> In *Les Quatre Cents Coups* the subject was so important that the film passed slightly into the background; I had so many scruples that I filmed humbly, as if it were a documentary. I wanted to make some formal discoveries, a desire I satisfied with *Le Pianiste*. *Jules et Jim* is in that measure a synthesis of the other films; it's simultaneously a great subject that sweeps you away—one you never regret having chosen throughout the filmmaking—and it's a creative venture that inspires ideas that are at the same time formal and moral, visual and intellectual.[8]

Truffaut, ever the critic, has described the dimensions of his film well. Having established the Truffaut hero at the center of his cinematic universe in his first two films, he was now free (if only for a while) to widen the circle of environment surrounding that hero. Or, more precisely—considering the passive, observant nature of Truffaut's sur-

Three *copains:* Catherine (Jeanne Moreau) as Charlot, Jim (Henri Serre), Jules (Oskar Werner).

rogates on film, let us rephrase that: the circle of the *observer* has widened to include a larger and more diverse panorama. Clearly the focus of the film is neither Jules nor Jim, but Catherine; yet the film is not misnamed, for the characters of the two friends form a broad, arching curve which is inclusive and demonstrative; Catherine is the space inside that curve. (Are women magic?) We observe her always from the male perspective. In effect, then, *Jules et Jim* is not so much about feminine freedom as it is about men's reaction to that freedom.

Circles of all sorts—arches, segments, spirals—are vital to both the imagery and the architecture of the film; they give it a sense of wholeness and effusive strength which is more than anything else responsible for the passionate responses of its audiences. Truffaut had seen in Henri-Pierre Roché's novel "a perfect hymn to love, and perhaps even a hymn to life," and he had worked off and on for more than eight years in correspondence with Roché to construct a film version which would capture that spirit. He thought so highly of the novel when it was first published in 1953 that years later he could write:

> Reading *Jules et Jim* . . . , the first novel of a man 73 years old, formed me professionally as a cinéaste. I was 21 years old and a film critic. The book overwhelmed me and I wrote: if ever I succeed in making films I will make *Jules et Jim.*[9]

Once again, it was the ambience, the spirit of the work that fascinated him rather than the details of character and structure: "what I admire in *Jules et Jim,*" he said in an interview shortly after he had translated it into film, "are not the facts, but the style of the book, the quality of the characters, the beauty of the relationship between them and the *morale* of the book."[10]

While it was the affirmative spirit of the film which attracted large audiences, it was rather the stylistic complexity and density which caught the attention of the critics. Two of the best essays written about Truffaut's work have dealt with this aspect of *Jules et Jim:* Michel Delahaye's "On *Jules et Jim*"[11] and Roger Greenspun's "Elective Affinities: Aspects of *Jules et Jim.*" Of especial use was Delahaye's emphasis on formal complexity, a central fact of Truffaut's work which has been, it seems, ignored ever since by most critics. Greenspun's essay is equally aware of Truffaut's mastery of the technical grammar of the medium. He is particularly informative on the circular motifs of the film and is worth quoting at length:

> The forms of life flourish within the protective circles of François Truffaut's *Jules et Jim.* Whatever is reflected in the kindly eyes of Jules *"comme des boules, pleins d'humour et de tendresse,"* tadpoles squirming in a round bowl of water, the slow, sensitive circling of a room by hand-held camera taking careful inventory of the pleasant labours of a reflective and observant man's life—circles enclose to promote and enhance the abundant vitality of this film's world and its creatures. Files of dominoes meander across circular tables. A young woman imitating a locomotive triumphantly puffs her way around Jules's room with a cigarette inverted in her mouth, followed in close-up by a rapidly circling camera. The camera races through an even more rapid circle in a cafe when the young woman, Thérèse, deserts Jules for another man. But after the camera's dizzy 360° pan Jules sits down, and draws on a round table top the face of another girl he might love. A figure of speech, the "family circle," becomes an image when the camera follows smiling glances from eye to eye at the German chalet. For the ways in which the film sees life, the cosmos itself according to Catherine's German authority being a great inverted bowl, the growing family ideally nurtures and extends possibility; the family circle can even improve the time, making a balance between an abstract symbol of perfection and all the inevitable signs of dissolution. Finally, the protective charm is lost when through the broken arc of a circle, a ruined bridge, Catherine plunges herself and Jim to death.[12]

Greenspun has caught the one salient characteristic of Truffaut's work which we have taken for granted so far: his uncommon ability to make sounds and images resonate with meaning. The subtext of *Jules et Jim* is the subject of language. There is much talk of translation; Jules's German accent separates him from the others, who will die; stories—by Thérèse, Jules, Jim, Catherine—are concrete correlatives for the film; books and paintings are ubiquitous; and of course both Jules and Jim are writers, like so many of Truffaut's protagonists.

Catherine fascinates all of them (Jules, Jim, and Truffaut) because she is immediate. "Catherine only revealed the things she wanted when she had them in her hand," the narrator tells us. Jim tells her, "I understand you, Catherine." She replies quickly, "I don't want to be understood." The esthetic tension of the film is not, as one might suppose, between Jules and Jim but rather between their passive, observant natures and the active will and concrete sympathies of Catherine. "Catherine doesn't like people being far away from her," Jules explains to Jim. "When she has the slightest doubt she always goes much farther than the other person."

If Catherine were simply a "blithe spirit" attracting and capturing the literary drudges, the film would be a grand cliché. But *Jules et Jim* is not such a simple portrait of Catherine; it is rather an essay on the space between her and her lovers. We share Jim's perspective: he "could only admire Catherine unreservedly by herself. In company she became something relative."

As Charlie was the type of the romantic hero first for Thérésa, then for Léna, so Catherine is such a type for the novelist and the entomologist. But whereas Charlie had been allowed only two masks, Catherine is forced into a whole series of roles. From one point of view it is Jules and Jim's romantic fantasies that she must serve. (The film is strewn with a variety of impetuous games and set pieces.) But from another, Catherine is forced into those roles by her society. Although the film focuses intently on the story of the three central characters, the social dimension is very much present. *Jules et Jim* is an essay about the period between the two world wars, about the end of cultural innocence which World War I has always represented and the beginning of the age of anxiety which the scenes of Hitlerite activity forecast at the end of the film. There are social realities mirrored in the activities of the individual characters, the most outstanding of which is obviously what we have come to call the "liberation" of women. Catherine's "liberation" ends in her death because she has been offered the ideal of it but not the actuality. Partly because of the male perspective of the film and partly because that's the way it was, Catherine must act out her liberation by mimicking men. This motif begins with her Charlie Chaplin costume; it ends with her in a jacket and tie, severe wire-rim spectacles, and very short hair efficiently manipulating the controls of the automobile headed for the broken bridge. Discovered as an art object (the image of Albert's photographed statue), she ends as a technician. In between, she is referred to as a grasshopper. We may sense that behind these roles there is a whole person, but we never really see it. And neither do

Another cafe: a protective circle, "formal and moral, visual and intellectual," above all vital.

Jules and Jim. These are *elective* affinities, romantic, ideal and unreal. That is why death must end the story.

When the two friends first meet Catherine and observe her Charlot act, the narrator carefully explains that "Jules and Jim were moved, as if by a symbol they did not understand." Catherine never escapes from the burden of symbol-hood; existentially, the only concrete choice available to her is to drive off that broken circle into the water. She has been an elemental presence throughout the film: she is prone to catch on fire on occasion and she is closely and fatally identified with water long before her final excursion. She is never understood. Even the first words of the film emphasize that:

> CATHERINE You said to me: I love you. I said to you: wait. I was going to say: take me. You said to me: go away.[13]

The dramatic tension of the film results from the imbalance between Jules and Jim's image of Catherine and whatever existential reality she *might* have had. The dialectic is geometric, moving between the circle of life the film describes and the eventually tragic triangle: the two are never made congruent. The "family circle" which Greenspun describes is not stable: the triangle destroys it. And here is where the politics of the film lie. Jules tells us that "the revolting thing about war is that it deprives a man of his own individual struggle." In a broader sense, the patterns of bourgeois society deprive the trio of successful conclusions to their own individual struggles. Throughout the film there are continual references to "the others." Merlin the anarchist paints on the wall DEATH TO THE OTHER[S] (MORT AUX AUTRE[S]). After the war Jules asks Jim, "How are the others?" A little later he instructs Jim to give his regards to "the others." It is the others against whom the three are trying to define themselves. The others win the battle. Jim concludes:

> It is a noble thing to want to rediscover the laws of humanity; but how convenient it must be to conform to existing rules. We played with the very sources of life and we failed.[14]

They failed even in death: "Catherine had always wished her [ashes] to be scattered to the winds from the top of a hill . . . but it was not allowed."

Truffaut is ever absorbed with the conflict between us and the others, and it will dominate most of the films that follow. *Les Quatre Cents Coups* had posed this dialectic as a song of innocence; *Tirez sur le pianiste* was a song of experience; *Jules et Jim* is an epic of the passage between the two. It surveys not one but many genres; it has a wholeness which many of Truffaut's genre films lack. It is a public rather than a private film. Having discovered that he could produce such a complete, finished, and satisfying product, Truffaut turned back to more personal, intellectual concerns. Like Jim he felt the need "for adventures, for risks," and he knew that a synthetic film, like a period of happiness, "holds little that can be related . . . it gradually uses itself up without anyone noticing the usury."[15]

4

TRUFFAUT
The Explosion of Genres

In 1963, looking back over Truffaut's very short career, most critics would have judged *Tirez sur le pianiste* to have been a move in the wrong direction. Why go that way when two other films, both more successful, had opened up such potentially fruitful territory? Truffaut could have built a very pleasant and productive career alternating between film versions of popular novels like *Jules et Jim,* full of stars and executed with professional panache, and more personal films on the model of *Les Quatre Cents Coups.* But he chose, almost perversely, to avoid the models of popularity and critical success and to follow instead the path first plotted out in *Tirez sur le pianiste:* the explosion of genres by the combination of them. Six years went by before he returned to the Antoine Dionel cycle (with *Baisers volés* in 1968); eight years passed before he used the personal essay form again (*L'Enfant sauvage,* 1970) or filmed a critically respectable novel (*Les Deux Anglaises et le Continent,* 1971). More than ten years passed before he tried to duplicate the humanistic breadth and sentiment of *Jules et Jim* (with *La Nuit américaine,* his most popular film since 1962).

Instead, he worked carefully on a series of genre films, all of which met with more or less disappointed reviews and none of which were very successful commercially. There is not much doubt that these four experiments in genres—*La Peau douce (The Soft Skin; The Silken Skin), Fahrenheit 451, La Mariée était en noir (The Bride Wore Black),* and *La Sirène du Mississippi (Mississippi Mermaid)*—are colder, closer, and more introverted than *Les Quatre Cents Coups, Jules et Jim,* and even *Le Pianiste.* They disappoint those who are looking for the spirit of freedom and compassion that suffused the earlier films. But Truffaut is after something quite different in these films: a methodical reworking of the formal elements of cinema with which he had grown up and which had structured his view of human relationships as well as his attitude towards film.

Truffaut agreed with Jean Renoir that the primary motive force of film art (and the other arts as well) was the result of the tension created between the traditional forms of a work and the filmmaker's struggle with them. There was also a certain sense of security involved. Like a child who molds his personality by interacting with and struggling against his parents' norms, the filmmaker had to grow and develop by confronting dialectically the established forms—the genres—of his art: genre versus auteur yields new genre. (Godard's view was also dialectical, but Godard preferred to situate himself outside this particular dialectic instead of within it.)

In an interview with Louis Marcorelles shortly after he had completed *Jules et Jim,* Truffaut explained in considerable detail what changes had taken place in his attitude towards filmmaking during the preceding three years. He was much more aware, now, of the manipulative power of his medium, and he was concerned about his relationship with his audiences. The success of *Jules et Jim,* in this respect, was a mixed blessing. Truffaut knew the value of the raw materials he had been working with. (The Roché novel was "truly a hymn to life. . . . There are forty women in the book—enough for forty pictures."[1]) And he had realized how relatively easy it had been for him to fashion an admired and moving film from it. He also explained, "I'm not really enthusiastic about any of my films because there's always something important that went wrong," and concluded:

> The question which really interests me now is this. Should one continue to pretend to be telling a story which is controlled and authoritative, weighted with the same meaning and interest for the filmmaker and for the spectator? Or ought one rather to admit that one is throwing on the market a kind of rough draft of one's ideal film, hoping that it will help one to advance in the practice of this terribly difficult art?[2]

Godard was obviously thinking along similar lines at this time and quickly came to the decision that "throwing the rough draft on the market" was the best course. But Truffaut seems to have shied away from the bluntness of that approach. Nevertheless, the films he made from this point on must all be seen in the context of these remarks. He retreated to a less defensible position; paradoxically, the genre films he now chose to make were less popular than the more personal films which had assured his future as a film director. Still, all of the genre films grew out of the same concerns which had marked the personal ones. Truffaut chose the specific genres not for their formal properties so much as for their rightness for his own developing themes. All are love stories, and most are triangles. *La Peau douce* begins the series with a revenge tragedy, one of the most ancient dramatic genres, which is classic in its simplicity and economy. *Fahrenheit 451* presented a chance to indulge multiple desires: as Science Fiction, it belongs to one of the most strictly stylized genres; the personality of its hero offered Truffaut an opportunity to film a man fainting, something he had always wanted to do; and its theme gave him a chance to portray concretely his love of books. ("There will be as many literary references in *Fahrenheit 451* as in all of Jean-Luc's eleven films put together," he wrote in his journal.) *La Mariée était en noir* was a long overdue homage to Hitchcock (Truffaut had just completed his book of interviews with Hitchcock) and a complement to *La Peau douce:* whereas the earlier film gives us the human and emotional dimensions of revenge, this tribute to Hitchcock focuses narrowly on the *business* of it. It is revenge suspense rather than revenge tragedy.

There now comes a break in the chronology. During the spring and summer of 1968 Truffaut returned to Antoine Doinel for the first time in six years; he was also deeply involved with the fight for the Cinémathèque and the stoppage of the Cannes festival that May. When he returned to the genre series the next winter he filmed a second novel by William Irish (*La Mariée était en noir* was the first). There is a sense of wholeness and sureness to *La Sirène du Mississippi* that the earlier films seem to lack; this film marks a plateau for Truffaut, the completion of one stage of development. He did of course return again to genre films (most notably in *Une Belle Fille comme moi*), but *La Sirène du Mississippi,* his first scope film since "Antoine et Colette", was a summation of what he had learned from the genre experiments of the mid-sixties.

Noting that he had made *Tirez sur le pianiste* "as a sort of antithesis to *Les Quatre Cents Coups,*" Truffaut explained in a 1964 interview:

> *La Peau douce* I made as a violent answer to *Jules et Jim.* It's as though someone else had made *Jules et Jim*— as if I were now saying *Jules et Jim* is a lie. To some people *La Peau douce* might seem to be sordid, but to me it is

> about love in the city, instead of love in the country, as in *Jules et Jim,* and love is necessarily less beautiful in the city. *La Peau douce* is truly modern love; it takes place in planes, in elevators; it has all the harassments of modern life.[3]

Besides being a dialectical response to the good-humored pastoral of *Jules et Jim, La Peau douce* is also Truffaut's first classical genre film. A melodrama of adultery, it has none of the mixture of elements which mark *Tirez sur le pianiste.* It tells its story straight and it focuses intently on the three corners of its triangle: Pierre Lachenay (Jean Desailly), a Balzac scholar who runs a little literary review and has achieved a certain degree of fame as a lecturer, his jealous wife Franca (Nelly Benedetti), and his compliant mistress Nicole (Françoise Dorléac), an airline stewardess. Yet, as Gilles Jacob pointed out, a closer examination of the film shows that the standard elements of the story of adultery have been subtly shifted.[4] Pierre's typical confidence is only a mask for weakness and indecision. His wife is not the usual resigned, mousy sufferer, but rather a voluptuous woman, attractive and desirable, whose rage—when it shows itself at the end of the film—is insanely simple. She hides a shotgun under her coat, goes to the cafe where she knows her husband will be, raises the gun and quickly pulls the trigger. No great recriminations, no forced dramatic scene, only the mathematical logic of revenge. She then slumps to the floor, relieved finally, and a vague smile crosses her lips. Neither is the "other woman" the traditional man-eating vamp, but instead a charming, intelligent, and rather wise young woman, less interested in money than in talking about her family.

These fresh shifts in the elements of the genre are so subtle and so precise that the total impression the film creates seems at first vaguely disturbing; for Truffaut has in fact insisted on filming the genre story in a style which we associate with non-genre filmmaking. He has thrown, not a rough draft, but something like an annotated second draft, "on the market." This is the record of his interaction with the genre.

If Truffaut's earlier films showed the raw talent of a man born to camera and lens, *La Peau douce,* stylistically, is the first film of a growing maturity. Gone is the wide screen; gone are the considered pans, exuberant tricks, and *frissons.* Visually, *La Peau douce* is much simpler than the preceding films. What is lost in humor and good feeling is gained, I think, in the clinical collection of objective details. Like Godard's *Une Femme mariée* of about the same time, *La Peau douce* is a collection of concrete images: these tell the "story." The film has a complex, Resnaisian montage of detail shots and close-ups which flip by in well-timed collages (Gilles Jacob suggests Truffaut was influenced by *Muriel*). The film is after all well aware of the delights of the skin, and its technical grammar is complementary. We are at all times more aware of surface than of depth—and the surface is beginning to break up. Lights are switched on and off arhythmically; gears shift lurching and grinding; camera shutters slice up time. The story, too, progresses as if in a dream of glittering surfaces. Neither Pierre and Franca nor Pierre and Nicole ever have much peace together. Even a weekend in the country away from the urban environment proves painfully difficult: patterns already so well-established, it seems, cannot easily be broken. In a way, Franca knows that the life she and Pierre lead is so tightly structured that it will be difficult if not impossible for him to escape. This is what makes her action at the end so startling—since as we know (even if she doesn't because of a busy phone), what she does is really not necessary. The affair of Pierre and Nicole was more an idea than an actuality. It was, for Pierre, a symbol of the potential contradiction of that structure which the language of the film so strongly enforces upon him.

Pierre is no fool and Nicole, despite her very evident charm, is no vamp. Like Alain Tanner's *Au milieu du monde*, produced a decade later, *La Peau douce* gives us adultery as existential act—an affirmation of freedom. In this world Balzac is understood only too well. Lachenay's lecture in Lisbon (which leads directly to his meeting Nicole) is titled "Balzac and Money." Unless he keeps his literature entirely separate from his life, we must assume he understands the Balzacian consequences of the affair he undertakes. If we doubt his consciousness, Truffaut reminds us of it again in Reims, where Lachenay begins another lecture with an apposite quote from Pascal: "All unhappiness stems from the inability to just stay put at home."

The story Truffaut wrote with Jean-Louis Richard nicely mirrors the problem which the film presents for Truffaut himself. Both Truffaut and Lachenay (named for Truffaut's boyhood friend and fellow cinéphile Robert Lachenay) have a certain formal knowledge of their genre. Each of them enters the genre (adultery for Lachenay, the drama of adultery for Truffaut) in order to test himself against its structure. These are objective acts of free will. Truffaut is luckier than Lachenay. Having analyzed the structural elements of the drama of jealousy, Truffaut has altered each of them in subtle but significant ways in order to see what happens. He has "de-dramatized" the narrative, attenuated it at certain points where we have learned to expect certain emotional payoffs. The passion of the romance is cool and fractured by the urban structures of the characters' lives. Franca's revenge is just as much an "obligatory scene" for her as for scholars of the genre. Like Julie Kohler in *La Mariée*

Nicole in focus, Pierre (and their relationship) out of focus in the mirror.

était en noir, she goes about her work efficiently and functionally, not melodramatically.

Moreover, like all of Truffaut's films *La Peau douce* is also an essay on the concrete reality of everyday life: a set of finely observed comments on the details of coping with ordinary physical reality. It is this aspect of the film that is responsible more than any other for the mixed response it has generated. A seemingly melodramatic story is couched in the language of very common people doing very common things. And despite occasional bursts of surprising energy they find that the material structures of everyday life are a formidable barrier to their attempts at high melodrama.

La Peau douce was an original screenplay; for his next genre experiment, Truffaut turned to a book by Ray Bradbury that he had long admired. He explained his use of novels as the bases for his next several films by noting:

> if I made a film each year from an original scenario, my films would all be too French, too full of nuances, too much a collection of little things, with not enough action.[5]

Once again Truffaut saw a projected film as a contrast to the one he had just completed. If *La Peau douce* was "too French, too full of nuances," then this American novel would provide a corrective. It must have sounded like an exciting action film, full of fire engines, book burnings (remember the scene in the movie theatre in *Jules et Jim*), and men with rocket belts chasing Montag, the hero, all over the countryside. But of course the *Fahrenheit 451* which Truffaut eventually did make neatly muted all of this American action.

Fahrenheit 451 must have seemed especially attractive to Truffaut because the genre of Science Fiction is so highly structured. The contrasts and tensions between author and genre would be all the more evident. As he explains clearly in his "Journal of Fahrenheit 451," his aim was to make the most eclectic and least clichéd Science Fiction film. To this end he designed a film in which "fiction" far outweighs "science." Not for Truffaut the great technical metaphors, replete with monumental morals, of such classics as *Forbidden Planet, The Incredible Shrinking Man,* or *2001: A Space Odyssey*. His main focus, as always, is people. "I wanted to make the movie because I wanted to show books in difficulty, almost as if they were people in difficulty," he has said. "I wanted the audience to suffer as if they were seeing animals or people burning."[6]

In some important ways *Fahrenheit 451* is Truffaut's least successful film. As he himself noted in the "Journal,"

> I like the film quite well when I see it in pieces or three reels at a time, but it seems boring to me when I see it end to end.[7]

Once again he had consciously, as the "Journal" shows, excised the clichés from the genre—but since the clichés were, and are, the source of the drama, the net effect is that the film has been de-dramatized. (The most significant difference between book and film in this respect is that Truffaut eschews the nuclear explosion which ends Bradbury's story.) In addition, Truffaut was working in English for the first time and experimenting with color as well, and these two factors further distance the film. He knew that the characters were "not very real or very strong" but attributed it to

> the exceptional nature of the situations. This is the chief danger in science fiction stories, that everything else is sacrificed to what is postulated.

Since he had already shifted the focus of the film from the "science" to the characters, he was therefore skating on thin ice. In addition, he worked intentionally to mute the characters even further. This was the source of his famous feud with Oskar Werner:

> Oskar's performance isn't as "cool" as I would like [he noted]. Clearly, he doesn't want to appear less intelligent than Clarisse, although that is the situation.

But as for Clarisse (Julie Christie),

> I have desexed Clarisse so as to get neither her nor Montag mixed up in an adulterous situation which has no place in science fiction. Not mistress, girlscout, nor "girlfriend," Clarisse is just a young woman, thinking, questioning, who happens to cross Montag's path and who makes him stray from it.

Finally,

> I don't want *Fahrenheit 451* to look like a Yugoslav film or an American left-wing film. I want it to remain modest, a simple film in spite of its "big" theme.

Yet the very nature of Science Fiction as a genre, as opposed to the drama of adultery or the revenge play, is just that it provides the novelist or filmmaker with a structure akin to parable and fable so that he can speak of grand themes convincingly. By muting that aspect of *Fahrenheit 451* Truffaut made it almost impossible for the film to succeed with audiences.

When *Fahrenheit 451* is compared with Jean-Luc Godard's venture into science fiction, *Alphaville,* made a year previously, it becomes even more apparent that what is missing in Truffaut's try at the genre is some sense of active resistance to the dismal, suffocating existence it postulates. Bradbury's original novel, like Godard's *Alphaville,* is deeply rooted in politics; Truffaut's film ignores them. The reality it pictures is excruciatingly passive; the human beings quite literally sacrifice their lives to the books. The actions of the book-*burners* do not inspire any sort of insurrection among the book-*people,* who instead escape into a pretty forest glade and retreat like turtles into the shells of their books. We are left despondent with the suspicion that Truffaut actually thinks the fairyland of the book-people represents some sort of victory for Montag and Clarisse.

If the substructure of the film revealed some political consciousness, something to separate audience and filmmaker from the characters so that they could be put into perspective, none of this would matter. The basic materials are there; the society of *Fahrenheit 451* operates with a brilliant McLuhanish intelligence. The wall-screen provides a unified field of experience that excuses Montag, Linda, and her friends from any responsibility for thinking or living. Aided by simple drugs and firemen who search out and burn books, the cool medium is in full effective control. For example, it is not in the least necessary for the authorities to find Montag after he has learned to read. There is no serious danger from him or from the book-people. It is only necessary to stage his death on TV; for the *real* reality is the wall-screen. The result is that the book-people must be seen as sublime but unconscious victims of liberal tyranny—they shall be *allowed* to exist, so long as they are passive. It is no accident that Bernard Herrmann's score for the film specifically recalls his score for *The Man in the Gray Flannel Suit.*

It seems clear that Truffaut was uninterested not only in the "science" of this piece of Science Fiction, but also in the politics of it. And since he had decided that passionate human relationships had no place in Science Fiction, he was left with a film whose main function was as a paean to books. Yet how to recapture the special magic of books in a medium so foreign to them? Ray Bradbury passes on to Truffaut a rather hokey solution: the book-people; but I think that ending is too fey. We become absorbed with the herculean dimensions of the job of memorizing even the shortest novel, and we cannot then generate the emotional attachment to books that both Bradbury and Truffaut wish to evoke. In short, Montag and Clarisse may yet *become* book-people, but as of the end of the film, despite their new names ("Tales of Mystery and Imagination by Edgar Allan Poe" and "Memoirs of Saint-Simon") they are still spaced-out, passive children of the TV-stoned generation they think they have escaped. They have advanced from narcissism to idolatry, no further.

But the images of the books Truffaut has so carefully photographed do succeed where the book-people fail. In fact, the film is visually one of Truffaut's most impressive achievements. Working with cinematographer Nicolas Roeg, Truffaut simplified his mise-en-scène even further than in *La Peau douce;* it would never again be so spare, fastidious, and carefully organized. The images of *Fahrenheit 451* dominate the characters, dominate the plot, and this is how Truffaut wanted it:

> half the film is strictly visual, which makes me really happy. In almost all films, the footage of acted dialogue scenes tends to increase during shooting whereas the mute part (action scenes, scenes of violence, love scenes, mute reactions) diminishes because there's never enough time to shoot all the scenes intended. Spurred on by all the silent films of the 1920s I have seen and seen again in the last two years, I cling to my "privileged moments" so that they don't get whittled down.[8]

Those privileged moments linger in the mind long after the plot has drifted out of memory: dull red fire engines against a backdrop of woods, fires, and books; simple rooms with antique touches; the scan lines of the wall screen; the mute antennae of the credit sequence; the effect of the aural credits; the narcissists passing time on the monorail; the Godardian shock of comic books with empty balloons; personnel files full of photos "including 12 back views"; an ambulance attendant stealing a look at his coiffure in the shiny surface of his kit ("in twenty

Fahrenheit 451: Montag (Oskar Werner) reads the "newspaper"—cartoons without captions; Laura (Julie Christie), earphone in hand, prefers TV.

minutes she'll be as good as new," he tells Montag, "we'll call you when she's done"); Montag making out the first few words of *David Copperfield* by the light of the blank wall-screen; the Antonionian emptiness of the streets; the sad snow falling on the reciting book-people; and—Truffaut's most privileged moment—Montag's fainting spell in the Captain's office. Clear, fresh, and evocative, these images and sounds create a strong mood for the film, as does Herrmann's music; but the mood can't carry the full weight of the de-dramatized and de-politicized Science Fiction.

Truffaut is right about the film: it works well enough in pieces, but it is boring when seen end to end. Near the end of his "Journal" he muses,

> . . . I think I still have quite a lot of blends to make, new quantities to try out. I am a French filmmaker who has maybe thirty films to make over the years to come. Some of them will succeed, some will not, and I don't really mind—so long as I make them.

As if in reaction to the passivity of *Fahrenheit 451,* Truffaut turned next to a story with a very aggressive character at its center. *La Mariée était en noir* afforded him an opportunity to apply what he had learned from Hitchcock: how to make the images of a film carry the story, how to free a film from dependence on dialogue. What he had not learned from

Hitchcock (what he had no desire to learn, we can assume) were the coordinates of anxiety and nightmare against which Hitchcock's films were plotted. So the result, once again, is a film in which the tension between the auteur and his materials is the main source of interest. Paradoxically, since the American murder mystery on which the film was based was already so Hitchcockian in nature, Truffaut was in the unusual position of working against elements of the narrative which Hitchcock would have emphasized. It was more important to maintain the dialectic of adaptation which now interested him than to underline the mystery and suspense in order to pay homage to Hitchcock. The result is a complex and tricky film which is only the more confusing because the plot seems so simple and straightforward.

Truffaut had first read William Irish's *The Bride Wore Black* (against his mother's instructions) when he was thirteen. Having decided that he wanted to make a second film with Jeanne Moreau, he set about acquiring film rights to this dark mystery, a process which took enough time to let Truffaut and Jean-Louis Richard adapt the story at their leisure. The whole tone and direction of their script is at odds with the original novel, and the changes they made are instructive. Irish's book had the conventional structure of a murder mystery. We don't learn the purpose of the murders Julie commits until the end of the book; she is arrested before she can commit the fifth murder; it turns out that she has murdered the wrong men; and a great deal of attention is given to the detective who follows her throughout the book. Truffaut and Richard de-emphasize the detective, thereby forcing us to see the film from Julie's point of view; and they inform us fairly early in the film of her motives, consequently reinforcing our identification with her. They also allow her to commit the fifth murder (so that she can neatly finish the job of revenge), and they leave the guilt for the killing of Julie's husband on her victims, which gives the story a fatalistic dimension. The effects of these changes are considerable. Our attention is shifted from the job of discovering why these murders are being committed to the question of how they are accomplished. Irish's rather complicated story (full of false leads and simplistic suspense) is streamlined in order to emphasize the fateful nature of Julie's mission. This, then, shifts our attention from the intrigue of the mystery to the human dimensions of the story—the personal relationships between Julie and the men. Then Truffaut and Richard set up a gallery of male types who are considerably humanized, much more sympathetic than their counterparts in the novel.

As Truffaut reworked the materials of the novel into his own scheme, his own special concerns were liberated. The result was a film even more fractured than its predecessors. The narrative materials are wholly American (even most of the American names have been preserved), but what is done with them is thoroughly French. (This national dialectic was also important to Godard, who was making *Made in U.S.A.* at about the same time.) *Tirez sur le pianiste* had been an American story told in a French style with the action transposed to France, *Fahrenheit 451* an American story filmed in English in an abstract setting. Both, Truffaut thought, had been hurt by these transpositions. He left the locale of *La Mariée était en noir* purposely vague. As C. G. Crisp has pointed out, the American aspect of the film is visual while the French is aural. The murders take place on the screen, but the soundtrack ignores them. The dialogue is devoted to the relationships between the characters. As Truffaut put it:

> If the soundtrack was played over the radio, people would be totally at a loss. They would have no reason for ever imagining that murders were taking place. . . . This decision to have the characters talk of matters external to the action is one Hitchcock would never accept: for him it would be a weakening of the structure.[9]

For Truffaut, however, it was the contrast, the risk, that counted.

At the center of this mix of contradictions is Julie Kohler (from her name we may infer a kinship with Charlie). Dressed throughout the film only in black or white, she is a woman with an almost religiously ecstatic vision of her mission. When she moves she glides, like a nun, or more pertinently like Hitchcock's Mrs. Danvers in *Rebecca,* with whom she shares a demonic and destructive obsession. She is the focus of the film, but she is a still center, and colorless. We learn far less about her than about any of her male victims, each of whom is defined in opposition to Julie; she becomes each man's ideal, and it is but a short jump of logic to imagine her as their creation, the personification of their own various guilts and desires. Bliss (Claude Rich) is the lady-killer, Coral (Michel Bouquet) his antithesis, the timid man. Morane (Michael Lonsdale) is the politician, pompous and self-obsessed. Fergus (Charles Denner) the artist, on the other hand, is sensitive and honest; he offers the only possibility of love. For them all, even Delvaux (Daniel Boulanger) the crook (and the last victim), she is a kind of objective correlative. Truffaut told Jeanne Moreau "not to be tragic; to play it like a skilled worker with a job to do, conscientious and obstinate." In her mechanical persona each finds a reflection of his own mortality. *La Mariée était en noir* does not do much to advance the development of Truffaut's study of genres, but it does give us a sharply etched emblem for the essential dramatic relationship of a Truffaut film.

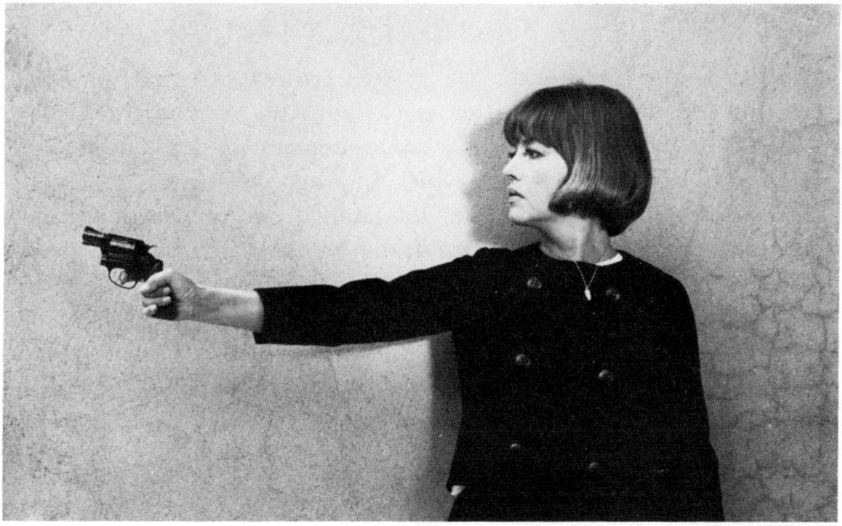

Jeanne Moreau: *La Mariée était en noir.*

Truffaut, having finished most of the work on *La Mariée* by the fall of 1967, had reached a dead end with his series of genre films. Each of them had been instructive, but none had had the popular success he felt was important. Before going ahead with another genre film, Truffaut returned to the Antoine Doinel series for the first time in six years and shot, during February and March of 1968, *Baisers volés.* At the same time he was deeply involved with the defense of the Cinémathèque and, later, with the closing of the Cannes festival. For the first time in his life he was involved in active politics, and the experience must have refreshed and revived him. He still maintained a certain skepticism; he still felt like an outsider. He did not join the short-lived Etats-Généraux du cinéma, nor the Director's Association which succeeded it. Whether it was the return to Doinel, l'affaire Langlois, the events of May, or simply a matter of time passing, he returned to the struggle with genres in December of 1968 with a new sense of assurance. *La Sirène du Mississippi* is the most successful film of the group, and a summary of what Truffaut had learned from his previous experiences.

Perhaps we should qualify that last sentence. The film, Truffaut's most expensive so far (it cost 800 million old francs—almost $2 million) and his first attempt at a glamorous "star" film (Deneuve and Belmondo were the highest-paid French actors at that time), met with uniformly confused reviews when it opened in Paris and was not financially successful. As with the earlier genre experiments, the "mix" was a problem. Neither audiences nor French critics, on the whole, were ready for it. But judged in terms of Truffaut's *own* intentions and against the background of his work in the mid-sixties, *La Sirène du Mississippi* marks the point at which his theories come together in a kind of critical mass which makes the film glow with energy. Fittingly, this genre masterpiece (and I mean that word in its original sense: a work submitted for admission to the rank of master) *was* appreciated by American critics, most notably Vincent Canby and Pauline Kael. Truffaut produced an American genre film, finally, that Americans understood and appreciated. Canby, who has always written well about Truffaut's films, put it this way:

> François Truffaut's "The Mississippi Mermaid" has the form of a preposterous romantic melodrama, but it is so full of lovely, complex things—of unannounced emotions, of ideas, of the memories of other movies (Truffaut's as well as those of two of his father-figures, Renoir and Hitchcock)—that it defies easy definition and blithely triumphs over what initially appears to be structual schizophrenia. It is the creation of a superior moviemaker who works eccentrically in the classic tradition.[10]

What initially appears to be structural schizophrenia is, of course, the concrete result of Truffaut's theory of exploding genres by combining them. For the first time, that idea got across to at least a section of the general public and the critics who represent them.

La Sirène du Mississippi is based, once again, on a novel by William Irish (also known as "Cornell Woolrich")—*Waltz into Darkness*, published in 1947. Again Truffaut stripped the novel down to its basic structure and rebuilt it according to his own specifications. He changed the locale from New Orleans to the Indian Ocean island of Réunion and France, shifted the time from the nineteenth century to the present, and softened and humanized both Julie, the femme fatale, and Louis, her "victim." Truffaut's Julie is not nearly so cruel and calculating as her counterpart in Irish's novel; his Louis is less naive and more intelligent. The result is a film which carries acceptable and intelligent human emotions within the framework of stylized melodrama. That framework is pure film noir material, but the sentiments it contains are worthy of Jean Renoir, to whom the film is dedicated.

Truffaut had recognized that the novel was especially valuable for its broad connection to genre filmmaking:

> What seduced me when I read *La Sirène du Mississippi* was that William Irish had treated in it a subject traditional in the pre-war cinema: it's *The Devil is a Woman, The Blue Angel, La Chienne, Nana.* This theme of the vamp, of the *femme fatale,* subjugating an honest man to the point of

> making a rag-doll out of him, had been treated by all the cineastes I admire. I said to myself that I must too. . . .[11]

But he realized also that he would be incapable of reproducing the broad dramatic clichés of melodramatic convention. This was one of the reasons why he thought it necessary to transpose the action into the present. He admired the scene in *Nana* "where the Baron gets down on his hands and knees to beg like a dog for *marrons glacés,* and the one where Emil Jannings crows like a rooster in *The Blue Angel,*" but these were not scenes that he felt capable of filming.

> That sort of woman isn't a tramp any longer, she's something much more comprehensible, and her victim is no longer entirely a victim. The black and white have become shades of grey. So despite myself, I weakened the contrast between the characters, as the risk of de-dramatizing the subject a little.[12]

The de-dramatization, as always, hurt the film at the box office, but this time, at least, all the elements came together concisely.

La Sirène du Mississippi begins as a mystery, evolves into a Hitchcockian chase suspense, and ends as a Truffautesque love story—altogether the most ambitious mix of genres so far. It is pervaded by the spirit of Renoir, not only because of its similarity with *Nana* and *La Chienne,* but more importantly because it investigates the bond between a man and a woman against a background of the full range of human experience. (Any summary of its antecedents should include Hitchcock's *Vertigo* and *Marnie,* as well.) Finally—and this is an entirely new element—*La Sirène du Mississippi* is also a "star vehicle." That is, it depends on the personas that Belmondo and Deneuve have created *outside* its structure. Our tendency always with a Truffaut film is to relate the personality of its hero somehow to Antoine Doinel. More often than not that approach is successful. But with *La Sirène du Mississippi* we must look not to Doinel but to Godard's films *A bout de souffle* and *Pierrot le fou* for the sources of Jean-Paul Belmondo's persona. The basic structure of all three films is precisely the same: *l'amour fou* leads to a mutually destructive relationship between a man and a woman, and a period—a long "privileged moment," if you will—in which the couple finds refuge outside society. In the end the man dies, a victim of the woman's betrayal (and his own), although in *La Sirène du Mississippi* the hero is allowed to survive, if barely.

Just as Léaud's work with Godard is a useful corrective for his Doinel persona, so Belmondo's one film with Truffaut serves to balance the persona he had developed working with Godard. So Truffaut is paying homage to Godard in *La Sirène du Mississippi,* as well as to Renoir and to forties genre romances. Since the mood of the film—the balance between guilt, obsession, and *l'amour fou*—also bears some resemblance to Chabrol's obsessions (especially in the series of films he was beginning just at this time), *La Sirène du Mississippi* is a kind of cinematic plaza where many roads cross: an emblem of the first decade of the New Wave, then concluding.

The function of the film as a vehicle for star personas developed outside the context of this particular film has a more general importance. Truffaut's humanization of Irish's rather harsh story gives it some of the flavor of American romantic films of the forties, and it does not take much imagination to see Bogart in Belmondo's role. There are significant differences, of course, but Godard's identification of Belmondo with Bogart in *A bout de souffle* ten years earlier still holds. This was Truffaut's first chance to deal with the phenomenon of "movie stars," which had fascinated him as a critic but which he had not yet tackled as a director.* ("I made *La Sirène du Mississippi* in cinemascope," he said, "so I could have both of them on the screen most of the time."[13]) The major reason Truffaut's previous genre efforts had been difficult for most audiences was the intentional lack of unity between their clearly generic form and their cinematic idiom of realistic narrative. The effect was of someone telling a fable or a fairytale in journalistic prose, or more precisely in the language of a highly personal letter. Now, with the stars of *La Sirène,* form and idiom were parallel, and there was less chance that audiences would recoil from the fusion of the two. Truffaut had finally created the "fairytale for adults" that he often spoke of making. What he meant to convey by the word "fairytale" was the combination of abstract formalism, moral point, and shared cultural experience that he found as a critic in genre films. These were the real contemporary fairytales; they had the same mythic resonances. The same stories were told over and over again because the *structures* of those stories had deep psychological roots. This is what intrigued Truffaut; this is why he had to go through the process of reworking those aging melodramas in contemporary terms. *La Sirène du Mississippi* is a synthesis of the work he had been doing during the preceding six or eight years, a great bouillabaisse of Renoir, Hitchcock, Bogart, Doinel, *Pierrot le fou, Tirez sur le pianiste,* Nicholas Ray, Belmondo, Audiberti

*Is it accidental that, having just given up so much of his control in *La Sirène* to an actor (and that actor's persona), Truffaut immediately made a film *(L'Enfant sauvage)* starring himself? The auteur as star—once again he had to complete the dialectic.

Louis (Jean-Paul Belmondo) and Julie/Marion (Catherine Deneuve): "I made *La Sirène du Mississippi* in cinemascope so I could have both of them on the screen most of the time."

(the "monorail" hotel alludes to a novel by Jacques Audiberti), Balzac (Louis reads *La Peau de chagrin*), Cocteau (the Clinique Heurtebise reminds us of the angel in *Orphée*), and so much else. Truffaut named the detective in the film Comolli, after the editor of *Cahiers du Ciñema*, because the *deep* mystery of the film (as opposed to the surface mystery) is cinematic: how can all the madly diverse elements of this weighty cinematic heritage be forged into a new cinema? While for Godard the problem was one of analysis, for Truffaut it was one of synthesis. In his next film he—like Godard—returns to zero (but in his own way) to investigate the essential nature of language and our relationship to it.

Truffaut's obsession with the mystery of genre films dominated his work during this period; but esthetic problems and formal dilemmas were not sufficient in themselves as justifications for his films. Significantly, he recognized the intimate connection between the structure of his film idiom and the themes of his films: he approached the art of film the way his characters approached the art of life. One chooses to do genre films, after all, because their formal structure allows a certain freedom. When one tells a story that most people have heard before, it is the method of the telling that counts, whereas, with the grand theme or "realistic" drama (i.e., non-genre films), the explicit interest of the story often masks its implicit substance. The genre film allows the filmmaker to work within and against a structure with mythic properties that encourages harmonic variations on a theme rather than the linear melodic development of more "realistic" modes. For Truffaut, working from secondary sources had a similar value:

> In adapting books describing a milieu other than my own, I end up saying things I daren't say in my original scenarios. In *Baisers volés,* for example, I had constantly to cover my tracks, camouflage myself, and transpose so that I wouldn't be too recognizable. In short, I wore a mask. In *La Mariée* or *La Sirène,* on the contrary, the mask existed *a priori,* and behind borrowed characters I felt freer to express my own personality.[14]

Except for *Les Quatre Cents Coups* and *L'Enfant sauvage,* every one of Truffaut's films to date has dealt with the relationship of men and women; in fact they share an intense and nearly exclusive focus on this phenomenon. All the films are seen from the male point of view, even *La Mariée, La Sirène,* and *Jules et Jim,* in each of which the woman is the central character. (Truffaut, talking about Antonioni, once said: "I don't like the way he deals with women, because instead of talking about them as a man would, he talks about them as though he had been told their secrets, like General De Gaulle telling the Algerians, 'I have understood you.' He flatters women, but it doesn't seem authentic to me.")[15] Psychologically, Truffaut's men are shy and timid; sociologically, they are always outsiders. Consequently, they are continually involved in an existential struggle to reaffirm their egos, a theme from the French literature of the forties and fifties which Truffaut has brought up to date. At their best, they tend towards the asymptote that Léaud traced in the Doinel films: "He's still an adolescent at heart," Truffaut explains, "and, of course, Léaud is like that as a person, full of good will and awkwardness, a combination of anguish and wholesomeness."[16]

The women, meanwhile, since they are seen from the male point of view, are seldom characterized with as much subtlety. More often than not, since the men are artists—musicians, writers, painters—the women appear as art works, mysterious and confusing, variable and a little frightening. When this happens the two questions of *La Nuit américaine* ("Are women magic?" and "Are films more important than life?") fuse: women and art become indistinguishable, and it is clear that the real question for Truffaut would be better phrased: How can we distinguish between the idealization of art and the concrete realization of our relationships with other human beings? If the ultimate iconic representation for Truffaut of the male situation is the scene of Montag fainting, then the ultimate fear of women—of the reality they represent—is more than adequately expressed by Julie Kohler—spiritual sister of Charlie, sharing a first name with "Marion" of *La Sirène* and the actress who played a dual role in *Fahrenheit 451*—who coldly murders five men. She isn't the only murderess in Truffaut. Women are exceedingly dangerous. In the genre films they murder; in the non-genre films they are merely difficult. Charlie Kohler, Louis Mahé, Fergus, Morane and company, Pierre Lachenay, Clovis, Prévine and Arthur, Montag, and Jim would all testify to that danger.

But, it must be remembered, it is not real women that men fear, but rather our distorted *image* of them. Truffaut's genre films of the mid-sixties are therefore attempts to exorcise the demons of the Bride and the Siren, to conquer the confusing appeal of the Soft Skin, and to neutralize the drugged, televised image of women in *Fahrenheit 451*.

Like all of Truffaut's films, in one way or another, *La Sirène du Mississippi* is about isolation, loneliness, alienation. It begins with a credit sequence against a background of newspaper "personal" ads as the soundtrack recites specific journalistic pleas for companionship in an accelerating crescendo of anxiety. It ends in a cabin in the mountains in the snow. As Julie/Marion notes—apparently having seen *Tirez sur le pianiste,* since it's literally the same cabin—"It's a fine place to end a gangster film." Truffaut has come full circle. *La Sirène* is a synthesis not only of his own films but of all the romantic, formalized genre films on which he (and we) were weaned. It leaves him free, in his next film, to begin again.

5

TRUFFAUT
Intimate Politics

Between the summer of 1969 and the autumn of 1972, in a period of three and a half years, Truffaut shot five films, including two of his best. After the triumph of *La Nuit américaine (Day for Night),* his most popularly acclaimed film since *Jules et Jim,* he ceased making films for two years, returning to the camera in early 1975 to shoot *L'Histoire d'Adèle H.* Practically speaking, the reason for the intense activity in the early seventies was simply that several scripts were complete and ready to be shot, and production money was available. *L'Enfant sauvage (The Wild Child)* had been gestating for eight years, ever since Truffaut had first been impressed by a stage production of *The Miracle Worker* in 1962. (He had tried to buy the film rights to the play, but Arthur Penn was already at work on the screen version.) *Les Deux Anglaises et le Continent (Two English Girls, Anne and Muriel)* had been in his mind ever since he made *Jules et Jim* from Roché's earlier novel. The idea of making a film about filmmaking—if it had not always been with him—certainly dated back to the time of his film about books, *Fahrenheit 451.*

The fallow period from 1972 to 1974 is also simply explained. When asked why he had stopped making films "at the moment of your greatest success," Truffaut replied:

> Well, for a very simple reason—I don't have any scripts. I usually keep three or four scripts in front of me, not concrete scripts, but rather 40 or 50 pages that describe the action, no dialogue. So I'm forced to stop, because I'd prefer to have four or five in reserve and then film them. It's a moral or mental buffer for me because if one film is very sad, I know I can put funny things into the next one.[1]

So the progress of Truffaut's career during the last six years can be simply explained. Yet, from the critic's point of view, there is also a metaphysical logic to it.

Overarching all the various contradictions which give life to Truffaut's work is the essential contradiction of criticism: that the mundane history of his career is one thing, while our *sense* of it is quite another. If accidental forces conspired to determine which films Truffaut made when, nevertheless the relationships between the films are not accidental. "I know that whatever picture I choose to make will inevitably contradict the one I have just made,"[2] Truffaut said once in order to explain why he no longer worried very much about choosing the next picture. He had become a bemused observer of his own work, intrigued by the unplanned yet valid relationships among his films and aware that the contradictions would inevitably illuminate.

For the man who had always regarded films as though they were people, for the critic turned filmmaker, one of the chief pleasures of his developing career was watching his creations take on lives of their own and find meaningful relationships with their cinematic siblings. "To be a filmmaker, you are almost forced to be surrounded by contradictions,"[3] he concluded.

L'Enfant sauvage was shot during the summer of 1969 (so as not to interrupt the education of Jean-Pierre Cargol, the gypsy boy Truffaut had discovered in the south of France to play the role). Truffaut had barely finished work on *La Sirène du Mississippi,* and once again one of his films neatly contradicts its predecessor. Having spent much of the preceding six years involved with de-dramatizing the high melodrama of the genre films, Truffaut now turned to a type of narrative structure which was new to him. *L'Enfant sauvage* has a mythic provenance and design which is in sharp contrast to the stylized drama of the genre films and even to the collages of personal memories of the Doinel films. The closest antecedent is, of course, Truffaut's first film, *Les Quatre Cents Coups.* During those intervening years he had concentrated on sexual relationships—the horizontal axis of family politics—but he remained equally interested in the generational relationship—the vertical axis. Indeed, in most of the intervening films, there is a child who serves as a reminder of this most personal theme. ("Fido," "Sabine," and "Christophe" appear in two films each.) Only *La Sirène du Mississippi* and *Baisers volés* have no notable roles for children.

Like *Les Quatre Cents Coups, L'Enfant sauvage* sets itself quite apart from most of Truffaut's films by the almost documentary quality of its narrative structure. This is a serious subject for Truffaut (if not quite the "grand theme" he had inveighed against), and his treatment of childhood has always been marked by an honesty and directness which shows itself in the tone he chose for both films. They tell their stories directly; there is none of the ironic distancing from the genre and memoir forms that is so important in the other films. Actually Truffaut could not altogether abandon his consciousness of genres in *L'Enfant sauvage*. He did, after all, make it in black and white and in the standard "academy aperture" ratio to express a sense of solidarity with the biographical films about science which he remembered from the thirties. But this effect is muted, like an antique "wash" which gives a painting some patina, and his concern for what might have been the genre of *L'Enfant sauvage* is nowhere apparent in the substance of the film. He has adhered to the strictest rules of narrative so that often the film looks and sounds more like an "educational" film that a fictional feature. Just as he had de-dramatized his melodramas, he has demythologized the mythic aspects of *L'Enfant sauvage,* of which he was well aware. In a passage quoted in publicity releases for the film he wrote:

> From Romulus and Remus through Mowgli and Tarzan, men have continually been fascinated by tales of beast children. It may be that in these stories of abandoned infants, reared by wolves, bears, or apes, they see a symbol of the extraordinary destiny of our race. Or it may be simply that they harbor a secret hankering after a natural existence.[4]

The mythic resonances are thus profound, but with his customary reticence Truffaut has given his film a quietly matter-of-fact tone which does nothing to artificially enhance those resonances. This makes them all the more meaningful, for we have the feeling that Truffaut is not grandly and self-consciously mounting the myth, but simply telling us an interesting little story, out of which *we* draw the mythic material. "I did not want to spell out my message," Truffaut told an interviewer after the film was released. Then, relenting, he added: "[It] is simply this: man is nothing without other men."[5] What impressed him about the story of Jean Itard and the "wolf-boy" Victor was not its "grand theme" but its emotional parallels with his own life; he was impressed with the opportunities this bit of history offered him to capture on film some of his own sentiments. In *Les Quatre Cents Coups* the Truffaut figure had been the boy entirely without a meaningful relationship with an adult. Now, twelve years later, the Truffaut figure is the adult (Truffaut plays the role himself), and there is considerably more understanding of the adult point of view.

As Truffaut noted, the myth of the wild child has an ambivalent attraction: on the one hand it posits the necessity for civilization and the socialization of children; on the other it offers a chance to indulge a "secret hankering after a natural existence." John Dryden gave voice to that "secret hankering" in 1667, in *The Conquest of Granada:*

> I am as free as Nature first made man,
> Ere the base laws of servitude began,
> When wild in woods the noble savage ran.

The attitude long pre-dates Dryden, but it was his phrase "noble savage" which symbolized throughout the eighteenth century and for much of the nineteenth the free, natural hero of the Romantics who stood in opposition to rational man. The doctor Jean-Marc Gaspard Itard chronicled his experiences with Victor of Aveyron, the wild child, in *Rapports et memoires sur le sauvage de l'Aveyron,* published in 1806, when, as it happened, the Rationalist and Romantic aspects of the myth were pretty much in cultural balance. Itard's attempt to educate this wolf-child is probably the first systematic study of a phenomenon of which there are documented instances dating at least two centuries earlier. The story of Itard and Victor, therefore, marks a turning point of sorts, as scientific logic is, for the first time, applied to the Romantic myth of the noble savage. It is the clash between these two sets of values—Rationalist science and Romantic nature—that is the source of the mythic dialectic of both the historical events and the film. By the time Truffaut made the film in 1969 the Romantic aspect of the myth had been resurrected (even if the flower-children of the sixties were rapidly becoming as rare as wolf-children). As a result, audiences of a particular kind had some difficulty with the film. In general, the immediate gut response of educated "hip" audiences was positive. But as they began to intellectualize the film, they realized that there was a criticism of the concept of the "noble savage" implicit in it which contradicted the Romantic ideal—and, for that matter, the *Whole Earth Catalogue* and Alicia Bay Laurel. But for Truffaut the "fairytale" of Victor of Aveyron in his natural state was simplistic and misleading (as by extension were all the then-current dreams of returning to nature). Victor, when he was discovered, was already tattooed with the scars that signified encounters with other, stronger beasts of the forest. It was clear to Truffaut that Victor would not long have survived as a "noble savage" in an environment which Truffaut saw as essentially hostile. (Truffaut lamented the financial limitations which prevented him from shooting scenes he had planned showing Victor's losing battles with the harshness of winter, a subject Itard emphasized.) So the film begins with a central compromise: to survive means to live in society.

Truffaut saw the wild child as essentially deprived, and therefore related to characters in some of his other films:

> I realize that *L'Enfant sauvage* is bound up with both *Les Quatre Cents Coups* and *Fahrenheit 451*. In *Les Quatre Cents Coups* I showed a child who missed being loved, who grows up without tenderness; in *Fahrenheit 451* it was a man who longed for books, that is, culture. With Victor of Aveyron, what is missing is something more essential—language.[6]

The Outsider is the one theme which recurs constantly in Truffaut's work. Most often (in the genre films, for example) it is love—or its absence—which separates the outsider from the rest of society. In the three films Truffaut mentions above, however, the quality of alienation is more acutely defined, giving a special urgency to these films, especially *L'Enfant sauvage,* where the dialectic is worked out in greatest detail. Truffaut shares this theme with his colleagues—especially Godard, who has given us possibly the most succinct expression of it. In his short film "L'Anticipation, ou l'an 2000," a Science Fiction fantasy, Godard creates an equation summarizing the dilemma when he shows us two people triumphant over an alienated society, who "are making love, conversation, and progress all at the same time." Maybe the third element of this formula (progress) is not so important for Truffaut, who has a deep-rooted distaste for practical politics; but the equivalency of love and conversation certainly works in his films. As Antoine explains to Christine the morning after, in his major declaration of love: "you teach me everything you know and I'll teach you all I know." Sharing knowledge—conversation—is the best evidence of love.

L'Enfant sauvage is, then, a love story; as Victor and Jean Itard learn to make conversation—and progress—they make love of a sort. When Freud was once asked "What is the secret of life?" he is said to have replied simply: "Lieben und arbeiten"—love and work. In *L'Enfant sauvage* Truffaut has managed to combine the two. Itard's love and his work are identical, as they must be in the best of all possible worlds. There aren't three scenes in the whole Doinel cycle (which are all original screenplays and therefore the best evidence) that don't focus precisely on either love or work, and the best of them manage to combine both: Antoine and Fabienne in the shoe store; Antoine and

Christine and the television set; Antoine and Kyoko at the model harbor. In *L'Enfant sauvage* love and work are united; every scene combines both. Through Victor's innocent obstinacy, Itard is forced to look at the world he *thinks* he understands with new eyes, to re-evaluate many of his basic assumptions, and finally to come to a new understanding of the process of learning in a manner I am sure Jean Piaget would find fitting. So the "education" (the "leading out") of Victor is also the education of Itard. The liberal image of the "teacher" as someone who molds a pliant, virginal student, who "fills an empty vessel" (the Miss Jean Brodie type), is eschewed in the film. Rather, Itard and Victor are engaged in the give-and-take of a dialectical relationship. Knowledge comes through the struggle with another's way of seeing, and also through a struggle with the material world.

The educational motif of the film naturally leads to some intriguing discoveries about language. For it is essentially his lack of language which separates Victor from his fellow human beings. He does, after all, have well-demonstrated emotions and a fund of knowledge about his forest world. He does not, however, express his feelings and thoughts in a way that others can understand. He wonders at fire, he yearns for the sun and sky, he bridles at constraint, he is warmed by the love of Itard and Mme Guérin, he is humiliated by curious tourists, he is proud of his own accomplishments; but he expresses these emotions in his own private language, the variety of which is one of the most masterful touches of the film. Truffaut has intuited an idiom of gesture and look which allows Victor to speak eloquently without words—and also makes him a powerfully cinematic character.

What Victor and Itard discover about language and its relationship to knowledge has a curiously modern flavor. It is hard to look at Victor matching things (scissors, comb, hammer, pen, key, book) with images of them and with the printed and spoken words for them without thinking about the categories of contemporary semiotics. Similarly Itard analyzes for Victor the rest of the structure of the civilized experience. The job begins slowly. First Victor must be sensitized to temperature, the most elemental differentiation of touch. Gradually, the tuning fork, the candle, the mirror, and Itard's other analytical devices develop Victor's discrimination of sights and sounds as well. Surrounding all of this sensual and linguistic education, however, is a structure of *moral* education which is still more important. The dramatic structure of the film (like the real-life experience) is concentrated in the painful dialectic of Victor's and Jean Itard's relationship. The battle may be taking place *within* Victor, but that only gives him an added weapon. Several times he devises ways to "cheat" in Itard's elemental

Language: object, image, and sign.

lessons, but Itard recognizes the value of this. At one point, when Victor has devised a method for accomplishing a task which short-circuits the lesson it was supposed to teach, Itard responds:

> That's very good, Victor. After all, you have invented a method which does not need any memory, comparison, and discernment. But I don't mind. This little invention is a tribute to your intelligence.[7]

The step-by-step education of Itard by Victor is one of the main pleasures of the film's logic. Gradually, Victor's natural intelligence shows Itard how to analyze a problem fully, without making civilized (and unscientific) elisions.

On an emotional level the conflict between the two is even more affecting. Itard is no stranger to the concept of the noble savage. Victor often falls into great rages at the arbitrary limitations of his captivity and escapes regularly. That Itard allow this makes him a more reasonable figure than the wardens of the Institute for the Deaf and Mute. But often Itard has regrets:

> At this moment, as at so many others, ready to renounce the task I had imposed upon myself, how deeply did I regret having known this child, and I condemned the sterile curiosity of the men who first wrenched him away from his innocent and happy life.[8]

The pain of the relationship culminates in the "dark closet" sequence at the end of the film, in which Itard, allowing his science to take precedence over his love of the child, realizes that he will never know whether Victor has a "disinterested awareness of the moral order" unless he subjects him to a "punishment as odious as it is unjust in order to see, precisely, if he will rebel." Victor does rebel, and Itard is deeply moved. A shot of long duration shows Itard gently stroking Victor's hair, as he explains, voice-over,

> How sweet it would have been at this moment to be able to make my pupil understand me, to tell him the very pain of his bite filled my soul with satisfaction. How could I rejoice half-heartedly?[9]

The two are united in pain and love, and separated by language: an emblematic image for all Truffaut's characters, from Antoine and his mother through Louis and Marion to Camille Bliss, her interviewer, and her victims. "Man is nothing without other men." But the relationship is never ideal; it is always unbalanced and therefore dramatic—and dialectical.

This is an image of Truffaut's politics as well, for his characters do make progress at the same time as they make painful love and halting conversation. This is not the macro-politics that so fascinates Godard, but micro-politics, an analysis of the basic political unit—the human couple. Most often expressed in sexual terms, in *L'Enfant sauvage* Truffaut's politics is de-sexed as well as de-dramatized, which makes its essential features all the more apparent. The idea of community is paramount, and the community begins at home, between father and son, woman and man—in this case among Itard, Mme Guérin—both surrogates—and Victor, so symbolically named. Itard's story is an object lesson not only for scientists and teachers, but for all "professionals" in a liberal society based on the axiom that expertise is the highest good. The relationship of Itard and Victor mirrors the politics of doctor and patient, lawyer and client, those with power and those without it.

The presence of Truffaut himself in the film emphasizes this political point, as does the dedication of the film to Jean-Pierre Léaud. Truffaut, wanting to preserve the film's documentary quality, had been searching for a non-professional for the role of Itard. Finally, since "the child has to be directed within the image," he saw that he "should have to try to play the part myself." The experience left him "with the impression not of having acted a role, but simply of having directed the film *in front* of the camera and not, as usual, *from behind* it."[10] His presence emphasizes the parallel with his own "professional" role as a filmmaker, engaged in an art which presents real ethical problems, since it "uses" human beings. What gives a doctor or lawyer the right to "use" patients and clients? What gives a filmmaker the right to "use" actors—and non-professionals? Truffaut has never thought of himself as a "director" of film ("I don't *direct* actors," he has said, "I *shunt* them"), but rather less pretentiously as a "metteur en scène." He has a cautious fear of the micro-political power of the "director," and he seems to understand as well as Godard that the best filmmaking, like the best work in many other professions, is—or should be—communal. His dedication of the film to Léaud re-emphasizes his debt to that actor and strengthens our sense of the relationship between this film and the Doinel series and, therefore, Truffaut's own life. *L'Enfant sauvage* makes concrete some concepts which have only been abstract until now: the director as teacher, the filmmaker as scientist-reporter.

The quiet tone of Truffaut's previous films was often misinterpreted as weakness; his effort to de-dramatize the stories he was filming often seemed self-abasing. What he had really been after was a more humane relationship with his audience. He left us some room in which to operate; he invited us to contribute. Accustomed to the oppressive power of the "American style" of contemporary filmmaking, we choose often to ignore that invitation. Yet the relationship between Victor and Itard (and that between Truffaut and Jean-Pierre Cargol or Jean-Pierre Léaud) shows us what the relationship should be between us and a film: a structure of mutual respect. As Lenin said, Ethics is the Esthetics of the future. Truffaut was proud to note, in his introduction to the published screenplay, that he thought the gypsy boy Jean-Pierre Cargol had benefited tremendously from the experience of making the film:

> . . . we saw that the cinema had helped his evolution. In my opinion, the difference between Jean-Pierre Cargol *before* the film and *after* it is astonishing.[11]

Is film, then, more important than life?

When he was asked in an interview in 1970 whether the past ten years had gone as he wanted them to, Truffaut took a long moment and then replied:

> I think they have. Except, sadly, for the death of several people. Actors. Françoise Dorléac, the star of *La Peau douce* and Nicole Berger, who played the pianist's wife in *Tirez sur le pianiste*, and Albert Rémy who played the father in *Les Quatre Cents Coups*. Also Guy Decomble, who played the teacher in *Les Quatre Cents Coups*, and Catherine Lutz, who played the lady detective in *Baisers volés*. And there were writers. William Irish, who

> wrote *The Bride Wore Black,* and David Goodis, the author of *Tirez sur le pianiste*. . . . And there are filmmakers whom I didn't know but loved a great deal. Jacques Becker. Jean Cocteau. . . .[12]

This sense of unexpected loss informs *Les Deux Anglaises et le Continent,* which he made the next spring. It is—until *Adèle H.*—his darkest film. As *L'Enfant sauvage* had marked a rite of passage for François Truffaut, so *Les Deux Anglaises* was intended to do the same for his cinematic double, Jean-Pierre Léaud:

> I had watched Léaud growing up since he was 13, and I wanted a film which would mark both his final goodbyes to adolescence and to . . . Antoine Doinel . . . and his entry into adulthood and ordinary films. I wanted people to stop seeing him as a character and begin to admire him as an actor.[13]

Truffaut had been working on a screenplay of *Les Deux Anglaises et le Continent,* the second novel by Henri-Pierre Roché, for many years, since even before shooting *Jules et Jim.* He had been angry at himself for not having made *Jules et Jim* before Roché died, and one can assume that that particular loss also motivated *Les Deux Anglaises.* He was anxious to make a film which would capture the sense of time passing (and the losses which that incurs). Orson Welles's *Magnificent Ambersons,* which Truffaut called his "Bible," does accomplish that, and it "informed the making of *Les Deux Anglaises.*"

Thus the film's autumnal mood; it was a passage into middle age. Truffaut began it in a funk which only lifted as filming progressed:

> What Claude says when he has finished his first novel made me smile: "I feel better now. I feel that it is the book's characters who will suffer in my place."[14]

So the film's characters suffer in Truffaut's. "Rather than a film about physical love," he said, he wanted to make "a 'physical' film about love, which explains the emphasis on fainting fits, nausea, blood and tears." The actors cried while making the film, he continued, and the audience should cry while watching it. The film is a close progression of images of pain. "The characters are in the grip of extremely strong emotions which they analyze among themselves and for themselves to the point of finally becoming lovesick." The characters were for Truffaut "romanesque," unnaturally distorted by their passions. Each image of the film contributes a detail to the canvas of time, loss, pain, loneliness, and the sickness of love. There are few indications of its pleasures, for the film, like its characters, is puritanical. Ultimately, the union of Claude and Muriel which, in terms of plot, is the aim of the story, is symbolized for us by the blood-stained bedsheet. At the end of the film (at the end of this love story) fifteen years pass, years full of corpses and shrapnel. There is an image of Rodin's *The Kiss,* lovers frozen in cold stone, and the film concludes with Claude alone in a taxi. "I look old," he says, and the image freezes. It is to be compared with the last frozen image of Léaud in *Les Quatre Cents Coups.*

Yet for all this darkness and cold, these purposes mistook and passions misdirected, the vomit and blood and blindness which are the materials out of which Truffaut builds the film, there is an anodyne. It lies, as Claude notes, in the process of art, the catharsis for the artist. Once again, as with the genre films, we have to look at the subtext of the film and its structure in order to find the logic which makes it comprehensible.

Henri-Pierre Roché published only two novels, both late in life and both semi-autobiographical, based on extensive journals and diaries which Roché had kept during the early years of this century. Even before Truffaut acquired the story, then, it had gone through a process of transformation as Roché molded his real experience into fiction. That diaries and letters form so large a part of the film increases our sense of life made into art (and also made the process of translating the book to the screen that much more difficult). Truffaut had been working on an adaptation for years, following the procedure he had used to good effect with *Jules et Jim,* reading and re-reading the book constantly, committing passages to memory, and marking certain passages with one, two or three x's, depending on their relative importance. He gave these annotations to Jean Gruault, who produced a 500-page screenplay which, after a lapse of several years, Truffaut edited down. He used Roché's journals as well as the novel, so that he had already created an esthetic dialectic for the film that the book didn't have—between the record of the experience and the art that was made from it.

While at work on the adaptation Truffaut and Gruault also read biographies of Charlotte and Emily Brontë, having seen similarities between the novelist-sisters and Anne and Muriel. "They, too, were English, romanesque, puritan, and exalted,"[15] Truffaut wrote. We might also add they they, too, were artists who used their novels as self-therapy; the psychological payoffs of their novels can be compared with the formalistic catharsis of *Les Deux Anglaises.* Truffaut also read the youthful memoirs of Marcel Proust, who raised this mixture of materialism, memory, and psychology to high art. "The hero of *Les Deux Anglaises,*" Truffaut informs us, "might in a sense be the young Proust,

Anne (Kika Markham) and Muriel (Stacy Tendeter), *Les Deux Anglaises. . . .*

who had fallen in love with Charlotte and Emily Brontë—loved them both for more than a decade without being able to choose between them."

But the hero, Claude Roc, is also clearly Henri-Pierre Roché as a young man. His surname is a pseudonym Roché had used, and his novel, *Jérôme et Julien,* is a bald allusion. The subtext of *Les Deux Anglaises* is then a story of artists in love with the work of other artists: Truffaut and Roché, Roché and himself, Proust and the Brontës: a matter of superfine allusions and cross-references which have far more importance for the artists than for the audiences. If there is an element of this mix that does come clearly across to us, it is just the necessity of being involved in the *process.* That is what gives comfort. "I feel better now. I feel that it is the book's characters who will suffer in my place." The *product,* which is what is available to the audience, is not so significant.

Where does that leave us? We seem to be closed off from much of the meaning and pleasure of *Les Deux Anglaises et le Continent,* Truffaut's most hermetic work. Yet the contrast between the material images and the transformations Truffaut works in the subtext is apparent. The old bicolor process of the thirties and forties which Truffaut mimics so well serves as a clue as to how we should approach the film. Not only *Magnificent Ambersons* informs it, but all the old historical romances of that period, as well. The knowledge we bring to the film of Truffaut's past artistic relationships with Henri-Pierre Roché and his novels helps. And there are material clues: portraits of the Brontës appear early, Muriel's hairstyle mimics Charlotte's, bits and pieces of the Brontës' lives provide some plot elements. (See Joseph Kestner's article for a thorough catalogue of these details.[16]) Even the structure of the characters' relationships suggests that we read *Les Deux Anglaises* as a commentary on the struggle of the artist's self with itself. Like so many Truffaut people before them—Charlie Kohler and Edouard Saroyan, Jules and Jim, Clarisse and Linda, Claude Roc and Antoine Doinel—they are doubled, one more real, the other more invented. Like Truffaut's earlier genre films, *Les Deux Anglaises* also twists the rules of the game: no happy ending here. Only the vague promise of art: novels, diaries, sculpture, and—eventually—film, which help us transmute experience into understanding.

The contradictions continue: Truffaut's next film, *Une Belle Fille comme moi (Such a Gorgeous Kid Like Me, A Gorgeous Bird Like Me),* was his first attempt at Slapstick. There have always been comic elements in his films—even *Les Deux Anglaises*—but never before had Truffaut attempted pure farce. The film is packed with pop posters, pulp detective and sex magazines, comic books, pratfalls, and other jokes of this sort. Yet it met with the usual mixed and vaguely disappointed reviews. The problem, as usual, is that Truffaut made not only a farce but a film about farce. The basic structure is classic Truffaut: *La Mariée était en noir* as farce, not melodrama. The woman is attractive and fatal; the men are victims. The source, for the fifth time, is an American genre novel, this one Henry Farrell's *Such a Gorgeous Kid Like Me* (a more evocative title than its French translation). If the new element of farce seems strange and forced, that is not entirely Truffaut's fault. Farce depends far more on actors than on directors, as all the greatest film farceurs from Keaton to Tati have demonstrated. Given an actor like Jean-Pierre Léaud, Truffaut can come close to Tati's beautifully cerebral style. In fact, in *Domicile conjugal* he had paid homage to Tati, whom he greatly admires, by having Antoine Doinel run into him on a Métro platform, watch his little routine, and mimic it. But none of the actors in *Une Belle Fille* are very well equipped for this sort of thing, and that leaves the film with rather a hollow center.

Still there are elements of interest in the film, if we decide not to ask too much of it in the way of farce. The comparison with *La Mariée* is instructive. Camille Bliss (Bernadette Lafont) manages only four murders as compared with the record five of Julie Kohler, but each of her victims is just as representative of a type—this time comic. Clovis

(Philippe Léotard), her erstwhile husband, is the ultimate drunken clodhopper of rural comedy, as his mother Isabel is the type of the miserly, tough-willed mother-in-law (Marjorie Main, if you will). Camille's first "fate bet" (as she calls her murderous gambles) is with her father, a psychological fact which does not escape her sociological interrogator and which makes comically blunt an underlying theme of *La Mariée*. Finally, there is Charles Denner's Arthur, an exterminator, expert in *"dératisation"* (should we compare this with de-dramatization?) who loves her blindly, is used by her more thoroughly than any other character, and who has serious puritan hangups about sex. Arthur is the comic type of the Truffaut hero. He has the same romantic idealization of women as Antoine Doinel (his phrase for Camille is "mon pauvre petit oiseau," which he repeats incessantly), his close brush with death by rat poison connects him with Louis Mahé (as does his obsession with Camille), and, most important, his total commitment to his work is a quality which we have come to regard as quintessentially Truffautesque.

Characters who don't die are equally important as types: Sam Golden, the absurd Americanophile, who mimics American music, sleeps under a poster of Vic Damone, and can't make love without the roar of the Indianapolis Speedway in the background; Murène and Marchal, the shyster lawyers—professionals who betray their clients; and the boy (Jérôme Zucca) who won't show Prévine his film because "it's still in rushes" but who then relents and enjoys commenting on the technique ("Regardez le zoom!" he exclaims).

Finally there is Prévine (André Dussollier), the young sociologist who, as he tape-records the story of her life, becomes implicated in her crimes because through his art he has been implicated in her life; because through his middle-class timidity he has fallen in love with her; and specifically because he faints, like the ultimately febrile hero who has always fascinated Truffaut, thereby allowing her to betray him. ("Moi, aussi, j'existe," she states, as if that were sufficient excuse.) The framework of the story, which allows most of it to be told by Camille to Prévine and his tape-recorder, is intriguing. First, it allows Camille to tell her own story; she is the first woman in Truffaut's films to do so. We see her strength and freedom from *her* point of view—also unique in Truffaut—which, however, would be much more interesting if the story were not set in a comic mode. Camille's narration also exemplifies Truffaut's recently increased interest in the distancing effect of the persona of the narrator: it does not give us an objectified story but instead focuses attention on how the character of the narrator has analyzed the material. This is another way of treating what Truffaut must regard as the single most absorbing (and fruitful) esthetic problem in film: it is not the story that counts, but how it is told; it is not the material, but the structure that speaks to us.

Although Camille occupies the center of the film and Truffaut has allowed her point of view considerable room, she is set against Prévine, whose point of view controls the beginning and end. What we see theoretically as a problem of narration represents personally for Truffaut the situation of the artist. Prévine is the comic type of his artist-hero: a sociologist, without the distancing irony that allows the others more or less to protect themselves from women and from death. Truffaut himself had narrated *Les Deux Anglaises* and *L'Enfant sauvage*—stories others had told him which he, like Prévine, had analyzed. The spinning reels of the tape recorder are significant punctuation points in *Une Belle Fille,* for they represent that attempt to transmute experience through art which has been the subject, first implied, then bluntly expressed, of so many of Truffaut's films. That this particular try doesn't end in catharsis either means that catharsis won't fit the comedy or that *Une Belle Fille comme moi* is ultimately even darker, underneath the farce, than *Les Deux Anglaises.* The film ends with Prévine, betrayed, sweeping a prison courtyard. The camera pans slowly up and over and then zooms in on his secretary Hélène (Anne Kreis), who has been a proper, quiet, and humorless foil to Camille, typing furiously on a balcony. The sound of the typewriter keys grows louder: "I will wait for you!" Women are still in control: Camille changed his life, Hélène will change his story. He has nothing left that is his own.

This connection between "life" and "story" was growing increasingly important for Truffaut. The tape recorder is a vital element of the film; Prévine's failure to capture Camille's life on tape and in print is significant. *Une Belle Fille* is a failed documentary, as the first scene shows us: in a bookstore someone asks, "Do you have *A Criminal Woman* by Stanislas Prévine?" The clerk replies, no, it was never published. That is our introduction to the film and Camille Bliss, the very antithesis of the weak and powerless nineteenth-century woman, *la dame aux camélias.*

In terms of sexual politics, Camille is a radical heroine. It is not that she kills—Julie Kohler did that—but that she does so with good-natured impunity. Julie killed for love and revenge, traditional motives, but Camille's "fate-bets" ("paris de la fatalité") are less easily explained. They really are gambles, wagers with fate, and with fatality. That is why she is such an insidious threat to the men she exploits: she does not fit any of the categories which enable them to hold power over women. Most important, together with her "accomplice," Hélène, she controls the story as well. As dangerous as her fate-bets are for others, for her they have an excellent existential rationale: "Moi, aussi, j'existe!"

La Nuit américaine may not be Truffaut's most seductive film, nor his most intelligent, nor his most deeply felt, but it is his most complete—a catalogue of his concerns, summarizing and synthesizing his work during the previous fourteen years. The presence of Jean-Pierre Léaud connects *La Nuit américaine* with the Antoine Doinel cycle. The Hawksian mood and tenor of the film make it closely comparable to the sixties genre films, as does Truffaut's announced intention of recapturing the breathless fascination with the way a job is done which for him was so characteristic of American films of the thirties and forties. Truffaut's presence in the film as the director Ferrand urges us to compare it with *L'Enfant sauvage,* the childhood flashbacks remind us insistently of *Les Quatre Cents Coups,* and the complex sexual relationships are reminiscent of both *Jules et Jim* and *Les Deux Anglaises.*

Having made *Fahrenheit 451,* an ode to books, Truffaut has said, it would have been "strange not to make a film about cinema." *La Nuit américaine* is a paean to filmmaking, full to bursting with appreciative detail and loving parody, and relatively free of the theorizing that marked the films of the late sixties and limited their appeal. Like *Fahrenheit 451* it is a very physical film: a collage of data which both visually and aurally caresses the materials of cinema. Unlike any other film about film, *La Nuit américaine* wants to convey some of the *practical* pleasure the filmmaker takes in his craft and its concrete reality. The film begins with credits on a black screen with a greatly enlarged soundtrack printed in white to the left. The soundtrack optically parallels the actual soundtrack which is then giving us both the noise and the music of a rehearsal of the film's music. The soundtrack is an abstract representation in code of the real sound; Truffaut has made it concrete so that we can observe the particular beauty it has in itself.

Throughout the film that follows, no matter what the nervous, busy, voluble characters are up to, we are constantly and quietly reminded of the physical fact of film. Several times we observe the frame counter on the camera totaling up the footage; cameras are ubiquitous; the fireplace is run on gas and the candle is really electric; rain comes from machines and—as the title tells us—night is a matter of filters. These are all technical details that interest the audience immediately because they reveal "tricks of the trade," how the job is done. But they also have a deeper significance as objective correlatives, objects with poignant connotations for Truffaut and for other filmmakers. At one point,

Opening shot of *La Nuit américaine:* the red camera crane (right) looms over the set at Studios La Victorine.

during one of several scenes in which we watch footage on the Moviola run backwards and forwards, slowed and stopped, Truffaut tilts precipitously down to the bin below the machine into which the film is spilling in luminous coils, both the blackish, liquescent picture film and the shiny tan sound film. We stare at the tangled coils of unreeled film in the bin for a second longer than may seem necessary: an image in film (of film) for the poignancy of loss, and a breathless "privileged moment" for Truffaut: carpe diem, carpe cinema.

This sense of loss and the emotions related to it are mirrored in the film structurally as well as by means of material images. The first scene of the film gives us an "acted" shot which is indistinguishable—until the "cut" command is given—from any of thousands of shots we have seen that we were supposed to accept as "real." Then the scene is reshot, but this time we hear the clipped commands of the assistant director: "Bring the white car in now," "Start the bus," "Faster Alphonse," "More action at the newsstand!" The third part of the sequence allows us not only to hear this encompassing reality but to see it. Truffaut cuts to a shot which reveals the huge red camera crane on the set of the square at the Studios La Victorine. He holds the shot as the music swells a little. Somehow it conveys both the sense of power that is so much a part of filmmaking as well as the gawky, limiting structure of the art which makes it so difficult. When the shot ends with the red crane aloft, lurching like a giraffe, this plangent exercise in demystification is complete. The French title of the film, *La Nuit américaine,* denotes the filter process which allows night scenes to be shot in full sunlight, a common practice until recently. But it also connotes the end of the studio films so closely associated with American cinema. The English title, *Day for Night,* then suggests the new dawn of realism that has effectively destroyed the old American system during the fifteen years since Truffaut made his first film on the sidewalks of Paris.

La Nuit américaine has a rich and closely worked fabric. The frame is always filled with useful detail. At one point Julie (Jacqueline Bisset) chats with Alexandre (Jean-Pierre Aumont) in the foreground while in the background Alphonse (Léaud) argues unintelligibly with Liliane (Dani). The counterpoint is all the more powerful because this very short scene immediately follows a carefully intercut sequence which includes Alphonse in character presenting "Pamela" (Julie) to his parents in the film-within-the-film; Lajoie and his wife; Joelle's characterization of Lajoie and his wife as *"Le Chagrin et la pitié";* and Alphonse out of character asking Julie if she has stage-fright at the same time as Liliane is necking with the photographer. Truffaut has compressed within the space of a minute or two of film time most of the *petits drames* the film will display.

At another point, earlier on, Truffaut ends a scene between the producer and the director by intercutting single white frames, the rhythm speeding up until the final cut to a shot of Julie arriving at the airport, striding purposefully down a wide corridor, preceded by photographers snapping flash guns: a rather unusual foreshadowing device that works perfectly to communicate the nervous tension which is central to Julie's character at the same time as it unites Julie's "nerves" with the solar plexus of the production office. Once again, it is the structure of the film that speaks, not the content.

The rhythms of the film, when they are not mimicking the quick breathless pace of Hawks and Walsh, are syncopated in such a way as to connect the broad volubility of *La Nuit américaine* with the more muted, introverted emotional landscape we have come to associate with Truffaut. This is clearest in the scenes with Alphonse. After Alphonse and Liliane have with some effort moved their beds together, Alphonse suggests a movie for the evening. Liliane has a list of restaurants she wants to try. Alphonse tells her they'll be lucky if they have time for a sandwich before the film. Liliane, not a cinéphile, explodes: she wants a leisurely dinner. Alphonse, continuing the rapid rhythms of the exchange for a moment, replies, "on one condition." A beat's pause. He goes over to a bouquet of flowers and with a typically bony gesture picks an imaginary bloom, conveys it to Liliane, and declares: "That you marry me!" She frowns slightly. Cut. That deafeningly quiet moment in the midst of the Hawksian chatter is Truffaut's signature. Again, at the end of the sequence in which Séverine (Valentina Cortese) flubs her cues four times running, Truffaut closes with a shot of Séverine in the arms of Alexandre, the two veterans together at the left edge of the frame, and punctuates the sequence with a wipe to black which isolates Séverine and Alexandre on the screen with the black void to the right.

This punctuation is representative of a kind of humility that permeates all of Truffaut's films. In resurrecting the punctuation of an earlier cinema—wipes, lap dissolves, and irises—he achieves the effect of softly distancing us from the power of his films as if to de-emphasize them. By blacking out part of the screen with a partial wipe as he so often does, he both isolates and cradles his characters. His montage, too, is modest and a bit shy—as the pair of sequences above illustrates; he often cuts a little too soon as if to convey the impression that a scene is perfunctory, making those "privileged moments," when the camera gazes in reverie, all the more pointed. This cinematic idiom is a mirror of the awkward, touching gestures of Truffaut's alter ego Léaud.

In *La Nuit américaine,* this shyness and awkwardness is expressed physically and directly. Truffaut's Ferrand, the director, wears a hearing aid, not on his shirt pocket like most people but on his sleeve, like the proverbial heart. As a result, he often has to raise his arm and cock his head to hear people—a superb image of Truffaut's own aggressive humility.

In *8½* Fellini dreamt elaborate psychological dreams of his childhood, parents, and family which explain much about the character, Guido, in which he masqueraded. Truffaut as Ferrand, in contrast, has one recurrent dream in which, as a small boy, he steals publicity stills of Orson Welles's *Citizen Kane,* detaching them carefully from a bulletin board. He is a collector, ordering the details of the film. He acts as the editor of the work of others; that is the dialectic which interests him. So his dream, as we should expect, is a modest one. Ferrand is not an entirely admirable character. He takes an early dislike to Stacey (Alexandra Stewart); yet Stacey proves herself wholly likeable and succeeds where everyone else has failed in comforting Julie, while Ferrand to Julie's helpless annoyance, steals her bitter lines from real life to improve a scene in his film. Again, when Alexandre is killed and everyone else is stunned by the human loss, Ferrand concludes, "What I had always feared had happened: a film was stopped by the death of an actor." Ferrand comes first in that sentence, then the film, then "an actor."

Only once does Ferrand become more than superficially involved with the other people of the film. When Alphonse decides to quit, Ferrand in an uncharacteristic gesture of empathy puts his arm around him and leads him back to his room explaining, with what we see as not a little effort on his part, that for the two of them, work is more important than their personal lives; whatever happiness they find must be in their work. These are the sentiments of *homo cinematicus:* the same empathy exists between Truffaut and Léaud.

In the main, Ferrand is defined not by his human relationships but by his relationship with films and filmmakers. The names of Welles, Vigo, Cocteau appear at various times, and there are many allusions to Truffaut's own work: the characters' names (Julie, Stacey, Alphonse), the actors, the situations, the two English women, the director-as-a-young-boy, the costumes, some of the sets, for example. The one obligatory scene, we sense, will then be some sort of homage to the forces which conspired to make François Truffaut a filmmaker: the filmmakers who came before him. In the production office, Ferrand is interrupted by a messenger with a package of books and magazines he has ordered. He cuts the string and unwraps them, spreading them out on the table, almost diffidently. The names confront us: Buñuel, Dreyer, Lubitsch, Bergman, Godard, Hitchcock, Hawks, Rossellini. The trick may be Godard's but the tone of respect is pure Truffaut. Those who know how thoroughly committed Truffaut is to the history of his craft can sense the special poignancy of this scene. Even in the hectic middle of his own film, Ferrand makes time to read about the work of others. But of course, he must already know these books. He must have sent for copies simply to have them near while he works, like a writer who keeps Joyce on the shelf close by the typewriter. This scene also points up the memorial tone of the film. When Alexandre dies, Ferrand informs us that a style of filmmaking dies with him, the studio film that Hollywood raised to its zenith.

From *Les Quatre Cents Coups* to *Une Belle Fille comme moi* Truffaut had concentrated, without exception, on the simple emotional geometry of pairs and triangles, family groups, and introspective, intense relationships. Now, for the first time he has at least fifteen characters with significant roles. The result conveys the fullness of life's experience with something of Renoir's breadth of vision. Alphonse, as we might expect, plays a pivotal role. He is decisively in love with Liliane, the apprentice script-girl, who has a flirtation with Pierrot, the mute photographer, and then runs off with Mark, the stuntman. Meanwhile, Alphonse gets himself entangled in another triangle with Julie and her husband Michael. Set beside this six-sided figure is the simpler triangle of Joelle, Bernard, and Odile—hardly a drama, really, since all three are hard-headed professionals; sex for them is a pastime between takes.

Arching over this complicated geometry are the relationship, now shadowy, between Séverine and Alexandre, a reminder of simpler days, and Alexandre's new and quiet obsession with Christian (a homosexual relationship which Truffaut characteristically expresses in terms of paternal affection: Alexandre has decided to adopt Christian). Stacey and Ferrand exist in relative isolation. On the one hand, Stacey, pregnant and something of a mother to all the cast; and on the other, Ferrand, alone, almost lonely, and thoroughly separate from all the others. In the background providing mute comment are Gaston and his wife, who knits furiously: *"Le Chagrin et la pitié"* as Joelle calls them, emblems of the darkness of married life.

This is a much broader perspective than we are accustomed to in Truffaut's work, but all these people are familiar. The men are relatively passive. Ferrand, half deaf and isolated as the director, almost doesn't count in the sexual equation. Alphonse, full of sound and fury, is as absurdly romantic as was Antoine. Alexandre is always the observer and commentator; Gaston is classically henpecked; Christian says almost nothing (although he does smile meaningfully); Michael appears occasionally, as if on cue, to be the colorless husband to Julie. Only Bernard seems in any way extroverted, but even he must be asked by Joelle to make love. Pierrot the photographer is utterly mute; always lurking darkly in the background and probing unwanted with his camera, he is the "foreboding presence" in this film, as the television actor was in *Domicile conjugal.*

As always in Truffaut, the women are the active principles and motive forces. (Only *Les Quatre Cents Coups* and *L'Enfant sauvage* are exempt from this rule.) However, before *La Nuit américaine* we always saw them as in a glass darkly, from the point of view of the male characters. Until *Une Belle Fille comme moi* they had always fit romantic stereotypes.

Liliane plays the "Camille" role here: tough, uncompromising, forward, and selfish. She has a certain *malin* quality which is rare and attractive. If the rest of the cast and crew don't particularly like her, it is not because she "plays around" but because she doesn't have the same commitment to her job as the rest. Séverine, one of the few "older women" in Truffaut, although she plays a role which is something of a stereotype, is nevertheless still independent, and as a successful cinéaste she is an important foil for the younger women. Julie, who is possibly the least active woman in the film, nevertheless impresses us with the strength of her image. Truffaut is obviously fascinated by the strong lines and purposeful expression of Jacqueline Bisset's face.

It is the technicians, however, who impress us most, mainly because they are not limited by roles as actresses. Odile (whose role would have been considerably larger had not personal difficulties kept Nike Arrighi away from the set, says Truffaut) is a quiet woman, but an effective worker and in some ways the most independent of the crew: more than the others she leads a life separate from the film, and she succeeds in a personal relationship where others fail. Stacey, although she hovers around the edges of the film, is clearly her own woman. It is Joelle, however, who most interests me. She has a sense of herself and her life which is notably assured. This is new for Truffaut; although in fact, she would be an unusually free woman in anybody's film. "I can see dropping a guy for a film," she says when she hears Liliane has left with Mark, "but I could never drop a film for a guy!" She means it. She can impatiently suggest to Bernard that they make love in the bushes, quickly, and then react with humorous indifference when she interrupts Bernard and Odile in bed a little later. More than anyone else except Ferrand, she is in charge of the film: it is no accident that Truffaut has made her the "script-girl," for that is the role in film production which women have been allowed to dominate. We can also assume that Joelle is an homage to Suzanne Schiffman, who has been Truffaut's continuity assistant for so long and who, we must believe, contributed a good deal to the screenplay for *La Nuit américaine.*

In one sense, this film about films and film people is a bit facile, concerned as it is with fifteen people isolated from the rest of the world for seven weeks of shooting, free to make temporary liaisons, untroubled by most of the limiting factors of daily life and work. Yet Truffaut has turned this cliché to good advantage, since a major theme of the film is the impermanence of relationships. The intense friendships and affairs that develop on a set must always have been somewhat painful for the introspective Truffaut, since they tend to end so quickly. He gives the expression of these feelings to Séverine, at her farewell party.* That scene is immediately followed by Alphonse's "breakdown"—placed there by the logic not of plot but of the emotional development of the film. The abstract freedom of the film set is thus joined with the

*Immediately after, we are told that Séverine has been such a great actress that she was called "Duse et Demi," which punningly reinforces the connection between her and Truffaut: he had made twelve *(douze)* and a half films.

Truffaut as Ferrand observes; Joelle (Nathalie Baye) takes notes.

sense of loss Truffaut wants us to share. Like his Alphonse (and like his Jean-Pierre), Truffaut now understands that adamantine romanticism causes, mainly, unnecessary pain.

Throughout the film the bullheaded, logical, romantic Alphonse has been conducting a survey: "I've been meaning to ask you," he inquires of his co-workers, "are women magic?" The answers he gets are of course various: "Yes, some of them . . ." "Yes, and so are men . . ." "No, only their legs; that's why they wear skirts." The answers aren't important; the question is. Léaud in any of his previous roles had never thought to formulate that question; he had always assumed that the answer was an indubitable "yes." Now that he has reached the stage where he can doubt, he understands considerably more about women: he is beginning to see them as human. If the self-centered Liliane rejects Alphonse for the same reasons Christine was chary of Antoine ("He needs a mother, a wife, a wet nurse, a sister," says Liliane; "I can't play all those roles"), we can sense that the next time around Antoine/Alphonse/Jean-Pierre will succeed.

Alphonse's second question is "Are films more important than life?" Again, the answer seems beside the point. It is the ultimate paradox of Truffaut's work that he has managed to construct some of the most affecting and accomplished humanist documents of the last decade and a half working not from the position of a Rimbaud, Hawks, or Hemingway who voraciously consumed life in order to make art of it, but rather from that of a cinéphile and bibliophile who has divined real truths by using mainly "secondary sources." *La Nuit américaine* is an homage to filmmaking but it is also only the thirteenth chapter in a continuing defense of the art. Each of Truffaut's films, by its masterful, reflective, allusive style, reinforces the union of life and film.

Jean Renoir has said about Truffaut's films that they are:

> the product of one man alone and that man looks with an equal eye on the problems of the actors, the sound system, the camera. There are no small problems, no great problems. There is only film. For Hindus the world is one; for Truffaut the film is one.[17]

And, it could be deduced, the two are the same.

Fellini's *8½*, that other great film about filmmaking, ends with one of the most strikingly affirmative scenes in cinema. Guido, the director, having decided *not* to make the film, organizes, instead, the people of his life. At dusk on the abandoned set (a half-built rocket ship) all the characters of his life join him in a circus ring: his parents, his wife, his mistress, his producer, his cast and crew, his friends and acquaintances. It is a surreal community, but it is a community nevertheless and has the strength and hope of the circle. *La Nuit américaine*, in contrast, ends more realistically on a dark note. Alexandre's death, an accident of "real life," has intruded upon the closed world of the film. *Je vous présente Pamela*, the film-within-the-film, will have to be changed in order to accommodate it. Alphonse can still kill his father (whom Alexandre had played), but he will have to shoot him in the back. Again we find ourselves on the set—for Truffaut a square, not a circle, but still a meeting place and, as we remember it from the beginning of the film, the vital and lively center of the community. It is dusk, as in Fellini, but the set this time is realistically empty, except for Alphonse and the stand-in for Alexandre. Alphonse shoots him in the back. Then he does it again for a second take. The patricide of Alexandre, who represents the "cinéma du papa," provides a fitting climax to "the American night."

But Truffaut, always balancing the elements of his film dialectically, can't end on so simply symbolic a note. *La Nuit américaine* has two codas after the "plot" and *Je vous présente Pamela* have ended in the darkened snowy square. The community of cast and crew breaks up and people go their separate ways, in the final attempt at demystification, both for the filmmakers and for us—as if the curtain hadn't come down at the end of the play and we stayed in our seats to watch the actors take off their makeup, chat awhile, then go home. Finally, reality intrudes upon *La Nuit américaine* as it did upon the film-within-the-film. An interviewer wants to ask questions about Alexandre. No one wants to talk; then Bernard volunteers. Speaking to us as much as the interviewer, he says:

> We hope everyone who sees the film enjoys seeing it as much as we enjoyed making it.

It is a highly ironic remark, considering that Alexandre's death has cast a pall on the set. It is also a hoary cliché. But it is the truth, as well. It reminds us that, for Truffaut, the relationship with the audience is paramount. The second part of the sentence reminds us that the real interest in film (as elsewhere) lies in the process, not the final product. The main difficulty we have with Truffaut's films is also their most attractive attribute: that they leave room for their audiences in which to operate.

The subject matter of Truffaut's films—work and love—mirrors this concern. It is the process of work that interests him—for example, Antoine's jobs—not the product. And it is the process of his films that he finds intriguing, not their ultimate value as commodities. This is why he decided to drop the fiction that he was giving his audiences anything but the roughest of drafts, "thrown on the market"; he wants a dialectical relationship, both with his films and with his audiences. This dialectical structure pertains to human relationships as well; sexual politics is probably the most underrated aspect of Truffaut's films. Catherine in *Jules et Jim*, Camille in *Une Belle Fille*, and the women in *La Nuit américaine* are fuller and more sophisticated as characters, and wiser, more powerful, and more human as women, than the huge majority of women characters in films of the sixties and seventies. Truffaut doesn't pretend to understand women; but he does understand a great deal about the relationships that exist between women and men.

Truffaut's micro-politics were not very impressive to most politically minded people during the maelstrom of the nineteen-sixties. But I think it is becoming clearer now that the study of the basic political unit of the family, the "community" of two or three, is vitally important. Politics begins at home; thus love stories are political. With *La Nuit américaine* Truffaut expanded the perspective to include a larger community, and we can hope that in the future he will feel confident enough to continue along this line.

He knows, too, every bit as well as Godard that "style is content," that fighting "Hollywood" is a political act, and that the structure of his films is as powerful as their content. Godard may have expressed these ideas more succinctly and more bluntly, but Truffaut's films nevertheless give us some of the best evidence that there is truth in them. Having developed a passion for the visual poetry of everyday life from Renoir and a sense of the power of the image from Hitchcock, he has created a strongly materialist cinema. (In a few cases—*L'Enfant sauvage* and *La Nuit américaine*— it would not be unjust to compare it favorably with Rossellini's.) His obsession with genre films and the myths they convey through their stylized form is often a source of confusion for his audiences, but it is also a highly useful and cathartic analysis. No matter how much we may desire to "return to zero," the genres will not go away. Truffaut has helped us greatly to understand how they operate.

This analysis of the "language" of cinema, subtle and unobtrusive though it may be, is a vital element of the political structure of Truffaut's films. To know how we live together and how we can change those arrangements, we must know a great deal more about the media through which we express the shared myths which define those arrangements. We have to know what Gangster films are really all about. We have to know why the vengeful bride in black and the "Mississippi mermaid" are images we find both attractive and disturbing. We have to know how books fit in the structure of media. We have to know what films have done to us and what we have done to films. Truffaut is not an essayist; he makes fictional films which sometimes succeed very well in the commercial marketplace. But he has left room in those films for us. Like André Bazin, he is a "moral realist" who is more interested in the relationship between author and film, or film and audience, than in static evaluations or frozen esthetics. And this is where the heart of Truffaut's films lies. As Truffaut is ultimately a cinéphile, a filmgoer—*homo cinematicus*—so we must be, ultimately, participants in the process, film*makers,* almost equal partners.

- "Are women magic?"
- "Are films more important than life?"
- "We hope everyone who sees the film enjoys seeing it as much as we enjoyed making it."

6

GODARD
Women and the Outsider

Where does one begin with Jean-Luc Godard? His work is global, demanding, and it doesn't admit us easily. He has become, in the decade and a half since the cultural shock of *A bout de souffle*, a phenomenon as well as a filmmaker. Maybe it's best to discuss the phenomenon first, so that we can then be left free to engage the filmmaker. Godard himself would certainly encourage this approach since much of his energy during the last eight or ten years has been devoted to freeing himself from the role of art "hero" that nearly smothered him in the early sixties. What follows, then, are some notes whose aim is the demystification of Jean-Luc Godard.

A bout de souffle (Breathless), his first feature, was regarded when it was released in March 1960 as a landmark. Truffaut, who had had a much more vicious reputation as a critic, had, a year previously, made his debut with a film which was immediately apprehensible to a large range of filmgoers. *Les Quatre Cents Coups* was fresh and new but it was also perceived to exist essentially within certain broad traditions. *A bout de souffle*, on the other hand, was clearly revolutionary. The story, while modern in tone, was certainly unexceptionable. Jean-Pierre Melville might have filmed it anytime within the previous ten years; indeed, Truffaut himself had conceived the scenario, though if he had filmed it himself it would never have been perceived as revolutionary. So it was not the substance of *A bout de souffle* that gave it its unique cachet, but rather its subtext—the attitudes of the filmmaker, his sensibility—that set it in stark contrast to the general traditions of film history. Godard had, with one cinematic stroke, established himself as an iconoclast in the closed world of film art; and his films would continue to be idiosyncratic to the point—for some—of being often unintelligible.

Ironically, the best-known innovation of *A bout de souffle* is the use of the jump-cut—mere filmic punctuation. It is as if a novelist or poet were to be praised for his "revolutionary" use of the semicolon! In all the reams that have been written about the jump-cuts of *A bout de souffle*, it is seldom mentioned that Godard hardly ever used the device again. Why did intelligent audiences look first at the style of Godard's films, for the most part ignoring their content? This question has haunted Godard ever since. It seems to me that there are two basic reasons for this misinterpretation, one simple, one complex. First, we look at style because we have been trained to do so and because it is easier to discuss than content.

Second, for nearly two hundred years, art, like all other human endeavor, has been subject to theories of progress. This is the legacy of the industrial revolution. In art as with machines, "progress is our most important product," and this is the source of the concept of the avant-garde: the cutting edge of progressive art. The idea that novels or poems, paintings or music, sculpture or films should somehow be "more advanced than" their predecessors is intimately connected with their function as commodities in capitalist civilization. In the history of the various arts the concept of progress is generally evident in the continuing development of abstraction. The esthetic focus moves from a concentration on the human element to a more intellectual level and finally to an exclusive concern with esthetics. We can see this process at work on the stage, for example, in the movement from the essential humanism of Ibsen and Strindberg, through the play of ideas of Shaw and Pirandello, on up to the highly stylized theatre pieces of Beckett and Genet, who said, "ideas don't interest me so much as the *shape* of ideas." In painting, the abstraction has become even purer: conceptual art no longer even needs paint and canvas.

This process of abstraction developed slowly throughout the nineteenth century and then reached a crisis point in most arts early in the twentieth, when such figures as Joyce, Schoenberg, and Picasso attacked the very foundations of their arts. At the time they worked, however, the young art of film was hardly adolescent. Although there has been an avant-garde movement in film since the 1920s, it was not until the late 1950s that it reached a critical point. Before that it had been isolated from the mainstream; after that it was able to challenge the establishment on its own terms. Godard's announced desire to "return to zero" fits the pattern. Consequently, critics have every right to compare him to Joyce, Schoenberg, and Picasso. The two best critics of Godard—Susan Sontag and Richard Roud—have described his contributions to the progress of the avant-garde with thorough intelligence. Here is Sontag making the connection:

> . . . Godard is not merely an intelligent iconoclast. He is a deliberate "destroyer" of cinema. . . . His approach to established rules of film technique like the unobtrusive cut, consistency of point of view, and clear story line is comparable to Schoenberg's repudiation of the tonal language prevailing in music around 1910 when he entered his atonal period or to the challenge of the Cubists to such hallowed rules of painting as realistic figuration and three-dimensional pictorial space.[1]

This is a succinct summary of Godard's position in the recent history of abstraction and avant-gardism. But he must also be seen in a political context. For better or worse, Godard is the Joyce, the Schoenberg, the Picasso of film; but he is also something more. For, unlike those earlier heroes, he revolted against his role: he moved on past the outmoded concepts of abstraction and the avant-garde into an entirely new area; he foresees a cinema (even if he has not yet quite articulated it) which is beyond capitalist progress, abstraction, and avant-gardism.

All this may sound excessively abstract, but the roots of Godard's struggle are concrete. Like Truffaut, Godard was formed by a critical dialectic. Whereas Truffaut buries that dialectic in the subtext of the film, in Godard it is strikingly evident in every frame. In an often-quoted interview in *Cahiers du Cinéma* in December 1962, Godard described his work this way:

> Today I still think of myself as a critic, and in a sense I am, more than ever before. Instead of writing criticism, I make a film, but the critical dimension is subsumed. I think of myself as an essayist, producing essays in novel form, or novels in essay form: only instead of writing, I film them. Were the cinema to disappear, I would simply accept the inevitable and turn to television [as he in fact did ten years later]; were television to disappear, I would revert to pencil and paper. For there is a clear continuity between all forms of expression. It's all one.[2]

So it is no surprise to discover that this critic-as-filmmaker has become a prime object of study for other critics. More has been written about Godard's films than about those of any other contemporary filmmaker save Bergman. This, too, has contributed to his mystique; but it is not necessarily a fair index of the value of his films. Critics much prefer to deal with his particular kind of intelligence than with the more humanistic intelligence displayed by, say, Truffaut or Renoir.

No doubt Godard's work has the *depth* that such critics as Roud and Sontag perceived and described. But if it is to be appreciated outside the strict limits of the film world it will have to exhibit a *breadth*—a popularity—that has so far eluded it. The problem with Truffaut's films is to show that there is "method" to them, and that that method is rigorous. The "sentiment" is obvious. The problem with Godard's films is the reverse: no one denies their method, but the sentiment, the breadth of human concern, is much less evident. If that can be revealed, Godard's artistic position will clearly be stronger. But the job isn't easy. Both Roud and Sontag, for example, in surprisingly similar introductions to their essays on Godard, include a disclaimer. For Roud, "one cannot hope to convince his detractors; on the contrary, a book which tries to explain Godard's aims and methods may well only confirm their objections; they will learn more exactly what it is they object to."[3] True enough, but what is the cause of this split?

First, that aspect of his work—the multiplexity of its language—which has made him, as Roud says, "for many . . . the most important filmmaker of his generation," is off-putting for others. At its best, this reaction evinces a healthy disrespect for effete estheticism and apolitical avant-gardism. At worst it is simply evidence of a closed-minded, rigid classicism which sees art as subject to a set of invariable laws and the critic's job as essentially judgmental. John Simon, in his essay "Godard and the Godardians: A Study in the New Sensibility," locates the moment of the birth of the "new sensibility . . . this disaster" in a scene in *A bout de souffle* in which Godard combines elements of Western movies with some lines from a poem by Apollinaire. "Now this is obviously nonsense," Simon writes. "What business have the characters in a vulgar American western reciting one of France's finest twentieth-century lyrics at each other—and antiphonally, at that, as though it were dialogue that they were improvising?"[4] Judged by an esthetics that makes a strict (and arbitrary) separation between "high art" and "vulgar art," Godard's films will always be found lacking; for it is just the combination of the two that he sees as the elemental heritage of film art. Likewise, anyone who thinks art should do one thing at a time will be confused and disappointed by Godard's multiplex films.

Second, and more important, Godard's films require participation. Trained as we have been to expect instant gratification from our cinematic commodities, we have too little preparation for appreciating the kind of open dialectic which forms Godard's films. They are not machines designed to measure out quanta of entertainment in effective rhythms, but, as he has said many times, essays—*tries.* They form questions; they don't draw conclusions. So as not to "cheat" his audiences, Godard announces this in the subtitles of many of his films: *Une Femme mariée:* "fragments of a film shot in 1964"; *Masculin-féminin:* "15 precise acts"; *La Chinoise:* "a film in the process of making itself"; *Weekend:* "a film adrift in the cosmos"; and, very simply, *Two or Three Things That I Know About Her.* These are not finely crafted, finished, esthetic objects meant for relaxed consumption; they are sinuous, struggling, quirky, unfinished, tense, and demanding essays. They are meant for active, not passive viewers.

The idea of participation is integral to Godard's films: it confronts us on every level. To paraphrase *Le Gai Savoir,* these are not the films that *should* be made, but when those films *are* made they will have to follow some of the lines these films have laid down. The main focus of Godard's energies, ever since he started writing about film in 1952, has been towards an understanding of the phenomenon of film (and by extension other arts): How does it affect us? More particularly, how does it change the way we perceive reality? What is its political value? What are the relationships between the various modes of fiction and documentary? How can the narrative language of cinema be reconstructed so that it is a more useful (and more honest) instrument? What are the differences between the language of film and the language of print? What is the relationship between filmmaker and film? Between film and audience? These are all critics' questions. But they are not abstractly esthetic. They are not particularly directed towards an evaluation of what is "beautiful" and what is not. They are, in essence, political, and have a profound influence on the way we live.

To appreciate Godard's films, it is necessary first of all to share with him a passion for understanding these matters, for analyzing them. In this sense, I suppose, he is a critics' filmmaker (or a "filmmakers' filmmaker"). But he is more than that, for he never loses sight of the vital connection between these theories and the human beings who are affected by their operation. Godard's films are, undoubtedly, films of ideas, but the ideas are often painful, personal, vital. This vitality must be emphasized. It is necessary, sometimes, when talking about difficult subjects to use difficult language. The complexity of Godard's idiom is not meant to confuse, it is meant to clarify, but it requires close attention. Godard's films never yield up all their meaning in one viewing; they reveal themselves through a dialectical process as we challenge and question them. They are not meant to be easily perceived fictions, nor are they meant to be cinema-vérité—frozen images of reality. They fall somewhere in between. As Godard has said,

> Generally speaking, reportage is interesting only when placed in a fictional context, but fiction is interesting only if it is validated by a documentary context. The Nouvelle Vague, in fact, may be defined in part by this new relationship between fiction and reality, as well as through nostalgic regret for a cinema which no longer exists.[5]

A new relationship between fiction and reality, a nostalgic regret for a cinema which no longer exists: these are the twin engines of the New Wave in general, and of Godard's dialectic in particular.

Biography

Jean-Luc Godard was born in Paris in December 1930. His father was a successful physician; his mother came from an important family of bankers. During the war, Godard became a naturalized Swiss citizen, but he returned to Paris in the late forties and studied at the Sorbonne, from which he obtained a certificate in ethnology. While he was still in school he became a regular at the Latin Quarter's ciné-club and the Cinémathèque, where he met André Bazin, François Truffaut, Eric Rohmer, and Jacques Rivette. With Rohmer and Rivette he founded the *Gazette du Cinéma,* which published several issues between May and November 1950. At the time, Rivette and Rohmer were making their first short films, and Godard acted in several of them.

Between 1952 and 1954 he wrote for *Cahiers du Cinéma* (and a small magazine, *Les Amis du Cinéma*), often using Hans Lucas, the Germanization of his name, as a pseudonym. During this period he also traveled extensively with his father in North and South America, memories of which would find their way into the reservoir of images for his films a decade later. After a brief return to Paris, he went back to Switzerland, where he got a job as laborer on the Grand Dixence dam. With the wages he financed his first film, a documentary in 35 mm about the construction of the dam, called "Opération Béton" (1954). In 1955 he made his second short film, "Une Femme coquette," in Geneva and then returned to Paris, where from 1956 through 1959 he wrote regularly, like Truffaut, for both *Cahiers du Cinéma* and *Arts,* and earned a living as a press officer for Artistes Associés. He made three more short films during this period: "Tous les garçons s'appellent Patrick" ("All Boys are Named Patrick") (1957) from a script by Eric Rohmer; "Charlotte et son Jules" (1958), a debut for Jean-Paul Belmondo; and "Histoire d'eau" (1958), salvaged from the footage Truffaut had shot.

Godard's work as a critic was overshadowed during the fifties by

Truffaut's. Godard was more elliptical, more personal, and altogether less strident. But he was often more reasonable and judicious. His work in *Cahiers du Cinéma, Arts, Gazette du Cinéma,* and *Les Amis du Cinéma* was anthologized and republished in 1968 in *Jean-Luc Godard par Jean-Luc Godard,* and the detailed survey this collection provides does much to convince us that both the theory and practice of Godard's films have deep roots in his early critical work. His prose is denser and more abstruse even than his cinema, but the two are both part of a continuous fabric. ("For there is a clear continuity between all forms of expression.")

His essays cover a wide range of topics and an equally wide stylistic spectrum, from the sublimely and incomprehensibly recondite pastiche of "Défense et illustration du découpage classique" his first manifesto in *Cahiers,* to the lengthy, comprehensive, but elegantly simple clarity of his two major essays on Hitchcock—"Strangers on a Train"[6] and "The Wrong Man."[7] There are panegyrics and homages in celebration of the expected heroes—Renoir, Rossellini, Nicholas Ray, Bergman, Ophüls and—yes—Frank Tashlin, and several reviews in which Godard analyzes images and metaphors which impressed him and which will later turn up, altered and rearranged in his own films; but the most important critical essays Godard wrote are a series of manifestos in which he struggles to define his own approach to cinema. There are four of them, stretched over a period of six years: "Towards a Political Cinema" (*Gazette du Cinéma* 3: September 1950); "Défense et illustration du découpage classique" (*Cahiers* 15: September 1952); "What Is Cinema?" (*Les Amis du Cinéma* 1: October 1952); "Montage, mon beau souci" (*Cahiers* 65: December 1956).

It is instructive, I think, that whereas Truffaut's critical stance (la politique des auteurs) could be outlined clearly and forcibly in just one essay, Godard's own struggle with the essence of cinema is stretched out over four abstruse pieces. "Towards a Political Cinema," written when he was nineteen years old, is a rather fumbling review of a group of Russian films, but it is notable for its evidence that Godard had been very much influenced by his studies in ethnology and had picked up several theories of knowledge that were to stand him in good stead throughout his career. The essay is studded with references both to dialectics and to semiology, two modes of thought that were to become central for Godard the filmmaker. He is already analyzing the films he watches as dynamically related to their viewers—connected to them semiologically and dialectically—and he quotes Brice Parain (who would later appear in one of his films):

> The sign forces us to see an object through its significance.

That phrase will be Godard's motto as a filmmaker a decade later: it is typically hermetic, almost mystical; it is as ambiguous as a line of modern poetry, yet it urgently wants to state a basic axiom: that there is no way we can sense the objective world without first understanding how our systems of signs—our languages, both verbal and non-verbal—"signify," how they mean, and how they thereby change our perceptions. Godard's career can be seen as a long struggle to work out the multiple possible meanings of Parain's deceptively simple sentence. He began this work in his criticism.

Awkwardly at first, in "Défense et illustration du découpage classique," and then with greater clarity in "Montage, mon beau souci," he developed a critique of Bazinian theories of mise-en-scène which, as we realize now that we have the practical evidence of his films, was going to move the theory of Bazinian realism forward by a quantum leap. Bazin had set up a dialectic in which montage and mise-en-scène were directly opposed. The former, he thought, served those filmmakers who were interested in creating an image of the event; the latter, those who wanted to capture the event itself. Bazin saw this in precise moral terms; cinema was an ethical enterprise, not a purely esthetic one. Those who created images at the expense of reality were to be condemned. Bazinian realism—a moral choice—depended on the elevation of mise-en-scène at the expense of montage, which Bazin considered an unethical abuse of power on the part of the filmmaker. Clearly, Bazin's theories are themselves in dialectical opposition to Eisensteinian theories of montage.

Godard does not contradict Bazin's theory; he simply carries it forward, Out of the thesis of mise-en-scène and the antithesis of montage, he forges a synthesis. In "Défense et illustration du découpage classique" he tries to accomplish this by setting up classical "découpage" (classical construction) as the synthesis of montage and mise-en-scène. He is severely hampered because the essay, as the title declares, is also a conscientious parody of Joachim du Bellay's famous eighteenth-century linguistic manifesto "Défense et illustration de la langue française." It is obviously important for Godard to do this since "the sign forces us to see an object through its significance." (Many of his films will reveal the same relationship between subject and form.) Yet if we read carefully and provide, from our knowledge of his later work, our own gloss on the essay, we can draw some conclusions.

The relationship between mise-en-scène and reality in Bazin's work is easily understood: it had to do with an ethical relationship between filmmaker and viewer. But what will be Godard's new sense of the relationship between découpage classique and reality? Because it includes montage, which has specific psychological dimensions, "découpage classique sticks even closer to *psychological* reality, by which I mean that of the emotions. . . ." Obviously Godard is trying for a union between plastic reality and psychological reality, although he isn't able yet to put it into words.

"Montage, mon beau souci," written four years later, is a reworking of the same theories, this time with greater clarity and assurance. "Montage," he declares succinctly, "is above all an integral part of mise-en-scène." (Since the phrase "découpage classique" won't work, he simply redefines "mise-en-scène" to *include* montage: a nice trick.) Godard sees montage doing in time what mise-en-scène does in space. Two corollaries follow: first, that mise-en-scène can then be every bit as oppressive and unethical as montage when the director uses it to distort reality—psychological reality, that is. "If direction is a look," Godard writes with his usual poetry, "montage is a heartbeat. To foresee is the characteristic of both; but what one seeks to foresee in space, the other seeks in time."

Second, looked at in this way, montage is not necessarily *a fortiori* evidence of bad faith on the part of the filmmaker. No doubt plastic reality is better served by mise-en-scène, which in the strictest Bazinian sense is still more honest than montage. But psychological reality may very well be better served by montage. And anyway, since montage is now, in Godard's system, simply a part of mise-en-scène, to do montage is to do mise-en-scène. What Godard has done, in his usual circuitous way, is to replace the simple, plastic, material universe of Bazin with a more complicated system in which perception is as important as the object perceived. Bazin's logic dealt with the object only. Godard's includes the perceiver.

Godard unites the two poles practically (as well as theoretically) by noting that "cutting on a look is almost the definition of montage, its supreme ambition as well as its submission to mise-en-scène." In other words, there is no way to define montage without reverting to mise-en-scène:

> [Montage] is, in effect, to bring out the soul under the spirit, the passion behind the intrigue, to make the heart prevail over the intelligence by destroying the notion of space in favor of that of time.

This is the psychological reality that Godard had been trying to grasp. He has neatly brought the heady theories down to earth.

Why is this question so important to Godard? Simply because in cinema the artist has the power to choose between montage and mise-en-scène; the novelist, the poet, the playwright, the painter, the musician do not. It may seem that all this discussion about what appear to be technical matters is dry theory. Quite the contrary. As we shall see, Godard, having seen the ethical nature of the technical debate, will eventually apply the logic in reverse: the technology has something to say about ethics. The filmmaker is an intermediary between the reality of the viewer and the reality of what is viewed. This is a responsibility which entails certain moral choices. Throughout Godard's criticism such phrases as "the logic of passion" recur. Logic and passion are inextricably intertwined for Godard, like montage and mise-en-scène. And the logic of the former technique and the passion of the latter are both directed towards the aim that psychological reality—where the heart and the heat meet—should be described, felt, comprehended. Therefore, it is the *synthesis* of cinema, rather than the analysis of it, which is Godard's greatest contribution and the synthesis of experience, not the analysis of it, which makes him a powerful artist.

Godard's criticism is just as compressed, intensive, quirky, and elliptical as the films which follow it. But the logic of his cinema is there, if we care enough to dig it out. For a preview of the substance of the films (as opposed to their dialectic), however, we must turn to the five short films he made during the fifties. All of them are very simple, none would have been judged extraordinary at the time they were made, but they all prefigure in one way or another the materials of the later films.

"Operation Béton," his first film, is notable mainly for its simplicity. It is a straightforward, no-nonsense documentary about the building of the Grand Dixence dam, but since, as its title indicates, it focuses on concrete (béton), we can use it as an exemplary epigraph for the body of Godard's work to follow: the materials he will use will be exceptionally concrete (*concrète* if not *béton*). The other four short films tell us considerably more. If they are described succinctly by their plots, their situations, or their milieux, there is nothing to distinguish them from the great majority of the features that follow (at least up to *La Chinoise*). Godard gives us "girls as we love them, boys as we see them everyday," and the background is the active and pervasive milieu of Paris. "Une Femme coquette" introduces the metaphor of prostitution which Godard will use so often in the future. The film is based on Maupassant's *Le Signe*, as is the film-within-the-film in *Masculin-féminin* ("Une Femme coquette" leaves off where *Masculin-féminin* begins). "Tous les garçons s'appellent Patrick," written by Eric Rohmer, presents a simple humorous love triangle which looks more Rohmeresque than Godardian. Two women have separately met the same man and each made a date. The film ends when they discover that their "dates" are identical. "Charlotte et son Jules" is the first film in which we can see Godard's attention shift away from the subject he is filming towards the technique of narrative. Charlotte (the name comes from Rohmer's "Charlotte et son steak" and from his script for "Tous les garcons . . .") has come back to see her ex-lover (Jean-Paul Belmondo). The focus of the film is a long monologue in which he berates her and pleads with her. But she has only returned to pick up her toothbrush. The frame of the story is no more complex than that of the earlier films, but here for the first time Godard has experimented with narrative point of view. The film is an excuse for the monologue, a device that will increasingly attract him.

The last short film of the fifties, "Histoire d'eau," also shows the developing complexity of Godard's style. Truffaut, who had always wanted to make a film about a flood, had managed to obtain some raw stock when the opportunity presented itself. After shooting most of the footage, however, he realized he had no idea what to do with it. Godard salvaged the film, dubbed the dialogue, and made of the botched footage the first really "Godardian" film, full of puns and wordplay (the title recalls the erotic novel *Histoire d'O* which had some notoriety at the time), in which our attention must be divided carefully between the subject of the film and its narrative style. Godard ignores, for the most part, the facts of the footage, the flood, and uses it as a stage from which to launch his dialogue collage. The key to the film lies in a story the young woman tells about Louis Aragon giving a lecture at the Sorbonne on the subject of Petrarch. (As she begins, she opens a car door and says, "Here I open a parenthesis: Everybody hates Aragon, but I like him, and I close the parenthesis." Whereupon she closes the car door.) Aragon, she tells us, started his lecture on Petrarch by throwing himself into a forty-five-minute discourse in praise of Matisse. Finally a student cried out from the back of the room: "Get to the subject!" whereupon Aragon, completing the phrase he had started before the interruption, said simply: "All the originality of Petrarch consists precisely in the art of digression!" "Histoire d'eau" is Godard's first Petrarchan invention, after the style of Aragon. Its interest is in its digression.

Writing about Godard's films one wants to mimic them. There is, for instance, no better way to describe the Godardian universe than to make a list. *A bout de souffle*, his first feature, yields a catalogue of elements:

> action vs. contemplation, the gray city, the ambivalence of women, the ambivalence towards women, lovelessness, the iconography of words, the power of popular culture, the grotesque distortions of capitalism, transience (no one has a home), cafes, the endless talk, the formal mise-en-scène, the syntax of sound vs. image, American culture, the B-movie, the film noir, the chilling romance with death, the difficulty of understanding, the commonness of death, the situation of the outsider, the political act, the importance of the sign, the "significance" (in semiological terms) of the sign, print vs. film, automania (both of the self and automobile), auteurism, digressions, the sociological treatise, the pun, Angst, Sartrean nausea.

What impresses us about Godard's films is their collage of cultural data and artifacts. Godard's characters—all of them, from Michel Poiccard and Patricia straight on through to "He" and "She" in *Tout va bien*—are afloat in a raging sea of images and sounds, metaphors and syllogisms, political half-truths and cultural clichés. And if there can be said to be one central action that unites and connects the various films, it is the battle to rescue life from abstraction, to return to the comfort of the concrete. If we must give this worldview a name, let us call it "existential semiology," since its main aim (even in the later political films) is the reaffirmation of the self, and it goes about this task by confronting and trying to analyze the plethora of languages that confound us. It is not, as it was for Sartre or Camus, a struggle with concepts and theories so much as a confrontation with the languages in which they are expressed—writing, film, popular art, billboards, packaging, advertising, and so forth.

None of this was as clear in 1960 when *A bout de souffle* was released as it is now, twenty-five Godard films later. Godard followed the fifteen-page scenario Truffaut had written fairly closely, and the result is a film which in terms of character and story comes closer than any of its successors to what we still regard as the norm for narrative feature films. *A bout de souffle* clearly has a beginning (Michel shoots the cop), a middle (he flees), and an end (Patricia betrays him, he is shot).* It also expends a good deal of effort developing the relationship between Poiccard and Patricia, and it is richer in incident than most of Godard's films. That it does remain so faithful to Truffaut's scenario is instructive, I think. However far the two filmmakers were to diverge in the future, *A bout de souffle* is strong evidence that they started from a

*Godard was once asked by an exasperated old-line filmmaker whether he would at least admit that films should have a beginning, middle, and end. "Yes," he replied, "but not necessarily in that order."

Michel (Jean-Paul Belmondo), a kid hidden under a Bogart hat, chewing a fat Gauloise, deep in the *fantaisies* of *Paris-Flirt:* print and image combined in the first scene of *A bout de souffle*.

common ground. We can expect that if Truffaut had made the film (he had vaguely conceived of it as a generalized sequel to *Les Quatre Cents Coups*—that was before he met Jean-Pierre Léaud) *A bout de souffle* would have paid much more attention to character; it would have had an altogether quieter, softer, and more compassionate mood. Yet the conceptual structure so evident in the final film is clearly present in Truffaut's scenario.

A bout de souffle is dedicated to Monogram Pictures, a "B-movie" studio of some repute among the *Cahiers* critics. Jean-Pierre Melville, who had for more than a decade been paying homage to the American film noir, makes an appearance—as the author Patricia interviews—which serves further to remind us of the *Cahiers* politique. *A bout de souffle* is a film noir, but set in the city of light, in the middle of summer. More precisely, it is a film *about* films noirs. By reversing the norms of that genre it hopes to explain something about it. The film's focus is not on the struggle between pursuer and pursued, but on the *image* of the situation.

The first shot of the film shows us the last page of the newspaper

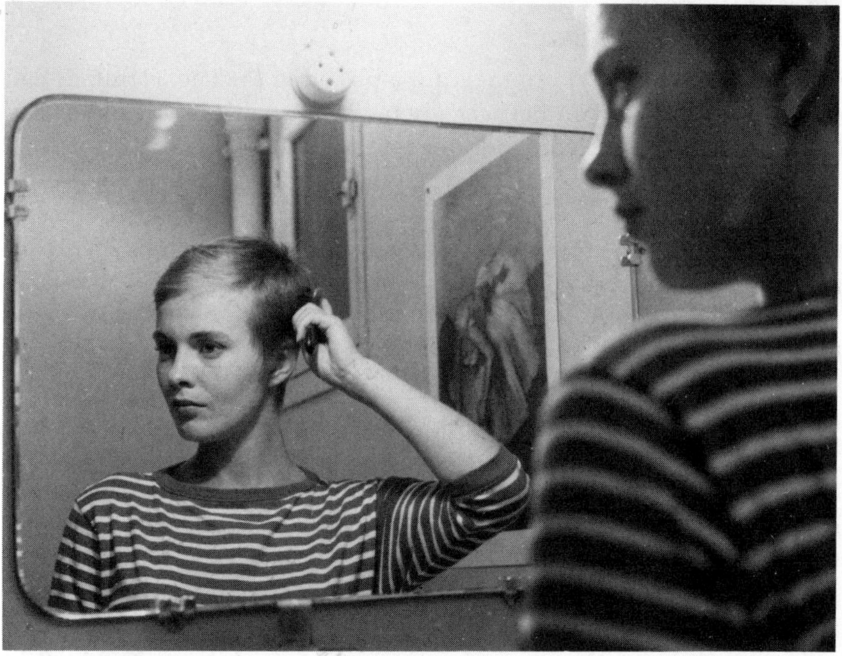

Patricia Franchini (Jean Seberg), the ultimate American girl in Paris in the late fifties, bracketing a Degas print.

Paris-Flirt: a pin-up. Poiccard is reading the paper, and hiding behind it, as he will often in the film to follow. The chase subplot is expressed almost entirely in terms of newspaper stories. Poiccard doesn't involve himself in the chase; he reads about himself. As "Laszlo Kovacs" (his pseudonym) he is separate from Michel Poiccard, the man for whom the police are searching. Poiccard is a character of popular journalism—a character Michel has invented. His infatuation with the image of Humphrey Bogart and his mimicry of Bogart further support this theme of mediated reality. What is important for Godard is not what we are, but what we think we are; not the object, but the medium through which it is expressed and which modifies it. This is the "psychological reality" he had spoken of as a critic.

Patricia Franchini sells the *New York Herald-Tribune,* the English-language Paris newspaper, and she wears a *Herald-Tribune* T-shirt, so she is a visual metaphor for the paper, and for the clash of languages that it implies. She wants to be a writer. At the end of the film, she succeeds: she rewrites Poiccard's legend by turning him in. For the first time since the beginning of the film he has to "act" in his own story. His melodramatic stagger up the street and his egregiously prolonged death are a bit hammy, but they put a period to the tale. (Truffaut had ended the scenario with Patricia's betrayal and Poiccard's curses.) His last words are: "C'est vraiment dégueulasse!" ("This is really disgusting!") It isn't clear whether he is referring to Patricia or to the hokey ending of the story he has just played out. In any event, Patricia hasn't understood him. She turns slowly towards us, rubbing her lips with her thumb in the gesture Michel had picked up from Bogart, and asks: "Qu'est-ce que c'est: dégueulasse?" She doesn't understand, but she has picked up the role nevertheless, and that is the point.

A bout de souffle is a montage of roles, images, models—vehicles for expression (and vehicles for transportation too—Patricia isn't the only "Belle Américaine" in the film; there are classic Cadillacs, Oldsmobiles, and Thunderbirds as well). But it is important to look also at the kind of stories being told. With Truffaut and Bogart Godard shares two characteristic themes: the isolation of the hero and the betrayal of women. He has taken the two to extremes. People in Godard's films seldom make any kind of human contact. There are no "Doinel" films, no *L'Enfant sauvage* to balance the stark alienation of *A bout de souffle, Le Petit Soldat, Pierrot le fou,* and so many others. Bogart was often betrayed by women, but he had some retribution. It is the strongly moral tone of his persona which has made him arguably the prime culture hero of the Hollywood star cinema. When Sam Spade tells off Brigid O'Shaughnessy at the end of *The Maltese Falcon* she understands and she is hurt. She may have betrayed him, but they share a set of ethics nevertheless. When Poiccard spits out his disgust at Patricia at the end of *A bout de souffle,* she doesn't even understand. Poiccard has caught the superficial image of Bogart, but it is no longer possible for him to fathom the moral basis of that persona. People in Godard's films (with very few exceptions) are paralyzed from the beginning. They may *talk* about love, about politics, but they seldom *make* either. At their best they reveal something of that terrifying internal battle between the paralysis of contemplation and the desire for action.

What is the cause of that paralysis? Godard will spend the next ten years working out answers to that question. *A bout de souffle* might be better translated "Out of Breath" than "Breathless." Godard is out of breath, beaten, at the beginning of his career. The dozen years after *A bout de souffle* are, for him, a struggle to regain composure.

Not much of this was evident to viewers of *A bout de souffle* in 1960. It was clear, however, that *A bout de souffle* had captured the moral ambience of the period. Young people who had felt an attraction to the existential image of Bogart found in Godard's film the first analysis of that phenomenon. And since Truffaut's first film was so personal, *A bout de souffle* was also in a sense the first "New Wave" film, since it dealt obviously with films as well as life. Critics may have appreciated this "instant classic" because it was technically fresh and innovative, because the hand-held Arriflex, the jump cutting, the location shooting and realistic lighting were invigorating renovations of cinematic language. But the general public found the film attractive for simpler reasons. It mirrored—with humor—the existential ennui that characterized the fifties, when we were all Michel Poiccards with dreams of writing our own "stories" and having them realized (i.e., made real) through the media. But Godard was to be a filmmaker of the sixties, and he quickly turned away from existential dilemmas towards the political debate which would characterize the succeeding ten years.

Le Petit Soldat was shot in April and May 1960, just after *A bout de souffle* had opened, but it was banned by the government until January 1963. No matter that its politics appear vague and unspecific to us now; it was enough that it dealt with the Algerian situation. Ironically, if the film has any political line at all, it is certainly one to which the French government should have been sympathetic. Bruno Forestier (Michel Subor), the hero of *Le Petit Soldat,* works for an anti-FLN organization, and the central sequence of the film involves the torture of Bruno by the FLN. Yet Godard has in fact been scrupulously apolitical. Forestier, who like Michel Poiccard is totally self-involved, although a little colder, harder, and more supercilious, is contrasted evenly with Veronica Dreyer, who works for the Left organization and with whom he falls in love, after his fashion. She seems only slightly more idealistically motivated than Forestier, who is a political assassin mainly because he enjoys the role of "secret agent." The materials of the film may be superficially political, but the tone of it is still existential—and this time rather effete. As Godard explained it:

> People talk about politics in it, but it is not politically oriented in a particular direction. The way I approached it was to say to myself: people complain that the Nouvelle Vague only shows people in bed, I'm going to show some who are in politics and don't have time to go to bed with each other.[8]

So the impetus for the film was reactive rather than active.

That Godard at the age of thirty really had no particular viewpoint about the Algerian situation is rather disturbing. Of course he intellectualizes the political stance of the film in such a way that he can almost be excused:

> I wanted to show a confused mind in a confused situation. Well, that could be considered wrong, because perhaps one should not have been confused. But that's how it was. . . .[9]

He calls the film "in any case, a kind of auto-critique." How?

> You mustn't forget, too, that I do not always maintain the same distance from my characters. You have to sense the moments when I am very close, those where I stand off. The first line of the film is: "The time for action is past, that of reflection is beginning." Therefore there is a critical angle. The whole film is a flashback: one never sees the present.[10]

Can *Le Petit Soldat* then be simply a sophisticated experiment in narrative theory? No doubt these were present concerns for Godard; yet the subject matter overwhelms the experimental tone. Algeria, the FLN, and the OAS are just too real to be treated as neutral materials. (Alain Resnais's *Muriel,* on the other hand, which is equally experimental, has characters who also operate in bad faith but manages nevertheless to convey a deep sense of the injustice of Algeria, because Resnais is able to establish his own voice as separate from those of the characters.)

Godard concludes his defense of the film by suggesting that a film about confusion must necessarily show confusion and that, therefore, "the spectator is free" (if, that is, he can suspend for a while his knowledge of the real Algeria). The theme was not "real but newsreel," as he put it.[11] This, too, connects it with *A bout de souffle;* what the newspapers did for the first film, the radio does for the second. There is a continual stream of news about OAS and FLN activities coming from the car radios in *Le Petit Soldat,* providing a background of "newsreelity" against which the consciously melodramatic story is played out. (That the government censored occasional words and phrases in the radio broadcasts, leaving black holes, only adds to their effectiveness.)

If we do disregard the political material of *Le Petit Soldat,* we have a much more understandable (and likeable) film. As in *A bout de souffle,* the characters aren't quite sure whether happiness is the cause of freedom or the other way round. For Bruno, as for Michel, existential freedom grows out of the barrel of a gun. However, if Forestier doesn't exactly have a set of ethics (he does admire Lenin's dictum that "ethics are the esthetics of the future"), he at least hesitates before he kills, and this makes him a more complex figure. Bruno narrates the film (it *is* a flashback), and the tone of his commentary, once again, is pure film noir. The melodrama is simplistic because it is Bruno's version of events, highly colored and romantic. This works to distance the film and make it appear more serious in intent than its predecessor. "I wanted to discover the realism I had missed in *A bout de souffle,*" Godard explained, "the concreteness."[12] Yet the subdued tone also has the consequence of making us take its politics seriously—and that is a large problem for the film.

Bruno is a reporter and photographer (he is continually snapping pictures: "When you photograph a face . . . you photograph the soul behind it. . . . Photography is truth . . . and the cinema is the truth twenty-four times a second. . . .")[13] and therefore a conscious artist rather than an intuitive one, like Michel Poiccard. He has long known that we all write our own stories; the problem is that Bruno has chosen to write the kind of distasteful story that he does. Unlike Poiccard's, his is a private story. "What's important is not the way others see you," he says, "it's the way you see yourself." But the character he constructs for himself is basically adolescent: interested in the *appearance* of action rather than the substance of it, wearing a macho mask, sophomorically full of bits and pieces of undigested cultural information, and of course totally unformed politically.

Bruno's adolescence is most clearly seen in his relationship with Veronica. He does not know how to talk to her (or to any woman, we conclude). He asks her silly questions. He tries to seduce her with his camera ("Shake your hair like this" [the classic Godardian gesture]. "Light a cigarette, take a shower . . .") Like Poiccard, he can only understand a woman by comparing her with art objects. Patricia was a Picasso; Forestier can't decide whether Veronica's eyes are Renoir grey or Velasquez grey. Like Patricia, Veronica speaks French with a foreign accent which is charming, mysterious, and esthetically attractive. Women

This attitude towards women, it must be admitted, is as much Godard's as Michel's or Bruno's. For Godard, at this point in his life, it is clear that women *must* be magic: they are wonderful works of art he can't fathom. He had just married Anna Karina before beginning to shoot *Le Petit Soldat,* and we can read the film as his own investigation of her mystery. In his next two films she will fill the central role, and he will at least attempt to see the materials from a female point of view. But, together with his political naiveté at this time, he reveals a pitiable ignorance of women. His shyness reveals itself in what seems to be a profound ambivalence about his women characters. They often betray the men of his films, and when they do not they are killed off. Bruno and his camera stand in for Godard and his camera in *Le Petit Soldat,* desperately hoping that the machine will reveal the soul of Veronica/Anna where the man has failed. When Bruno learns that Veronica wants to be an actress, he explodes:

Still life, Veronica (Anna Karina), a cigarette, a rose: "When you photograph a face you photograph the soul behind it."

> Actors! It's stupid to me. I despise them. It's true, you tell them to laugh, they laugh. . . . You tell them to cry, they cry. You tell them to crawl, they do it. To me, that's grotesque . . . they're not free.[14]

In *Le Petit Soldat,* Bruno may be free ("Up to now my story has been simple. It's about a fellow without ideals. And tomorrow?"), Godard may be free ("I wanted to show a confused mind in a confused situation"), even the spectators may be free ("If it is important for Subor to ask himself these questions, it is no less important for the spectator to ask them"),[15] but Veronica certainly isn't. She's captured, tortured, then killed. With the next film, her liberation begins.

Godard began shooting *Une Femme est une femme (A Woman Is a Woman)* in November of 1960. It was his third film in fourteen months—an extraordinary beginning. Since *Le Petit Soldat* had been censored, *Une Femme est une femme* was the second film by Godard that the public saw, and like Truffaut's *Tirez sur le pianiste* (with which it shares some characteristics), it was generally misunderstood. Both of these second films happen to be more personal and more eclectically ambitious than Godard's and Truffaut's first films which, "through a concatenation of circumstances," Godard explained, had become "much too successful."[16] Truffaut had expressed similar sentiments. Both of them, it seems, were not only surprised but also a little frightened by the popularity of their first efforts. The pressure of success was disturbing to them after having spent a decade criticizing film from the position of outsiders. No one denies the evident merits of those premier films, but Godard, like Truffaut, began the real work of his career with his second and third films, and *Une Femme est une femme,* like *Tirez sur le pianiste,* deserves more serious attention that it has so far received.

Like *Le Pianiste, Une Femme* is a study of genres. Truffaut's film may have been the greater shock, since there was no evidence whatsoever in *Les Quatre Cents Coups* to indicate that he was interested in genres, but Godard's essay in the Musical was also unexpected—we may see *A bout de souffle* as a study in Film Noir now, but at the time it was taken rather straight. Certainly, no one expected the charm, the music, the lyrical quality of *Une Femme est une femme* from the author of *A bout de souffle.* Godard explains that:

> The over-all conception of the film came from something Chaplin had said: that tragedy is life in close-up and comedy life in long shot. I said to myself, I'm going to make a comedy in close-up: the film will be tragicomic.[17]

The results are, if not actually tragicomic, at least tinged with the poignancy that the French alone seem able to bring to comic subjects. The main mood of *Une Femme est une femme,* however, is neither tragic nor comic; this is a love story, one of the few successful ones of the sixties. It is set in the frame of the Musical genre which is so closely associated with that theme, and it includes a muted but nevertheless clear critical distancing from the genre which sets things in perspective. Early on Angéla and Alfred (Karina and Belmondo) announce that they want to be in a "musical by Gene Kelly, with choreography by Bob Fosse," but Godard knows those days are gone. *Singin' in the Rain* will never be reproduced and, as a result, an air of nostalgia suffuses *Une Femme est une femme.* That nostalgia was doubled and redoubled within just a few years after the film was released, for it quickly became not only a paean to the Musical Comedy but one of the last and most charming vestiges of that brief period after the cultural miasma of the fifties had lifted but before we were overtaken by the realities of the sixties. It is the only one of Godard's thirty-six films that celebrates the life-force wholeheartedly, a song of innocence. (The scenario had been written before Godard began *A bout de souffle.*)

The romance of *Une Femme est une femme* is not, however, as anachronistic as it may seem. One of the strands which weaves itself throughout French film in the 1960s is just this attempt to recapture the aura of romance in American films of the thirties. Godard makes it clear by giving Alfred the last name Lubitsch that this is a conscious homage to that era. (The similarity with *Design for Living* was intentional.) But what makes *Une Femme* successful is that this mood of affirmation is expressed on many different levels. If the film is a warm love story, it is because Godard is moved not only by admiration for romantic Musicals, but also by love: of his new wife Anna Karina; of the classic genre of thirties American comedy; of his new-found "toy," color; of his discovery of direct sound; and of the freedom of widescreen composition.

The motivations, then, are manifold. Compare the wide range of *Une Femme est une femme* with the narrow focus of the two best-known French romances of the sixties—Jacques Demy's *Les Parapluies de Cherbourg* and Claude Lelouch's *Un Homme et une femme.* Music is essential to both these films (as it is to Godard's); but Demy forces the issue to extremes in his operatic fairy tale, and Lelouch's film, although it manages to catalogue just about every element of contemporary romantic culture—from Brazilian sambas to automobiles to filmmaking and even children—nevertheless rings hollow, draws no conclusion.

Does Godard's adventure in romance need a defense? I think not. *Une Femme est une femme* is one of the few absolutely necessary films in Godard's canon. It describes lyrically the sentiments which, when later contrasted with method, will yield his politics. As Che Guevara said: "At the risk of seeming ridiculous, let me say that the true revolutionary is motivated by great feelings of love." At the risk of seeming ridiculous, Godard made a Musical.

The contradictions of *Une Femme est une femme* make it interesting as well as charming. Needless to say, Godard's love story is underpinned with theory. It is a musical without much time for music. On the recording of the soundtrack of the film that he made (but which was never distributed) he describes, in his usual elliptical way, his theoretical motive:

> The invention of cinema is based on a gigantic error: that of recording the image of man, and reproducing it by projecting it till the end of time. In other words, believing that a strip of celluloid is less perishable than a block of stone or even memory. This strange belief means that, from Griffith to Bresson, the history of cinema and the history of its errors are one: the error of trying to paint ideas better than music, to illustrate actions better than a novel, to describe feelings better than painting. One may say

> in short that *errare cinematographicum est.* . . . But this error . . . becomes fascinating in a thriller, arresting in a Western, blinding in a war film, and alluring in what is normally called a musical.[18]

This profusion of possibilities and the confusion of media are what make genre films so seductive. The clash gives them life: "To make movies is to make mistakes." In an interview, Godard spoke more precisely about the genesis of the film:

> . . . I conceived this theme within the context of a neo-realist musical. It's a complete contradiction, but this is precisely what interested me in the film. It may be an error, but it's an attractive one. And it matches the theme, which deals with a woman who wants a baby in an absurd manner whereas it is the most natural thing in the world. But the film is not a musical. It's the idea of a musical.[19]

The *idea* of a musical, *Une Femme est une femme* is therefore an analysis of one. If the most obvious aspect of a Musical is its music, Godard will separate that element from the rest and concentrate on direct sound instead. If color is an integral part of a Musical (as it was of the ones of the forties and fifties he had in mind), then Godard's color will be controlled, forced, dialectical. His palette concentrates on primary colors and white ("Blue coat, white fur, red beret, for Angéla the day of glory is come"). To focus our attention on the film rather than the action in it, he sometimes stops the story so that the actors can speak to the audience. Because a genre film is highly stylized our interest usually lies in its method, not its content; so that most important is the structure of the fable Godard is narrating. *Une Femme est une femme* is an adventure in narration, indicating the main direction Godard will take hereafter. For the first time, printed words appear on the screen to call attention to the teller, not the tale. The film is marked off in epigrams which summarize the action: "Emile takes Angéla at her word because he love her, and Angéla lets herself get caught in the trap because she loves him." Or,

Be-cause-they-love-each-oth-er,
Every-thing-will-go-wrong-for-E-mile-and-An-gé-la.
They-have-made-the-mis-take-of-think-ing-they-can-go-too-far.
Be-cause-their-love-is-both-mut-ual-and-e-tern-al-as-we-have-al-read-y-said.

These words are stretched across the wide screen as well as spoken on the soundtrack. The aptly named Angéla and Emile Récamier and Alfred Lubitsch have been caught up in the inexorable logic of their tale.

Words on the screen

Still life: Flowers, wine, Jean-Claude Brialy (Emile), and Anna Karina (Angéla): "a realist Musical Comedy."

In the very first year of The Pill Angéla and Emile live together, spiritually united but not legally tied. Angéla has doubts, Emile doesn't. Angéla wants a baby; she may have to turn to their friend Alfred (Jean-Paul Belmondo), who loves her from the far corner of the triangle, to find a father. Godard prefigures the lifestyle that was somewhat daring in the sixties and has become commonplace in the seventies, and he forecasts the problems of liaisons like these which are in some ways more intense than traditional marriages. We know these sentiments well; the pleasure is in the mounting—and in the distancing Godard provides. The film's world captures for us a mood in which Musical Comedy fantasies are a very real and present refuge, a world in which romance is as simple as the reds and blues of the palette, in which bicycle races and plaid skirts and white blouses determine the limits of reality, in which the magical powers of film Méliès had discovered sixty years earlier are part of the fabric of everyday life—the flipped egg that waits in the air while Angéla answers the phone, the instant costume changes. A film about film, in other words, and about telling stories on film, and about the kind of fabulous tales that once were told.

At the center of this collage of colors, poses, milieus, songs, jokes, routines, gestures, objects, games, and memories there is Angéla, the woman of the title. Godard's attention has turned from the outsider who occupied the center of his first two films to the representative woman who will provide the focus for nine out of his next eleven films. He still knows pitifully little about women, but here it doesn't seem to matter that he obsessively tries to capture a woman on film by triangulating her culturally ("Two blue eyes: Giraudoux. A red umbrella: Aragon. That is Angéla . . . rather like Camilla in Renoir's marvelous film [*La Carrosse d'or*], . . . If Angéla were called Marianne it would be Musset. . .").[20] That technique fits the mode of the musical. The partnership between Karina and Godard is going to yield some of his most impressive films (six in the next seven years) and be just as instructive for Godard as were the relationships with Masina for Fellini, Vitti for Antonioni, and all those women for Bergman. Like Angéla, like Renoir's Camilla, we can wonder "where theatre ends and life begins."

At the end of the film, after the dilemma of the baby's father has been resolved, after the conversation in book titles, after the sobering Aznavour song "Tu te laisse aller" has been heard, after the boys have learned that the girl has a particular life of her own, after the celebration of the Musical is complete, Emile turns to Angéla in bed and declares:

> Angéla, tu es infame!

But Angéla has the last word. No, she replies, I'm not infamous,

> Je suis *une* femme!

The victory is small, but on it Karina and Godard will build. As Jean-Claude Brialy has exclaimed earlier, talking to us about the film he's acting in,

> I don't know whether it's a comedy or a tragedy, but in any case it's a masterpiece!

The film that follows, *Vivre sa vie* (*My Life To Live, It's My Life*), is as dark as *Une Femme* was light, as close and direct and restricted as its predecessor was open, free, and vivacious. The Film Noir aspect of *A bout de souffle* and the political tendencies in *Le Petit Soldat* come together with the feminine focus that was established in the comedy. The result is a summary for Godard, and a step forward. The narrative freedom and experimentation of *Une Femme* revealed an important new source of power, and *Vivre sa vie* is Godard's first film to take serious advantage of it. It is his first filmed essay. essay

After finishing post-production work on *Une Femme est une femme* in early 1961, Godard encountered a period of forced inactivity of the sort that has plagued independent filmmakers in the last two decades. During 1961 he worked on two projects—"Eva," from the novel by J. H. Chase, and "France la douce," which he described as the story of "a woman of the right and a man of the left"—both of which fell through.

In the fall of that year he also made a sketch ("La Paresse," "Sloth") for the compilation film *Les Septs Péchés capitaux (The Seven Capital Sins)* and acted with Anna Karina in a parody sequence in Agnès Varda's *Cléo de 5 à 7.* In early 1962 he shot *Vivre sa vie* in less than four weeks. He says,

> I didn't know exactly what I was going to do. . . . In fact, I made the film right off the bat, as if carried along, like an article written at one go. *Vivre sa vie* had the kind of equilibrium which means that you suddenly feel good about life for an hour, or a day, or a week"[21]

Both the fallow period of the preceding year and the rushed (even for Godard) shooting schedule seem to have had beneficial effects. *Vivre sa vie* is the first film in which his own cinematic voice is clear and forceful; he has emerged from the shadows of the genres.

In order to combine the modes of fiction and documentary Godard went to the logical source, Brecht, and adapted some of Brecht's distancing devices for the narrative of the film: he drained the drama from it, paralleled the action with a factual commentary, used direct sound exclusively (often with only one microphone picking up both dialogue and background sound), rigorously chose long shots over close-ups, and used extended mise-en-scène (long takes and slow pans) as opposed to the more intimate and lively montage of the earlier films. Raoul Coutard, whose work in both black-and-white and color for Godard in the early and mid-sixties set standards which have not yet been surpassed, provided starkly black and white images whose strength surprised even Godard. ("What astonishes me," he said, "is that it seems to be the most carefully composed of all my films, whereas it certainly wasn't . . . Coutard brought off his best camerawork."[22]) The dull settings, the lengthy narrated shots, the distant voice of the narrator (Godard) reading statistics, and the total insouciance of the characters towards the presence of the camera (they speak with their backs to it sometimes) all further contribute to the controlled distancing. *Vivre sa vie* is a demanding film, and in that sense classic Godard. But it is also classic in being, as Richard Roud has pointed out, exquisitely balanced. It is divided into twelve sections ("why 12? I don't know; but in tableaux to emphasize the theatrical, Brechtian side"), and, like a classical tragedy, is structured neatly into exposition, development, crisis, and conclusion, all progressing inexorably. Chaste title cards announce and summarize the sequences, like "arguments" in an epic poem:

The first shot of *Vivre sa vie:* forced distancing. The entire shot is played in the mirror. Nana (Anna Karina), Paul (André S. Labarthe).

1. A cafe—Nana feels like giving up—Paul—the pinball machine.
2. The record shop—200 francs—Nana lives her day.
3. The concierge—Paul—The Passion of Joan of Arc—a press agent.
4. At the police station—Nana is being questioned.
5. On the street—the first client—the room.
6. Running into Yvette—a cafe on the outskirts—Raoul—Machine gun fire in the street.
7. The letter—Raoul again—On the Champs Elysées.
8. Afternoons—hotels—money—client-pleasing.
9. A young man—Luigi—Nana thinks maybe she's happy.
10. The street—a client—pleasure is no fun.
11. Afternoon cafe—the stranger—Nana doesn't know she's a philosopher.
12. The young man again—the oval portrait—Raoul sells Nana.

As in Classical tragedy, many of the most "dramatic" events are kept off-screen, and the greater part of the work is devoted to the development of the consequences of events—in other words, talking.

But *Vivre sa vie* is more an essay than a play. With "Documentation from 'Où en est la prostitution?' by Marcel Sacotte," the film reintroduces the theme of prostitution Godard had first tentatively explored in

"Une Femme coquette"; here it is "realistic," in the future it will become the grand Godardian metaphor through which many of his political ideas will be developed. Nana's name reminds us that the film exists in a tradition that goes back through Renoir to Zola. Like the novel and film before it, *Vivre sa vie* is pervaded with a naturalistic sense of fate. As Truffaut described the film: "There is a girl, she is in a fixed situation, desperate straits, and from the beginning. At the end of the road lies death."[23] There is no exit.

Many of Godard's films are built along similar patterns. In these, the ones Truffaut calls Godard's "sad" films, "the role of autobiography in each is greater than the role of invention." *Vivre sa vie* may be esthetically distanced, it may be something of a factual essay on its subject, but it is this personal (and painful) atmosphere which makes it finally such an affecting film. There isn't that much in the film about prostitution per se: in "The first client," for example: Nana and the client enter the room; close-up on the man's pelvis as he pulls the money out of his pocket; he tries to kiss her on the mouth; she resists; slow fade. But there is a great deal about the terror of Nana's situation: she has lost Paul at the beginning of the film; she has tried modeling; she has tried the movies; she has had a job as a shopgirl (200 old francs a day); Raoul the pimp is the only alternative. Like her sisters Patricia, Veronica, and Angéla, she is an object (sometimes venerated, sometimes detested). She is compared with Falconetti in Dreyer's *La Passion de Jeanne d'Arc* (the sublime) and with Elizabeth Taylor (the ridiculous). In the last scene, the young man she has recently met reads to her from Poe's "The Oval Portrait," which, significantly, is about an artist whose wife dies just as he finishes her portrait. Nana, however, is now not only an object, but a commodity as well. As Raoul drives her to the "marketplace" where she will meet her death, they pass a theater showing *Jules et Jim*. There are long lines of people waiting to get in. Catherine is free, Nana is emprisoned: still both meet the same fate. Nana has had her conversation with Brice Parain about communication and freedom, but she hasn't broken free soon enough. Unlike her sisters, she has begun to work out the logic of her own life, she has started to ask questions, but the questions aren't sufficient to guarantee her freedom.

Most of Godard's characters before *La Chinoise* (and a good number after) face this same trap. The films so often end with death, not only because that is still the most effective dramatic period, but also because an important facet of Godard's own romantic, existential cinematic personality is Keatsian, half in love with easeful death. Politics will bring him out of that bind, but politics are still a good distance off at the time of the ironically titled *Vivre sa vie*. If we are works of art, we may be eternal, but we are frozen in that eternal moment, as Pirandello pointed out. If we are commodities then we must eventually be disposed of. Obviously the search is, then, for a condition of existence beyond commodity, even beyond art. *Vivre sa vie,* combining fiction and reality, begins the search.

7

GODARD
Modes of Discourse

In what we have determined, with the characteristic blitheness of abstract criticism, to be Godard's "second period" the modes of discourse of the films are an important focus of attention. Godard shares with Truffaut the twin concerns of method and sentiment. Their common heritage pointed these different personalities in the same direction: towards a scrutiny of the medium of film and its connection with everyday life. The two elemental questions Truffaut asks—Are films more important than life? and Are women magic?—would serve just as well for Godard, if we translated them into his language. The first question is political; it seems to have caused Godard more pain than it did Truffaut. The second question Godard also seems to have taken more seriously—at least many of his films have been more painfully confused about women and their roles.

Truffaut's cinema is materialist, structural, and dialectical. Godard's cinema certainly shares those characteristics; but since, unlike Truffaut's, it is so often self-referential, it announces these qualities. Godard and Truffaut both intuited and intellectualized the formal essence of the art and its ramifications; having studied under and worked with André Bazin, they shared his view that realism was the foundation of cinema and that "realism" was an ethical system as well as an esthetics.

So much depends on that overburdened term "realism." Godard was fond of quoting Brecht, who said, "Realism doesn't consist in reproducing reality, but in showing how things *really* are." Christian Metz, who has pioneered in the attempt to describe the phenomenon of cinema in semiological terms, makes an important distinction between the reality of the substance of a film and the reality of the language in which that substance is expressed. "On the one hand," he writes, "there is the *impression* of reality; on the other the *perception* of reality. . . ."[1] The simplest definition of "realism" is limited to the first area—what is *represented* (an auto crash looks "very real," or, as we say, "this is a realistic portrayal of working-class life"). The realism of Brecht, Bazin, Godard, and Truffaut, however, is concerned not only with substance but with language. In other words, each of these artists demands a certain honesty of himself in his relationship with audiences. This is what Godard was driving at in his early critical essays when he spoke of "psychological realism." The struggle for realist language (as well as realist substance) has been Godard's major motivation ever since. It is the reason why his own voice as narrator becomes increasingly important in his films; why even his political films of the Dziga-Vertov period talk more about film than they do about politics; and why so many people find his films difficult—because they are talking about themselves as much as their ostensible subjects—they have that dual voice.

Film is necessarily materialist. Because it shows objects and because it has the optimal power of realism, film comes perilously close to reproducing—or replicating—the objects. But in fact it doesn't—it only gives us images of them. And we are aware that these are images, not objects. To be honest, then, we can't avoid the objects, but neither can we avoid the images. Hence film must be structuralist as well as materialist, for the images are summations, symbols, signs, indices of the objects. This fact leads us on the one hand into the ethnographical side of structuralism (since the images are summations and thus mythic), and on the other into the linguistic side—semiology—since the images form a system of signs. Remember Godard's quotation (when he was not yet twenty years old) of the dictum of Brice Parain: "The sign forces us to see an object through its significance" *("Le signe nous oblige à nous figurer un objet de sa signification.")* The very phrasing of that sentence suggests an ethical question. If the image "forces us" to see an object through itself, then anyone who uses images should operate with a set of ethical or moral principles concerning their use. Politics is film.

Finally, we should add that, since this realist power of film is sustained by the wealth of images and sounds that can be collected and by the availability of tropes from so many other arts that can be used, the arrangement of all these elements (montage and mise-en-scène) makes the art of film naturally dialectical. When one image is juxtaposed with another, one sound with another, an image with a sound, it is almost impossible not to think dialectically. It is not always the artist who works this way; sometimes it is only the observer.

While with Truffaut we could avoid this theoretical superstructure, with Godard we cannot. It is too much a part of the fabric of his films from the mid-sixties on. Materialism, structuralism, semiology, dialectics are not only tools which we use to discuss Godard's films, not only tools which *he* uses to make them, but also the *subjects* of his films. And as such they have grown organically out of the nature of the medium itself. Is film more important than life? Evidently, judging by Godard's actions in recent years, no. But if we can understand the system of film, he suggests, possibly we can then better understand the system of life. Film is politics.

Materialism, structuralism, dialectics are all useful and vital methods of examining the world (and film)—but all can be subsumed under semiology. Before we can understand the dialectics of a film, before we can sense its materialism, before we can learn about its structure, we must first get past the barrier of the sign. "The sign forces us to see an object through its significance." Is there, then, a system to the "language" of film? Is there a way that we can codify the relationships between the object, the sign, and the significance? If there were, then Godard's job (and ours) would be considerably easier. If we could go to a "grammar of film" to discover the laws that were operating, we would find it a lot easier to understand how film manipulates both the reality in front of the camera and the observers in front of the screen.

Christian Metz confronted this problem directly. If film were a language *system,* like English or French, which could be codified, the film semiologist could simply apply the science of linguistics to the "language" of film, making the necessary changes. But Metz discovered—and had the courage to admit—that cinema was not a language system. It had too close a relationship to the reality it described. Metz concluded that "the cinematographic image is primarily speech [*parole*]"; that is, it is a *language,* since we can understand it, but it is not a *language system,* since we can't codify how it works. "The word, which is the unit of language [systems], is missing; the sentence, which is the unit of speech, is supreme. The cinema can speak only in neologisms."[2] So no one can really learn the language of film, though everyone can "speak" it. And it follows that everyone can understand it. In Metz's terms, cinema is composed of "short-circuit" signs: that is, the signifier *equals* the signified; it is identical to it rather than merely a representation of it.

Metz summarizes the problem succinctly in a sentence which should be dear to anyone who has ever written or talked about film:

> A film is difficult to explain because it is easy to understand.[3]

Because it so closely mimics reality, a film can be understood by anyone who can understand reality. But it is nevertheless *not* reality. It needs explication all the more, then, because it is so seductively, duplicitously "real."

The same dilemma confronts Godard as well as Metz. Metz can't very well study the semiology of film if there is no language system, so he avoids the dilemma by raising the level of his discussion to another plane: if we can't have a semiology of cinema because it is not a language system, then maybe we can describe a semiology of *narrative structure*. Godard stops considerably short of this flight. True, he evinces a strong interest in the phenomenology of narrative techniques, but he is even more absorbed by the *ethical* implications of the "short-circuit sign." If film is both easy to understand and difficult to explain, then the critic as *filmmaker* must confront that dilemma; he can't skip over it. We are back to the essential Bazinian ethical problem of realism: "The meaning is not in the image," says Bazin, "it is in the shadow of the image projected by montage [and mise-en-scène] onto the field of consciousness of the spectator."[4] This is another way of saying "the sign forces us to see an object through its significance."

To be honest, a filmmaker must explain his language as well as its content. This is a chore that writers do not face. Where the signifier is separate from the signified, the difficulty of understanding is what makes the "spectator" aware of the language; where signifier and signified are identical, as they are in film, there is an extra burden of separation (and identification) placed upon the artist. The burden is especially vital because film is not just another art like sculpture or painting but an entirely new *medium* which directly challenges the written and spoken language itself. This is why the analysis of the phenomenon of film is politically important for Godard.

The parallel with the problem Bertolt Brecht faced is clear. Like Godard, Brecht insisted that his audience maintain a consciousness of the "vehicle" (in his case the stage). To that end, he worked out the theory of the *Verfremdungseffekt* (the "estrangement-effect"). "The object of this 'effect,'" he wrote, "is to allow the spectator to criticize constructively from a social point of view."[5] Consciousness of the vehicle not only allows but demands the participation of the viewer in a continual process of analysis of the images, sounds, and other phenomena with which he is confronted. A great deal to ask? Possibly, but the only way either Brecht or Godard could see to be honest with their spectators.

Godard had no particular, codified theory like Brecht's. In a series of films he worked out the problems practically; "modes of discourse" had to be tested. Before we go on to examine some of those modes, we must define "discourse"; it is a kind of narrative. As Metz puts it, drolly,

> What distinguishes a discourse from the rest of the world, and by the same token contrasts it with the "real" world, is the fact that a discourse must necessarily be made by someone (for discourse is not language), whereas one of the characteristics of the world is that it is uttered by no one.[6]

This suggests another way of looking at the difference between film and literature. In literature, a reader is always aware of a narrator: someone is speaking or writing those words on the page. In film, however, one tends to dismiss the concept of narrator (unless one hears the voice on the soundtrack) and accept the images and sounds as the *equivalent of reality*. Hence the moral burden. Hence, too, the attention the New Wave paid to auteurs very early on. Again, in order to be honest, it is necessary to remind observers at every turn (even if the filmmakers have not) that film *is* discourse, *does* have a narrator or author. Metz later suggests that *irréalisation* ("unrealization") is at the "heart of every narrative act." *Irréalisation* is broader and more general, but it parallels Brecht's *V-effekt*.

The question now is: what modes of discourse did Godard examine and experiment with and how did they serve to "unrealize" the narratives? *Les Carabiniers,* as it happens, is clearly Brechtian; *Le Mépris (Contempt)* is Godard's only real attempt at a Hollywood film; *Bande à part (Band of Outsiders)* takes us back to the fables of *A bout de souffle* and *Le Petit Soldat;* and *La Femme Mariée (The Married Woman)* breaks through to entirely new ground—it is a landmark film for Godard, a major achievement.

Les Carabiniers was shot in and around Paris during a period of a month or so in the winter of 1962–63 from a script that Godard, Jean Gruault, and Roberto Rossellini had fashioned from the stage play *I Carabinieri,* by Benjamino Joppolo. The stagey simplicity of the source fit Godard's purposes well. All his earlier films had depended on sets of logical problems which Godard had posited for himself, but until now, never had a Godard film been so strictly organized around it's logic. The result was his coldest film up to then—a film that met with considerable opposition when it was released. The honeymoon with the New Wave was over.

The subject of *Les Carabiniers*—war—is the ultimate testing ground for theories of distancing and "unrealization": how else can the absurdity and absolutism of that phenomenon be treated? In the first place, "war" is what Truffaut or Chabrol would call a "grand" subject—too large to be encompassed in art. To film war, to paint it, or to write about it realistically would be to make it comprehensible, when the salient characteristic of it in the twentieth century is its very incomprehensibility. How can one conceive of the dimensions of World War II, for example? We can state a fact: "six million were exterminated in the German death camps." But how can that statement be made real? Simply counting to six million, working eight hours a day, would take more than a lifetime. There is no way, really, to comprehend the actuality of war. Somehow, some kind of leverage of logic must be brought into play. Alain Resnais, for example, in his films about World War II focuses on memory. Memories are structured by the limits of the mind; we have a gauge by which to judge their size and impact. The equation is set up: the memory gives us a comprehensible index of the incomprehensible phenomenon. In *Dr. Strangelove,* Stanley Kubrick utilizes the equally effective distancing of absurdist satire: if we can understand the joke of war, then, too, we have a satisfactory index. Throughout the late fifties and the sixties, anti-war films provide a range of answers to this esthetic-political problem. Godard's *Les Carabiniers* is one of the clearest expositions.

Godard begins by personalizing the phenomenon. This will be a film not about war but about Ulysse's and Michel-Ange's reactions to it and participation in it. But personalization allows us to concentrate on a human and therefore comprehensible drama and avoid politics. So Godard distances the characters by making them unsympathetic. The visual organization further heightens this separation, the film was shot on Kodak XX negative and then printed on special high-contrast stock to force the grain and to duplicate the dramatic high contrast of old orthochromatic stock. The intertitles are scrawled in Godard's own handwriting. The stylized play on which the film is based provides narrative materials which work in parallel: deaths are superfluous, violence arbitrary, sympathy dead. What looks like a traditional (and therefore relatively unaffecting) "human drama" is, it turns out, an essay on the political problems involved in the esthetic of war films. For Godard, the necessary leverage is not memory, satire, or irony, but the language of film itself. The experience of war is one thing; the knowledge of it which we gain through film and literature is quite another. If we know, generally, the difference between "film" and "real life," we should be able to extrapolate from the filmic image some sense of the actuality.

Must of *Les Carabiniers* looks like it might be a documentary; in fact there are quite a few newsreel shots intercut mainly to suggest this. Godard compared the film to a recent "successful" documentary, *Mourir à Madrid,* which he suggests imposes significance on its newsreel shots:

> This is what I call cheating—even if the intention is pure—because making a documentary compilation does not mean stealing the life which sleeps in the archive vaults: it means stripping reality of its appearances to restore the raw reality which is sufficient unto itself. . . . Filming, therefore, is simply seizing an event as a sign, and seizing it at the precise second when . . . the significance springs freely from the sign which conditions and prefigures it.[7]

In other words, Godard is suggesting that any complication of "real" film—news*reel,* that is—immediately defuses (and diffuses) itself. It gives us not the reality behind the film, but the fiction of the newsreel. It allows us to "integrate" the experience (even if we never had it)—it "steals the life which sleeps in the archive vaults." What *should* be done is to make a documentary (or better, an essay) about the pieces of film evidence themselves: How do they relate to the actuality? How do they connect with our memories of the actuality? Of the film? How can we use them here, now? "Filming, therefore, is simply seizing an event as a sign." What we need are not so much films about war as films about war films. Before we can understand the reality, we must understand the signs which represent it. Much later, in *Letter to Jane,* Godard will spend 45 minutes of film analyzing a single image (see pp. 245–50). This semiological analysis is difficult business, but *Les Carabiniers* makes a good beginning simply because it works out its analysis in practice rather than in theory.

> Each shot, each sequence, corresponds to a particular idea: the Occupation, the Russian campaign, the regular army, partisans, and so on . . . or a particular feeling: violence, confusion, indifference, derision, disorder, surprise, desolation. Or a particular fact, a particular phenomenon: noise, silence, etc.[8]

Clearly, the interest for Godard has shifted slightly but pointedly from the narrative—the human story—to the image and its function as a sign.

Michel-Ange and Ulysse live within this semiological world, not merely as objects of it; they share Godard's perplexity with the confusion of signs. They are enticed into the army with promises of plunder ("you can take anything you want, Hawaiian guitars, elephants . . ."), but it turns out there is no reality behind those words; they return to their wives, Vénus and Cléopâtre, at the end of the film with only a box of picture postcards. They have captured the images, not the objects. In a long and riveting sequence they take each picture from the box and slap it down on the table, almost as an offering to their wives: a series of buildings—the Eiffel Tower, the Empire State; a series of sights—the pyramids, the Grand Canyon; a series of paintings; a series of women—all commodities. This is the first of the great Godard catalogues, and its power is magical. Neither Michel-Ange nor Ulysse can ever quite make the distinction between the sign and the object (or more precisely, the signifier and the signified). In the middle of the film, Michel-Ange goes to see his first movies. They are also *our* first movies, homages to early films by the Lumières. When a woman appears on the screen in a bath, Michel-Ange charges forward, tries to peer over the edge of the bath-tub to see more of her, and, stymied, attacks the screen itself. At a Maserati dealer, Ulysse tries to buy a car, showing the letter he has from the King. It doesn't work. (Is it any less logical to think that a letter from the King will be worth a car than to think that a banknote with his picture on it will?) Michel-Ange and Ulysse want the realities of cars and girls, but they can't quite tell the difference between reality and image; this is why they so matter-of-factly kill, loot, and rampage. As they write to their wives, "we left a trail of corpses . . . a fine summer all the same," and "a lot of blood and corpses. We kiss you tenderly."

Separating sign and object, signifier and signified, is thus clearly a political point. If we know the difference between an image of a woman and a woman who lives and breathes we are less likely to kill the latter. If we can separate our image of a country like Vietnam, built up of wild, fantastic racial and political myths, from the reality of it and its people, we are less likely to pepper the land so efficiently and thoroughly with twice as much bomb tonnage as was dropped in all of World War II. The signifiers betray us: "anti-personnel bombs" are conceivable, shrapnel imbedded in a womb is not; "body counts" are acceptable, while the blood and guts of a single mutilated death are not. To be able to abstract

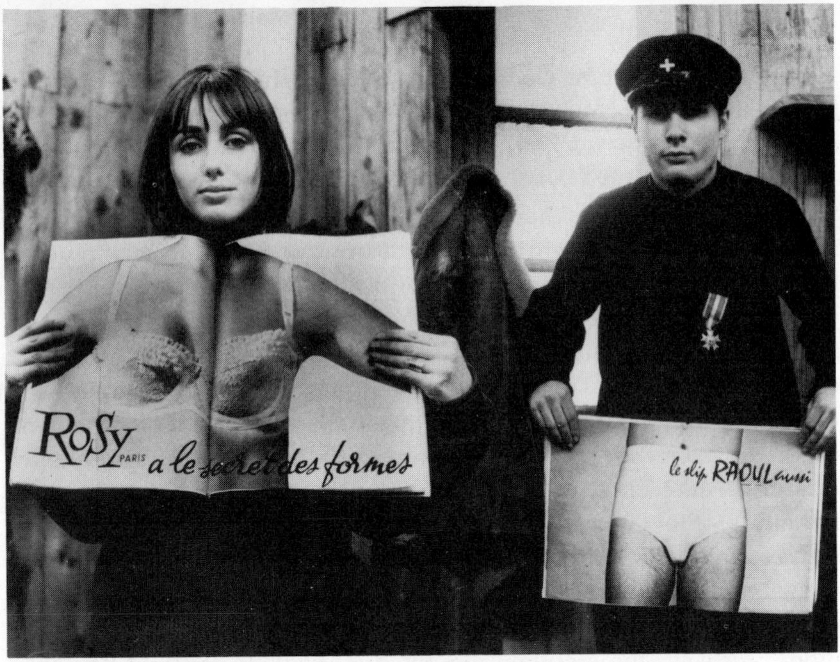

"The secret of forms": Godard's semiological mythologies begin in *Les Carabiniers.*

is to be able to wage war and commit murder. The battle for Godard is to rescue life from abstraction. For him "the really horrible thing about" images of desolation should not be "their horror but their very ordinary everydayness. *C.Q.F.D.* [i.e., QED] *Les Carabiniers Quel Film Dangereux.*"

The possibilities of the metaphors of stage art which he explored in *Les Carabiniers* intrigued Godard so much that even before he had finished shooting, he was already planning to film Alfred Jarry's absurdist classic, *Ubu Roi* ("in much the same style") and Jean Giraudoux's *Pour Lucrèce* ("because I simply want to record a text, record voices speaking it").[9] But with typical impatience he never returned to stage properties—leaving the exploration of theatre to his former colleague Jacques Rivette—and instead turned to the opposite pole of the continuum of acted reality: cinema. As *Les Carabiniers* was an essay in stage metaphor, so *Le Mépris* is an exercise in cinematic metaphor—specifically, Hollywood. Of course all Godard's films are to one degree or another essays in cinema, but *Le Mépris* takes the world of commercial filmmaking as its subject matter as well as its subtext.

It is also Godard's closest approach to the orbit of a dying Hollywood. *Le Mépris* shows all the evidence of being his "coming of age" as a commercial director: it had a script from a well-known novel, it was produced by international moguls Carlo Ponti and Joseph E. Levine (who got his start with cheap Italian Hercules movies), and its international cast of stars includes Brigitte Bardot, Jack Palance, and Michel Piccoli. The theme of prostitution takes on new dimensions: Godard signs with a big-time producer and is given the great sex star of the late fifties to work with in a film which is itself about the prostitution of a writer in similar circumstances. The result is a droll commentary on Godard's own tenuous position as a hired hand.* *Les Carabiniers*—Godard's only theatrical film—understandably studied its genre by concentrating on the most significant esthetic advance in that genre: Brechtian distancing. *Le Mépris,* being about cinema, can be more precise and subtle. Its focus is not so much esthetics as it is the economic infrastructure of the medium of Hollywood movies: the relationships between producer (Jeremiah Prokosch) and director (Fritz Lang), producer and star (Camille), producer and writer (Paul).

As the credits end, the camera we have been watching track across an open yard turns its lens towards us (as if we were the subject of the film), and Godard gives us the film's epigram, a quotation from André Bazin:

> The cinema gives us a substitute world which fits our desires.

As if to illustrate this theorem, the first scene of the film shows us the writer Paul Javal (Piccoli) and his wife Camille (Bardot) lying in bed. Bardot is totally nude. Joe Levine has required this scene. But Godard, satisfying the letter of Levine's requirement, destroys the spirit of it. Paul and Camille do not touch; the dialogue is painfully unerotic; the scene is shot through red and blue filters. The images are beautiful, but they are not erotic. The dialectic of the film has already begun. What Levine and Jeremiah Prokosch want is a substitute world that fits our desires. What Godard and Lang (and Godard again within the film as Lang's assistant) are going to give us is something quite different: not a substitute world but a real cinema, not a reflection of our desires but a challenge to our intellects. This is the basic dialectic of the genre films that fascinated the contributors to *Cahiers du Cinéma* in the fifties. It was foreordained that, having learned so much from Lang and Hitchcock,

*Michel Piccoli told an interviewer that Godard wanted him (Piccoli) to wear Godard's tie, hat, and shoes. Raoul Coutard said: "I'm positive that . . . he's trying to explain something to his wife. It's a letter that is costing Beauregard [the producer] a million dollars."[10]

Ford and Walsh, Nicholas Ray and Frank Tashlin, Godard would eventually face this rite of passage.

"Moravia's novel is a nice, vulgar one for a train journey, full of classical old-fashioned sentiments in spite of the modernity of the situations," he explained, "but it is with this kind of novel that one can often make the best films."[11] His plan is to strip the novel of the satisfaction of bourgeois narrative which is, after all, the main commodity it is selling, and rework the materials of *Il Disprezzo* into "a simple film without mystery, an Aristotelian film, stripped of appearances. . . ."[12] The novel was a fine example of bourgeois psychological melodrama; the film will be its opposite—a classically constricted epic in which psychology will be eschewed and the personal conflicts dedramatized. The film Fritz Lang is supposed to be making is a version of *The Odyssey*. Why should Prokosch think to produce such a film? If Levine can make money on Hercules, why shouldn't Ulysses prove equally profitable? But Lang has other ideas. His Ulysses is epic, not dramatic, and the shots of the "film within the film" exist more as footnotes—static restatements of the theme—than as dramatic reflections of character and plot. Lang's film works as the chorus to Godard's.*

Until this point, we have always referred to the characters of a film by the names Godard has given them, rather than by the names of the actors who play the roles, even though there is often little difference between the character and the actor. It is a function of that special cinematic confusion of reality and fiction that so often in film criticism the names of characters are ignored in favor of the names of the actors, who are, after all, recognizable as the characters are not. In Godard's films—and in most European cinema—it is the characters who count. But with *Le Mépris* it becomes increasingly difficult to stick with characters and avoid actors. This is, after all, a Hollywood film, and that particular mode of discourse (which was dying at the time; *Le Mépris* is a kind of eulogy) depends far more on the identifiable persona of the actor. Here is the single strange point of confluence between the Brechtian theatrical mode of the previous film and the Hollywood mode of the present one: in each, the actor's persona takes precedence over the character's. It is more important, in each, that we look at the acting, not at the character; in this sense both modes are anti-realistic. The first

*Godard gives this a nice twist: Lang plays himself. The truth is that Fritz Lang did not shoot the scenes from *The Odyssey*—Jean-Luc Godard did. Godard has Lang say that the scenes were shot by the second unit; Godard plays the part of Lang's assistant director, who would have been in charge of that second unit.

shots of *Le Mépris,* for example, we identify as images of Brigitte Bardot, not of the character, Camille, whom she is ostensibly playing. There is a dramatic dialectic at work here which will become increasingly important for Godard in years to come. Prefigured in Belmondo's and Karina's play-acting in Godard's first two films, the conflict between actor and role is much more specific in *Le Mépris* because this was the first time that Godard worked with actors who had previously established strong personas. Not until *Tout va bien* did he choose to work this way again, although *Alphaville, Weekend,* and *One Plus One* make obligatory nods in this direction.

To elaborate, "Jack Palance" is the persona that a man named Walter Palunuik fashioned through numerous roles in Films Noirs and Melodramas in the fifties. There is no perceivable difference between the Jack Palance we have come to know and Jeremiah Prokosch. Prokosch is, in fact, one of Palance's best roles simply because Godard and Palance do not attempt to individualize it. Palance can play Palance "to the hilt." Within this simple framework, Palance is further identified as an "actor" (or more precisely, Prokosch is). We first meet him on a ramp elevated above the other characters, who follow him as he struts and declaims proverbs from the little "bible" he always carries with him. Behind him is the word "Teatro," if we need further explanation. Often in the film Palance/Prokosch will hesitate dramatically, shift levels of reality, and mimic or act out elements of the film (either film). In the screening room we see him against the screen hurling film cans as if they were discuses. Prokosch understands the relationship between himself and the films, and he knows how useful it can be to "act out" in "real life."

Meanwhile, "Paul" (Michel Piccoli) has much less leeway. Piccoli had not at this time established the decadent persona that was to serve him in the late sixties and seventies. He is, in terms of this film, an unknown. Paul's character is therefore provided with a set of other characters to which to relate. "A character from *Marienbad,*" Godard called him, "who wants to play the role of a character in *Rio Bravo,*" he wears his hat at all times like Dean Martin in *Some Came Running.* Then there is Bardot, whose body is the main commodity of *Le Mépris.* Fritz Lang and Godard play themselves.

The film is then almost an essay on portraiture, role-playing, acting. At the center of the group is Francesca (Giorgia Moll), Prokosch's assistant and translator who must interpret for the characters, who speak four different languages. She is a symbol of their separation and isolation, but also something more. She allows Godard to duplicate lines of dialogue, further de-dramatizing the materials of Moravia's

Personas. The quotation from Lumière below the blank screen reads: "the cinema is an invention without a future." Harsh angles and blank squares work to separate Prokosch, Paul, and Fritz Lang.

novel; and she is his defense against dubbing. In the fourteen months since making *Vivre sa vie* he had accorded ever more importance to direct sound. He was now going to make a film in Italy, notorious for post-dubbing dialogue, and he needed insurance against it. A character on screen much of the time whose sole function is to translate would be difficult to work around if the film were to be re-dubbed in a single language.*

Much of the flavor of *Le Mépris* depends on this device. It not only slows the film up but also calls attention to Godard's own situation and therefore to the infrastructure of the film which is his real subject. This is his *Two Weeks in Another Town* (Vincente Minnelli's film about making films in Rome), but the comparison is not so much with the story of Minnelli's film as with Godard's own experience of it. Rossellini's *Viaggio in Italia,* which the characters of *Le Mépris* logically screen for themselves, is possibly a more direct antecedent since its style is much closer to Godard's (remember that he had just worked with Rossellini on the script of *Les Carabiniers*), and since the theme of the confrontation of Anglo-Saxons with the milieu of Italy compares so closely. Unlike most of Godard's color films of the sixties, *Le Mépris* is suffused with natural light and earth colors. The dialectic of France and Italy, of Godard's kind of filmmaking and Levine's and Ponti's, is

*Nevertheless, the Italians managed to do just this, inventing an entirely new role for Francesca. Godard took his name off this version.

reflected in the conscious shift between the outdoor scenes—full of brown, amber, and green—and the more abstract reds, blues, and whites of the indoor scenes. The primary colors are Godard's; the earth colors those of the strange environment.

There is also a human dimension to *Le Mépris.* For Godard it is "the story of castaways of the western world, survivors of the shipwreck of modernity who, like the heroes of Verne and Stevenson, one day reach a mysterious deserted island, whose mystery is the inexorable lack of mystery, of truth, that is to say. . . ."[13] As we might expect, even the passion of the film is expressed in cinematic metaphors. As José Luis Garner has pointed out, whenever the act of filming appears in *Le Mépris* it takes on a ceremonial significance. Godard expressed it this way: "the eye of the camera watching these characters in search of Homer replaces that of the gods watching over Ulysses and his companions." At the end of the film, after the personas of Prokosch and Camille, Palance and Bardot, have been destroyed by the *deus ex machina* ("la macchina" in this case being a red sports model), we return to the peace and security of the mechanics of film. Lang and his assistant are in action again, filming a shot of Ulysses surveying the wine-dark sea. We are brought in the end to the source—of life, the sea; of the film, Ulysses. Godard calls for silence. The camera pans out to sea. The last image of *Le Mépris* is the water, the sky, the sun. It fits, of itself, and it also reminds us of a basic trope of Italian film, of Rossellini and Fellini. Godard himself concludes, a little too patly, that

> *Le Mépris* proves in 149 shots that in the cinema as in life there is no secret, nothing to elucidate, merely the need to live—and to make films.[14]

In December 1963, Godard shot a sketch entitled "Montparnasse et Levallois" for a compilation film, *Paris vue par . . .* (*Six in Paris,* the first production of Barbet Schroeder's Films du Losange; each of the episodes—by Rouch, Rohmer, Chabrol, among others—is located in a particular district of Paris, which it is supposed to summarize.) Shot in 16-mm color (one of the aims of the production was to prove that inexpensive 16 mm would prove a viable alternative for feature films), this 12-minute film is a further exploration for Godard of modes of discourse.

The anecdote "Montparnasse et Levallois" relates is identical with the "news item" Belmondo had read to Karina in the cafe in *Une Femme est une femme.* ("In fact," Godard noted, the story, "which I altered, was taken from a short story by Giraudoux."[15]) A woman (Johanna Shimkus) thinks she has mixed up two letters she has written to a pair of lovers and visits each of them to apologize. It turns out she was wrong: the letters were mailed in the proper envelopes, and only her subsequent explanations let each lover know of the other's existence. Godard gave the actors—all inexperienced—a large degree of freedom and directed Albert Maysles, the well-known American documentarist who shot the film, to act like a newsreel cameraman, involving the camera in the action as inquisitor.

> The interesting thing is this sort of fluidity [he wrote], being able to feel existence like physical matter: it is not the people who are important, but the atmosphere between them. Even when they are in close-up, life exists around them. The camera is on them, but the film is not centered on them. The film is a district, a particular time. It is Montparnasse.[16]

If *Le Mépris* was Godard's *Six Characters in Search of an Author* (or Producer), then "Montparnasse et Levallois" is his *Each in His Own Way*. In the feature Godard had experimented with the opposition between character and actor, as Pirandello had before him. In the sketch, he moves on to the more complex relationships among cameraman, director, actor, and setting:

> I wrote the script and said: "That is what is going on. This is what it means." I had the meaning, the actors brought the sign, and Maysles gave the signification. The three stages of semantics.[17]

Like all of Godard's short films, "Montparnasse et Levallois" is limited to the strict development of a single idea: "sketch" aptly describes their function. He has made six altogether, not counting his contribution to *Loin du Vietnam*.

"La Paresse" (*Les Sept Péchés capitaux*, 1961) is an exercise with Eddie Constantine: his character is so slothful and exhausted that not even sex excites him. "Le Nouveau Monde" (*RoGoPaG*, 1962) illustrates a parable that had long intrigued Godard: "a man goes out into the street; everything seems normal, but two or three little details reveal to him that everyone—including his fiancée—no longer thinks or reasons normally." Cafes, for example, are not called cafes anymore. He discovers that he is the only man left on earth who has escaped the effects of an atomic explosion. "Everything is the same and yet different. What has happened is that all notion of cause and effect has disappeared."[18] "Le Nouveau Monde" is a preparation for *Alphaville*.

Several years later Godard returned to the science fiction mode for one of his most beautiful sketches—"Anticipation, ou l'an 2000" (*Le Plus Vieux Métier du monde*, 1967). He shot the film in color but monochromatically; various scenes are tinted red, yellow, blue, and black. A soldier of the Sovietoamerican army (Jean-Pierre Léaud) is discovered to be sexually deprived and is sent to receive treatment. The first prostitute, representing "physical love," does not excite him. The second, Anna Karina, who is "spiritual love," does. Together they invent the kiss, using the one part of the body which can both speak and make love. The screen bursts into full color, and the ubiquitious p.a. system announces that the couple is dangerous because "they are making love, progress and conversation—all at the same time." Godardian ecstasy was never so succinctly expressed.

"Le Grand Escroc" (*Les Plus Belles Escroqueries du monde,* 1963) gives us a cinéma-vérité reporter, Patricia Leacock (Jean Seberg), who discovers a man in Marrakesh (Charles Denner) who is cheating poor people—he gives them fake money. But he reminds her that she also sells ersatz goods: her cinema is false because it pretends to be reality. The truth of subjectivity is missing.

Godard's last sketch, "L'Aller retour des enfants prodigues" (also called "L'Amour"), was made for an Italian producer in 1967 for inclusion in a compilation film called variously *Vangelo '70, La Contestation,* and *Amore e rabbia (Love and Anger).* The two main characters are a French bourgeois woman and a man from the Third World. She speaks French, he speaks Italian, and two observers translate most of the dialogue. The film bears obvious connections with *Le Mépris* (and also with the project "France la douce" which was never realized), but it also points toward the politics of the late sixties.

Bande à part, Godard's seventh feature film within five years, was shot during February and March of 1964. It is a film, as Pauline Kael has said, "about a girl and a gun." It was also a relatively simple and relaxed project for Godard. It offered him a breathing space and a chance to summarize before the beginning of the furious activity that marked the two years between the summer of 1964 and the summer of 1966 (during which time he completed six films). *Bande à part* is not, like its immediate predecessors, an exercise in narrative modes—unless, that is, we decide to see it as an epitome of the earliest Godard films. It shares the witty, good-natured elan of *A bout de souffle* and *Une Femme est une femme.* Like the former, it revels in the sentiments of the Gangster genre; like the latter, it puts Anna Karina at the apex of a triangle and is suffused with a gentle, lyrical quality and a nostalgia for the American movies of his youth that motivated Godard in the first place. ("As soon as you can make films, you can no longer make films like the ones that made you want to make them.")

All the familiar Godardian devices are in evidence here. For the first time, he seems to be repeating himself, summarizing the film world he has been constructing for the past five years. We are therefore free for once simply to take pleasure in Godard's collection of images, sounds, gestures, and juxtapositions. The credits announce that this is a film by "Jean-Luc / Cinéma / Godard." That's his middle name. If anything sets *Bande à part* apart, it is this *joie de film:* the characters have it within the structure of the film; Godard shows it outside the structure.

Arthur, Franz, and Odile, three superannuated students, have decided to commit a robbery, but they are motivated not so much by any thought of gain as by that particular brand of ennui that leads so many of Godard's characters to try to reformulate their lives in terms of cinematic fiction. The point is to have a story to tell. Cinema offers the security of known modes of discourse and protection from the emptiness and absurdity of what film people insist on calling "real life." Like so many of Godard's people, they gain comfort from seeing the world in terms of the metaphor of film, speaking in its language, acting through its formulated gestures. This is why Godard's interest in modes of discourse is more than just esthetic: If we can find out new ways of telling our stories, we might be able to discover new ways of living our lives. There is a danger here: "Franz did not know," the narrator Godard tells us, "whether the world was a dream or the dream was the world." The confusion between reality and cinema can be dizzying. But for the most part, *Bande à part* is satisfied to catalogue an ebullient collection of illustrations of this phenomenon.

Arthur, for example, dies twice. His first death, a fake one, is very effective. He knows how to recreate death cinematically. But then he dies "really" in a shootout with his uncle, and his final death, however fatal, is highly melodramatic and a lot less convincing than the first. When they actually find themselves committing the robbery, none of the three has much stomach for it. The boys are reticent about breaking a window. Odile stops in the middle to pet a dog. Franz stops to steal a good book. It's *not* the way it was in the movies. Like all Godard's films from here on, *Bande à part* has a distinct consciousness of itself. Godard narrates, and for the first time his persona becomes part of the fabric of the film. Our attention then is not focused on the relationships among the characters, but on the connection between the characters, the narrator-filmmaker, and us, the audience. After a few minutes of film, Godard stops to explain: "A few clues for latecomers: a girl, money, a country house. . . ." "Out of respect for second-rate thrillers," he tells us later, "they won't do the job until nighttime." After Arthur's final death scene, as Odile and Franz drive off into the cinematic sunset (and take a boat for Buenos Aires), Godard tells us, "we'll end our story here." We see a shot of a globe whirling in space, and he concludes, "sequel in cinemascope and technicolor!" Even the credits joke—about

Michel Legrand, who composed the music for this quasi-musical gangster film.

There are a number of ways to "speak" about ideas, characters, feelings, and *Bande à part* uses many of them. Arthur, Franz, and Odile meet in English class—language is the matrix of the film. The sign above the door announces forebodingly: "Loui's Cours" (sic). "Today," the teacher explains, "we must know how to spell Thomas Hardy or Shakespeare." She reads a long passage from *Romeo and Juliet* which the class is supposed to translate into English. (Shakespearian English? modern English? the English of Loui's Cours?) Arthur, meanwhile, writes a love-note to Odile: "Tou bi or not tou bi contre votre poitrine, zat iz zi question." His writing is a combination of his French accent and our comic transliteration of it. The teacher continues to recite Shakespeare, much too rapidly.

What about the other cultural languages? Later, the trio decide to "do" the Louvre, beating the American record of nine minutes, forty-five seconds by two seconds. In the Métro, Arthur asks Odile what interests her about him. She replies: "Marriage," and then half-sings, half-recites a song about lonely sad people. We have a few images of those people in the train. They stop at a station. The doors open: LIBERTÉ, says a huge sign. Franz is planning to go north after the job, "to Jack London territory." Speaking directly to the camera, he tells a long yarn from Jack London. Next it is Arthur's turn to do a monologue as they drive. Odile tells Madame Victoria: "I hate cinema . . . I like nature." It is more a wish than a truth. As if to prove the point, the next scene shows us Odile leaving the house and running free, with jazz on the soundtrack, while Arthur and Franz wait for her in the woods by a stream reading about murders in newspapers. In the cafe, someone suggests a minute of silence. The soundtrack is cut off (but only for forty seconds: film time is not real time!), and then Arthur, Franz, and Odile do their Bob Fosse dance. Previously, Odile has visited the powder room to discover the message: "Mascara for beauty—and happiness too!" It is an advertisement for Godard's next film, which will deal specifically with the commodity of "beauty."

In *Bande à part,* Godard has found a kind of equilibrium; each of his previous films was motivated in some specific way such that he was forced to work dialectically, in opposition to the given materials of the film. In *A bout de souffle,* the struggle was with Truffaut's scenario; in *Le Petit Soldat* and *Les Carabiniers* with the political material; in *Une Femme est une femme* and *Vivre sa vie* with his own pre-conceptions and with the enigmatic persona of Karina; and in *Les Carabiniers* and *Le Mépris* with the modes of discourse. Now, in *Bande à part,* he is free of those

Arthur (Claude Brasseur), Odile (Karina), and Franz (Sami Frey) demonstrate the "madison" in the cafe.

pressures. The result is a film which is less tense, less stimulating, but more open and easier to apprehend. We can lay the film out flat on the table to trace the essential elements of Godardian cinema. In his careful and conscientious essay on the film, Robin Wood tries to grapple with what he calls "the textual unevenness of [Godard's] films: the way in which passages of great complexity and denseness exist side by side with passages whose significance and interest strike one as thin in the extreme."[19] Wood offers many perceptive suggestions as to why this may be so (Godard's "method of working," his "Brechtian bent," the freedom that is gained), but he analyzes strictly from the point of view of the observer. Looked at from the filmmaker's point of view, each of the elements of *Bande à part* (many of which were indexed above) has a validity all its own. The "reader" of the film, then, must work deductively rather than inductively. Wood asks, "If you are no longer bound by any of the traditional principles of organization, then what replaces them as a means of preventing your film from falling into chaos?" The answer lies, simply, in working experientially with the materials of the film at hand—working towards potential principles of organization, rather than judging the materials by preconceived principles. We start by giving Godard the benefit of the doubt (as we do with all artists): we assume that meaning adheres to this shot, that cut, this gesture, that line of dialogue. Then we try to discover what that meaning might be, always remembering that "the sign forces us to see an object through its significance."

This is the best approach to all Godard's films. They *do* often require study; they don't always reveal themselves wholly on first viewing. But it is especially important to think this way with *Bande à part,* in which, for once, character, plot, theme, and theory are muted, offering us a rare opportunity to examine the layout of the film, its basic construction. Early in the film, just about when a conventional film director would be concentrating on delineating character, Franz, Arthur, and Odile decide to cut class and take a joyride in the convertible whose top stays down even in winter. Rather than opening a parenthesis to explain the characters, Godard tells us, "we'll let the images speak." If we let them, they do. They do not "advance the plot," or "explain character"—those traditional principles of organization—but they do help us to comprehend the universe of the film and the sardonic existence of the band of outsiders. A few seconds later we find ourselves in empty suburban streets. Odile, in long shot, rides away on her bicycle making careful hand signals that no one will see. The shot has its own poignancy. It may not connect to what comes before or after, but the sum of shots like these is the quotient of our experience of the film. A collage if you like, a cubist fracturing of experience, but apprehensible nevertheless. Having mastered this fictional mode of discourse, Godard can now pay more attention to the substance of the discourse. The stories are over; the essays are about to begin. As Franz says at the end of the film, "each goes his own way, distrustful and tragic."

La Femme mariée is the midpoint of the road between *Vivre sa vie* and *2 ou 3 choses que je sais d'elle*. Between the former, a personal portrait of a prostitute, and the latter, a semiological essay on the metaphor of prostitution, we have *La Femme mariée,* in Godard's original title. The film was not passed by the French censors until four minutes of it had been cut and the title changed to *"Une" Femme mariée,* lest the unsuspecting viewer make the generalization from the definite article that Godard very much intended! We can restore the definite article even though we can't restore the lost footage. Subtitled "Fragments of a film shot in 1964," it is a passionate essay about women, men, and the culture of sex. The film is obviously a portrait of its eponymous heroine, but it views its subject through a complex semantic screen. At the center of the film we find Charlotte, *a* married woman, but we see her through a glass darkly as *the* married woman—a concept rather than a human being, for she has been formed and molded by the languages of the media that surround her: film, magazines, literature, records, advertisements, billboards, TV, radio. It is the relationship between *a* married woman and *the* married woman that fascinates Godard; the connection between the specific and existential and its reflection in the general culture. *La Femme mariée* is a shimmering network of interferences among several levels of significance: *the* married woman (concept), *a* married woman (person), and the media that formed the person through the concept and also formed *our* conception of the subject (separate from the specific instance of the film itself). Charlotte's breasts, an objective correlative for the theme of the film (it could have been titled, on the model of the shorts of the fifties, "Charlotte et sa poitrine"), will serve to illustrate the levels.

First, we have the real breasts of Macha Meril, the actress who plays the role. While we may assume that the censor's cuts have shifted some interest away from them, they are still an object of interest for Godard's camera: the concrete, esthetic reality. But these breasts have a specific meaning as well. Charlotte calls attention to it early in the film when she dares her lover, Robert, by running around his roof dressed only in a pair of panties. Breasts have a cultural function more specific and more powerful than any other part of the female body. They are sexual weapons. Having been taught their function by aptly named Triumph brassiere ads, Charlotte is intent on developing her capacities. In the middle of the film she reads from a magazine an absurd calculus of the bosom:

> "Take your measurements and compare them to the ideal silhouette. There's an ideal bust dimension. Compare the breast of Venus de Milo with its tip on a horizontal line, a centimeter below the center of the arm. Stretch your tape from the armpit to the inner elbow. Deduct one centimeter, divide by two and you have the bust measurements proper for your height. Measure the distance from the base of your neck to the tip of your right breast. This should be 20 centimeters. Trace another imaginary line from the base of your neck to the tip of your left breast. Measure the distance between the tips of your breasts. All three form an equilateral triangle.[20]

In the same way, the lines between the ideal married woman of the magazines, Charlotte, and Godard's conception of the absurdity of the role also form an equilateral triangle. The three are connected by media. At the base is the mathematics of the breast, behind Charlotte loom the majestic bosoms of the billboards, to one side is Charlotte's new bra, more architecturally advanced, to the other the erotic records ("How to

The Married Woman measures up.

strip for your husband") that instruct her on how to use her new, improved weapons. We are beginning to see the factual development of the theme of commoditization that began with *Vivre sa vie* and will reach a peak in *2 ou 3 choses.*

Godard could have chosen to discuss this theme in the usual way by placing a character who thinks about things like this within a plot that would have allowed her to come to the same conclusions. But he did not. Instead we have a film, as Godard describes it,

> where subjects are seen as objects, where pursuits by taxi alternate with ethnological interviews, where the spectacle of life finally mingles with its analysis: a film, in short, where the cinema plays happily, delighted to be only what it is.[21]

No better way to describe the success of the mode of *La Femme mariée:* "the spectacle of life finally mingles with its analysis." Those abrupt shifts of the level of discourse—from fiction to essay to poetry to music to portrait and back again—should no longer trouble us as they once might have, since now, for the first time, we approach the film as an essay rather than a fiction. It is the freedom of the form that makes *La Femme mariée* so direct, refreshing, and passionate. We are finally relieved of the burdens of the conventions of fiction in general and genres in particular, and we can now accept each image, each sound, each juxtaposition for what it is. The relationship between character and observer is no longer the focus; it has been replaced by the relationship between filmmaker and observer. Godard, at last, can speak in his own voice.

La Femme mariée has been almost universally praised by commentators on Godard, and generally for this reason. Tom Milne in his excellent essay "Jean-Luc Godard ou la raison ardente," borrows a phrase from Roger Leenhardt's monologue in the film to describe its peculiar attraction.[22] Leenhardt quotes Guillaume Apollinaire:

> Soleil voici le temps de la raison ardente. . . .

It is this *raison ardente,* this passionate reason, which attracts us irresistibly to the film (and to Godard).* In fact, Leenhardt's monologue could serve as a declaration of conscience for Godard at this point in his career. It is given the title "Intelligence":

> . . . I think this is the best definition of intelligence: "Understand before you act." In order to search further, to reach the depths, the heights, to understand others, to find a small bridge between oneself and the other, between pro and con. . . . Not everybody cares for this intellectual approach. Especially nowadays, when things are either black or white, and seeking shadings seems a bit gray. But to me, it's the fanatics who are boring; you always know what they are going to say. . . . But people who like paradox are fun. Paradox offers an alternative to the self-evident. And then there is compromise, the finest, most courageous of intellectual acts. . . . It's come to mean lack of conviction. Still, I'll go on looking for the proper synthesis and I insist the world isn't totally absurd. And intelligence is precisely the attempt to inject a little reason into this absurdity.[23]

It is significant that Leenhardt, like *la raison ardente,* is a visitor to this film and that Pierre and Charlotte are slightly uncomfortable with him (and it). As dutiful consumers, their moral universe is better defined by *la raison argente.* Godard's intelligence is precisely the attempt to inject reason into this absurdity.

Leenhardt's homily is the third in a series of seven monologues which punctuate the film's logic. The series starts at the dinner party Pierre and Charlotte give for Leenhardt, and the married couple precede his remarks with essays of their own: Pierre on "Memory," Charlotte on "The Present." These two set-pieces describe the tension of their marriage. As Charlotte explains:

*I quote from Milne rather than directly from the script in order to honor Milne, who first called attention to the significance of the phrase, but also so that I can insert a fourth-generation quote.

> Memory . . . you don't need it. I prefer the present! The present's more exciting. I like music. Things that die—flowers—love—of course love. Love must be lived. You have to live in the present of course, because, if there is no present, it can't live, it dies. To me the most important thing is to understand what's happening to me, . . . and to understand what's happening I try to compare it to things I know, that I've seen before . . . That's difficult in the present, that's why I like the present, because in "the present" I have no time to think. . . . No, I don't understand . . . I can't understand the present, it's beyond me. What I like of course is this thing that escapes me—that I can't control in the present. . . .[24]

Charlotte's circular, paradoxical logic gives her a human dimension that would otherwise be lacking from Godard's portrait of the married woman. We now know that she is at least attempting to understand the forces which operate on her, even if she never comes to the "proper synthesis" that Leenhardt advocates. Nevertheless, there is enough reason in evidence here for Leenhardt later to make the connection between Charlotte and Apollinaire's *raison ardente*.

Immediately after Leenhardt's speech, the couple's child, Nicolas, provides a dissertation on "Childhood" which is a singularly charming moment (and a rare venture for Godard into the world of children):

> To do it:
>
> 1) You pay attention
> 2) You figure it all out
> 3) You tell everybody
> 4) You do it
> 5) You buy paint
> 6) You check everything
> 7) You paint it
> 8) You recheck
> 9) You work the whole thing over some more
> 10) You make it go.[25]

No way to tell what the child is describing, but it might just as well serve for Godard's attitude towards his film.

In the fifth essay, the aptly named Madame Céline, Charlotte's housekeeper, recites a passage from *Mort à credit* that gives us in words the earthiness that has been missing from the images of sex in the film. The sixth set-piece, "Pleasure and Science," consists of Charlotte's interview with the gynecologist who posits some neanderthal attitudes towards birth control and sexual freedom. The last titled essay, "Theatre and Love," concludes the film, as Charlotte and Robert re-edit Racine's *Bérénice* in order to provide dialogue to match the end of their affair and the film.

These numbered sequences form the basis of the film's découpage. Intercut with them are equally separate illustrations of the commoditization of sex. The scene of the two young girls in the cafe is possibly the most important of these; the complexity of its narrative structure serves as a model for the whole film. Just before the scene begins, we have had one of the stream-of-consciousness poems with which Godard punctuates the film. Charlotte leaves the house, passing in front of a fresco of Jean Cocteau. This is followed by a pan over the letters "AMERI . . ." and negative shots of mannequins posing by the pool. Charlotte thinks:

Ah! l'harmonie, trouver l'harmonie	Ah! bliss, to find bliss
Comme au cinéma.	Like in the movies.
Le ciel est bleu.	The sky is blue.
Abolir le passé.	The past is wiped out.
Mettre du rouge à lèvres.	Put lipstick on.
A quoi tu penses?	What are you thinking?
J'hésite.	I hesitate.
Le lendemain matin.	The next morning.
Il ne savait pas.	He didn't know.
Dans les nuages.	In the clouds.
Se déshabiller.	To get undressed.
A ta place, je n'irais pas.	I wouldn't go, if I were you.
Le lendemain soir.	The next evening.
Mardi après-midi.	Tuesday afternoon.
Très rapidement.	Very fast.
Pendant plusieurs jours.	For several days.
En janvier 64.	In January 64.
Et puis, ça m'amuse.	It's fun.
C'est nerveux.	It's alive.
Délivré de cet espoir.	Free of this hope.
Il n'y avait rien de changé.	It was still the same.
Une dernière fois.	One last time.
Le nouvel appartement.	The new apartment.
Le téléphone sonne.	The phone's ringing.
Il fait très beau.	It's lovely out.
Ni à lui, ni à personne.	Not him or anybody.
Pour quoi faire?	What for?
On ira où tu voudras.	We'll go wherever you like.
Il ne pleuvait pas.	It's stopped raining.
On n'entendait rien.	Not a sound.
Il faut choisir.	Make up your mind.
D'abord, je n'ai rien dit.	I said nothing at first.
Qu'est-ce que tu as?	What's the matter?
La Tendresse.	Tenderness.
Evidemment.	Obviously.
Tout le mal possible.	The most harm.
Un visage noyé de larmes.	A tear-streaked face.

Caresser mes cheveux.	To caress my hair.
Je restais silencieuse.	I said nothing.
Regarder autour de soi.[26]	To look around.

This cryptic, broken collage of verbal images comes as close as possible to duplicating in print what Godard does on many levels cinematically.

As if to illustrate the topic more concretely, Charlotte then observes from the background in the cafe as two young girls present a dramatic representation of what we have just had poetically. They talk about horoscopes, monokinis,* and what to do with boys. Titles announce: WHAT EVERY WOMAN SHOULD KNOW, then SHE KNOWS and SHE DOESN'T. A quick shot of *Elle* magazine reminds us of the provenance of the girls' knowledge of sex. Then the background noise of the bar is amplified and we resort to subtitles for the girls' conversation: "I sleep with a boy." "I don't know what to do." "He'll kiss you, he'll hold you, turn off the light." "I'll have to undress! He'll be completely naked. I'll be completely naked." "In the dark. No time. No more thinking. Mood." "Still frightened. He'll see my breasts."[27]

And we are back where we began. But Godard's catalogue of media is not over yet; there are first a yé-yé song on the jukebox by Sylvie Vartan, then more ads, then a cartoon strip, and finally, the last word on the subject, a "poem" in homage to brassieres: "Don't be jealous. You too can have the line—young, modern, dynamic—that you envy."[28]

A tour de force? Yes, but more important, a tour de la femme mariée, an approach from every mediated angle to the phenomenon of the woman whose sole function is the development of her sexual assets and her capitalization of them. This is a film, as Godard said, in which "subjects are seen as objects." Even the words speak as signs: The word "EVE" appears on the screen. The camera pulls back to reveal the whole word, "REVES." Then the word "DANGER" warns Charlotte, and the camera tracks in to reveal "ANGE" at the heart of "DANGER" Eve is lost in dreams and the angel in danger.

As Tom Milne notes,

> none of these apparent digressions really digress, nor are the puns as simple or extraneous as they may seem. As in Joyce's linguistic dislocations, they throw out hooks in all directions, forming a mesh of meaning [Charlotte's web?]. . . . With Godard an image can be, at one and the same

*Most of the footage now missing from the film comprised a sequence Jacques Rozier had shot on the Riviera documenting the charms of the fashion sensation of that year, the "monokini."' Godard had inserted it here. The censor cut it.

> time, a private joke, a public gag, a clue, an imaginative link, or a serious statement."[29]

It is this multiplex set of significances that rivets our attention. For the most part, the images themselves are extraordinarily clean, precise, almost classical. The film opens with a shot of a hand on a white sheet and closes as a hand withdraws, leaving the empty, blank, white sheet. Close-ups predominate: profiles and shots squarely from the front. Bodies are seen mainly as fragments. Godard has limited the "story" (or narrative content) of each image in order to leave room for the connotative material. The simplicity of the images, the complexity of their meanings rival the combined emotional and intellectual effect of music. *La Femme mariée* needs to be "watched" (both guarded and regarded) many times:

"Qu'est-ce que ça veut dire exactement, 'regarder'?[30] asks Charlotte. Pierre replies: "'Regarder' . . . J'sais pas . . . Ça veut dire garder deux fois . . ."

Charlotte: "Si c'est deux fois . . . alors, c'est précieux."

8

GODARD
A Season in Hell: Icy Poetry

There is a refrain in *Pierrot le fou* that goes:

> Chapitre huit: Une Saison en enfer.

That echo of Rimbaud will do as well as any other name we might give to the period of intense productivity during 1965 and 1966. There is a time when the structures of criticism break down, and we have reached it with Godard. The five films he made during this time were, each in its own way, *cris de coeur,* and, though the language of criticism serves well enough to describe what Godard is about from the point of view of *la raison ardente,* there is another metaphor for his work, what we might call *la poésie glacée,* which does not yield so easily to categories and comparatives. What we have already described in terms of genres and logic, by way of semiology, we should now repeat via poetry. Best to let Jean Cocteau, whom Godard quotes more than any other poet, do it. In *Le Secret professionnel* (1922) he described poetry in words that fit Godard's cinema equally well:

> Do you know the surprise of finding yourself suddenly facing your own name as if it belonged to someone else, seeing its form and hearing the sound of the syllables, without the blind and deaf habit which a long intimacy provides?

> The same phenomenon can take place for an object or an animal. In a flash we *see* a dog, a cab, a house *for the first time*. What is special, mad, ridiculous, beautiful in them is overwhelming. But immediately afterwards, habit rubs out this powerful image with its eraser. We pat the dog, hail the cab, inhabit the house. We don't see them anymore.
>
> That is the role of poetry. It unveils, in the full meaning of the term. It strips bare, under a light which shatters our indifference, the surprising things around us which our senses register automatically.[1]

This is pretty close to the function of narrative that Christian Metz gave us: *irréalisation;* the stripping bare under a light which shatters our indifference. That is the task Godard has set for himself. Cocteau further makes an important differentiation:

> It is useless to look far afield for strange objects and sentiments, with which to startle the day-dreamer. That is the method of the bad poet, and it gives exoticism.
>
> He should be shown what his heart and his eyes touch on each day, but so viewed and with such speed that he see it and be moved by it for the first time. . . .
>
> Put a commonplace in place, clean it, rub it, light it so that it will give forth with its youth and freshness the same purity it had at the beginning, and you will be doing the work of a poet.[2]

It is almost as if the old poet turned filmmaker were speaking directly (from his youth) to the young filmmaker-poet. For it becomes clear during this period of Godard's career that he is a poet of the commonplace. He shows us what our heart and eyes touch on each day, but so viewed and with such speed that we are moved by it as if for the first time. First in the fables of *Alphaville* and *Pierrot le fou,* then in the more direct essays of *Masculin-féminin, Made in U.S.A.,* and *2 ou 3 choses,* we are presented with a rich collection of the objects, sentiments, and events of everyday life. This is a cold, icy poetry, balancing the fiery reason—the two poles of Godard's cinema.

Now these are both profoundly personal endeavors, and it must be said that the major quality these five films share is the real existential pain that motivated them.* Godard is driven to explain, to analyze, to capture the elements of what he so often perfunctorily refers to as "modern life." In this middle period he concentrates intently on this task. ("Thinking," he said in *Le Petit Soldat* "comes after defeat and before action.") It may seem that that analysis is the work more of an

*Cocteau also deals with this aspect of the artist's work, in *La Difficulté d'être* (1947): "A work is to such a degree the expression of our solitude that you can wonder what strange need for contacts urges the artist to release the work to the public."[3]

essayist than a poet—and so it is; Godard is a graduate in ethnology, after all—a more demonic Jean Rouch, if you like. But it is also the work of a poet, the difference between the two being that the poet realizes (in both senses of the word) the power of words (and images and sounds), their validity in and of themselves without reference to the world outside. Once again, the sign forces us to see an object through its significance. Like most contemporary poets, then, Godard is intent on helping us first of all to understand the language so that we can then comprehend the world it represents.

The three major soliloquys of *La Femme mariée* provide the basis for what Godard is in the process of doing.

- Memory. As Pierre explains it, memory should deal not with the frozen image of the past (for Cocteau that is "exotic"), but with understanding the changes that have taken place.
- The present. Charlotte half-coherently expresses Godard's own sense of the terror of the present moment: "To me the most important . . . is to understand what goes on . . . and to understand what goes on I try to compare it to things I know."
- Intelligence. For Leenhardt, it is "precisely the attempt to inject a little reason into this absurdity."

The films of 1965 and 1966 are Godard's most passionate attempts to inject reason into this absurdity, and he does so by combining *la raison ardente* with *la poésie glacée:* In his own phrase, these films are *"contes de fée"* . . . but they are also *contes des faits,* fairy tales and fact tales.

Alphaville was shot in the gray, wintry streets of Paris in January and February of 1965 in black and white. *Pierrot le fou* was shot five months later in the vivid early summer of the Côte d'Azur in color and scope. Both films are global, encompassing summations of his moral universe. Both are love stories; one ends in life and re-invention of love; the other ends in death and negation. Both are highly "poetic"—general, abstract, and moral, and as a consequence lyrical rather than exegetical narratives.

Alphaville, especially, shows its roots in poetic literature. Paul Eluard's *La Capitale de la douleur,* written in the early twenties and capturing the newly demonstrated truth of the metaphor of the wasteland, provides the text. *Alphaville* is also, on the face of it, the "City of Dreadful Night." And finally, the basic plot line (and some of the images) echo Cocteau's cinematic poem *Orphée:* Lemmy Caution leads Natasha von Braun from the dark city in much the same way that Orpheus leads out Eurydice. *Alphaville* is "science fiction," but like much of the best science fiction it prefers to see the poetry of science

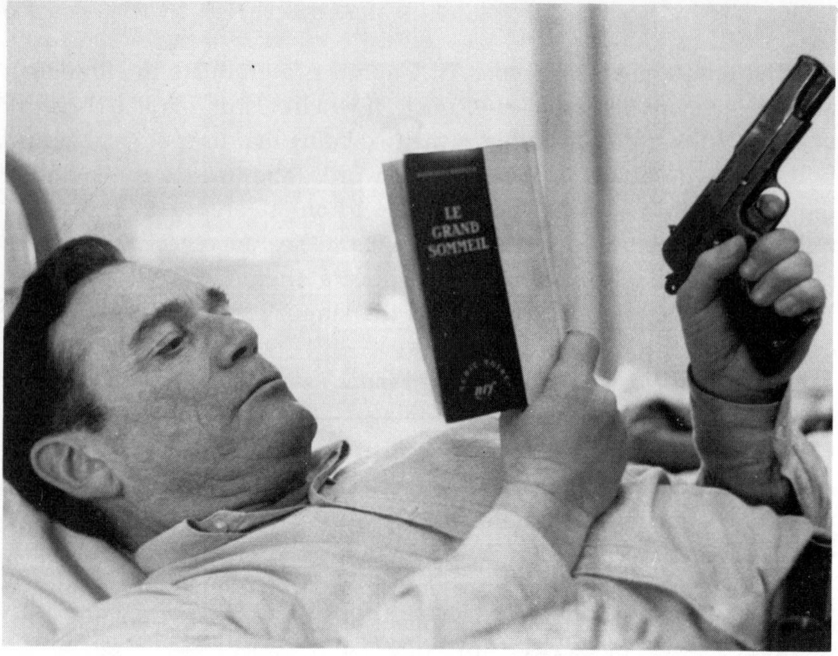

The Big Sleep: the private eye, the book, and the gun.

rather than its mathematical logic, and the relevance of fiction rather than its fantasy. Like Truffaut's *Fahrenheit 451* which began shooting just a month later, *Alphaville* wants us to see that it is not the future which is frightening, but the present. As Mephistopheles told Faustus in the play which is the prototype for many of the basic mythic structures of science fiction: "Why, this is hell, nor am I out of it!" Godard sees Lemmy Caution less as a traveler in the future than as a man from the past visiting in the terrible present. *Alphaville,* which is sub-titled "Une Etrange Adventure de Lemmy Caution," takes that persona from a series of French parodies of American detective fiction that starred Eddie Constantine. Lest we miss the point, Lemmy is shown early in the film reading a copy of *The Big Sleep* and has been preceded to Alphaville by Harry Dickson (another French model of the American private eye) and Dick Tracy. Like *The Big Sleep, Alphaville* is more a moral mystery than a whodunit, and Lemmy Caution shares with Bogart's Marlowe an existential moral character that separates him from the inhabitants of a city that is marked by the total absence of ethics or love.

Alphaville is perhaps better seen as *cultural* futurist fiction than as *science* fiction. Like all Orpheus and Eurydice myths it deals in darkness and light and the struggle to get from one to the other. This time the underworld is contemporary Paris, a land so dark that it is necessary to use flashbulbs to take photographs in broad daylight. Alphaville is a city of signs rather than of humans (although Roland Barthes refused Godard's request that he appear in it). Signs are everywhere: the circle and the arrow, the announcements of directions (always confusing), the loudspeaker instructions from the computer Alpha-60, the foreboding neon Einsteinian formulas that punctuate conversations. This underworld is semiological; Lemmy succeeds in conquering it because he challenges the logic of the simple signs with the poetry of his own intelligence and the literature he knows. "People have become slaves to probability," we are told; Caution champions the *possible.* The critics Fièschi and Comolli from *Cahiers du Cinéma* play Heckel and Jeckel (remember the cartoon ravens?), assistants to Dr. von Braun, the inventor of Alpha-60. But Caution is on the side of characters, not critics; experience, not analysis.

The politics of Alphaville (both the city and the film) are also anti-analytical. Natasha reads from *Capitale de la douleur:*

> Nous vivons dans l'oubli de nos metamorphoses. . . .*

And Alpha-60 tells us,

> Nor is there in the so-called Capitalist world, or Communist world any malicious intent to suppress men through the power of ideology or materialism, but only the natural aim of all organizations to increase their rational structure.[4]

The line from *Capitale de la douleur* reminds us that the real battle is with the images—the metamorphoses—not the reality they represent. Alpha-60's analysis calls attention to the organic insidiousness of unbridled logic and the terror we feel in the face of its aggrandizement. Lemmy will destroy Alpha-60 by turning it against itself. His secret, Lemmy tells the machine, is

> something that never changes with the night or the day, as long as the past represents the future, towards which it will advance in a straight line, but which, at the end, has closed in on itself into a circle.[5]

Alpha-60 can't understand this metaphor (or any other). If it does find the answer, Caution warns, "you will destroy yourself in the process . . . because you will have become my equal, my brother."

*"We live in the void of our metamorphoses . . .", from "Notre Mouvement."

Alpha-60 dies eventually of a nervous breakdown, the seeds of which it has carried since its birth. Its last words:

> The present is terrifying because it is irreversible . . . because it is shackled, fixed, like steel. . . . Time is the material of which I am made. . . . Time is a stream which carries me along . . . but I am Time . . . it is a Tiger which tears me apart . . . yet I, too, am the tiger. . . . For our misfortune, the world is a reality . . . and I . . . for my misfortune . . . I am myself—Alpha-60.[6]

The machine has broken down into metaphor. The speech is reminiscent of Charlotte's struggle to conquer the terror of the present. Like its cousins in contemporary science fiction (I am thinking not only of HAL-2000, but also of the libidinous monster of *Forbidden Planet*), Alpha-60 is made in the image of its creators. It is itself only a final metaphor for our own psyches; the ultimate Rorschach: a projection of our fears and inadequacies. "I'm very well, thank you, not at all," is the constant contradictory refrain of the film.

Caught in the present, caught in the logic, caught in the signs of the logic, how will Lemmy deliver us? Again, the salvation is expressed in signs: Lemmy offers Natasha not the gift of love but the gift of the word "Love." It is the ultimate weapon against Alphaville. Like their predecessors in "Le Nouveau Monde" they have been thrust into a world of inhuman, alien logic. Like their successors in "Anticipation," they free themselves by "making love, conversation and progress—all at the same time." Love and progress are easily understood as terms in this cosmic joke of Godard's, but pay attention, too, to the second element, conversation. It is equally important: it is where *la raison ardente* flickers into life. Love is too simple by itself.

Lemmy's first gift to Natasha is the volume of Eluard that was Harry Dickson's last testament. He tells her to read the passages he has underlined, and the first cracks in her armor of logic appear as she does so:

> Nous vivons dans l'oubli de nos metamorphoses . . .
> Mais cet echo qui roule tout le long du jour
> Cet echo hors du temps d'angoisse ou de caresses . . .
> Sommes-nous près ou loin de notre conscience. . . .*

"There are words here I do not understand," says Natasha. The key word is *"conscience,"* which in French carries with it both the English

*"We live in the void of our metamorphoses . . ./But that echo that runs through all the day / That echo beyond time, despair, and the caress . . . / Are we close to, or far away from our conscience. . . ."

Natasha at the window, a copy of *Capitale de la douleur* in hand.

senses of "conscience" and "consciousness." The two are semantically identified for Godard: to be conscious of our selves as existential beings, to be aware of the environment in which we exist, is to have "conscience"—an ethical sense of relationships and actions. In Alphaville people only say "Because"; Lemmy asks "Why?" Not the answers, but the questions are alive. *Alphaville* is not *science* fiction at all, but a new, higher endeavor; *con-science* fiction: "to know together," if we etymologize the word literally, in order to distort out of it a deeper meaning. That is love.

From the word "*conscience*" (which sounds vaguely familiar) Natasha progresses to "Why?" and from there to an understanding of the difference between love and sensuality. She phrases the question and Godard gives us one of his most deeply felt sequences to answer it:

> *Montage of close-ups of Lemmy and Natasha embracing, perhaps dancing, against the light and alternately illuminated by it, Lemmy gently kissing her, a front medium shot of Natasha against a white wall . . . in which the light intensifies until it is painful, and then fades away again; both of them against the jukebox, he kisses her hand, she puts her hand to his cheek, she passes her fingers through his hair, and they dance ritualistically as the light flashes off and on. . . . Intercut are images of the police in their car, coming to the hotel, as the morse-like bleeps direct them.*[7]

We hear Natasha's voice:

> Your voice . . . your eyes . . . our silences, our words . . .
> Light that goes . . . light that returns . . . one single smile between us both . . . From needing to know, I watched the night create the day . . . without change to our appearances . . .
> O, Beloved of all beloved of one alone . . .
> In silence your mouth promised to be happy . . .
> Further and further, hate says . . . nearer and nearer, love says . . .
> Through a single caress we leave our childhood. . . .
> More and more I see the human predicament as a dialogue between lovers.

Then we have the stunning image of Natasha looking out of the window with the book clutched close to her which has become the emblem of the film.

When Natasha finally learns to pronounce haltingly the words "I . . . Love . . . You," the film is finished. She has learned how to separate "I" from "You." More and more Godard sees the human predicament as an argument between lovers.

Pierrot le fou, shot a few months after *Alphaville,* continues and completes the process begun in that film. Many of Godard's earlier characters had talked of going south, of escaping the sadness of the city. Ferdinand and Marianne accomplish it for all of them. There are many echoes of the earlier films in *Pierrot,* as well: Ferdinand is reminded by Marianne that it has been five and a half years since they last met. "It was October," the time of *A bout de souffle.* Belmondo and Karina last acted together in *Une Femme est une femme,* whose color scheme in reds and blues is echoed here. Like Veronica and Bruno, Marianne and Ferdinand find themselves caught up in a set of vaguely political adventures, and the real world of politics is never very far removed: Algeria for the earlier film, Vietnam for the later. Ferdinand is tortured in the same manner Bruno was. Marianne's name, as Michael Walker has pointed out, echoes both Nana *(Vivre sa vie)* and (la) Mariée, and the Paris from which the pair escape is expressed in the language of *La Femme mariée.* Ferdinand's wife is her twin: "I'm wearing my new invisible panty-girdle which you can't see," she explains, and hands him a magazine: "under my new panties . . . SCANDALE." The party which finally drives Ferdinand to escape is a collage of ads for automobiles, soap, and cologne. Much of it is shot in primary monotones, which reminds us of the beginning of *Le Mépris,* as does the presence of a filmmaker, the one voice of sanity. This time it is Samuel Fuller; last time it was Fritz Lang. Like *Le Mépris, Pierrot le fou* describes the disintegration of a relationship in the heat of the southern sun and ends with a shot of the symbolic sea; this time, however, the pan continues to the sky, as well. Like *Bande à part, Pierrot* gives us characters who find refuge from reality in the plots of pulp fiction; and like *Alphaville* it presents us with a fabric of literary and poetic references in which the themes of the film are worked out.

So *Pierrot le fou* is clearly a summary for Godard, but not, however, a conscious catalogue. In an interview in October 1965 he noted,

> . . . it is a completely spontaneous film. I have never been so worried as I was two days before shooting began. I had nothing, nothing at all. Oh well, I had the book [Lionel White's novel *Obsession*]. And a certain number of locations. I knew it would take place by the sea.[8]

The spontaneous nature of the film is vital to him, for *Pierrot* grew out of a set of very personal emotions. He had reached a point in his career when he had begun to call the whole activity of cinema into question. The very foundation of his art was threatened. In a prefatory essay ("Pierrot mon ami") to the published interview, he went into detail about this attitude. He begins by explaining that the motivation for the film was to capture "life itself" ("I have big ideas"),

> by way of panoramic shots of nature, fixed shots of death, brief shots and long takes, sounds loud and quiet, what else, movements of Anna and Jean-Paul, actor or actress free and enslaved, but which rhymes with man and woman. . . .[9]

Then he describes the threatening paralysis that he faced in this attempt:

> . . . here, parenthetically, I take the opportunity of telling you that as if by chance the only great problem with the cinema seems to me more and more with each film when and why to start a shot and when and why to end it.

Needless to say, this way madness lies. There are the beginnings here of the aphasia that Richard Roud protests in the films of the late sixties. Godard knows this. He continues,

> One might as well try . . . because everything fits, as they say, in life, without ever knowing whether it fits because that's life or the opposite, because I am using words, and words can be reversed and replace each other, whereas can the life they represent be reversed? A question as dangerous as it is perplexing and a crossroads where ideas wonder which

> road to take next . . . and so it was for me filming a true cinema image, its true symbol, but a symbol, no more, for what was true of Marianne and Pierrot, not asking what came first, was not true of me because that was precisely what I was asking, in other words, at the very moment I was sure I had captured life, it escaped me for this reason. . . .

I have edited parts of these two long sentences, but the grammatical awkwardness is not the result of the editing. The words are cheating Godard, going limp on him just when he needs them. He goes on to define the problems of cinema,

> where the real and the imaginary are clearly distinct and yet are one, like the Moebius curve which has at the same time one side and two, like the technique of cinéma-vérité which is also a technique of lying. It's pretty disconcerting, to say the least.

Agreed. Yet at first it seems as if this is the kind of fear that only filmmakers are subject to. Not for Godard. He goes on to express this terrible confusion in terms of spectators, as well, and their identity with what happens on the screen. "This double movement, which projects us towards others while taking us inside ourselves, physically defines the cinema."[10] So what seems like a problem of esthetics is really a much more vital question of ethics. Godard *approaches* the problem of *Pierrot* on the level of esthetics, but we see the questions he raises in terms of ethics.

> In this sense, one can say that Pierrot is not really a film. It is rather an attempt at cinema. And the cinema, by making reality disgorge, reminds us that one must attempt to live.

The attempt at cinema forces the attempt at life. Both are tentative.

This moral-psychological dilemma is part of the material of the film as well as the approach to it. There were various attempts throughout the earlier films to inject the persona of the filmmaker directly into the film, either as narrator, via titles, or through Brechtian distancing. But in *Alphaville,* Godard finally hit on a device which suited him well: the notebook or diary. From *Pierrot* onwards, Godard's handwriting becomes a visual reminder of his presence, as his voice is an aural aide-mémoire. It is typical that the aural representation is insufficient; he must draw his own diagrams and pictures, use his own handwriting as well: all semiological fields must be covered.

What kind of diary is Ferdinand/Pierrot writing? We have only fleeting images of it, but a few illustrations might help to define it:*

> "I have decided to keep a diary. Such is the essence of that being, face to face with nature, who is unable to believe. *The urgency to describe it with language* [my emphasis]. We live by hunting and fishing. Tuesday: nothing. Friday: *(in English)* my girl Friday. Experience of the flesh. The eyes; human countrysides. The mouth; onomatopoeias which disappear by becoming language. The language of poetry rises from the ruins. Friday: the writer decides to . . . *(the rest is incomprehensible).*[11]

"The urgency to describe it with language" is an apt subtitle for *Pierrot le fou*. Ferdinand has found an idea for a novel, as well:

> No longer to write about people's lives . . . but only about life, life itself. What goes on between people, in space . . . like sounds and colors. That would be something worthwhile. Joyce tried, but one must be able, ought to be able, to do better.[12]

That is the goal of *Pierrot le fou* and of all Godard's films from this point on. As Godard says,

> The important thing is to be aware one exists. For three-quarters of the time during the day one forgets this truth, which surges up again as you look at houses or a red light, and you have the sensation of existing in that moment.[13]

How close this is in spirit to the passage from Cocteau with which we began this chapter. If we give a name to this mood, it is evidently "Angst" or "la Nausée"—the global fear of existential thought (and I mean the ambiguity of that phrase). It has been stated before, but when it is experienced, one can do nothing but state it again. Godard phrases it in cinema.

Out of the matrix of this fear and sickness unto death, Godard fashioned what he saw as "the story of the last romantic couple, the last descendents of *La Nouvelle Héloise, Werther,* and *Hermann und Dorothea.*" *Pierrot le fou* is a romance in the older sense of that word as well as the most modern. Like Godard's own *Le Mépris* and Truffaut's *La Peau douce* and *La Sirène du Mississippi* (with which it bears many

*Godard's language is such an important focus of his films by this time that it is almost a requirement to have printed scripts in order to appreciate the poetry fully—not the visual "poetry," not the aural "poetry," not the poetic sentiments, but the real, old-style, printed-on-the-page poetry. It seems to me (though this is not the place to try to prove it) that Jean-Luc Godard is one of the most vital French poets working today. Luckily, many of his scripts (especially from this period) are available.

resemblances) it is a film about obsession and sexual betrayal. But it is also a type of medieval romance since, like its precursors, it deals with a voyage of discovery. It may not be accidental that *Pierrot le fou* takes place in the same general locale as so many medieval romances. Because of Godard's own emotional motivations for the film, however, his characters allow themselves to be guided by events. "They are abandoned to their own devices," he elaborates. "They are inside both their adventures and themselves." In other words, they have the self-awareness that Lemmy Caution taught to Natasha. In *Vivre sa vie,* Brice Parain had told Nana the story of Porthos, the musketeer who when he thought for the first time to consider how it was possible to put one foot in front of the other, ceased immediately to be able to do so, and consequently died as the bomb he had just set exploded. Like Porthos, Marianne and Ferdinand are caught up in the logic of their selves and their adventures, and their self-awareness will lead inexorably to their deaths.

Looked at another way, *Pierrot,* like so many of Godard's films, is driven by the tension between the active principle of Marianne and the passive principle of Ferdinand. If Ferdinand can't even communicate sufficiently with this woman he loves to get her to call him by his right name, then it is equally true that, as Marianne tells him, "You speak to me with words and I look at you with feelings." *Pierrot le fou* is a tragedy because the active intelligence of Marianne and the passive intelligence of Ferdinand will never combine, must always remain separate—as opposite as L'Allegro and Il Penseroso. From the position of the contemplative consciousness (which is certainly Godard's position), there is no more poignant and frightening tragedy than this. Marianne will never accept the existence of Ferdinand—she will insist that he be what she wants him to be, Pierrot the clown of commedia dell'arte, not what he is. For his part, Ferdinand's single act is to light the fuse of his own destruction. Typically, he immediately contradicts this action—but it is too late. As Ferdinand has said, "Love has to be invented all over again." It is going to be necessary to return to zero before the balance between action and contemplation can be redressed.

Despite all the profuse elements of romance and adventure, gangsters and blood, drama and pain, *Pierrot le fou* is just as much an experiment in narrative form as any of Godard's other films. It is still an essay; this time, however, the motivation of the film and the spontaneity which that necessitated add a new element: the struggle with time. Even for some adamant Godardians (Roud, for one), *Pierrot le fou* seems disjointed, either too much a story or not enough of one. In *Pierrot* Godard allows shots to find their own optimal length and this creates a new, more aleatory rhythm: at times we have a rush of images which are next to impossible to accept, at others, long takes which impress by their diffidence. This is the idiom Godard will employ for the next several films, and there is no doubt that it is demanding.

Similarly, *Pierrot le fou* prefigures the group of films which follow it by being heavily laden with cultural references. For the moment, these are only used, as by T. S. Eliot, to reinforce the thematic materials; in the films following *Pierrot* they will form the basis of Godard's cultural critique. Picasso is important, as ever, but in keeping with the Romantic warp of the film, Auguste Renoir's paintings take pride of place. Marianne's surname after all is Renoir, and she is compared often to her spiritual grandfather's women. And of course, this is the country of Matisse. The literary references, however, give us a better sense of the mood of the film. Several novels of Céline are cited (Ferdinand's name, of course, is also a reference). Marianne quotes the suicide Pavese. Chateaubriand's *Paul et Virginie* is offered for comparison, and Garcia Lorca's "Lament for Ignacio Sanchez Mejias" provides Ferdinand with one of his most affective plaints: "Ah! What a dreadful five in the afternoon!" There is Rimbaud, who provides the motto for the film: "Chapitre huit: Une Saison en enfer"; and Joyce; and Proust.

The quotations and allusions provide Godard with comfort as well as artistic leverage. In front of a sign that says "S.O.S." Ferdinand lights a cigarette and flashes a look at the camera. On the soundtrack we hear his words (and Godard's):

> For words in the midst of shadows are a strange power of enlightenment.

Marianne adds:

> Of the things they signify,

and then qualifies ironically,

> in effect.[14]

Immediately, we see a close-up drawing of Rimbaud with colored vowels dotted over his face, like a disease. Marianne's voice: "Language often retains only purity." As if in answer, Ferdinand is seen drawing in red in his diary. He breaks down Marianne's name into

MER, AME, AMER, ARME, ARIANE.

Sea, soul, bitter, arms, and an allusion to the famous lines from Racine:

> Ariane, ma sôeur, de quel amour blessée
> Vous mourûtes aux bords où vous fûtes laissée!*

If Marianne is Ariadne, then Pierrot is Theseus. Ariadne has helped him escape from the Labyrinth. He is about to abandon her.

In the following scene, in which Ferdinand goes to the movies to watch newsreels of Vietnam, Godard quotes himself to explain what is happening. Jean Seberg, holding a movie camera (the shot is from "Le Grand Escroc") notes,

> We are carefully looking for . . . that moment when one abandons the fictional character in order to discover the true one . . . if such a thing exists.[15]

Ferdinand stares at the screen. Seberg points her lenses at him, across the void of years, defiantly. Only those in the past who have "the gift of death," who have already committed their words to paper and to film, can help us.

Ferdinand longs for the freedom from life that the authors he quotes celebrate. Near the end he tells Marianne:

> The only thing I want is for time to stop. You see, I put my hand on your knee which is marvellous in itself . . . that is life. Space . . . feelings . . . but instead of that I will follow you, and continue our story of blood and thunder. It's the same for me either way.
>
> Allons-y, Allons-o.[16]

Pierrot le fou begins with Ferdinand in his bath, reading to his daughter at length from a copy of Elie Faure's *Histoire de l'art* about Velasquez at the end of his life. This long citation is very important to Godard, for it sets the theme of the film precisely:

> After he had reached the age of fifty, Velasquez no longer painted anything concrete and precise. He drifted through the material world, penetrating it, as the air and the dusk. In the shimmering of the shadows, he caught unawares the nuances of color which he transformed into the invisible heart of his symphony of silence. . . . Space reigned supreme. . . .[17]

If *Pierrot le fou* is frightening (as I think it often is) it is because it is full of emptiness. Space reigns supreme between these people. They are on the very margins of the film, in time and in space, and they never close the gap.

After reading a couple of paragraphs which describe the desolation of

Phèdre I:iii. "Ariadne, my sister! Wounded by what love / You died abandoned on the shore."

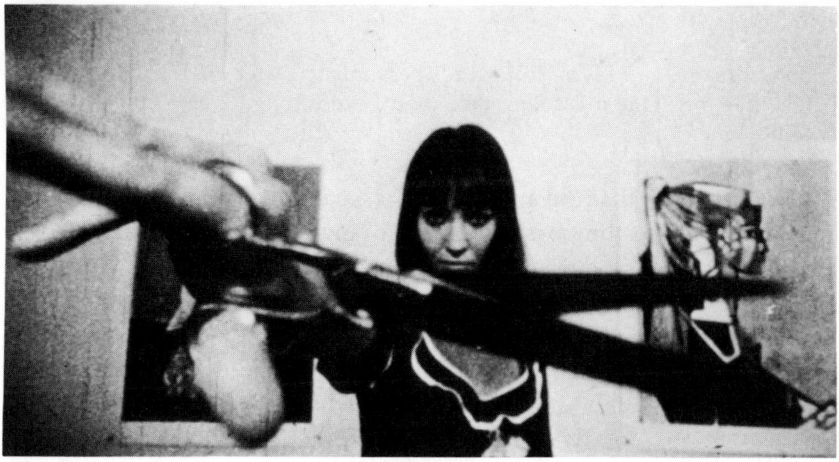

The Cubist intelligence/Marianne the active principle/ARIANE/MER/AME/AMER/ARME/the danger of women. (Frame enlargement.)

the world in which Velasquez managed to survive, Ferdinand comes to Faure's description of him as "the painter of the evening, of the plains, of the silence, even when he paints in broad daylight. . . . Spanish painters never went outside except at those times in the day when the air was radiant, when everything was burnished by the sun. They discoursed only with the evening. . . ." Ferdinand thinks that is beautiful. I think Godard would like to be that way. *Pierrot le fou* ends with son ami Pierrot setting aside the Pieds-Nickelès comic book which he has carried like a talisman ever since the first frames of the film, painting himself blue, wrapping himself in red and yellow dynamite—primary colors and primary significances—and lighting the fuse on the top of a hill. He explodes far away from us, quietly. The camera pans slowly to the calm open sea and then sweeps up into the sky. Marianne and Ferdinand are heard on the soundtrack. They whisper intimately the lines from Rimbaud:

Elle est retrouvée.	It's found again.
Quoi?—L'Eternité.	What?—Eternity.
C'est la mer allée	It's the sea gone
Avec le soleil.	With the sun.

At last everything is burnished by the sun and the discourse is only with the evening.

Shortly after finishing *Pierrot* and just before he began shooting *Masculin-féminin,* Godard described his state of mind this way:

> Two or three years ago I felt that everything had been done, that there was nothing left to do today. I couldn't see anything to do that hadn't been

> done already. . . . I was, in a word, pessimistic. After *Pierrot,* I no longer feel this. Yes, One must film, talk about, everything. Everything remains to be done.[18]

There's no doubt that the anguish expressed in *Alphaville* and *Pierrot*—the anxiety about the possibilities of loving and communicating—was deeply personal. Godard could have said with Ferdinand: "I'm worn out. I've a mechanism for seeing, called eyes, for listening, called ears, for speaking, called mouth. I've got a feeling they're all going their separate ways . . . There's no coordination. One should feel they're united. I feel they are deranged." Yet Ferdinand's odyssey and death, and the filming of it, must have been, at least in some respects, cathartic, for Godard moved on with new energy in the years that followed.

And the cure for his Angst? At the age of thirty-five, Godard finally discovered politics. Here was a system in which one could still believe. It was not so much that politics offered answers, but that it offered a valid framework in which to work. "Times had changed," Paul explains at the beginning of *Masculin-féminin* with characteristic irony.

> This was the era of James Bond and Vietnam. A great wave of hope had risen in the French Left with the approach of the December [1965] elections.[19]

Godard's plunge into politics was, as it is for all of us, a kind of Pascalian wager: the odds are still enormous against success, but to lose is to lose nothing, while to win is to gain a great deal. Semiology had led Godard perilously close to total anomie and aphasia. Dialectical materialism was to bring him back, at least part of the way. It is important that we see Godard's politics not so much as a subject for his films but as a way of making them, indeed a way of life. As always, method and subject were inextricably linked, and the job at hand, he was to discover, was "not to make political films, but to make films politically."

Godard's intense identification of what he was doing with how he was doing it is basic to an understanding of his art. This concern with process is a significant parallel between him and François Truffaut. However different their films may appear on first viewing, they nevertheless share a strong common heritage. Their worldviews are not identical but they are congruent; the products may seem worlds apart but the processes share certain similarities. I have specifically avoided trying to explain the films of one in terms of the other because I think that would skew our perspective on each. It might be worthwhile, however, to take a moment just to pair off films that seem to me to have common grounds and aims: *A bout de souffle* and *Tirez sur le pianiste; Jules et Jim* and *Une Femme est une femme* (and *Bande à part*); *La Femme mariée* and *La Peau douce; Alphaville* and *Fahrenheit 451; Pierrot le fou* and *La Sirène du Mississippi; La Nuit américaine* and *Le Mépris; Le Gai Savoir* and *L'Enfant sauvage; Masculin-féminin* and the Doinel cycle. Without a doubt, the styles of the two filmmakers diverge radically; nowhere is this more evident than in the darker, more self-conscious tone of Godard's films. Yet there is still enough in common in terms of subjects, heritage, and raw materials for the comparison to be useful.

The most obvious difference between Godard and Truffaut seems to be political, but the gap is not so broad as received opinion has it. Godard's politics are certainly more explicit, but I hope I have shown that there is a rich vein of implicit politics in the films of Truffaut as well. It's instructive that the film which marks Godard's turn towards politics in the late sixties, *Masculin-féminin,* comes close to being a fifth episode in the life of Antoine Doinel—mostly as the result of using Jean-Pierre Léaud, who was in the process of creating one of the vivid and dominating personas of the New Wave. Between 1962 and 1965, when Léaud had found it difficult to get work as an actor, Godard had used him behind the camera first as apprentice on *La Femme mariée,* then as assistant director on *Alphaville* and *Pierrot le fou,* so that he could keep his hand in. When Godard decided to make a film about "the children of Marx and Coca-Cola," Léaud was an obvious choice. Not only was he the right age, but Godard must have known that his sometimes absurd, sometimes affecting romantic persona would add a personal dimension to the film. Léaud was only twenty-one, but he had some of the same romantic qualities that Godard had given to the heroes of his previous films who were almost a generation older. During the late sixties, Léaud worked for both Godard and Truffaut. He has said, "if Truffaut was my 'father,' then Godard was my 'uncle.'"

Godard eases into politics slowly. Before 1968 it was still a subject that he approached from the outside. "A purely political subject is difficult to do," he said in late 1965. "For politics you need insight into the points of view of four or five different people, and at the same time have a broad over-all grasp. Politics involves both past and present."[20] He is thinking, of course, of politics in the limited sense, which is peripheral to *Masculin-féminin:* we have the obligatory Vietnam scene and some talk about workers alienated from their tasks, but they go nowhere. Godard still hasn't understood these issues experientially, and he doesn't trust himself. But the Movement of the sixties did make one large advance over previous leftist politics in two relatively new areas of thought and action which Godard was well equipped to deal with: sexual politics and the media. These are the themes of *Masculin-féminin*. Godard intuited political truths that he could never have explicated in the language of the old politics.

Masculin-féminin is a realist mirror image of the romantic *Pierrot le fou*. Paul, like Ferdinand, is obsessed with a woman, but Paul has no thought of escape. The film is another story of betrayal, but now the dialectical nature of the argument between the feminine, active principle and the masculine, passive, and contemplative principle is sharper. As always, the active force wins; the man is betrayed and destroyed. But before the logic works itself out in the plot, Godard has had a chance to capture a number of precise truths about the way men and women interact. The long, tentative, shy conversations between Paul and Madeleine and Robert and Catherine (the first is nine and a half minutes long, the second, eight minutes) give us a cinéma-vérité analysis of sexual relationships which are painfully forced. Paul and Madeleine in the bathroom of the magazine office make the usual small talk; he is trying to get something started, she is trying to decide whether or not she wants him. The dialogue moves from a typical opening ploy—"What about the twenty-third? You told me we could go out together on the twenty-third"—to a quiet direct challenge—"And when you say 'go out,' you mean go to bed? Come on, tell me honestly. Answer me," Madeleine counters.[21] But the real knowledge of the scene is in the faces: Léaud pops a cigarette into his mouth with studied nonchalance; Chantal Goya fiddles with her compact and plays with her hair; Léaud suddenly grins, lowers his head, stops smiling, looks up in surprise, bites his lip; Goya, surprised by his answer ("Yes, I would, I would like to sleep with you") and his riposte ("And you?") breaks into a smile; the mask has dropped for the first time.

But the affair which begins with such traditional foretalk is going to go nowhere in particular. Madeleine (Chantal Goya was a real Yé-Yé singer, not an actress) is best described by the youth-cult magazines she used to work for:

> . . . a lively little creature, sociable and tender, she strives to create a universe all her own. . . . The precision of her frame is upset by the flash of her smile, the mischief that sparkles in her look, the mobility of her face, the gracious ease of her movements. Endowed with a great artistic sensitivity, she demands authenticity from herself as well as others. The far-out bores her, not from any laziness of spirit, but because of an instinctive mistrust of everything which may not be sincere and clear.[22]

When we read between the press-agented lines, we have the real Madeleine, a true child of the Pepsi generation, whose emptiness is a void in which Paul loses himself. She not only strives to create a universe all her own, she denies his, which, if not mature yet, nevertheless makes room for poetry and politics.

Madeleine is a commodity, formed by the newly powerful youth culture. Godard caught this phenomenon very near its birth and described its fatuity as well as anyone since. Madeleine is a product of magazines and records, a close cousin of Charlotte. The emptiness of the culture is reiterated by Paul's six-minute interview with Elsa in the middle of the film. Titled "Dialogue with a Consumer Product," it is composed of one long take in which "Mademoiselle 19 ans" is seen, like so many of Godard's women, in violent contrast in front of a brightly lit window. Elsa smiles a lot, plays with her hair, but she isn't much good at answering Paul's questions about politics. About the best she can do is define "reactionary" as "being in opposition, reacting against a lot of things, not accepting just anything that happens," which she decides is a good thing.

The basic mode of dialogue in the film is the interview. Many questions are asked, but few are answered. The media culture continually acts to separate the characters from each other, and after a while we sense that Paul, who has gotten a job with a public opinion firm, has become just as much an outsider as his mentor Godard. In the penultimate scene of the film Paul explains:

> Little by little during these three months I've noticed that all these questions, far from reflecting a collective mentality, were frequently betraying and distorting it. . . . Without knowing it, I was deceiving [the people I was questioning] and being deceived by them. Why? No doubt because polls and samples soon forget their true purpose, which is the observation of behavior, and insidiously substitute value judgments for research. I discovered that all the questions I was asking conveyed an ideology which didn't correspond to actual customs but to those of yesterday, of the past. Thus I had to remain vigilant. A few random observations came to me by chance and served me as guidelines:
>
> A philosopher is a man who pits his conscience against opinion: To have a conscience is to be open to the world.
>
> To be faithful is to act as if time did not exist. Wisdom would be if one could see life, really see, that would be wisdom.[23]

So Paul shows his solidarity with the heroes who have preceded him and also points the direction for the future.

His romance has run its course in a city filled with perfunctory, matter-of-fact violence. There are five inane deaths in the film to which no one particularly reacts. Leroi Jones's *Dutchman,* a play which created a myth that is central to this film, is quoted; a man comes up to Paul with a knife and then stabs himself in the stomach; a man asks Paul for a match, takes the box and then goes around the corner and quietly immolates himself. He leaves a note: "Paix au Vietnam." A woman shoots her husband; nobody seems to care. This is the background against which masculine and feminine play out their vital dialectic. But even in bed with two women, Paul is every bit as alone as his older brother Ferdinand. Like him, Paul believes that "one cannot live without affection." When Madeleine suggests that Elizabeth move in with them in their new apartment, Paul takes a fatal step backwards, off the edge, into the air. We don't see this; it is recounted to us by the girls. His death/suicide is just as ambiguous as Ferdinand's, for we are also told that he "wanted to take some pictures" and stepped too far back to get the right angle. The desire for objectivity kills, too.

Yet the objectivity of *Masculin-féminin* is one of its greatest achievements. It captures the taste and smell of Paris in the winter of 1965 with such rich detail that it is one of the masterpieces of truth-cinema (Godard had said that since Marker and Rouch had done Paris in the spring and summer—in *Chronique d'un été* and *Le Joli Mai*—he wanted to do it in the winter.) And it explicates with great sympathy and intelligence the dilemma of being young in the sixties. The relationships the film describes may be characteristically empty (and fatal), but *Masculin-féminin* is still an optimistic film. It is cooler and less anguished than its predecessors, and Paul is asking questions: the political landscape can be glimpsed on the horizon. If Paul/Godard can transcend the obsession with romantic love, there is good work to be done and a community of workers to do it with. There is a sense that the old movies and the life they described are dying and will be replaced by the new films of a new reality. After he has been to see a film (and complained to the projectionist about the aspect ratio!), Léaud says:

> We often went to the movies. . . . The screen lit up and we trembled. . . . But more often than not Madeleine and I were disappointed. *(Close-up. He closes his eyes.)* The pictures were dated, they flickered. *(He reopens his eyes.)* And Marilyn Monroe had aged terribly. It made us sad. *(He looks to his left and then back to the camera.)* This wasn't the film we'd dreamed of. This wasn't the total film that each of us carried within himself . . . *(he closes his eyes again; his eyelids flutter)* the film we wanted to make, or, more secretly, no doubt . . . *(he reopens his eyes)* that we wanted to live.[24]

Masculin-féminin is not quite that film either; Godard is still a stranger among the generation of Marx and Coca-Cola; but he is now definitely involved in the struggle for a new life and a new cinema.

The difficulty for Godard (and for us) during the succeeding years will be this unique conflation of life and cinema. The more Godard struggles for a wider sense of politics in his films, the more he will be thrown back into the logic of cinema, which imprisons him. If he was criticized earlier for false consciousness and a fatuous political line, maybe it was more because his political critics made the understandable mistake of looking for his politics in the content of his films, while his real political contributions were best revealed in their style and construction. Godard is never very far removed from cinematic conceptualization: even when we find an affective human element in the films (as in *A bout de souffle*, for instance, or *Pierrot le fou*), it is almost required that we perceive that emotional content by "reading" the style of the film. Our identification with Michel Poiccard, for example, depends on our understanding of him as a character existing within the cinematic traditions of Bogart and the Film Noir. With Ferdinand Griffon, it is even more essential to see the closely woven texture of the fabric in which art is the warp and life the woof.

Nowhere is the intensity of this confusion of life and art so apparent or so difficult as in Godard's next film, *Made in U.S.A.* Godard had already begun work on *2 ou 3 choses que je sais d'elle* when Georges de Beauregard, who had produced five of Godard's first half dozen films, and to whom Godard had been close, approached him with a request. Beauregard was in some financial difficulty due to the banning of *La Religieuse*, and asked Godard if he could possibly make a very quick film for him. "It was the only way for him to get out of the mess," Godard wrote. "It would allow him to hang on. He told me: 'Only you can do things quickly.' I answered: 'It's true.'"[25] Godard accepted. The challenge of making two films at once intrigued him. (Later he was to suggest that the two films be shown together, possibly with a reel of one alternating with a reel of the other, on the model of Faulker's *Wild Palms*.)* So for about a month during the summer of 1966, Godard found himself working on the set of *2 ou 3 choses* in the mornings and *Made in U.S.A.* in the afternoons. This last film, made symbolically in place of Jacques Rivette's *La Religieuse*, which was to become Anna Karina's most successful film without Jean-Luc Godard, ironically was to be the last film Karina and Godard would make together. The marriage, both in cinema and in "real life," was coming apart, and within a year Godard would mark his commitment to the generation of

***Made in U.S.A.* has never been distributed in the U.S.A. due to a legal contretemps between Beauregard and the author of the American novel on which the film was ostensibly based, Donald Westlake ("Richard Stark"). A wonderful Godardian irony. See Albert Nussbaum, "An Inside look at Donald Westlake," *Take One* 4:9 (May 1975) for further details.

the sixties by marrying Anne Wiazemsky. *Made in U.S.A.*, like *Alphaville* and *Pierrot*, is a hymn to the image of Karina which had obsessed Godard for more than five years. This was not just a matter of love or infatuation, but a legitimate cinematic inquiry. A decade earlier, Roland Barthes had described the significance of the "absolute mask . . . the archetype of the human face" in his famous essay about the image of another Scandinavian, "The Face of Garbo." For Barthes,

> Garbo's face represents this fragile moment when the cinema is about to draw an existential from an essential beauty, when the archetype leans toward the fascination of mortal faces, when the clarity of the flesh as essence yields its place to a lyricism of Woman.[26]

Godard could have said the same of Karina, from whose essential beauty, as wife, he drew an existential one, as actress. Characteristically, he could express even simple passion in intellectual cinematic terms.

The image of Karina's face is at the center of *Made in U.S.A.* "Paula" is on screen most of the time and the other characters are only vaguely realized; they all play minor supporting roles. Paula is also the first of Godard's women to be allowed to play the game of cinema in life, for she is modeled, Godard tells us, on Humphrey Bogart in *The Big Sleep*, which he had recently seen. Paula, therefore, supersedes Michel Poiccard. So the image at the center of *Made in U.S.A.* is once again a "double exposure" of cinema and life.

This conflation is recognizable in the thematic material of the film as well, and here it is even more confusing. "At the beginning," Godard wrote,

> I tried to make a simple film, and, for the first time, to tell a story. But it's not in my nature. I don't know how to tell stories. I want to mix everything, to restore everything, to tell all at the same time. If I had to define myself, I'd say that I am a "painter of letters" as others would say that they are "men of letters."[27]

Godard also wanted to say something about the Americanization of France and thought he could link this theme to a marginal episode in the Ben Barka affair, the French political scandal of the day.

> I imagined that Figon [a double agent involved in the affair] was not dead, that he was hiding in the countryside, that he had written to his girlfriend, asking her to join him. She went to the rendezvous, and upon her arrival found him dead. . . . No one knows why he is dead. . . . She gets caught up in a network of policemen and crooks and she ends up wanting to write an article on the whole episode [she is a journalist].[28]

So we have Karina as Bogart, an essay on the "coca-colonization" of

France, and an attempt to comment on the underside of French politics as seen through the Ben Barka affair. Yet these various motivations, in themselves, would not have resulted in the dark reconditeness of *Made in U.S.A.* if Godard had not also decided once again to film the "spaces between people." We see very little of the anecdote Godard recounted above; the film concentrates on episodes and images which are often all but unintelligible. It is meant to follow directly in the tradition of *The Big Sleep,* whose incidents confused even Raymond Chandler. Chandler's world was dark, impenetrable, and paranoid, and the angst which pervaded it had first attracted the critics of the New Wave in the fifties; Godard is simply transferring the breakdown of logic and ethics which frightened Philip Marlowe from the Private Eye metaphor to a more specific mode. In case we should overlook this basis for the film, an early sequence, the fourth, takes place in a bistro which is straight out of Alice's Wonderland (and Ionesco's theatre of the absurd). The Waiter, Paula, and a workman are trying to define their milieu:

WAITER — Yes, yes. Well a bar is . . . it's a place, I mean a room . . . that is I mean it's several people gathered together under the gaze of a barman, and then it's also a room where liquids are poured out. In fact, what I mean is it's at the same time several people gathered together under the gaze of a barman, and then it's also a room. . . .[29]

This quickly degenerates into Hegelian absurdity:

WAITER — That'll do. You're just making a list of words any old how. That's no good, you must do something with them.

. . .

WORKMAN — If you like, I'll try to show off with sentences. But I don't like doing it.

WAITER — And why don't you like doing it?

WORKMAN — Because sentences are collections of words which make nonsense. It says so in the dictionary. . . .[30]

But the workman tries, nevertheless:

> The glass is not in my wine. The barman is in the pocket of the pencil's jacket. The counter is kicking Mademoiselle. The floor is being stubbed out on the cigarette. The tables are on the glasses. . . . I am what you are. He is not what we are. They are what you are. He has got what they have. They have got what we haven't.[31]

Godard's film is likewise a series of tentative statements whose provenance is the logic of structure, not the making of sense.

Paula is surrounded by characters out of a filmmaker's nightmare. David Goodis (Yves Alfonso) appears as a poet ("In this mirror I am enclosed alive / And true like we think angels. / And not like reflections are") who eventually becomes the only ally she can trust. Donald Siegel (Jean-Pierre Léaud) wears a huge button with the words "Kiss Me, I'm Italian." There is an Inspector Aldrich, a girl named Doris Mizoguchi, and nemeses named Widmark (Laszlo Szabo), Richard Nixon, and Robert MacNamara. Needless to say, Paula never discovers who killed her lover, Richard Politzer, and *we* can't even find out his last name (without resorting to interviews with Godard), since every time a character mentions it a jet roars overhead or a bell rings. There are parallel monologues at one point (which makes both of them incomprehensible) and counterpointed dialogues (in the manner of Ionesco) at others. The visual field of the film is equally disorienting: a jumble of posters, mannequins, signs, bludgeoning colors and shapes, often couched in a montage whose very insistence cries out in pain. If the narrative of *Made in U.S.A.* can be understood, then the film has failed. Paula knows this. Very early in the film she tells us,

> Already fiction carries away reality. Already there is blood and mystery in the air, already I seem to be plunged into a film by Walt Disney, but played by Humphrey Bogart—and therefore a political film.[32]

Godard dedicates the film to "Nick [Ray] and Samuel [Fuller] who taught me respect for image and sound." In *Pierrot,* Fuller had defined cinema: "Love . . . Hate . . . Action . . . Violence . . . Death. . . . In one word . . . Emotion."[33] And that is the sum of *Made in U.S.A.,* which was not made in the U.S.A. but in a country that was frighteningly like it.

But there is a subtext which controls our reaction in the face of this violent clash of images and sounds which seem to signify nothing. Roland Barthes wrote a few years later that there is "no semiology which cannot, in the last analysis, be acknowledged as *semioclasm.*"[34] The thorough breaking-down of signs, of the languages we take for granted in order to rebuild them on stronger foundations: a good motto for *Made in U.S.A.* Marianne Faithfull has sung "As Tears Go By." We see Paula in a left-hand profile against a dark background. She tells us,

> Whatever I do I can't escape my responsibility towards another person. My silence acts on him, just as my words do. My going away worries him as much as my presence. My indifference may be as fatal to him as my interference. My sometimes thoughtless concern is deadly to him. *(Reverse angle. Her eyes are full of tears.)* Either this life is nothing or else it must be everything. By contemplating the possibility of losing it rather than submitting it to action, I place in the very center of my relative existence a point of absolute reference: morality.[35]

This speech may seem out of place in the jumble of images that is *Made in U.S.A.*, but in fact that moral responsibility, which Karina had first phrased in *Vivre Sa Vie*, is at the heart of the film, awash in semioclasmic images and sounds. Richard Politzer appears to us in the film only via the medium of audio tape. (It is Godard's voice.) He is recording a manifesto, shortly before his death. His voice is urgent. The tape is played at a painfully high volume, a bit distractingly. It is not the content of Politzer's manifesto that is so important (although it does have some substance); it is the tone. He mentions Robespierre and St. Just, and if we unconsciously place Politzer in the role of Danton (or Marat) we are not far wrong. The same urgency, the same sense of the absolute necessity of beginning again, continually, pertains. Several times in the film, we see the title of a book: *Gauche, année zéro*. Other people are reading a *série noire* crime book, *Adieu la vie, adieu l'amour*. *Made in U.S.A.* is about the confluence of those titles; out of the sentiments they express and the genres they represent there grows an as yet amorphous hope.

At the end of the film, Paula is alone, on her way out of this French Atlantic City which is really the suburbs of Paris. She is standing by a traffic light. She comments on the film we have just seen:

> The drama of my consciousness is that having lost the world I try to recover myself, and in this very movement I am lost. . . .[36]

A yellow car drives up—once again, an *ex "macchina"* ending. Philippe Labro, the journalist who himself will soon begin making political films, gives Paula a lift, out of fiction, back to reality. She tells him what's happened. There is a close-up of *Gauche, année zéro*. On the soundtrack: the beginning of a movement of Schumann's fourth symphony. They talk about fascism, Ben Barka, and personal responsibility. Philippe says,

> You remember, Elisabeth in [Cocteau's] *Les Enfants terribles*. . . . The right and the left are both the same, they'll never change. The right because it's stupid and vicious. The left because it's sentimental. Besides, the idea of right and left is an equation which is totally out of date, one can't put it like that.[37]

Paula then asks the last question of the film, the one which motivated it:

> Well how?

She puts up her hand, turns, straightens her hair, and moves restlessly in her seat. The film ends with a red, white, and blue title: FIN.

Godard might easily have taken some lines from *Une Saison en enfer* as an epigram for *Made in U.S.A.*:

> Ce fut d'abord une étude. J'écrivais des silences, des nuits, je notais l'inexprimable. Je fixais des vertiges.*

But *Made in U.S.A.* was a glance backward, toward the fiction and movies that were rapidly receding into the past. Its companion piece of the summer of 1966, *2 ou 3 choses que je sais d'elle,* looks toward the future. In a direct line of development that began with *Vivre sa vie* and continued on through *La Femme mariée* and *Masculin-féminin,* it eschews fiction—even the reality of fiction—in order to fix, not frenzies, but facts in their flight. For Godard, this was a far more ambitious undertaking.

2 ou 3 choses, which began with an article about prostitution in the new suburbs of Paris by Catherine Vimenet (published in *Le Nouvel Observateur*), is a carefully reasoned project. Godard thought of it as "a continuation of the movement begun by Resnais in *Muriel:* an attempt at a description of a phenomenon known in mathematics and sociology as a 'complex.'"[39] The villain of the film is Paul Delouvrier, De Gaulle's Minister of Planning for the Paris region. Like Resnais's fascinating film, *2 ou 3 choses* attempts to divine the particular in the general and the general in the particular by forcing a fusion of viewpoints: the "her" of the title refers not to Juliette or to Marina Vlady who plays her so much as to the city of Paris. Juliette does not personify the city, but the stories of the two, on separate, parallel levels, are congruent. The housing "complex" in which she and her family live is a microcosm of the new, alienated Paris, and the name that is given to this new kind of domestic environment allows Godard to shift the level of meaning of the film back and forth between the complex that is sociological and that which is psycho-political. So the materials of the film have various dimensions: the personal, the architectural (or better yet, structural), and the political.

The film's narrative also has a varied set of dimensions. Godard explained in an essay:

> Basically, what I am doing is making the spectator share the arbitrary nature of my choices, and the quest for general rules which might justify a particular choice.[40]

We are reminded once again that the underlying struggle always for

*"At first it was an experiment. I wrote silences, I wrote the night, I recorded the inexpressible. I fixed frenzies in their flight."[38]

Godard is the matter of choice and responsibility, especially as it reveals itself in artistic activity. He continues,

> I watch myself filming, and you hear me thinking aloud. In other words, it isn't a film, it's an attempt at a film and is presented as such.

He is not moving away from fiction because fiction is in some way not "real" or "true." Godard doesn't believe that. But fiction doesn't leave enough room for the persona of the artist, and his voice; therefore, it is incomplete—almost dishonest. Only the tentative essay, the "attempt at a film," allows that freedom and honesty that Godard increasingly needs. The personal dimension reveals itself most clearly in the structure of the narrative, the authorial voice; observers who ignore this aspect of Godard's cinema miss a great deal. One might find it relatively easy to dismiss the sociology of *2 ou 3 choses* as fatuous or stillborn. But when we take into account Godard's own relationship with his materials, the film comes painfully alive. There is a passion here to make images, sounds, and words serve our understanding, and a knowledge of how they so often do not. "During the course of the film—in its discourse, its discontinuous discourse, that is*—I want to include everything, sport, politics, even groceries." Only in the clash of these elements of our culture can a sense of the truths about it emerge.

In a second essay Godard analyzes the discourse more precisely: there are four principal "movements."

The first is "Objective Description (or at least attempt at description, Ponge would say)"

- of objects ("houses, cars, cigarettes, apartments, shops, beds, TV sets, books, clothes, etc.")
- of subjects ("the characters, Juliette, the American, Robert, the hairdresser, passers-by, Marianne, the old man, the children, etc.").

Second is "Subjective Description (or at least attempt)"

- of subjects ("particularly by way of feelings, that is through scenes more or less written and acted")
- of objects ("settings seen from the inside, where the world is outside, behind the windows, or on the other side of walls").

Already we have a demandingly thorough analysis of the patterns. But there is more: the combinations. The third movement consists of the sum of the first two. Godard calls it "The Search for Structures (or at least attempt)."

*Typically, Godard here makes a pun *(cours—discours—cours discontinue)* revealing the logic of etymology: "discontinuous discourse" is a phrase which is important in Christian Metz's definition of narrative.

> The sum of the objective description and the subjective description should lead to the discovery of certain more general forms; should enable one to pick out, not a generalized overall truth, but a certain "complex feeling," something which corresponds emotionally to the laws one must discover and apply in order to live in society.[41]

Godard is advocating a structuralist ethnology which proceeds from two poetic approaches: the objective (or Concretistic—Francis Ponge is a good example) and the subjective (or Confessional—Rimbaud serves here). "Don't think, but look," advised Wittgenstein. "To the things themselves!" cried Husserl. "Let's make poetry from the things' side of it," suggested Ponge.

The sum of movements one, two, and three is the fourth movement; "Life":

> having been able to define certain complex phenomena while continuing to describe particular events and emotions, this will eventually bring us closer to life than at the outset . . . maybe then will be revealed what Merleau-Ponty calls the "singular existence" of a person. . . .

So much for theory. What about practice?

The advertising poster for the film (designed by Godard, as usual) announced a film about "two or three things that I know about her":

> HER, the cruelty of neo-capitalism
> HER, prostitution
> HER, the Paris region
> HER, the bathroom that 70% of the French don't have
> HER, the terrible law of huge building complexes
> HER, the physical side of love
> HER, the life of today
> HER, the war in Vietnam
> HER, the modern call-girl
> HER, the death of modern beauty
> HER, the circulation of ideas
> HER, the gestapo of structures.

These topics all find their way into the substance of the film. Godard uses titles from the series of essays published by Gallimard called "*Idées*" to punctuate the sequences and call attention to their purposes. Raymond Aron's *Eighteen Lessons on Industrial Society* is the first and most prominent of these—a model for the film. (Others: *On the New Classes, The Psychology of Form, Introduction to Ethnology, The Great Hope of the Twentieth Century, The Sociology of the Novel.*) In addition, each of the scenes fits into the general plan of twenty-four hours in the life of Juliette Janson: we begin with her one evening, follow her to Paris the next day; at the end of the film she returns home. The

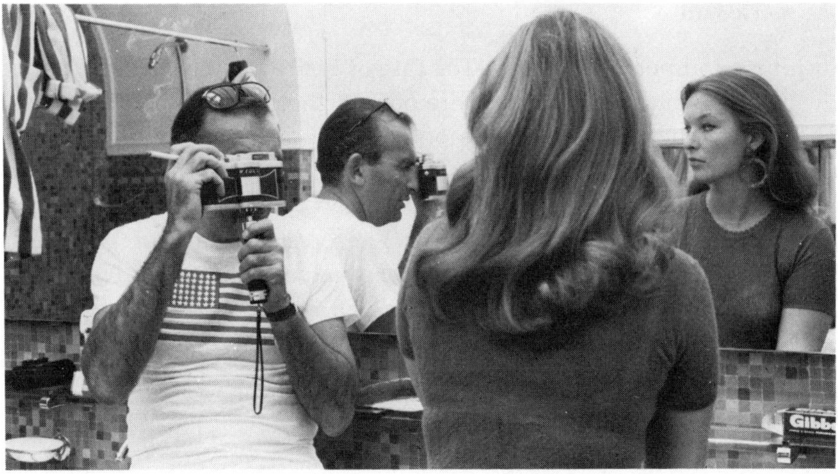

Reading from left to right: The American photo-aggressor with the camera without a lens/Raoul Lévy (a filmmaker himself)/Juliette (Marina Vlady)/Juliette at work.

incidents are explainable in terms of this minimal plot, but the book titles (and other intertitles) call attention to the deeper significances.

Each sequence of the film is a microcosm of Juliette's world, and each provides a new angle of attack for the demonstration of Godard's thesis. The level of discourse shifts often within the sequences as well as between them. In the first scene, for example, Robert (Roger Montsoret) and his friend are listening to "Lyndon Johnson" on the shortwave radio. The words Robert translates for the others are not taken from Johnson's speeches but from a well-known cartoon by Jules Feiffer. At the end of the scene there is a large close-up of the radio equipment which is clouded in the smoke of cigarettes. On the soundtrack: the roar of airplane engines and the thud of bombs. Cut to a violent red and blue sign which fills the screen: MADE IN U.S.A. PRISUNIC A PARTIR DU 16 AVRIL. Then back to the radio equipment "under attack." Godard on the soundtrack: "O, dear George Washington, what madness made you play the cruel role of William Pitt?" Then a new shot: red letters on a white field: PAX. Godard's voice: "Pax Americana . . . Supereconomical brain-washing." Then immediately, a shot of Juliette (Marina Vlady) in her kitchen, surrounded by soap powders. There is a wonderful continuity here—not of plot but of poetic logic. There *is* a connection between soap powders and Vietnam. In 1967 this may have been a difficult train of thought for many to follow; but not today.

The two most significant scenes of the film take place in cafes. Godard's people have always spent much of their time there. They either have no homes, or they live in apartments relatively bare of furniture and personal effects. The cafe or bistro is their meeting place; the meetings, most of the time, are only further evidence of alienation. The first of the two cafe scenes of *2 ou 3 choses* opens with Juliette's definition of herself. She turns to the camera, answering unheard questions and says "To define myself? . . . in one word? 'indifference'!" She talks to her friend for a while. She orders a pack of Winstons. Meanwhile, the pimp, who looks like an advertising executive in suit and tie, is talking in the background with another one of his girls. Juliette orders a Coke. A young woman is smoking, in a reverie. A man reads *France-Soir.* Juliette writes a few words in her notebook. The sound of the pinball machine is abnormally loud. Juliette watches as the young woman thumbs through a magazine—*Lui*—the images of women that we see include one with lips painted with stars and stripes, another, like a cartoon, with a blank balloon issuing from her open mouth. She is wearing a "mod" backless dress. Her breasts are clearly seen. Godard speaks on the soundtrack. He describes the scene we are looking at. Then there is a series of quick shots, each one a closer enlargement of a coffee cup, until finally the cup fills the center of the scope image. Godard:

> Perhaps an object like this will make it possible to link up . . . , to move from one subject to another, from living in society, to being together. But then, since social relationships are always ambiguous, since my thought is only a unit, . . . since an immense moat separates the subjective certitude that I have for myself from the objective truth that I am for others, since I never stop finding myself guilty, even though I feel innocent, since every event transforms my daily life, since I always seem to fail to communicate. . . . since . . . since . . . since I can't tear myself away from the objectivity that crushes me, nor from the subjectivity that isolates me, since it isn't possible for me either to raise myself into Being, or to fall into Nothingness . . . , it's necessary that I listen, it's necessary that I look around me more than ever . . . the world . . . my fellow creatures . . . my brothers . . .

This is not a film talking, it is a man. It is the most personal—and most painful—moment in all of Godard. Poets sometimes speak this privately and directly to us; filmmakers seldom do. All the while, the eloquent, liquescent, shimmering black coffee swirls in the swollen cup. The spoon stirs the sugar, the sharp light refracts in the bubbles that form, turn slowly, slowly on the surface, and then annihilate themselves, the currents calm, the turbulence clears. Cut to a shot of the man smoking a cigarette, in profile, Juliette watching from behind, out of focus. Street sounds. The pinball machine. Then silence. Extreme closeup of the bubbles in the coffee. Godard continues:

The café universe. (Frame enlargement.)

> . . . the world today, alone, where revolutions are impossible, where bloody wars haunt me, where capitalism isn't even sure of its rights . . . and the working class is in retreat . . . where progress . . . the thundering progress of science gives to future centuries an obsessive, haunting presence . . . where the future is more present than the present, where distant galaxies are at my door [the coffee looks like galaxies]. "My fellow creatures . . . my brothers."

The man looks at Juliette. An extreme close-up as a piece of sugar tumbles into the coffee and breaks into showering crystals. The circle of the cup scintillates with bubbles. Godard concludes:

> But where to begin? But where to begin with what? . . . We could say that the limits of language are the limits of the world . . . that the limits of my language are the limits of my world. And in that respect, I limit the world, I decide its boundaries. And when logical, mysterious death finally abolishes these limits . . . and when there are, then, neither questions nor answers . . . , everything will be out of focus. But if, by chance, things become clear again, they would only be so through the phantom of conscience. Then, everything would connect.[42]

Slowly the coffee has become clear again. A few more seconds of the image, calm now. Cut.

Godard's pensive, restive, ineffable coffee cup does make it possible to "link up, to move from one subject to another." It is the bridge between poetics and politics. After telling us two or three things that he knows about her, Godard decides to listen more, to look around him more. He is finished with film as an end in itself. He moves on to film as a means to another, larger end, "a new world where people and things would find harmony among themselves."

A bit later in the film, Godard finds a trope through which he can express this confusion of "dead objects, always alive" with "live people, often already dead." It is late in the afternoon. Juliette has gone to visit her husband at the gas station where he works. A red car, a profusion of signs. An extreme close-up of the gas pump as it adds up the price, running quickly from F13.20 to F16.45. Godard:

> It is 16:45 [4:45 p.m.]. Should I speak of Juliette or these leaves? Since it is impossible, any way, to do justice to them both . . . let us say that both tremble gently at the end of an October afternoon.[43]

The camera zooms slowly into the leaves of the trees. Cut. The world of things, the world of human beings. Godard has given us the "things' side of things" in hopes that we can puzzle out the people as well.

The second cafe scene occurs two-thirds of the way through the film. We are coming out of that moment of paralysis. The film is opening up. The cafe is more active. Robert is talking to a young woman he has just met. (Juliet Berto in her first appearance, an echo of Karina.) She asks him a few questions as he writes in his notebook. He replies abruptly. She decides to ignore him. His interest is piqued. "Don't you have anything else to say to me?" "No . . . not especially . . . and you?" They talk about the weather. They talk about talking about the weather. His explanation for the trend of the conversation: "Me, I think that in movies you never quite get to speak the truth. That's what I would like to do with you."[44] We are back to the beginning: the idle talk of the first approach between two people. They talk about sex. They talk about talking about sex.

Meanwhile, another young woman is sitting with a writer, asking him to explain Communism to her, while two men, identified as Bouvard and Pécuchet (Flaubert's characters who wanted to absorb all knowledge) sit in the corner, behind a mound of books, picking phrases at random from them, tying them together, as "one subject links up with another," aleatorically. Godard has triangulated the problems of communication: first, sexual; second, political; third, artistic.

The tempo of the film picks up. A black man and woman make love quickly. Juliette and Robert leave the service station in their red Austin. A shot of a cashier at the Prisunic. A huge housing development. An interview with some children. Juliette and Robert return home. Christophe reads his composition to his mother, which explains why it is possible to be friendly with some girls but not with others ("Some girls are very nice, very honest"). Robert and Juliette put the children to bed. For the first time in Godard, we are seeing a family, all together. Yes,

Domicile conjugal in the new Paris: Vance Packard meets the fashion magazines; the hand struggles to pull Robert and Juliette together.

it's true, there is no love apparent among them, but they are a family, nevertheless. The last scene: Juliette and Robert in bed—she in blue, he in white, the blanket is red—under the painting of the hand grasping the edges of two abstract profiles (or squeezing the space between them) which perfectly summarizes the film. Juliette smokes a cigarette. Godard speaks. We watch an extreme close-up of the cigarette as it dies down, then glows again as Juliette smokes. Godard:

> I listen to the ads on my transistor . . . thanks to Esso I'm happily on my way, on the route of dreams, and I'm forgetting the rest. I'm forgetting Hiroshima . . . I'm forgetting Auschwitz . . . I'm forgetting Budapest . . . I'm forgetting Vietnam . . . I'm forgetting the housing crisis.[45]

He cuts to a group of household products on the grass, looking like the isolated, blockish apartment houses and office buildings which have been the world of the film: Lava, Omo, Dash, Ajax, Schick, Lucky Strike. Godard:

> I've forgotten everything, except that, since I've gotten back to zero, it will be necessary to start over again from there.

Juliette, the apartment complex, prostitution as a way of life, the magazines, the radio, the cafes, the gas station, the road, the noise of construction, the noise of the pinball machines, the children, the posters, the painting, Robert, Marianne, canned goods, detergents, the coffee cup, the cigarette end—objective description of objects, of subjects; subjective description of subjects, of objects. The search for structures. Life. The job is complete. La Capitale de la douleur has become La Capitale des choses. Ponge had written,

> Out of the typographical thickets that constitute a poem, on the road that leads neither beyond things, nor towards the spirit, certain fruits are formed from an agglomeration of spheres that a drop of ink fills up.[46]

Aragon, who had followed a road from art to politics similar to Godard's, said of him:

> The disorder of our world is his raw material—all this shantytown of our lives without which we couldn't live, but which we manage not to see. And of this, as of accidents and murders, he creates beauty.[47]

9

GODARD
Returning to Zero (Picture and Act)

The films Godard made in 1965 and 1966 were informed by a harrowing vision of his own existential situation. He was enveloped by structures, both political and esthetic, which appeared increasingly meaningless and destructive. They truly oppressed him. He was at sea in a phenomenological nightmare: things bore down on him with the weight of their Being while people were depersonalized, vapid, ephemeral. A cup of coffee, a cigarette become more poignant, more affective than a human face. *2 ou 3 choses que je sais d'elle,* for example, ends with an ironic *Déjeuner sur l'herbe* in which the characters are consumer products. Godard also felt the pressure of the filmmaker's responsibility. The more he learned about images and sounds, the more he understood how false they were. The harder he tried to find the right combination of tropes to express what he felt and thought, the more obvious it became that the precision he strove for would never be achieved; his art was out of joint. It was the dilemma of the critic as artist, not content simply to make art, but always analyzing what he has done: practice never catches up with theory.

In his most accessible films, he was content to use the traditional forms to try to convey the texture of this particular anxiety. But they were never sufficient. Rather than static, romantic evocations of mood and spirit, Godard wanted dynamic, logical analysis of the situation. Like Brecht, he wanted his art to be active. Love and conversation may have value in themselves, but as in the theorem he expounded in "Anticipation," they should lead, as well, to measurable progress. Hence, the experiments with the stricter, more active form of the essay—*La Femme mariée, Masculin-féminin,* and finally *2 ou 3 choses.*

But each time, no matter what the mode, the questions the films raised outnumbered their tentative answers. It became increasingly obvious to Godard that they were only attempts at cinema, not complete or finished; and therefore the idea of the *attempt* would loom ever larger in his work from now on (see, especially, *Letter to Jane,* pp. 245–50). What this meant in practical terms is that each film would include its own "autocritique," it would have an evident dialectical relationship with itself, and therefore the elusive specter of the "complete film," the *finished* product, would recede. The apologias of the later films sometimes seem superfluous—they are often annoying to new audiences—but they are necessary in this scheme. One has to understand Godard's own reaction to the films that came before to grasp fully the purpose of the films that come after. There are only two dramas in the films Godard made after 1966: first, the battle to find a politics that will make life livable; second, Godard's own personal semiological battle with the medium of film.

2 ou 3 choses que je sais d'elle was Godard's last attempt at a comprehensive summary of these concerns, just as *Made in U.S.A.* was his last venture into fiction. *2 ou 3 choses* had made all the connections that Godard found possible: politics were people, culture was architecture, feelings were objects, esthetics were ethics. He had caught the pure rhythms of the *temps morts* out of which we weave most of our days and had effectively made the equation between people and environment—buildings, machines, rooms, products, highways, clothing, signs, gauges. The life of those "things" had been captured and the relationships between people had been adequately described in terms of negative space.

But after *2 ou 3 choses,* what? Godard had closed the door on pure fiction. He could have left cinema altogether to work in politics, but, as he was to express it later, there was a certain moral imperative that he use the knowledge and talents that he had been given. And, anyway, there was still the lurking suspicion that he could not survive without film, either as artist, thinker, or militant. The obvious solution was to investigate politics through film. Which he did, of course, but in his own particular way. He did not make documentaries or cinéma-vérité, nor did he turn to political melodrama of the sort that Costa-Gavras was rediscovering at about this time and which became a popular mode of expression for quite a few French, German, and Italian filmmakers during the next few years. Instead, he continues to make self-conscious "Godardian" essays about politics—or, perhaps, his own relationship to politics.

As always, Godard was a little in advance of cultural and political trends, so that the four films he made during 1967 set themselves apart. It is not inappropriate to look at the features (as Richard Roud does) as a trilogy which mirrors the trilogy that preceded them. Like *Masculin-féminin, La Chinoise* is about the culture of the generation that succeeded Godard's and focuses on a group. *Weekend,* like *Made in U.S.A.,* has fictional overtones and depends on a large measure of fantasy for its effect. As their English titles indicate, they are also both about the Americanization and embourgeoisement of French life. Finally, *Le Gai Savior* might just as easily have been called *2 ou 3 choses que je sais d'elle;* both are profoundly personal and intensely epistemological.

La Chinoise, ou plutôt à la chinoise, un film en train de se faire, to give it its full title, is a film "about a Chinese woman, or rather, the Chinese style: a film in the process of making itself." A tentative film: an ambiguous essay, a "try." "We must oppose vague thoughts with clear images," reads one of the slogans painted on the walls: it is a good motto for *La Chinoise.* The ideas are not so much vague as preliminary. Godard is no longer a tourist in the city of youth as he was in *Masculin-féminin;* he is now an invited immigrant settler who is about to marry one of them, Anne Wiazemsky, La Chinoise herself. (As Karina had played Veronica in her first film, so Wiazemsky plays Véronique in her debut with Godard.) But there is an ambiguity about the politics of the film which led, when it was released, to its being condemned with equal fervor by both the French Communist Party (P.C.F.) and the Maoists. Clearly, the film is sympathetic to the aims of "cellule *Aden-Arabie*" (they name their collective after a novel by Paul Nizan). Yet one of the group of five, it turns out, is a revisionist, another is a romantic suicide, and the single concrete action of the group is performed by an individual—and bungled. Véronique, the leader, mistakes apartment number 23 for 32 and kills the wrong man. Finally, we discover that this activist commune is only a vacation bungalow, a bourgeois apartment borrowed without their knowledge from parents of a friend. It seems as if the *Aden-Arabie* collective is only playing at revolution, and they aren't very successful, even at that.

There are several ways to explain this ambiguity:

- first, as critics of the right, left, and center (we'll put the P.C.F. at the center) all charged: Godard himself was only playing at revolution; he was a dilettante who didn't really believe in the politics of the "groupuscule";

- second: Godard was criticizing les Chinois from the perspective of the P.C.F., which is represented in the film by Francis Jeanson and Henri, the revisionist;
- third: Godard thought he was making a film in favor of the Maoists, but unconsciously revealed his own fears of commitment;
- fourth: Godard was constructing a Brechtian distancing machine so that the questions he raised would of necessity have to be discussed by the audience and answered.

There may be some merit in the first three explanations, but they are not, I think, worth elaborating on if there is any truth at all in the fourth explanation. They are the province of "intentional criticism" which seeks to find reasons outside the film for elements which exist within it. The fourth "explanation" rather invites a dialogue with the film. There are several keys within the film to assure us that this is what Godard is about. One is Véronique's dissertation on how it is possible to do two things at once (see below). Another is the prominence of Brechtian thought. In the first extended sequence, Guillaume talks about his function in the film (he is speaking in response to a question from Godard):

> . . . you believe that I'm playing the clown because I'm in the process of making a film, or because there are technicians around me *(a quick shot of Coutard at the camera),* but not at all. It's because there's a camera in front of me that I'm sincere.

Then Guillaume paraphrases in his own way what he calls "a very beautiful passage from Althusser on one of Brecht's plays":

> I turn around and suddenly—irresistibly—the question confronts me: [what] if these several words which I've just read in my maladroit, blind fashion, were nothing else but fragments of a huge, unknown play happening inside myself—me, a worker in the theatre of the world—their sense still unknown. . . . That's why I speak. *(A shot of Réné Levert, the sound man. A shot of Coutard.)*
> GODARD'S VOICE: Cut. Very good.[1]

We should ask the same question. This film in the process of making itself does not show us "reality," but insists that we use it as an instrument of discovery. "Le réalisme, ce n'est pas comment sont les choses vraies, mais comment sont vraiement les choses," Godard quoted Brecht.* *La Chinoise* is meant to be *used;* it doesn't *present* a truth, it *leads* to it.

How can we use it? The film gives us a set of contradictions which we must resolve. Mao said:

> We are confronted by two types of social contradictions—those between ourselves and the enemy and those among the people themselves. The two are totally different in their nature.[2]

The main reason the film has been misunderstood is that people expected Godard to deal with the first type of contradiction when he was really exclusively concerned with the second. (In fact, this is true of nearly all the films that follow with the possible exceptions of *Weekend* and *Tout va Bien.*) In other words, he doesn't make propaganda, he makes Brechtian *Lehrstücke*—teaching-pieces—for those who are already committed to the struggle.

La Chinoise focuses on two precise contradictions: the first, the question of violence, was the most immediate argument separating the old French left from the new at the time. The second, how to achieve stability and solidarity within the groupuscule, was going to prove, in the years that followed the euphoria of 68, one of the main problems of the left. This is not the analysis of a dilettante. The film also focuses our attention, historically, on the students of the University of Nanterre who, precisely a year after it was made, were to find themselves in the avant-garde of the events of May 1968. The film opened in New York only a few weeks before the symbolic uprising at Columbia University that year, and Godard was happy to hear that many Columbia students had seen it. Coincidence? Well, probably; but such coincidences certainly speak well of Godard's political acumen.

The "cellule *Aden-Arabie*" is composed of five members, only one of whom—Véronique, La Chinoise—has the kind of hard-headed, thorough-going commitment to the revolution that we might expect to be archetypal of the New Left. The others—Guillaume, an actor (and still a romantic), Henri, the revisionist and worker at the Institute for Economics, Kirilov, the painter and suicide, and Yvonne, a peasant from the provinces who has been a hooker for a while—provide a broad and humanized spectrum. The main problem that confronts the group is to find a common bond and the stability that comes with it. They never quite do. In the end, Véronique is left alone to return to the university. Guillaume and Yvonne have gone off to make political theatre (as

*"Realism isn't about how things are real, but about how things really are."

The image analyzes: this is one frame from the tracking shot past the windows that give onto the balcony to the real world where the Aden-Arabie collective exercises. To the left, Véronique (Anne Wiazemsky) and Henri (Michel Semeniako), the more highly politicized members; to the right Guillaume (Jean-Pierre Léaud) and Yvonne (Juliet Berto), the less committed gauchistes.

indeed Léaud and Berto did in real life), Henri is ousted, and Kirilov (Lex de Bruïjn) is dead.

The question of the usefulness of violence as a tactic receives more explicit attention. Henri represents one pole of the contradiction: he is against it, on humanist terms. Kirilov represents the other: he has a Dostoevskian obsession with self-destruction. Véronique is in the middle, cool and logical. The argument is played out for us almost in cinéma-vérité in the long scene in which Anne Wiazemsky discusses the issue with Francis Jeanson. Jeanson, like Henri before him, is no theory-ridden clay pigeon. He makes some excellent points and, indeed, within the limits of the film, could be said to win the discussion. Véronique doesn't have as sure a grasp of the theory. But she shares with her generation an intuitive grasp of the necessity of violence. Yet, since May 68 ultimately failed, Jeanson may be correct in practice as well as theory. What is important is that the discussion still provokes argument and analysis. Again, the film doesn't force a point of view, but sets up the contradictions so that we may better examine them. Earlier, Véronique has spoken of "the analysis of contradictions inherent in things and in phenomena." Yvonne, who is the least politically-minded of the group, asks why it is necessary to analyze.

And Henri answers quietly, "Because, in this world, things are complex and many factors go into their determination." It is a key that *La Chinoise* is not so simple as it seems.

There is much material in the film having to do with film, theatre, art and their relationship with politics. *La Chinoise* has a relatively narrow field of inquiry for Godard—more than two-thirds of the film takes place in the apartment whose walls are progressively covered with quotations—but the metaphor of theatre and film is very much present, even if less insistent than before. Godard explained this aspect of the film in a 1967 interview. His interlocutors had asked him how he felt about the influence of structuralism and semiology on film criticism, and Godard had replied to the effect that most of it was too dry, lifeless, and speciously theoretical (although he found Metz "the easiest to like of them all: because he actually goes to movies; he really likes movies"). This led him into a discussion of arguments he had had with various people regarding *La Chinoise,* especially one in which he had been reproached for "talking 'in examples.'" Philippe Sollers

> said I kept saying "it's the same thing as," or "it's like." But I don't talk "in examples," I talk in shots, like a movie-maker. So I just had no way to get him to understand me. I'd have had to make a movie we could have talked about afterwards. What it signifies on the screen for him is maybe what "signifies it" for me.[3]

In other words, there is a basic confusion (on Sollers's part and on the part of much of Godard's audience) between the value of the *signifier* and the value of the *signified.* No one before Godard had tried to make the medium of film serve such complex constellations of meaning; much of that meaning is contained in the shape of the discourse, not in the object of the discourse. It is necessary to "read" Godard's films (especially from this point on), the way Louis Althusser (whom Godard quotes several times in *La Chinoise*) talks about "reading" Marx in his book *Lire le Capital.* Specifically, Marx (and Godard) should be understood through "symptomatic reading" *(lecture symptomale)* which, as opposed to "superficial reading," discovers the "unconsciousness" of the text and sees it in terms of its "problematic" (the theoretical or ideological framework). Symptomatic reading shows us the text that is not there (the shape of the discourse) as well as the one which is and analyzes the mechanism which produces the split between what we might call the "text" and the "anti-text." *La Chinoise* is a film "en train de se faire," which means we had better be willing to participate in that process; *La Chinoise* is not an end, but a means.

The presence of actors as actors and material about cinema and film reconfirms that fact. Kirilov quotes Paul Klee: "Art doesn't reproduce the visible, it makes visible what isn't." Véronique explains how it is possible to do two things at once when she tells Guillaume (whose last name, by the way, is Meister) that she doesn't love him any more: "I no longer love your face, I no longer love your eyes, I no longer love your mouth, I no longer love the color of your sweaters," she says while she plays a record of romantic music. The point is that Guillaume should listen to the music, not the words: "Music and words," she says. *"It's necessary to struggle on two fronts."*[4] (This phrase will become a refrain for Godard.) Music? Godard was interested to hear that Jacques Demy had liked *Made in U.S.A.* "The movie *Made in U.S.A.* resembles most is *Les Parapluies de Cherbourg,*" Godard commented. "The actors don't sing but the movie does."[5]

La Chinoise is a group song. It has a melodic line. Even the titles lead us along: several of them build slowly. First, an intertitle that makes the statement "The Imperialists still live." A bit later, "The Imperialists still live, they continue to force." Still later, "The imperialists still live, they continue to force their reign." Five titles later: "The Imperialists still live. They continue to force their arbitrary reign in Asia, Africa, and Latin America. In the East, they still oppress the popular masses of the respective countries. This situation . . ." Four more titles slowly build this last sentence. The effect is to force the idea of linear incremental logic. Technically, Godard leads us in this direction with the long lateral tracking shots on the balcony of the apartment, which force us to pay attention not to what we see but to what it means. We have to build on them. Likewise, Godard's camera refuses on occasion to follow the action—actors leave the frame, re-enter, go out the other side. The camera waits for them. This both calls attention to the environment rather than the actor and gives us room to think while the actor is off-screen. Like the sound of Godard's muted voice on the soundtrack and the shots of the clapper boards, the effect is to distance. We must take part, "fill in the blanks," ourselves. The techniques of distancing are often misunderstood as functioning to alienate the audience; but that was not at all what Brecht had in mind.

Finally, Godard invents dramatic tropes to fit this cinematic tone of voice. The greatest of these in *La Chinoise* is clearly the blackboard filled with names, each of which—in his own order—Guillaume slowly erases, until only Brecht is left. Goethe, Voltaire, Feydeau, Duras, Cocteau, Sophocles, Adamov, Dumas, Kleist, Montherlant, Giraudoux, Labiche, Genet, Racine, Williams, Sartre, Lorca, Beaumarchais all disappear, their existence negated, as Guillaume conscientiously returns

Guillaume begins to erase names: "a film in the process of making itself." And a politics of art, as well.

to zero. The effect is stunning. It reverses the great catalogue of *Les Carabiniers*.

As a political act, then, how does *La Chinoise* measure up? First, even Godard admits that it does not deal precisely with the most important, relevant contemporary issues. "I say it over and over again, the one movie that really ought to have been made in France this year," he told *Cahiers*, "is a movie on the strikes at Rhodiacéta." But Godard doesn't know that world; he is completely isolated from it. The workers would have had to make the film themselves. That compartmentalization of society is one of the main subjects of *La Chinoise*. Véronique outlines the contradictions: "one, the difference between manual and intellectual labor; two, between city and country; and three, between agriculture and industry."[6] But Godard can't deal with those contradictions concretely. He is in the position of the scholar who knows in his heart that the true duty of an intellectual is "haute vulgarisation" but who can't, try as he will, write a book that is a best-seller. He has isolated himself by thinking too well, in too much detail, and can speak only to professionals who have learned the language he has had to invent to deal with phenomena that have never before been discussed. "Union militants have realized," Godard said, "that men aren't equal if they don't earn the same pay; they've got to realize that we aren't equal if we don't speak the same language."[7] This is the primary dilemma for all Godard's political films. But it is a question for us as well as for him. If he doesn't make films (as Ken Loach, for example, does) that can be apprehended by the people who are actively involved in the struggle; if his films don't lead directly to political action, nevertheless they provide a wealth of information on the structures of politics (and their relation to the structures of art and communication) which we are just now beginning to assimilate.

Véronique speaks quietly at the end of the film:

> When summer ended, classes started again, and so did the struggle, for me and many of my comrades. But, on the other hand, I had fooled myself. I believed I had made a great leap forward, but I understood now that I had only made the first timid steps of a very long march.[8]

The last title of the film: END OF A BEGINNING.

"Caméra-oeil" ("Camera-Eye"), the episode Godard contributed to the collective film *Loin du Vietnam (Far from Vietnam)*, made in the summer of 1967, gives us a more detailed analysis of what Godard means when he talks about the "cultural prisons" that prevent him, as filmmaker, from producing active, direct cinema. How does one make a film about Vietnam? *Loin du Vietnam*, which was organized by Chris Marker, and on which Resnais, William Klein, Joris Ivens, Agnès Varda, and Claude Lelouch also worked (along with many of the best-known technicians of French film), is a collection of approaches to political filmmaking. It gives us the necessary statistics; the obligatory scenes of carnage and suffering; scenes of the people fighting back; a "flashback" which outlines the historical situation; an interview with a Vietnamese woman who lives in Paris; a song by Tom Paxton; scenes of the April 15, 1967, peace march in New York City and demonstrations in Paris; shots of American bombers taking off from carriers; and an interview with the widow of Norman Morrison, one of the first Americans to immolate himself in protest against the war.

The two most complex sequences of the film—and the two which take its title most literally—are those by Godard and Resnais. There is no evidence that they conferred beforehand, but there are surprising parallels between their sequences. Resnais gives us the only acted sequence (though Godard's may be considered to be acted): Claude Ridder, a writer, has been assigned to review Herman Kahn's notorious book *On Escalation*. In a monologue he explains why he won't review the book. "It's all very complicated," he says. The narrator tells us that Ridder is "the honest voice of Bad Conscience, that is, of Bad Faith." And the episode clearly demonstrates that peculiar mind-set that intellectuals use as an excuse for inaction. We are angry with Claude Ridder, and our disgust with his philosophical waffling is only increased by later episodes, which speak of Norman Morrison's sacrifice, from a Vietnamese point of view and from Morrison's widow's perspective—an example of *complete* commitment: the ultimate act of sacrifice, whatever else we may think of it.

But Godard's segment follows Resnais's directly. Godard is seen standing next to a huge Mitchell camera which is fitted with two lamps, almost like eyestalks. There are shots of the mechanism of the camera as it starts and stops, the lights going on and off, Godard operating the pan and tilt controls (as if it were an antiaircraft gun), some scenes from *La Chinoise,* some from North Vietnam, and at least one shot (a 360° circular track around a Vietnamese soldier) that was apparently taken especially for "Caméra-oeil." Most of the footage, however, shows us Godard at the camera, in profile, as he speaks to us.

He begins by narrating some war experiences.

> What terrifying explosions *(sound effects).* If I'd been a cameraman for ABC in New York or San Francisco, that's what I would have filmed. . . . but I live in Paris. . . . Last year I tried to go to North Vietnam *(shots of Vietnamese children),* . . . it took eight months for them to turn me down. . . . [they must have thought] I was a guy whose ideology was a bit vague . . . they couldn't trust me. I guess they were right. . . . It's difficult making movies in France. I was going to go to Cuba or Algeria, but I decided not to. *(Scenes from* La Chinoise: *the puppet theatre.)* . . . It is difficult to talk about bombs when you haven't experienced them. I realized that as a Parisian I should make films in Paris. . . . I thought of using a woman's nude body, and then showing in the style of Robbe-Grillet (or Flaubert, because I don't really like Robbe-Grillet) what fragmentation bombs would do to it . . . but it took special effects . . . it wasn't natural. . . . I wanted to show everything—defoliation, etc. . . . But we are far away, so the best we can do is make films—let Vietnam invade us—come in to our everyday lives, instead of invading Vietnam with our own sensibilities. Instead of our invading them with a generosity we impose, we should let them invade us and see what happens.

Godard is obviously in a position quite similar to Claude Ridder's. Those who find him a dilettante in matters of politics will seize on this episode of confession as proof of their analysis. Yet, Godard has a valid point to make—a political point. There is no doubt about the high level of his commitment; he has given up enough over the years, materially, to prove his intentions. What may be in doubt is his effectiveness; and he may doubt it as well as his critics. He quotes Che next: "Let us create 2, 3, many Vietnams," speaks of the strikes at Rhodiacéta as an example of what French filmmakers should really be about, and plaintively concludes:

> I am cut off from the working class but my struggle against American movies is related, yet workers don't come to see my films. It is a split like our split with Vietnam. We are all in cultural prisons.

Godard's anguish for at least the next six years, will be that he cannot find a way to increase communication between these cultural prisons. In his own quirky, intriguing way he can demonstrate his solidarity with the people who are engaged in concrete struggles—with the Vietnamese, with the French working class, with the students of the left, with the Chicago Eight, with black militants, with radical filmmakers, even with the troubadours of rock and roll—but he can never quite find the precise methods that would allow him to serve them broadly, to make cinema which would be wholly active, not contemplative. There is a sorrowful line of isolation that runs straight from "Caméra-oeil" to *Letter to Jane* (with its similar gestalt), five years later.

Weekend, which was shot during September and October of 1967, is subtitled "A Film Lost in the Cosmos" and "A Film Found on the Scrap-heap." In the tradition of *Made in U.S.A.* and *Alphaville* it is a static, distanced portrait of an absurd, Americanized society. It is also, strangely enough, very nearly a comedy. It does not significantly advance the political theory that was beginning to develop in *La Chinoise*. The absurd bourgeois universe of Corinne and Roland with its inimitable mix of sex and consumer capitalism is reminiscent of the cocktail party of *Pierrot le fou* and the general milieu of *La Femme mariée*. (We are reminded that Godard has seldom dealt with bourgeois characters unless they were in rebellion against their society and outside of it.)

Most of all, *Weekend* reminds us of the closed universe of Claude Chabrol. Jean Yanne, who made one of his first appearances in the film, went on in the next few years to do several important films for Chabrol, and I think it is not accidental that Paul Gégauff (Chabrol's perennial scriptwriter) appears in the film as well, for *Weekend* strips naked for us the heart of Chabrol's world: the violent, demonic, and destructive forces which the shimmering veneer of bourgeois civilized manners is barely able to hide from our view. Chabrol, in the numerous films which fit this pattern, delights in the dialectic relationship between the patina of manners and the crudeness of the violence that lurks underneath.

Many films have made a good deal of money by pleasantly shocking the very class they pretend to satirize. The tradition of *épater les bourgeois* is an old one. Godard's problem with *Weekend,* then, is how

to avoid being co-opted. His tactics are twofold. Fir
revolutionaries of the second half of the film aga
world of Corinne (Mireille Darc) and Roland (Jean Y
in the first half. As Kalfon says, "We can only ov
the bourgeoisie by even more horror." The reason
of the bourgeoisie are so readily and pleasurably c
class is just that they—unlike *Weekend*—pose the proble
terms. The characters on the screen, for whom we develop natural contempt are then easily seen as "others," not "ourselves." The presence of the revolutionaries in *Weekend* forces a bourgeois audience to see the film from the point of view of Corinne and Roland. Second, Godard has tried to ensure the *affect* of the film by exaggerating the violence of his images. The cannibalism of the revolutionaries, the pornography (a fish shoved up a vagina, Corinne's opening monologue), the blunt language, the blood, the sacrifice of animals (the skinned rabbit, the slitting of the pig's throat) are all meant to serve as barriers against the film's co-optation. This second tactic is not so effective. With a huge irony Godard must appreciate, it is just these elements of the film which have become commonplaces in bourgeois cinema since 1968. Godard had underestimated the capacity of that class for self-mutilation and, as a result, *Weekend* is now an unintentional landmark in the history of contemporary grand guignol: animal slaughter, sexual self-abasement, blood, and cannibalism have become valuable commodities in the marketplace.

In addition, because Godard is, after all, motivated by humane, moral concerns, he does not really exploit the psychic violence of the film. The blood is obviously fake (there are theoretical esthetic reasons for this—but ethics is the esthetics of the future); the pornography has a point: to give the film a dark and forbidding vision. As Kalfon explains at the end of the film, speaking, I think, for Godard,

> [There is] a boundless horror which man feels for others of his species. Perhaps I may be wrong when I say this. But perhaps I may be right too. . . . I know that there must probably exist a more terrible affliction than the swollen eyes which come from meditating on the strangeness of man's nature, but I have yet to discover it.[9]

Gros Poucet, one of the "imaginary characters" whom Roland and Corinne encounter in the middle of their journey, further explains Godard's own attitude to the project of the film: after Roland has immolated Gros Poucet's companion-in-costume, Emily Brontë, Gros Poucet muses,

> d to myself; what's the use of talking to them? They only buy knowl-ge and sell it again. All they're looking for is cheap knowledge they can sell for a higher price. They are determined to win and they are not interested in anything which stands in the way of victory. They don't want to be oppressed, they want to oppress . . . they don't want progress, they want to be first. They will submit to anyone so long as he promises that they can make the laws. What can one say to them? I wondered.[10]

There is a mood of ironic resignation in *Weekend* not dissimilar to that Bertolt Brecht expressed in his poem "Vom Armen B.B." ("Concerning Poor B.B."), which Godard alludes to. Like Brecht, Godard hopes that

> In the earthquakes to come. . . .
> I shan't allow bitterness to quench my cigar's glow.

Weekend is Godard's most desolate film. There is no real political analysis in it; even the word itself is treated contemptuously. In a title, Godard discovers its root by breaking it up:

ANAL

YSIS

and the title itself is shoved up the middle of Corinne's opening monologue. And certainly the F.L.S.O. (Liberation Front of Seine et Oise!) offers no real alternative. They exist (as they themselves seem to know) only as the mirror-image of the obscenity of the bourgeoisie; they are tools for Godard, not, like their predecessors in *La Chinoise*, political characters who describe a concrete problematic so that we can learn from it. In fact, serious politics appears only once in the film: in the scene in which the two garbagemen speak about Black and Arab liberation. But even here, there is more rhetoric than logic. *Weekend* is a farewell dirge. The last title, which intrudes on Corinne and Kalfon as they munch on bits of stewed English tourists, seasoned with the leftovers of Roland, announces:

END OF STORY END OF CINEMA

Yet the ennui with bourgeois cinema that hangs over *Weekend* like a miasma is counterbalanced by a profound comic energy. Before we wind down in the vertiginous territory of the F.L.S.O. Godard indulges himself—as if he knew he might never again have the chance—in cinematic pyrotechnics. The first half of *Weekend* is a black-humorous ode in celebration of the sublime absurdity of the carnage and automania of capitalist civilization.

The film opens quietly enough in a Parisian penthouse. There is some chit-chat dialogue. Then a line slips out—"Wouldn't it be great if when Roland drives your father home, both of them died in an accident?"

asks Corinne's friend.[11] Then, after the main title, we see in the street below that a red Matra coupe has collided with a blue and white Mini. There is much furious honking. One driver leaps out, tears open the other driver's door, and throws a punch. The fight is furious and wild. But we are looking on it from a high angle and we sense the distancing which will suffuse the rest of the film. The next sequence is Corinne's monologue. Dressed in bra and panties, she is sitting on a table, outlined (once again) against a window. Her story of her erotic adventures with Paul, Monique, milk, and eggs (but no butter—butter is left for Bertolucci) is told quietly: narrated, not illustrated. The monologue is bracketed by another violent, slapstick car episode, which ends as Roland drives off, tires squealing. The adventure has begun.

Next the centerpiece of the film and one of the most exhilarating sequences in all of Godard: a slow, deliberate tracking shot down a country road jammed with stalled cars, which lasts more than seven minutes. There is an ear-splitting symphony of horns to accompany the shot as we move with stately pace past men playing cards on the hood of their car; a man playing catch with a boy standing up through a sunroof; a crashed car lying upside down; a crowd of kids running around; a traveling circus (monkeys, lions, a llama); an empty bus; a horse and cart; some schoolchildren; more ballplayers; a Dauphine which has smashed into a tree; a huge red and yellow gas tank truck; a white Fiat coupe; people playing chess; more cardplayers; a man in oilskins in his yacht on a trailer hauling up sails; a driver urinating; and then finally, the cause of the jam, a majestic multiple crash: a collage of color, crumpled steel, broken bodies, and blood.

The wonderful humor of this tableau vivant depends on how we read the sequence. Essential to our sense of it is a consciousness of the deliberate pace of the track, the cinematic equivalent of a yarn-spinner taking his own time with a well-polished shaggy-dog story. The shot moves forward (following Roland's car as he tries to circumvent the jam on the far shoulder of the road), but the action does not. In *La Chinoise*, Godard's first experiment with the long tracking shot had been "edited," in effect, by the frames of the windows which gave onto the terrace. But now he has found a way to make the shot edit itself; each car is a new "frame," a new focus of interest. The tension between the action (or lack of it) and the movement of the camera is the source of the humor, which is as cinematic as it is cosmic.

Several other evocations of automaniacal carnage follow, but none is quite so exhilarating as this seven-minute track. The whole film is pervaded by this bemused sense of wonder at the havoc it surveys; Godard maintains a distance from it all. Chaplin had said: "Tragedy is close-up, comedy is long-shot." Close-ups had been vitally important to nearly every one of Godard's previous films. *Weekend*, however, depends almost exclusively on full- and long-shots. They are images of finality: cinema is riding off into the red, blue, and yellow sunset.

Despite its mood of apocalypse, *Weekend* is then nevertheless the kind of film that can stop for a while to listen to Jean-Pierre Léaud sing a telephone message in a glass booth by the side of the road while Roland tries to steal his car (Léaud responds to the attack on his "petite Japonaise," his little Honda, by grabbing a spare tire to use as a shield and brandishing a lug-wrench like a broadsword), or it can pay perfunctory, blunt homage to the Italian lire that co-produced it: Corinne and Roland pass a trio of Italians who intone: *"Siamo gli attori italiani della coproduzione!"* "What are those guys doing?" asks Corinne. "They're the Italian actors in the coproduction," translates Roland.[12] Cut to black—the cinematic equivalent of the comedian's "take." Unlike most of Godard's films of the middle sixties, *Weekend* is also crammed with cinematic references and in-jokes of the sort we associate with the earliest days of the New Wave.

Perhaps it is better to end a discussion of *Weekend* not at the sour end of the film, but rather in the precise middle of it, where Godard has placed the sequence entitled MUSICAL ACTION. Corinne has just "seduced" a truck to stop for them by lying in the middle of the road with her legs spread. The driver will take them to Oinville if they promise to help him with his concert first. Paul Gégauff then proceeds to play a section of Mozart's piano sonata K. 576 in the middle of a barnyard as the camera tracks slowly in a circle around him. Once again, as in the linear shot earlier, the camera is not following the action; it is surveying a scene, examining the fabric of the reality that surrounds Gégauff and his piano and his music. Gégauff is smoking a cigar as he plays. He stops several times to speak to the audience, almost in the manner of Victor Borge:

> Basically, there are two sorts of music: the sort you listen to and the sort you don't. Quite obviously Mozart belonged to the category you listen to. . . . the sort of music people don't listen to is so-called serious modern music.[13]

The single long take encompasses three full circuits of the barnyard; the circular pattern is directly opposed to the linear shot earlier and isolates this sequence-shot from the rest of the film. As Robin Wood notes, it also insists on the "total irrelevance of the Mozart performance—and the Mozartian sensibility—to the world of pile-ups and general disintegration outside."[14] Here is a moment of ironic peace in the still center of the apocalypse; it is also a tribute to a nearly dead past in which the artist was free to retreat from the world, to compose balanced, humane harmonies.

Godard does not give us the end of the world in *Weekend,* but "the end of *our* world" (as Wood notes). Valerie, as she lies dying in Kalfon's arms, sings the *envoi:*

> I want so much for you to realize,
> You whom I shall leave tonight,
> That though one may be suffering agonies,
> Yet still to others all may seem all right.
> With a broken heart one can still smile,
> Apparently indifferent,
> When the last word has to be written,
> In a novel which has come to a . . . bad end.[15]

END OF STORY. END OF CINEMA.

Weekend had been intended as a global portrait and as a political instrument. As a portrait it succeeds, but as a psychological weapon which might shift the level of consciousness of those who watched it, it was not particularly successful. Clearly, something more was needed. It was not going to be possible to make the new cinema by using the language of the old, hence *Le Gai Savoir,* Godard's ultimate effort at "semioclasm."

The French national television network, O.R.T.F., had offered Godard an opportunity to make a television film, and late in 1967 he turned to the task. He shot *Le Gai Savoir* in December 1967 and January 1968, after the intense experiences of *La Chinoise,* "Caméra-oeil," and *Weekend,* and just before the Langlois affair and the events of the spring of 1968—at the last possible moment before contemplation would be overtaken by events and surpassed by action. It is one of his finest films, and also one of his most difficult. The offer from O.R.T.F. was salutary. The new medium would allow him new liberties and force him to redefine his cinema. The small screen would force him to focus on the essential. A straight essay on the order of *Le Gai Savoir* would never have been commercially viable in theatrical cinemas, but the intimate personal nature of television suited the form well. In fact, Godard chose the most common and effective form of television—the interview—as a model for *Le Gai Savoir.* The film is one of the rare examples of the use of the medium of cinema for what is almost pure intellectual discourse. If Godard has filmed a "summa," then this is it; the title of the film expresses the essential spirit of Godard's work as well as any phrase I can think of: Le Gai Savoir, The Joy of Learning.

Emile and Patricia. (Frame enlargement.)

Emile Rousseau (Jean-Pierre Léaud) and Patricia Lumumba (Juliet Berto) stumble over each other one night in a disused television studio. They embark on a series of seven late-night dialogues during which they try to develop a rigorous analysis of the relationship between politics and film. They meet for seven evenings (that is the structure of the film), and more often than not one of them is late (that is its plot). Needless to say, in an hour and a half of film time Godard, Emile, and Patricia cannot give us the kind of detailed, closely reasoned exposition that we (and they) would like to have. What we can expect, however, and what we do get is a filmic summary of the areas that *should* be investigated. *Le Gai Savoir* is a *poetic* essay—qualitative, not quantitative. It is therefore at the same time simple and complex, structured and anarchic, clear and ironic, revealing and confounding. It is, after all, using the language of film to discuss that language, so the meaning will be as much in our response to the totality of the film as in its syllogistic narrative. Because we can't use the convenient shorthand of "character," "plot," and "significance" to describe the film, it is unusually difficult to discuss it in still another medium. Here, for example, is a précis of the "First Night":

> Radio sounds . . . narration: "8,247 frames, 22,243, 72,000, 125,000, . . . about 7,500 feet. 127,000 feet." Patricia comes in (the background is a black void), dressed in red and blue, carrying a clear umbrella with yellow stripes. It is her "anti-nuclear umbrella," she explains. She trips over Emile. He tells us about her, she about him. She is Patricia Lumumba, the Third World delegate to the Citroën plant. He is Emile Rousseau, great-great-grandson of Jean-Jacques. She announces: "I want to learn, to teach myself, to teach everyone that we must turn back against the enemy that weapon with which he attacks us: Language." "We are on TV," he says. "Then let's go into people's homes and ask them what we want to know," she replies. Frame: SAVOIR. Pan to black. A montage of street scenes and pictures ending with the cartoon (p. 211) which "identifies" Godard mathematically with zero. Muddled radio voices. The story of Les Afraniches ("Les Français"), after the "computer mutations." "Let's start from zero," he says. "No," she replies, "it is necessary to return to zero first." It is necessary to dissolve sounds and images in order to analyze them. "Images: we meet them by chance, we don't choose them. Knowledge will lead us to the rules for the *production* of images." "In 'isolate' you have 'island.' We are on an island." Things and phenomena. Video pictures and sounds. "The first year we collect images and sounds and experiment. The second year we criticize all that: decompose them, reduce them, substitute for them, and recompose them. The third year we attempt some small models of reborn film." "It's almost dawn." They walk away, out of the frame. Pictures, streets. Che. Mao.

Static is the metaphor for the film (which this condensed summary of the "First Night" can't convey). What we will be able to seize from this essay will come in bits and pieces, even as it does to Jean-Luc, Emile, and Patricia. They are awash in a bubbling sea of images and sounds, radio static and video ghosts, incessantly bombarded with bits of information, almost all of it designed by the "enemy" to serve its purposes. Patricia and Emile find some precious respite in the dark studio in the quiet of the night. For a while they exist alone in this shimmering black void. There is no horizon, there is no ground level. (There are only three other speaking characters in the film—an old man, a young boy, and a young girl who are interviewed.) But there is always the voice of the narrator (Godard), incessantly commenting on and expanding the logic of the film, his urgent whisper accompanied by the electronic noise that pervades a media-ridden society.

Le Gai Savoir is a quest for the purity and comfort of "zero." There are no reasoned maxims in the film, no directives or conclusions that one could take home and pin on the wall as incentives to action. That kind of work comes later. As the narrator says, "half the shots of this film are missing." They are left to "Bertolucci, Straub, and Glauber-Rocha." "Zero" is the key to the constellation of concepts which is *Le Gai Savoir*.

The metaphor of the film is mathematical—a dialectic of asymptotes, those conceptual lines which curves on an algebraic graph approach but never touch. It is not the *location* which is significant, but the *approach* to it, not the *object*, but the *sign*. "It's necessary," says Emile, "to be very careful not to fall into the ideology of being true-to-life, a trap not always avoided by filmmakers as important as Dreyer, Bresson, Antonioni, Bergman." Again, we remember: "realism does not consist in reproducing reality, but in showing how things really are."

The dialectic out of which will grow our understanding of "how things really are" has three aspects: First, there is the dialectic between Patricia and Emile (the dramatic dialectic we have understood since childhood). Second, there is the dialectic between characters and the narrator-filmmaker. They are his creations, of course, but as soon as they say what he has written for them, it is necessary for them to qualify, react. (This tension is heightened by the history of the film's production. O.R.T.F. rejected the film and later sold it back to Godard. It appears that he edited it sometime *after* the spring of 1968 when his own ideas, we may assume, had changed appreciably. It was not shown publicly until June 1969.) Third is the dialectic between the film and the audience—the most difficult, but in the end the most important. If we become too involved in the *subject* of the argument between Emile and Patricia, then the narrator raises us to another level. If we become fixed in the relationship between the narrator and his invented characters, then the film itself, by its very density and conflation of images and sounds, will distance us. It's essence is process.

In order that we not take the specifics of the film at face value, Godard sets them in a mosaic of fantasy. What do Patricia and Emile do between sessions? One day, "Michel and I are going to steal the dreams of two pop stars and sell them and send the money to North Vietnam." Another day, Patricia is going to bomb an Italian theater because they won't "let films be shown in the original language" (Italian films are almost always post-dubbed). Still another day Patricia is off to show movies to strikers—*Lola Montès* and *The Great Dictator*. Near the end Emile speaking with Patricia's voice explains "how I killed Kennedy on orders from Lautréamont's ghost." At dawn he goes to visit the Bolsheviks Litvinov and Bukovski.

It is necessary above all for Godard that the film not deal with tangible actuality. That would make it just another false mirror of reality. The film must be *presentational*, and avoid the fallacy of the *representational*. It cannot—no film can—reproduce reality honestly. It can only produce itself, and in order for it to do that honestly, it will have to reinvent itself after discovering exactly what it is about the way film is used today that makes it false (*"fauxtographie,"* as the title in *Weekend* has it). Godard's aim, (as always, but here more explicitly) is not to *divorce* film from life, but to *distance* it, so that we can integrate it into our lives. When we see no qualitative difference between film and life, we then have no sense of film *as itself* and it is therefore useless—even insidious. Like *2 ou 3 choses,* this film reminds us that for Godard process is more important than achievement, the questions are more valuable than the answers, and attempts are more admirable than successes. What was the point of all those advisory subtitles—"a film in the process of making itself," "a film lost in the cosmos," "fragments of a film . . ."—if not to insist that we recognize that the films were not complete or "perfect," but only the premises of syllogisms to which we must provide the conclusions?

Godard tells us at the end of *Le Gai Savoir* that he and his film have

> not wished to, cannot wish to, explain the cinema, nor even become the goal it seeks, but more modestly to offer a few effective methods for reaching it. This is not the film which must be made, but shows how, if one is making a film, that film must follow some of the paths indicated here.

This apologia is basic to *Le Gai Savoir* and to the experimental Dziga-Vertov films that follow. It also represents one of the main reasons why people find these films tedious. In order to appreciate what Godard is up to after 1968, I think it's necessary to understand and accept the logical and psychological premises that led Godard to give us this warning. It will be repeated in each of the Dziga-Vertov films and will reach a self-parodic climax in the introduction to *Letter to Jane,* in which Godard spends nearly half the time of the film cautioning us to approach its substance with care and reservation.

Is this just evidence of Godard's own anxiety and sense of inadequacy in the face of the task he has set for himself (a task, we should remind ourselves, that many people regard as abstract and futile)? In a way, I suppose it is, but we think of it as such only when we don't share Godard's passion for the semioclasmic work of rebuilding cinema. We might as well charge Pirandello, Brecht, or Beckett with small-mindedness: they did the same kind of work in the theatre. As intellectually distant as it may seem, *Le Gai Savoir* is also an impassioned cri de coeur. This is dangerous ground, returning to zero. As Richard Roud points out, "It takes great effort to look at everything afresh, to call everything, even words, into question."[16] Our wonder is not that Godard made this film (and the ones which follow it), but that he survived the experience. Roud, who has a healthy ambivalence about

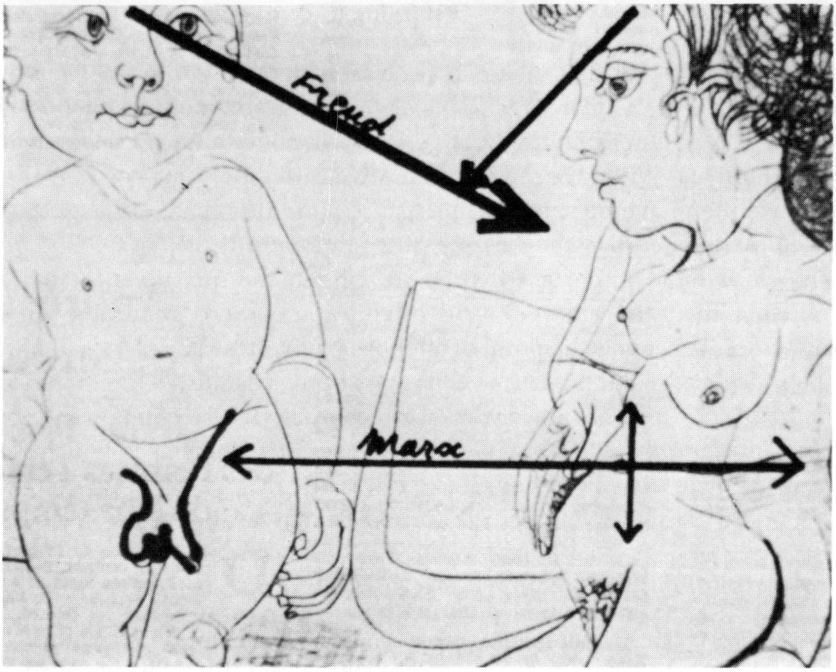

The intersections of Freud, Marx, and Picasso: "a constant current between man's biological nature and his intellectual construction." (Frame enlargement.)

the film, also wonders whether its austerity is entirely due to its ideological premises and function. He suggests that it might also be "a kind of psychological despoiling, a masochistic denuding."[17] It is; that is part of its strategy. The primal question Godard raises—how is it possible to make films (or any other art) that are honest and life-affirmative?—is maddeningly elusive. We prefer not to *think* about all that. We would rather just go ahead making films. Aren't questions like that, after all, the province of wizened professionals and deadly critics?

Maybe so. Yet for Godard, the very existence of the medium of film is one of the three or four major political phenomena of this century, and a filmmaker, a craftsman, who has not set his own house in order—who has not ideologically and technically seized the means of production—can hardly hope for any ulterior political success. One of the great sadnesses of *Le Gai Savoir* (the title is at once ironic and joyous) is that we now know about these problems and therefore can't avoid confronting them.

So the apologia, and the involuted, reticulated form of the film, are necessary for psychological reasons. They make us personally involved in Godard's knotty struggle, as do the hand-written signs and words that punctuate the film. To read print is to be conscious only of the meaning, the "significance." To read handwriting is to recognize the iconic importance of the words and the intelligence behind them, the "signifiers" and "the signifier."

There is a strict logical provenance for this method, as well. The involutions, the parallel articulations, the spiral patterns, the self-references, the metaphorical contradictions, the sometimes purposeful inscrutability of the discourse, the dependence on dependent clauses (both strictly, in prose, and metaphorically, in cinematic equivalents)—these are all characteristics of modern dialectical thought. Louis Althusser, for example, rings some beautiful changes on the Marxian concept of Causality, which, he explains, is "structural, complex" rather than "linear." In "Structural Causality" the effects are caused by the global whole of the structure of causes—ideological, economic, epistemological, political. The metaphor for cause-and-effect is then not a linear "chain," but rather a "critical mass" which, when reached, gives forth an explosion of "effects."[18] This is why Godard has to "put everything" into his films. Only then can the critical mass be achieved.

And while making this foray into the wilderness of dialectical metaphysics, let me add an apology of my own. This is not the study of Godard's work that should be written, but it shows how, if one is making such a study, that study must follow some of the paths indicated here. I realize that I have given you nothing clear and concrete that you can carry away, nothing that "pins down" *Le Gai Savoir,* but as Fredric Jameson says in his Preface to *Marxism and Form:*

> In the language of Adorno . . . density is itself a conduct of intransigence: the bristling mass of abstractions and cross-references is precisely intended to be read in situation, against the cheap facility of what surrounds it, as a warning to the reader of the price he has to pay for genuine thinking.[19]

And likewise to the viewer of the price *he* has to pay. This method of thought-as-art is probably more familiar and more comfortable for French observers of Godard, accustomed as they are to the theoretical psychedelics of Althusser, Metz, and Lacan, than it is for Anglo-Saxons. There *is* a validity to this method, then, even if there is also a strong criticism to be made of it.

All this, I realize, is coldly abstract. *Le Gai Savoir* is a film of ideas, of Method, but also a film, like any other, composed of images and sounds, and they are striking in themselves: the yellow-ribbed umbrella; the liquescent blackness of the studio; the side-lighting and back-lighting that make icons of Léaud's and Berto's faces; the face of the old man who is interviewed; the Cuban revolutionary hymn that punctuates the film; the dialectical pans which move from Emile to Patricia and then, still moving in the same direction, through the black void back to Emile; the simple cartoon which is so poignantly self-effacing, yet complex and sarcastic; the muddled radio static juxtaposed with Godard's tense, sad whisper; Patricia riding a bicycle around Emile like Brialy around Karina in *Une Femme est une femme* (again, Berto's resemblance to Karina should not be ignored); the usual stark, strong reds and blues, here isolated against the black and therefore even more balanced and assured; Patricia in yellow and purple against cartoons of comic-book heroes; above all, the vast, noisy, jumbled, careful collation of sounds and images which "dissolve themselves in order to analyze themselves."

The "Seventh Night" of the film gives us the planned "third year" of the struggle, which will be devoted to building "a few models of sounds and images" for the future. It is a catalogue of types of film discourse:

- the Historical film (Patricia in costume);
- the Imperialist film (we see the back of Patricia's head; she sings scales, Emile sings a single note, finally overpowering her and forcing her to do the same),
- the International film (the image is missing; the narrator makes suggestions);
- the Experimental film (Mozart and a magnetic line drawing);
- the Psychological film (He is reading. She reads. "The Sweet being two"),
- the Guerilla film (he describes her face as a Molotov cocktail);
- the film tract (a collage of slogans: "Read, Criticize, Listen, Watch");
- and finally the "film d'Role," as good a label for this film as can be found—Emile (like Jean-Pierre) is off to Bratislava to shoot a film with Skolimowski. "Half the shots of this film are missing." Emile and Patricia talk about them. Finally, the word

  MISOTODIMAN

  appears: "the word I finally found for sounds and images," Godard tells us, a mixture of "Method" and "Sentiment."

The Method of *Le Gai Savoir* is clear; or at least it is clearly a film *of* method. What about the "Sentiment"? *Le Gai Savoir* is propaedeutic, elemental, almost paranoid at times because of the fear of language on which it rests. But it is also, like *2 ou 3 choses,* a painful personal essay. Its aim is nothing less than the beginning of a rigorous examination of the systems of signs through which politics, love, beauty, and existence are expressed and understood. It speaks of love and eroticism, workers

"What is really at stake is one's image of oneself." (Frame enlargement.)

and bosses, language and meaning with sad but incisive humor. As it destroys the language it would analyze, it creates sounds and images of intuitive sense.

"What is really at stake," Patricia discovers, "is one's image of onself." Film and politics are as much a part of the self as one's eyes and ears. ("The eye should listen before it looks.") Or, as the song Emile sings puts it, there is

> a constant current between man's biological nature and his intellectual construction.

This is the ultimate Godardian struggle—to fuse Method with Sentiment, to overcome the fact of the self, to reconstruct the expression of self, finally to give rebirth to the self, and so to sanity. *Le Gai Savoir,* one realizes, is a film about a man and a woman: a love story of sorts.

At the end Emile, Patricia, Godard, and we are left with the neoseme MISOTODIMAN. Method is the vertical axis of Godard's own moral coordinates, Sentiment the horizontal. He is himself a true descendent of Rousseau, courting the daughter of the Third World: if the marriage is ever effected it will doubtless be through the proper combination of head and heart, Method and Sentiment. We have abrogated the social contract which Emile's progenitor spoke of two centuries ago, and *Le Gai Savoir* is a film about form, not content, which explains, subliminally, how we have done so.

On the third night, at 3:00 A.M., in the exact middle of the edifice of the film, Godard quotes Che Guevara:

> A revolutionary—an authentic one—is guided by great feelings of love.

This is the deepest meaning of *Le Gai Savoir*. But Godard does not give us the introductory clause of that sentence. Che had originally said, "At the risk of seeming ridiculous, let me say that a revolutionary—an authentic one—is guided by great feelings of love." Godard, at the risk of seeming ridiculous, has given us a deeply felt essay which reflects with all its confusions and self-induced paralysis his own frightening sense of the media universe in which we live.

PATRICIA	It's more or less nothing that we have discovered, no?
EMILE	Not at all. Listen: what better ideal to propose to the men of today, one which would be above and beyond themselves, if not the reconquest, through knowledge, of the nothingness they themselves have discovered?[20]

10

GODARD
Theory and Practice: The Dziga-Vertov Period

From 1968 through 1973 Godard was engaged in the processes of Patricia Lumumba's three-year plan for revolutionary cinema: "The first year we collect images and sounds . . . the second year we criticize all that: decompose them, reduce them, substitute for them, and recompose them. And then the third year, make two or three models of reborn film." The plan did not work itself out sequentially, as Patricia had suggested, but rather all at once. The nine films Godard completed during these years, either working alone or in collaboration with Jean-Pierre Gorin, came out of a matrix of contradictions, both political and esthetic, personal and public. The spirit of paradox which had motivated so many of Godard's earlier films was now expressed in political rather than philosophical language, but it is still in the struggles with those contradictions that we find the energy, wit, and feeling of Godard's art.

He wanted to make a new cinema which was political, concrete, active, and collective, but the evidence of the Dziga-Vertov period shows how very difficult this was. The words "theory" and "practice" take on iconic significance as they are repeated continually in these films: they are spoken, written, drawn, printed, and illustrated as Godard tries mightily to transform the lessons he can express theoretically into cinematic practice. But, as before, theory always outstrips practice, and the iron hand of logic oppresses. In *One Plus One* Godard has Eve Democracy agree that "the only way to be a revolutionary intellectual is to cease being an intellectual." It is an intuitive truth. But Godard does not cease being an intellectual and a few years later has to retract that statement: "The only way to be a revolutionary intellectual," he has to admit, "is to be a revolutionary intellectual." Which is not much comfort.

The contradictions:

• Godard's films during this period certainly qualify under the broad rubric of "politics," yet nevertheless deal increasingly with esthetic questions. He knew film; he did not know politics. He could deal with the structural nature of politics because he could compare it with the structural nature of film, and so his politics were expressed in filmic terms and his films spoke the *language* of politics though they seldom came to grips with the concrete issues of politics. He had often quoted Lenin's "Ethics will be the esthetics of the future," but he read that sentence backwards. So what we have is not a cinema about politics, but a politics of cinema. One remembers that rather poignant and self-effacing line from his contribution to *Loin du Vietnam:*

> I am cut off from the working class, but my struggle against Hollywood is related, yet workers don't come to see my films.

Increasingly, through these years, he speaks in interviews about that struggle with Hollywood. Even now the sign still forces us to see an object through its significance, so that even if it were possible for Godard to make "political films," it would be necessary first for him to learn how to "make films politically." The correct content is useless without the correct form. And the "correct" form doesn't exist. So political questions will have to wait until esthetic questions are answered.

• The films would have to be not only "political," but also "concrete." They would have to deal with analysis of concrete situations. But the materials of the Dziga-Vertov films* were concrete only as they dealt with cinema. For various reasons, not the least of which was money, Godard paid relatively little attention to the political realities of France during the late sixties and early seventies; he spent more time outside France during these years than he had in the twenty years previous. He made films in the U.S., Czechoslovakia, England, Italy,

*Not all of the films made between 1968 and 1973 are strictly "Dziga-Vertov" films, but I will use this phrase as shorthand to refer to all the films of this period.

and Palestine which dealt, rather abstrusely, with political issues that existed in those countries, but he made only two films that dealt directly with French politics—*Un Film comme les autres* and *Tout va bien*—and this last spends a good deal of time focusing on the specific situation of an American living in Paris (Jane Fonda). Indeed, Godard left France to make his first film abroad only weeks after the events of May 1968. The contract had been signed six months earlier, but the question is not whether Godard intended to exile himself, only that he did.

• If the films he had made had been both political and concrete, then they would have played an active role, as well—at the very least they would have had the potential for direct political influence, a fortiori. We assume Godard desired this. Yet if such things could be measured it would be clear that the Dziga-Vertov films are considerably less effective and demonstrative than, say, *La Chinoise* or *Weekend*. They are, if anything, more exquisitely intellectual than anything Godard did before. By nature, most of the Dziga-Vertov films have to be directed to a very small audience—those interested in learning more, not about politics, not about political films, but about how to make political films politically.

• Finally, Godard also wanted to break with the past and his status as an auteur, a "star," by making films collectively. This would be a way to become a revolutionary intellectual without, possibly, ceasing to be an intellectual. It is also the necessary first step towards making "political films politically." But the Dziga-Vertov collective was hardly ever large enough even to be called a groupuscule. It never included more than two people—Godard and Jean-Pierre Gorin—and several of the films which are "signed" by the Dziga-Vertov group were nevertheless wholly Godard's work. It is true that, especially after the motorcycle accident in June 1971 in which Godard nearly lost his life, Gorin took over more of the work, but, as Gorin himself says, "basically all I have done comes from Jean-Luc's previous work, and that's why some of our last films are considered highly Godardian, even though I made them."[1] In attempting to widen the basis of the authorship of his films, to "depersonalize" them, Godard had succeeded only in discovering a filmmaker who was even more Godardian than himself. "I had a need," Gorin says, "to go back into his early work and even discover some aspects of his work that he had not discovered himself."

Yet it is precisely in this mass of contradictions that these films have their greatest interest. It is their obsessive logic that yields their truths. If complexity and theory have any place in politics at all, then the Dziga-Vertov films have real value. These films were not what their audiences wanted them to be—that is their problem. But they were also, we sense, not exactly what Godard wanted them to be. His own politics had its source in a personal anguish which, as Tom Milne has pointed out, reached "a point of no return in *Pierrot le fou,*" when the anatomy of social despair began "to filter through like a watermark."[2] Politics had offered a chance for action, that existential grail that had eluded Godard. To find out that one was still an intellectual, imprisoned in that passive role, must not have been pleasant. Even in politics Godard found himself an outsider.

But the Dziga-Vertov films also demand to be judged in *simple* political terms. Godard is open to three basic criticisms in this respect:

• First, his films don't really serve the "people" or the "revolution"; he has not used his talents—the materials he has been given—in the most effective way. There is some truth to this criticism when it is phrased this way. But of course, this is inductive reasoning and assumes that there was some other way Godard *could* have acted. Deductively, he did what he could do best. His films are not Molotov cocktails, it's true, but given his situation, he acted with some courage.

• Second, the Dziga-Vertov films have often been charged with "anti-humanism," and I think there is considerable evidence in support of this. The provenance of the films is almost exclusively theoretical, not practical. The film which dealt with the most specific and concrete political reality, *Jusqu'à la victoire,* the Palestinian film, remained unfinished for five years. Godard has never been the kind of realist who allowed reality to reveal itself. He was (and is) rather the poet of an interior reality. In politics, that interior reality is theory, and therefore the Dziga-Vertov films are exceptionally cold and distant. Their subjects are: first, themselves; second, the *shape* of political theory; third, political theory. There is little room for human beings in them. *Le Gai Savoir* had forecast a fusion of Method with Sentiment. But so far, Godard has been overwhelmed by the ogre of Method and its iron logic. He gave us *Vivre sa vie* and *La Femme mariée* when feminism was still only a term in history books; yet there is nothing in the Dziga-Vertov films that comes close to matching those films for their insight into the female condition. When the subject is approached through theory rather than through poetic practice, it dies for Godard.

• Third, despite the intellectual value of Godard's essays on the subject of "making political films politically," all the Dziga-Vertov films are tainted by a sense that Godard protests too much. The elaborate, elegant structures of Marxist-Leninist theory are the last refuge of the bourgeois intellectual, protecting him by the very majesty of their labyrinthine and eloquent rhetoric from the concrete truths of the struggles of street politics. Like Bertolt Brecht, Godard has used Marxist theory to his own ends, yet there is nevertheless a nagging feeling that he also shelters himself under the profuse and obfuscatory foliage of high Marxian theory. Even though there is some evidence that the rich bouquets of rhetoric in the Dziga-Vertov films are meant at least in part as analytical parody, there is still entirely too much theoretical "noise." The Dziga-Vertov films continually ring changes on the concept of "concrete analysis of concrete situations," repeating those words again and again until they become almost a chant. But Godard himself worked from books, not from reality. The result was the production of an ingenious "Marxist cinematics," a theory of cinema couched in the language and theory of dialectical materialism. Eloquent, truthful, but lacking in one very important respect. Ironically, Godard—whose political consciousness was forged in the cauldron of the sixties—ignores the political lessons of those years. The New Left, in both France and the United States, had brought new life to militant politics by championing practice in the face of theory and by re-humanizing left politics. Both these modifications were historically deductive. The New Left learned as it grew (and then partially forgot as it declined) that the power of militant politics needs decentralization and that it stems from action, not rhetoric. As Brecht said, "Erst kommt das Fressen, dann kommt die Moral!" ("First comes the grub, then the moralizing.")

It should be stated in Godard's defense that he probably knew all this and also that these contradictions only mirrored a general situation. The ultimate characteristic of the Dziga-Vertov films is their rigorous spirit of auto-criticism. They were never meant to be finished products, but rather exploratory forays down certain paths of cinema. What was important to Godard and Gorin, as we can see from numerous interviews they have given, was first to do the film, then to see what went wrong. "Failed" experiments often teach more than "successes." This is the real spirit in which the Dziga-Vertov films should be read.

And then, too, we can see that Godard and his films during this period clearly reflect one of the central contradictions of the politics of the left, especially as it was demonstrated in the sixties. Godard symbolizes the dilemma of the bourgeois intellectual revolutionary: thoroughly commited to radical politics, but prevented by his class and role from participating existentially in the struggle—the dilemma of the "unoppressed" white, male, middle-class, middle-aged professional. If we can learn, from an examination of Godard's work, something about the tenuous relationship of bourgeois intellectuals with militant politics, then the Dziga-Vertov films will be continually useful. Again, we come back to Godard's struggle to define himself as the central interest of his work. This time the definition is to be in the language of class politics. In an interview he described his evolution this way:

> I was raised in a bourgeois family, and then I escaped. I went to the Sorbonne for one hour, and that was enough. I still had to escape this bourgeois family, so instead of going to LSD or marijuana I got into show business. Then I discovered—and it took me fifteen years—that show business was an even more bourgeois family than the one before. So I tried to escape again, at first just by feelings and instincts. I just wanted to be free to do what I wanted, but even in show business you can't do what you want. So although I was a bourgeois, I was an *oppressed* bourgeois. (Of course, if you compare that to being in a ghetto or being a peasant in South America, it's a very privileged situation to be oppressed in show business.) Then, after fifteen years of being a bourgeois fighting other bourgeois, when the May–June events arrived I was ripe to make a break with what I was. It can't be done in just one day—it's going on, and it will go on until my death. Probably, my son will continue it.[3]

Godard had met Jean-Pierre Gorin as early as 1965, while Gorin was connected with a political group that published *Cahiers Marxistes-Léninistes.* A few years later, while he was doing research for *La Chinoise,* Godard started discussing politics with Gorin and, as Gorin says, "It went on as a kind of loose relationship the following years." At the beginning of 1968, Gorin had been working in a factory (after having been fired as literary critic for *Le Monde*) when Godard approached him with a project for a film which would survey all the various groups "trying to live in new ways: groups involved in politics, music, theatre, etc." As Gorin explains:

> It was going to be a 24-hour film called *Communications,* and he asked me to make the Maoist part of it. So I started writing a script called "A French Movie," based on the experience I had had for two years organizing political groups. I gave the script to Jean-Luc. It was an attempt to put political points into an esthetic form, and it was never filmed. But all the films we made after 68 are in some way a transformation of this original script.[4]

The project for *Communications* was overtaken by the events of the spring of 1968. Godard had been involved in the work of the Committee for the Defense of the Cinémathèque in February and March. For the first time it was possible to act politically within a cinematic context. Film was an important part of the system of communication that was set up in Paris during the student strikes; and, just as a beginning of sorts was marked when the cinéastes took to the streets in defense of Langlois in February, so the climax of the turbulent spring can be said to be the closing of the Cannes festival on Saturday, the eighteenth of May. Truffaut seems to have made the first public suggestion that the festival should not take place. Godard suggested that the "grande salle" be occupied, which the *Comité du Défense de la Cinémathèque* proceeded to do. At three in the afternoon the organizers of the festival attempted to resume with a screening of a film called, of all things, *Peppermint Frappe*. Godard and Truffaut hung on the curtains to prevent their opening, someone cut the sound cable, and the Cannes festival was stopped.

This provides us with a wonderfully cinematic image of the "struggle against Hollywood," but of course it is more symbolic than substantive. There was an attempt to reorganize the means of production and distribution of French film in the succeeding months, through the actions of the general committee which took the name "États-Généraux du Cinéma," but neither Godard nor Truffaut took a large part in these discussions. During May and June Godard occupied himself with shooting *Un Film comme les autres* and several of the "cinétracts" put out by the états-généraux. In late June he left for London to shoot *One Plus One*, and he was in England, intermittently, throughout the summer.

In the fall of 1968 he came to the United States to film a project called *One American Movie (One A.M.)* with Leacock and Pennebaker, but the film was abandoned after a while. In February 1969, Godard made *British Sounds* in England for London Weekend Television (which refused to show it). This is the first film to be signed by the Dziga Vertov group, although Gorin informs us that both *British Sounds* and *Pravda* were really Godard's own work. *Pravda* was shot in Prague in March 1969. Two months later Godard was in Italy to shoot *Vent d'est*, the first real collaboration with Gorin. *Luttes en Italie* was shot in December 1969, but not finished until many months later. Early in 1970, Godard and Gorin went to Palestine to shoot *Jusqu'à la victoire*.

In the spring of 1970, Godard and Gorin were in the United States for a lecture tour of college and university campuses with their Dziga-Vertov films.* At this time they contracted with Grove Press to make two films. *Vladimir et Rosa* was shot early in 1971. The second film, "18th Brumaire," was never made. Grove was also distributing *British Sounds* and *Pravda*, which led to many jokes about the contradictions

*Godard and Gorin had named their collective after the Russian filmmaker and inventor of the concepts of Kino-Eye and Kino-Pravda simply to draw attention to his work. "It was a way to oppose Eisenstein's glory," Gorin notes, "and especially the way his glory had been reconstituted into the loose category of bourgeois esthetics." Vertov's theories about the relationship between politics and esthetics were also, of course, very close to Godard's and Gorin's.

inherent in making revolutionary films for capitalist producers. But Godard had no compunctions about where the money came from. It was important, he felt, not to worry about how the films would be distributed, but simply to produce them the best way possible. Distribution would take care of itself, after the films existed. In 1969 he had even signed a contract with United Artists to make a film of Jules Feiffer's *Little Murders* with Elliot Gould. "My intention," he explained, "was not to shoot that picture, but to take the money and make a picture on a subject I chose." United Artists, hearing about *British Sounds,* reneged. Another important source of funding during this period was television networks. Claude Nedĵar was instrumental in getting three of them to put up money (London Weekend for *British Sounds,* O.R.T.F. for *Le Gai Savoir,* and RAI for *Luttes en Italie*), but all three eventually refused to show the films that were made.

Early in June 1971, Godard was involved in a serious motorcycle accident. (His mother had died in a similar accident.) He was not yet fully recovered when shooting began on *Tout va bien* early in 1972. It appears that Jean-Pierre Gorin was mainly responsible for the direction of this film. In September of 1972, Godard and Gorin made *Letter to Jane,* which was shot in one day (being mainly composed of stills), processed in one day, and edited in one day (although the writing, they inform us, took two weeks). In the fall of 1972, they accompanied *Tout va bien* and *Letter to Jane* on a tour of American universities. (Taking their films personally to their audiences so that they could engage them in direct dialogue was essential to the Dziga-Vertov concept.) In 1973 the Dziga Vertov group disbanded. Within a year Gorin had moved to California and was at work on a variety of projects. Godard, meanwhile, set up an elaborate film and videotape studio (or "laboratory") in Paris near Place Pigalle and began experimenting intensively with video. He worked on a formal film/tape, entitled *Moi/Je,* and at the same time was involved with sketches and studies for an elaborate project he called *The Decline of the Dollar.* Early in 1975, citing the pressures and conformity of life and work in Paris, he moved to Grenoble, where in the spring he shot the film/tape *Numéro 2 (A bout de souffle)* and quickly followed it with *Comment ça va,* another mix of film and video which at least from its title seems to have a connection with *Tout va bien* (the relationship is question and answer). None of these film/video projects have been publicly screened, at this writing. Yet we can tell from their titles and Godard's cryptic published descriptions of them that they mark a turning inwards, a period of renewed self-analysis, and—probably—an attempt to rephrase what he had learned from the Dziga-Vertov films in a personal psychological language.

> Where do correct ideas come from? Do they drop from the skies? No. Are they innate in the mind? No. They come from social practice, and from it alone; they come from three kinds of social practice: the struggle for production, the class struggle and scientific experiment.
>
> —Mao Tse-Tung[5]

Two basic esthetic-political problems dominated the films of the Dziga Vertov group. The first of these Godard phrased this way:

> The old principle says "go and fetch images and then try to edit them." The point we are at now is to *build* images—build images as simple as possible so that you can build your analysis.[6]

This is the logical outgrowth, many times removed, of the ideas Godard first expressed in "Montage, mon beau souci." The second problem, a corollary in a way, was the "tyranny of image over sound." Images and sounds would now be "built" and opposed to each other in strictly dialectical fashion, for "realism does not consist in reproducing reality, but in showing things as they really are," and "photography is not a reflection of what is real but what is real in this reflection."[7] It follows that the Dziga-Vertov films will shift the virtual focus from the "reality" in front of the camera (and "behind" the screen) to the "reality" of the screen's own surface. Image will be opposed to image, sound to sound, image to sound, and sound to image. Rewriting Althusser, Godard declared in the fall of 1969, "A political film is obliged to discover what it has invented . . . television and film do not record moments of the real but simply moments in the dialectical process. Areas/Eras of contradiction that have to be examined. . . ."[8]

The first step along the Dziga-Vertov road to correct ideas, *Un Film comme les autres (A Film Like Any Other),* was a sublimely simple statement/illustration of these two basic concepts. Godard was not quite yet ready to build images, but he was clearly through "fetching" them, and the tyranny of image over sound was about to be broken. *Un Film comes les autres* is not at all like other films. There are only two major visual sequences in the entire film (which runs close to two hours). The first includes several differing scenes of students from Vincennes and workers from the Renault plant at Flins, sitting in a meadow outside Paris discussing where they have been politically and where they will go. It is punctuated with the second set of shots: clips from the Cinétracts shot by Godard and others during the "events of May." We seldom see the faces of the people in the film (once one is glimpsed—possibly by accident) and, although it seems like a very pleasant, balmy afternoon and there are some interesting shots of wildflowers and occasionally an interesting newsreel shot from the Cinétracts, obviously anyone looking for the interest of the film on the *screen* is going to be vastly disappointed—which is the point. The soundtrack—a collage of speeches, newspaper reports, and street sounds—is, finally, dominant. For those who were (or are) at least mildly interested in the events of May, the discussion of the students and workers holds some interest, if only documentary and historical. For those who aren't interested in May 68, the film is a huge bore. Godard reinforced the objective humor of this cinematic parable by suggesting that audiences flip a coin to decide which of the two 16 mm reels of the film be shown first, and that they vote after the end of the first reel whether or not to continue.

Clearly, the interest of *Un Film comme les autres* lies not in its literal substance but in our experience of it, as with some of the early Warhol films. *Un Film comme les autres* is the *l'Arroseur* of the new cinema.

One Plus One, in contrast, is Godard's "last bourgeois film," in his own words, yet there are surprising echoes of the theory which underlay *Un Film comme les autres. One Plus One,* as its title announces, is a film of elementary arithmetic. The equation is not complete; the problem is left to be worked out. The main sequences of the film record a series of taping sessions as the Rolling Stones painstakingly put together, track by track, their song "Sympathy for the Devil." In Godard's version of the film* we never hear the complete song; the sixteen tracks on the monstrous tape deck never add up. The completion of the song's equation, like that of the film, is left to the observer.

Interspersed with the footage of the Stones at work are several other, possibly parallel sequences: black militants in a junkyard, discussing possible courses of action; scenes in a pornographic (political) bookstore—passages of *Mein Kampf* are read; snips of a fantastic porno-political novel on the soundtrack; shots of Anne Wiazemsky painting Joycean slogans ("Freudemocracy," "Cinémarxism") on most available walls, and finally, Wiazemsky as the costumed character Eve Democracy being interviewed by various media types in a green wood. They ask her complicated political questions (Is the only way to become a revolutionary intellectual to cease being an intellectual?) which she answers (sometimes with prompting) either Yes or No.("Because she is Democracy. What else can Democracy say?") A fine Godardian joke.

Un Film comme les autres announces its new approach; no one can avoid confronting it the way it wants to be confronted, and its first screening in New York resulted in a small riot at Lincoln Center. *One*

*The producer, Iain Quarrier, changed the title of the film to "Sympathy for the Devil," and stretched out and froze the last images so that he could dub in the completed version of the song at the end. Godard punched him.

Plus One does not, and therefore leaves itself open to misinterpretation. It is abstract and static, and it makes a statement even simpler than the film which preceded it—at least in *Un Film comme les autres* there was the sound collage. *One Plus One* is no more complicated than the puns Wiazemsky scrawls on London walls. Its content is not the basis for any kind of progressive discussion, and hardly any of its images are "built." Yet the sequences with the Stones do have a certain power: what better way to announce the beginning of the liberation of sound from image than to force images to portray the construction of sounds? Modern recording techniques require the same lonely, isolated, meticulous and repetitious work as film. Sounds coalesce very slowly into music. Each of the Stones works generally alone, separated from the "group" by earphones and acoustic baffles. A phrase is repeated and repeated again until it is honed to final sharpness, then preserved on tape, later to be mixed with literally thousands of other, separate phrases, the whole to give the illusion of passion and unity. We might infer that the structure of the revolution is parallel: it, too is composed of thousands of separate acts and words, the whole not yet come to critical mass. We can see why Godard was angry with the producer's changes. *One Plus One* cannot end with the sense of completion that Quarrier's version implies; nor is it advocating "Sympathy for the Devil," but rather sympathy for the artist-revolutionary who is beginning to *build* sounds and images rather than fetching them. ("I was very arrogant to make [*One Plus One*], to think that I could talk about revolution just like that—just to take images thinking I knew what they meant."[9]) *One Plus One* ends with one of the most stunning "built" images of Godard's recent work: the "heroine" (and by implication, the theory and practice of bourgeois film) hoist by her own petard, the camera crane, into the windy blue sky above the beach, as the black and red flags attached to the crane snap briskly. It is another of the countless ends-as-beginnings in Godard.

Godard's next project was to have been *One American Movie (One A.M.)* In the fall of 1968 he planned and shot, with the aid of Leacock and Pennebaker, footage for the five "actual" and five staged sequences he had planned: interviews with Eldridge Cleaver, Tom Hayden, The Jefferson Airplane, a woman Wall Street executive, and a young girl from Harlem together with matching "acted" sequences in which Rip Torn worked out theatre pieces commenting on the five "actual" sequences. The project was finally abandoned in 1970. The original plan had obviously been to oppose fetched images (the interviews) with built images. The fetched images fail because Godard simply doesn't have sufficient information about American politics, and, since the built images were based on the interviews, they don't have much chance of success either. Pennebaker later took the footage Godard had shot and combined it with some of his own documentary footage about the shooting to produce a melange, which he called *One P.M.* (*One Parallel Movie*, or *One Pennebaker Movie*.) That film is organized out of three basic elements: American politics as seen by Godard, Godard and his film as seen by Godard, and Godard and his film as seen by Pennebaker (this last view none too flattering). The film is of some interest just because of the clash of styles between the embryonic materialist filmmaker Jean-Luc Godard and the New American documentarist Pennebaker. Godard had often criticized the films of Pennebaker in the early sixties (which he felt partook of the cinéma-vérité fallacy), yet *One P.M.* does give us a rare chance to examine footage that Godard felt had failed. The best criticism of the film is carried within the sequences Godard had shot with Cleaver and Hayden. The major topic of the Cleaver interview is his view of the relationship between the struggle of Black people and what he calls the "Film Mafia," in which group he includes Godard. Hayden is also troubled by his "role" in the film.[10] In general, Godard agreed with this criticism. His first attempt to deal concretely with a political situation was not successful.

British Sounds, however, made in February 1969, seems to me the most representative Dziga-Vertov film and possibly the most successful, except for *Tout va bien*. The film, produced by Kestrel Productions was shot on location at the BMC plant at Abingdon and the University of Essex, and, at least in part, was the product of collaboration between Godard and British militants. *British Sounds* is composed of six balanced sequences (each about a reel in length) which operate as separate, complete Brechtian teaching pieces of such clarity and simplicity that it is hard to figure out why Godard didn't proceed further along this line. The range of the sequences—from students to workers to women's liberation—indicates that Godard was still intent, as he was in the failed projects of *Communications* and *One A.M.*, on presenting a panoramic survey of the various elements of society engaged in militant political activity, with the inference that by setting them side by side in a film, he could indicate various areas of agreement and conflict.

As the title indicates, *British Sounds** is at the same time another blow for the equality of sound and image. Because its politics are more

*The film is also known under the distributor's "hipper" title, *See You at Mao*.

concrete than those of most of the other Dziga-Vertov films, and because Godard has achieved a delicate balance between the political material and the esthetic structure, *British Sounds* has a clarity and force that makes it considerably more effective politically. The sequences are carefully staged and highly structured and are in no sense to be taken as "documentary." On the contrary, they present, in some cases, political ideas to which Godard may be opposed. The aim, as with Brecht's *Lehrstücke,* is to incite political discussion, to present a concrete situation in such a way that an audience is forced into a mode of productive analysis. *British Sounds* might work even better if it were broken up into discrete sequences, so that each could be dealt with by audiences before moving on to the next. In the spirit of the film, let me describe it by outlining each sequence in order and presenting some typical, if arbitrary, questions that might be raised:

1. *The Image:* A ten-minute tracking shot moving slowly down an automobile assembly line. The car we follow is, of course, red. *The Sound:* The excruciating screeches, clangs, and hootings of the assembly line, the words of Marx and Engels, and the voice of a little girl memorizing her Marxist catechism, the dates and events of the history of the British working class.

Question: Immediately, the audience has to deal with a concrete cinematic as well as political reality: how do we react to the interminable boredom and the real physical pain of the assembly line? Cinematically, is this sequence more or less effective as a criticism of the dehumanization of the assembly line than, say, Chaplin's *Modern Times?* What is the best sound for this sequence? Should it be Marx and Engels? Or would it have been better to listen to the workers, which could have turned the shot into a "documentary"?

Like the tracking shots of *Weekend* and *Tout va bien,* this majestic sequence-shot is a major objective correlative for Godard. The simplicity of the image versus the complexity of the sound sets up a kind of semiological "distortion" which reinforces the psychological reality of the assembly line.

2. *The Image:* First, a static shot of a staircase: a nude woman walks in and out of doors on the top landing, and up and down the stairs. The final shot is a long take, a medium-shot of the nude torso from waist to thighs. *The Sound:* The same woman, a writer for a British underground newspaper, reads texts on women's liberation she has written. Mixed over her voice, a masculine voice challenges with suggested "topics for research," such as "a Marxist-Leninist analysis of the most natural position to fuck."

Question: This may be the most nearly perfect illustration of the

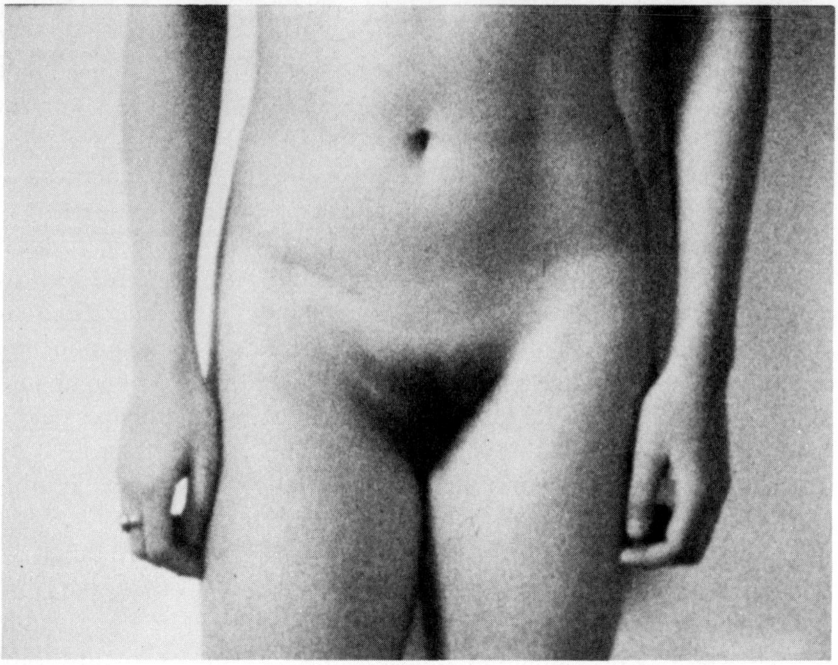

British Sounds: the demystification of the body. (Reproduced by permission of Grove Press Films; frame enlargement.)

dialectic of sound and image that Godard is after. Audiences immediately seize on the image as opposed to the sound of the sequence and jump to the conclusion that nudity exploits women. The mix of the soundtrack, however, is the real focus of the shot. The liberationist texts are directly opposed to the contemptuous "leftist" masculine attitude revealed in the "suggested topics for research." The sequence, then, immediately induces a discussion of the dialectic of the images and sounds. Tom Luddy has written that the nude shots are "a bold attempt to present the image of a naked female in a way that does not reduce her to a depersonalized sex-object—an image of sexuality and feminity that cannot be consumed by the pornographic appetite created by capitalism."[11] Yet it isn't at all clear from the image that the woman is presented as "sexual and feminine"—in fact, the opposite might be true. The point of the sequence is not to make statements, but to invoke dialectical argument. It is markedly anti-erotic. Does the sequence *not* depersonalize the woman? Does it re-personalize her?

3. "Capitalist Sound." *The Image:* A man with an exaggerated upper-class accent is seen in black and white, as if on TV, reading a blatantly racist, chauvinist, arrogant speech. This is intercut with shots of work-

ers and slum-dwellers. *The Sound:* Relatively simple this time—the speech.

Question: The sequence is placed near the center of the film, which is ideologically correct since it is "Capitalist Sound," as conveyed by the media, to which the workers, students, and women in the rest of the film react. The technique is simple exaggeration. It is as if one of Enoch Powell's speeches has been rewritten to state explicitly what is usually only implied. How can we react to this kind of rhetoric? Is there an element of militant guignol to the sequence?

4. "Workers' Sound." *The Image:* A meeting of Trotskyist union men. The camera pans, but we seldom see the face of the speaker, only the reactions of the listeners. *The Sound:* Again simple—the discussion, sometimes interrupted by the little girl's recitation of dates, places, and events.

Question: The discussion itself raises specific issues which lead to further analysis. The sequence emphasizes the collective nature of the group by focusing on the listeners rather than the speaker, a device which also raises the issue of the way films are usually shot and edited to focus on action rather than reaction.

5. "Student Sound." *The Image:* A group of students who have occupied a University of Essex building are shown lettering signs and rewriting the lyrics to a few Beatles songs ("You say Nixon, I say Mao" replaces "You say Goodbye and I say Hello"). *The Sound:* The songs and discussion of tactics.

Question: The dialectic is as strong here as in the first two sequences. Especially as juxtaposed with the serious discussion of the workers, the students' simplistic analysis and practice appears negative. The sequence almost insists that we criticize the students, especially in terms of their shoddy analysis of class struggle in the sixties and seventies. How will the Dziga Vertov group resolve their ambivalence towards students? How will we?

6. "Sound of Revolution." *The Image:* A shot of long duration: a bloody arm is moving slowly across dirt and snow to take up a red flag which lies on the ground. The flag is raised. Paper Union Jacks are repeatedly smashed by fists. Finally, a red frame with the words NO END TO THE CLASS STRUGGLE. *The Sound:* A complex montage of revolutionary songs and slogans and voices in affirmation of the struggle. At the end, the phrase from the song of *Marat/Sade:* "We want our revolution, . . . Now!"

Question: Tom Luddy describes the central shot of the bloody arm picking up the flag as "maybe the most beautiful revolutionary image in all cinema." Yet the problem with the sequence may lie just in our response to it as "beautiful." The sounds of revolution are analyzed (if that is the word) from an esthetic rather than from a dialectical point of view.

So at least three sequences of *British Sounds* (one, two, and four) exhibit clearly one method of using film effectively in a political context: not for statement or explanation, but to incite discussion and dialectical analysis. The other three sequences fail variously to capture the balance and objectivity necessary for a teaching-piece to work, yet despite their "finished" nature, their passive role, the fact that we consume rather than challenge them, they still work, on a lower level, as filmic posters. It may be that Godard wanted this mix of active and passive sequences; but I think not. The first two sequences of *British Sounds* have a power that we don't see again until *Tout va bien*.

Godard shot *Pravda* clandestinely in March of 1969. So far as is known, no Czechs or Slovaks were involved in either the theory or the practice of the film, and the result is the worst possible product of Dziga-Vertov theory. *Pravda* has an interesting and ingenious semiology, but bad politics. The title is ironic (the word means "truth," but it is also the name of the Russian newspaper, a clarion of "revisionism")—and it may possibly be itself a critique of the film. The film is narrated by a man named "Vladimir" and a woman named "Rosa," two portmanteau revolutionary characters who will soon have a film of their own. In the English version an extra dimension of commentary is added, since the English-speaking narrators are rather confused and rushed by the narration they are reading; the words have the sound of a printed text, and this further distances them from the images. *Pravda*'s central concern is revisionism, and the background is Czechoslovakia, filmed on the sly.

Judged purely cinematically, *Pravda* offers a profusion of interesting images—there is one long-duration shot of a lathe and its operator which conveys very effectively the dehumanization of industrial labor. The metaphorical structure of the film has to do with the movement of the color red in the frame. *Pravda* was shot on Agfa film, and the color is very poor in quality; Godard makes this a part of the metaphor by having Vladimir apologize to Rosa for it (as we look at a faded red neon Agfa sign): "The color is bad. It's West German film processed in Soviet labs." Red objects move continuously through the film, and their movement has meaning. Red roses are trampled in the mud of revisionism. Red street cars shot from above continually enter the frame from the right traveling left, disgorge their passengers, and go off to the right again: revisionism moving to the left, then turning around leaving the masses behind. At the end of the film, we focus on a red flag on a truck fender as it moves quickly left. The camera tracks alongside, slowly gaining until it passes it and, while the truck is still moving towards the left in reality, the camera has overtaken it and the flag is seen to move towards the right on the screen.

These are ingenious devices, but they can't hide the essential political poverty of *Pravda.* The first part of the film, by its own admission, is no more than a political travelogue. The second part, however, announces itself as "a concrete analysis of a concrete situation." It investigates the similarities between Westernism and Revisionism, which are the same for Godard: a matter of prostitution, meaningless work, and the tyranny of the media. The film treats, in turn, students, peasants, the army, the working class. And it shows disdain for all of them as they exist—now—in Czechoslovakia. It explains superciliously that they "are not thinking correctly." For example, during the Czech revolution of 1968, the students flew the black flag, not the red—and the "black flag of suicidal humanism," at that, rather than the black flag of anarchy. Vera Chytilova, an important figure in the Czech film renaissance of the early sixties (which was, of course, thoroughly imbued with "suicidal humanism"), is interviewed. Vera Chytilova, we are told bluntly, does not "speak correctly." She speaks "like Arthur Penn or Antonioni."

But *Pravda* ends with an important clue. After a discussion of the Third International, Vladimir tells his co-narrator, "Listen, Rosa, you're acting dogmatically. You thought you were taking one step forward when in fact you were taking two steps backward." This is the autocritique: and it is right on target.

The First Step Backward: Godard chose to discuss Revisionism (a good intention) in Czechoslovakian terms (a mistake). He has taken on a more complex concrete reality than he can analyze effectively. His effort to link Westernism and Revisionism closely makes him ignore much of the significant struggle of the Czech and Slovak peoples during the previous year since, as he points out disdainfully, they opposed Revisionism (the Russian repression) "only" with "suicidal western humanism." By forcing a "concrete situation" into an abstract paradigm, he misses the point of the Czech revolution and thoroughly belittles its importance for the sake of making a symmetry which doesn't really exist. This is a highly destructive misinterpretation which can't be overlooked.

The Second Step Backward: Pravda shows a diffident contempt for the people who are its subject and for their society, and this is a more direct and damaging error even than the mistaken analysis of the "first step backward." There are several interviews with workers, students, and peasants in the film—none of them translated from the Czech. Don't worry if you don't understand, says Vladimir at one point, it is not necessary because people say the same things in any language. This is certainly no way to conduct a concrete analysis of a concrete situation! France and Czechoslovakia shared a moment in history in the spring of 1968; the response of the Czechs and Slovaks to a severe repression that summer was heroic, while the response of the French to a comparatively mild and gentle repression was simply not of the same order. For a Frenchman, then, to criticize the Czech and Slovak peoples barely a year later in such unfraternal ways is inappropriate, to say the least.

Godard realized his failure here. A year later he explained,

> . . . we made the effort to finish it, and not to quit and say it's just garbage. But having made that psychological effort, we must also put a notice on it. This is a garbage Marxist/Leninist movie, which is a good way of titling it. At least now we know what not to do anymore.[12]

In its failure, *Pravda,* points up the two parallel difficulties which haunt the Dziga Vertov group: first, their curious propensity for examining distant situations rather that the immediate realities of their comrades' lives and their own; and second, the tendency for baroque, dogmatic, effulgent ideology to cloud the images and sounds of "concrete analysis of concrete situations." The two failures are linked, for both make it possible for the Dziga-Vertov films to ignore people in order to celebrate the esthetics of dogma. In the battle between theory and practice, the former too often wins out. What is missing is an understanding of the deep truth Brecht expressed when he wrote, "Brains can't fill the pantry of the poor."

Vent d'est, (Wind from the East), which was shot on locations in Italy, on the Western town set at Elios Studios, and the soundstages of De Paolis Studios, is probably the most complete and thorough of the Dziga-Vertov films. It takes the broad view and tries to summarize the contemporary Marxist political situation, the position of the militant filmmaker, and the relationship between the two. As a result, it is a dense and tricky film which, more than the others, requires that the viewer become deeply involved in the process of the film before it can be comprehended. The "pre-credit" sequence, for example, indicates the mode of discourse of what is to follow: in a high-angle shot, we see a couple in costume lying motionless in a field. They are bound together by a chain. After a long pause, we hear a woman's voice on the soundtrack narrating the ersatz "story" of the film—"We went to see my father's family in May as we did every year. My uncle managed the exploitation of aluminum for the Alcoa Company near Dodge City."[13] As the narration continues, voices of people in the "story" break in: a union delegate, a striker. Then a second woman's voice begins to comment on the story. All this while the image does not change. The soundtrack carries the primary montage of the film. We are *listening* to what may as well be called a Marxist Western, but what are we watching? The image of the man and woman in the field alternately puzzles, bores, intrigues, hypnotizes. If we are participating correctly in the dialectic of *Vent d'est,* we have already realized that the real interest of the film will lie first in the struggle between sounds and images, and second in the critical analysis of the political metaphorical value of the stories, images, and other tropes. Then the story breaks off. The second, commentative, narrator speaks directly to us:

> The two voices have continued to lie; the two others have continued to stammer. Which one is speaking for us? How can we find out? Today the question "what is to be done?" is urgently asked of militant filmmakers. It is no longer a question of what path to take; it is a question of what one should do practically on a path that the history of revolutionary struggles has helped us to recognize. *(Long pause.)* Yes, what must we do? Make a film, for instance. That means to ask ourselves, "where do we stand?" And what does it mean for the militant filmmaker to ask himself the question: "where do we stand?" *(Long pause.)* And what does it mean for the militant filmmaker to ask himself the question: "where do we stand?" It means first of all, but not exclusively, opening a parenthesis in which we can ask ourselves what the history of revolutionary cinema can teach us.[14]

Questions, and more questions. These form the fabric of *Vent d'est* and the films that follow it. I have quoted the statement at length and verbatim because the rhetorical style of the narration from now on takes on special significance. Long periodic sentences, often with parallel structures, leading to questions, then questions about questions, then corollary questions: rhetorical Chinese boxes. Always the primal question hangs overhead: "What is to be done?" For the essayist Montaigne the question was: "Que sais-je?" For the essayist Godard the question is: "Que fais-je?"

After several illustrative episodes of militant film history, we have the identifying title, and the first part of the film proper begins. The commentator repeats the last few sentences of the paragraph I have just quoted and then adds two new sentences, continuing the train of logic. This, too, is characteristic of the style of the next several films: to make a statement, to make a statement and draw a conclusion, to make a statement, draw a conclusion and then state a corollary. Then begin again. The general structure of the first half of the film parallels this rhetorical device. Titles announce: 1. THE STRIKE; then, 1. THE STRIKE, 2. THE DELEGATES, and so on until we have built up the whole sequence: 1. THE STRIKE, 2. THE DELEGATES, 3. THE ACTIVE MINORITIES, 4. THE GENERAL ASSEMBLY, 5. THE ACTIVE STRIKE, 6. THE POLICE STATE. We are analyzing the structure of *the* strike through a depiction of *a* strike, in France, in the spring of 1968, as phrased in terms of the Western. In addition, throughout the construction of this multi-part political syllogism, we are also analyzing the history of militant film styles. When, for example, the study of the model strike has reached the stage of the "General Assembly," Godard films, as an example, a general assembly of the filmmakers themselves (and there are many of them, with conflicting opinions).

The second half of the film develops two theories (labeled "A" and "B") that grow logically out of the dialectic of the first half. One of those theories, "The Worker-Directed Factory," is condemned. The other, "The Armed Struggle," also presents problems, but offers more possibilities. Before discussing these theories, which are organized according to the interrelationships of "Struggle," "Critique," and "Transformation," Godard interpolates a section of Auto-critique. "It's not enough to have an aim, you've got to solve the problem of the methods which will allow you to accomplish this." "You forget that this film has one name—the Western—and that this is not by chance." "In this film the principal task is theory."[15]

After the direct auto-critique, two filmic parables: In the first a pregnant woman goes up to Brazilian director Glauber Rocha at a crossroads and asks, "Which is the way to political film?" He points down two roads: "That way is the unknown cinema, the cinema of esthetic adventure. That way the Third World cinema, a dangerous cinema—divine, marvellous." The woman starts down the road of Third World Cinema, but stops. She then goes back and proceeds down the road of esthetic adventure.

Then a second instructive sequence. The second narrator explains: "In ten seconds you will be looking at a character on a bourgeois film screen. He is a Western character from a psychological drama, a thriller, a historical film. It doesn't make any difference. In fact, he's always the seducer. He describes the room where you are sitting." He speaks in Italian, with voiceover translations in both French and English. He invites us up on the screen, where it's a beautiful day.* The point? "Struggle against the bourgeois notion of representation."

*James Roy MacBean, in "*Vent d'est,* or Godard and Rocha at the Crossroads," analyzes these sequences and several others superbly and at length.

Finally, an introduction to the second half of the film which is a catalogue of advice to militants. "Miss Althusser" is selling books. A union delegate selects "Reading *Das Kapital.*" But the narrator explains that "Reading *Das Kapital*" is not enough; one must know how to *use* it.

I have only been able to suggest the complicated theoretical structures of *Vent d'est.* It attempts an extensive catalogue of Godard's thinking on politics and film and their interrelationship, and his theories are not easily summarized. In the end, however, the basic fear of inadequacy for the task which haunts all the Dziga-Vertov films (as it had the bourgeois films before them) makes itself known:

> What is to be done [the second narrator asks]? You've made a film. You've criticized it. You've made mistakes, you've corrected some of them. Because of this you know a little more about making images and sounds. Perhaps now you know better how this production can be transformed. *For* whom and *against* whom? Perhaps you have learned something very simple.[16]

But what, precisely, has been done to advance the struggle? Despite the richness of its theory, *Vent d'est* is, like the countryside in which it is set, langorous and a bit too quiet. It does not have the direct power of *British Sounds* or the humor of *Vladimir et Rosa.* It was more a communal effort than the films which preceded and succeeded it, but even here there was a kind of ultimate failure. "What happened," Godard and Gorin explain, "was that the two Marxists really willing to do the film took power, and . . . all the anarchists went to the beach."[17] There is a diffident, divorced tone to the film which is only emphasized by the fact that it was made in five languages. Again we have the feeling that theory is not enough; that practice—revolutionary practice—cannot be achieved in the secondary activity of cinema.

Late in 1969, Godard and Gorin made their fourth film of the year, *Luttes en Italie (Struggles in Italy),* in which they turned to the specific question of their own personal relationship vis-à-vis revolutionary praxis. A young militant goes through the details of her daily life until she finally sees clearly her relationship to the working class. In this respect, the film is an attempt to deal with the contradictions of the first of the self-criticisms offered in *Vent d'est:* "Be critical of your lack of liaison with the people. . . . You still talk in slogans, in poster language: you're still apart from the people."[18] *Luttes en Italie* has been seen only rarely, and no English version of it exists. Gorin and Godard describe it in an interview:

GORIN: *Luttes en Italie* is a film about the transformation of a girl who, in the beginning, says she is involved in the revolutionary movement and is a Marxist. The film has three parts. During the first part of the film, while she speaks, you discover bit by bit that she isn't really as Marxist as she has said. . . . What we try to explain in the second and third parts is how things have happened. So the whole film is made of reflections of the few images in the first part.
GODARD: In the second part, she realizes that there was something wrong in the first part. She realizes this, and we realize it with her (because we are more or less the same kind of people that she is), but she doesn't really know how to find out what has happened. In the third part, from what she has discovered in the second part, she has to go back to the first part and try to really find out what had happened.[19]

The first part is made up of a series of chapters of her life—university, family, home, militancy—which are announced by a voice which says only, "Militancy," "Sex," "Family," "Relationship Between Father and Mother." "This voice," Gorin explains," is the voice of the bourgeois ideology which separates things." These sections are punctuated by stretches of black leader which have a jarring effect.

The second part of the film, Gorin explains, asks

"why these black spaces?,""what have they been taking the place of?," "who organized these black spaces?," "who put those black spaces in her speech?" Little by little, those black spaces will be replaced by other things, which are the real . . . *rapport de production,* the real economic and social pattern which governs ideology. . . ."
GODARD: The basis for *Luttes en Italie* was our attempt to organize our personal lives with our wives. We had problems as individuals, but these related to the general problem. So we deliberately chose a subject which was strongly related to our ideology, because even when you speak to a woman you are in love with, or the woman speaks to you, this is ideology.
We tried, and it was a complete failure, because we finished the movie alone, and our wives thought of it, at that time, as only *our* work—you know, "This is your job. I have my job too, and this is *your* job."

So *Luttes en Italie* is, at least in part, an attempt to find the method of sentiment.

In February of 1970 Gorin and Godard went to Palestine to film *Jusqu'à* la victoire (Till Victory). There was apparently considerable friction between the militants of Al Fatah and the filmmakers of Dziga Vertov, which was one of the reasons Godard and Gorin later had so much trouble putting the film together. They worked on the footage off and on over a five-year period; it wasn't until 1975 that the film was reportedly finished. In an interview in 1974, Gorin had suggested that if the film ever were completed it would have to be more "a film on how to film history," than a film about the Palestinian situation, which had changed so much since the footage was shot that any film they could construct out of it would be misleading. Gorin continued,

> One of the interesting things about the film is our impossibility [sic] to edit it, but I think we've found some kind of creative possibility to reflect on the impossibility of editing the material.[20]

Whatever film did eventually result (I haven't seen it), the fact still remains that, when confronted with concrete political realities and an active militant movement, the Dziga Vertov group was stymied.

Vladimir et Rosa, which was shot in late 1970, began life as "Sex and Revolution," a project designed for Grove Press. Godard explains at the beginning of the film:

> Why are we making this film? Well, the last film was the Palestinian film. We are making this film to pay for that film. Economic necessity. But that doesn't mean this film can't be a good one.

Even before this aural apology we have been given an image of and for the film: a picture of Lenin with the words *théorie* and *pratique* handwritten across it. The latter word has been crossed out. *Vladimir et Rosa,* then, will be another film of theory: the theory of making political films politically. Three times in the film we stop to watch a sequence in which a group of correctly dressed bourgeois play mixed doubles on a tennis court while Godard and Gorin, running back and forth, discuss the problems of making the film. They stutter and become increasingly incoherent. The image is dialectically correct, and the comment is well taken. The more one knows about theory, the more difficult practice becomes.

Like its predecessors, however, *Vladimir et Rosa* tries to be about politics outside film as well as within it, and here we run into the usual difficulties. The film is nominally about the Chicago Eight trial, which is parodied effectively in a series of scenes (Ernest Menzer scathingly burlesques Judge Hoffman), and about the real and the metaphorical connections between our lives and the symbol of the trial. The characters have a mixture of names, some "real", some commentative: Anne Wiazemsky and Juliet Berto play themselves (but as defendants), "David Dellinger" is played by Claude Nedjar, but Bobby Seale becomes "Bobby X" for the film, and William Kunstler becomes "John Kunstler." The effect is to make us re-examine the interrelationships of the various levels of cinematic reality. This is not the Chicago Eight

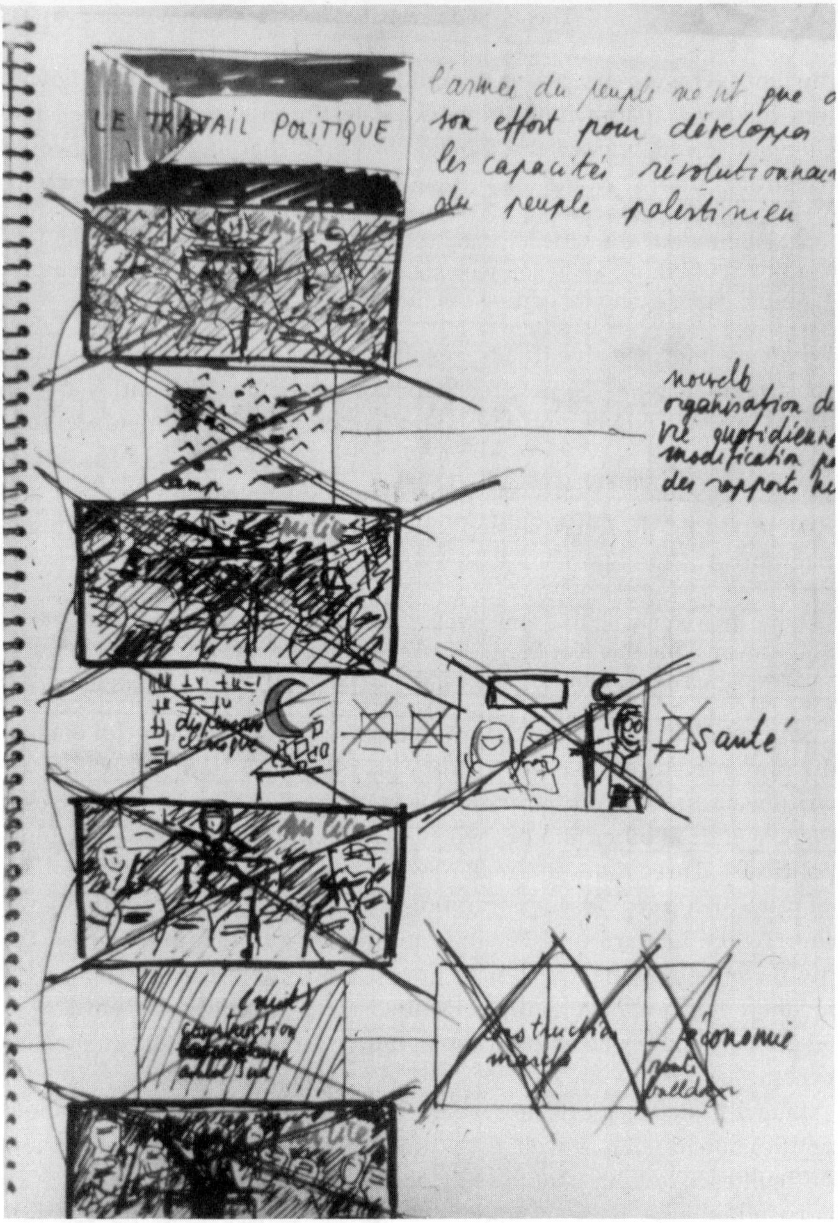

A page from Godard's notebook for *Jusqu'à la victoire* which storyboards a sequence dealing with "Political Work." (Photo: Robert Altman.)

trial, it is a film *about* the trial; more precisely, it is a film about some people making a film about that trial. As Godard says in the tennis court scene, the purpose is TO EMPHASIZE THE CONTRADICTIONS. Another quick shot gives us a Marx Brothers poster over which has been written: "Sometimes the *first* meaning of a film is not apparent until the *second* viewing." How does this work?

One glaring change has been made in the composition of the cast of characters for the trial. Godard and Gorin have added a worker as a defendant—just because there was no working-class defendant in the real trial. "To emphasize the contradictions." The Dellinger figure and the Seale figure (who represent two of the most important radical groups operating in the U.S.) are vague and distanced; Godard and Gorin's real sympathies, as the number of scenes allocated to this character show, lie with the figure of the young worker, who didn't exist in the real trial and represents only a potential rather than an actual militant force in the U.S. He is there because he makes the trial a *French* political metaphor, but he is also there simply because he was *not* there in reality. His presence will lead to a discussion of his absence.

At the other end of the spectrum of public-private politics we are given several scenes which comment on French domestic political life, one in particular: Jean-Pierre Gorin (who plays "Vladimir") comes into a room where Anne Wiazemsky is silkscreening some T-shirts with the women's liberation fist symbol. They have a discussion of the subject, obviously drawn from printed texts. Vladimir says he understands. Then Anne reads him something really rather simple, and he changes his mind: he doesn't understand. There is a certain difficulty with *Vladimir et Rosa* in that several of the scenes appear to be more in the naturalistic mode which we take for reality, so that we don't necessarily have to approach them dialectically and materialistically. For example, most of the film is made with direct sound as opposed to the commentative sound of the preceding films. Nevertheless, sequences such as this one still must be approached analytically. *Vladimir et Rosa* makes only the most simplistic statements about sexual politics, but it is not just "slogans, poster language." The crudeness of the dialogue is the spark for further discussion.

There are two especially effective sequences in which the world of the filmmakers and the world of the film (and the political reality behind it), which have been separate for the most part throughout, finally meet—a fusion that is quintessential Godard (and essential Dziga-Vertov):

- After Bobby X has been bound, gagged, and removed from the courtroom, the screen goes black. We hear Godard explaining, over the black void:

> You may wonder why we have this shot of a black screen. Well, we finally got a chance to use it. We've been carrying it around since the summer of 68 and we didn't know what to do with it. At first we thought it represented shots we could not envision, such as the damage of bourgeoisism and imperialism; then we realized that it represented shots we were incapable of making—the same. So now we are using it to represent the absence/presence of the Black man at the trial; after we have shown you shots of the others, then we show you this black screen.

This is the struggle of Dziga-Vertov: to fill up that black hole; to discover meaning in it; to find out how to build images that speak correctly. There may be some subconscious significance that Godard and Gorin don't realize in the fact that the leader is always black—never red. It may be that the greatest contributions of the Dziga Vertov group are best interpreted in terms of humanist anarchism rather than pure Marxism/Leninism. We have that shot of the anarchist Marxists (Groucho and his brothers) as evidence, too. Godard may not like this; he may crave the comforting and elaborate Marxist/Leninist structures and fear the perfect freedom of the anarchist non-structures, but he may be freer than he either knows or wants to be.

• The second sequence is the press conference the defendants hold. Since Bobby is absent, they force the press to focus their cameras on a bright red empty chair—to photograph his absence. It is a political lesson achieved by political means, a nice ploy with a complicated dialectics. At the end, there is a very quick shot of Godard pointing a gun at the head of a TV cameraman as the narrator speaks of taking over.

After the sentence is read at the end of the film, we hear Bobby X speaking as the shot shows a television screen image of a tape recorder, from which Bobby's voice is coming. This is the crux of the problem: Godard is so far away—all he has is a report of a report of a report. As the title implies, the film is really about Gorin ("Vladimir") and Godard ("Rosa"). It's tempting to criticize it on strictly informational grounds: we want to know more about the implications of the presence of the worker and the absence of Bobby X. But *Vladimir et Rosa,* like all Dziga-Vertov films, refuses to work out the logic of the situations it presents. That is left to us.

At least the film has a renewed sense of humor about the multiple contradictions of Godard and Gorin's position. That black screen is, for the revolutionary filmmaker, the equivalent of Paul's and Ferdinand's

This is the still that represents the absence/presence of all the stills that should be in this book but aren't. (From *Vladimir and Rosa;* reproduced by permission of Grove Press Films; frame enlargement.)

fatal suicidal humanism: true, but not useful. This is the bind. As much as Godard might like to avoid it for ideological reasons, there is a real drama here—the implicit struggle between *théorie* and *pratique*—just as the real emotions of Godard's "bourgeois" films were inherent in the tension between the contemplative male characters and the active women. Dziga-Vertov simply translates the emotional metaphor from people to ideas. How can we resolve the opposition of *théorie* and *pratique?* Godard can't escape himself.

The motto, the identifying sign of *Vladimir et Rosa,* was ROMPRE, "to break"—to break the rules, to break away, to break into, to break through to the other side of the black frame. The time for analysis had now passed and the time for construction was at hand. Gorin and Godard's next project was a "love story," a film for a large public, which synthesizes what had been learned through the Dziga-Vertov experiments. In Godard's words:

> I passed through a time of disrespect for the public in order now to respect them better. To respect them better means to no longer treat them as the public, but as man or woman, there where they are, with their specific problems. It means to be able to make films in which one no longer speaks about the film itself. The fact of talking about the film returns each person to their specific problems.[21]

The product of this new attitude is *Tout va bien,* materialist fiction for a large audience: a film that balances the microcosm of sexual politics against the more general politics of class struggle; a film that uses the conventional elements of fictional cinema in order to enlarge the Brechtian theory of *Lehrstücke;* a film that admits it's a film, but doesn't become paralyzed by that knowledge; a film about reality—the way things really are—but one which does not "reproduce reality" (in Gorin's words, an example of Brechtian realism rather than bourgeois realism or socialist realism); in other words, a film that proves that the knotty, difficult experiments of the last four years were productive and could be assimilated and used. Underlying *Tout va bien* are the lessons learned in *British Sounds* (whose concreteness it shares), *Vent d'est* (whose complex intelligence is basic to it), *Luttes en Italie* (whose analysis of the relationship between the intellectual and the working class provides a foundation for its structure), and *Vladimir et Rosa* (whose humor and sexual politics are influential).

A love story—but "lovers are not alone in the world; there's a lot of noise happening and they'd better realize it" (Gorin).[22] But also a "blackboard film," on which Godard and Gorin have drawn "three elements, three social forces, which are represented by three 'noises.' The management, the voice of the boss; the CP voice; and the leftist voice. . . . These are the three social forces at work in France today" (Godard).[23] A love story and a blackboard film—achieved through a "certain process of irréalisation": a film full of theatrical metaphors with a soundtrack of "social music," based on contradictions, even within acting styles. A film about workers which uses out-of-work actors to portray them: the boss is played by a film director, naturally, but one who is also a Brechtian actor. In the middle of all this, two "stars," Yves Montand and Jane Fonda, stars not only in the box-office sense of the word (which made it possible to raise the money for the film) but also within the terms of the film itself, since both of them have developed images as politically active human beings; so we look at them as playing roles very close to their own lives. We can identify with them in the old way, but they are themselves confronted with contradictions which are unresolved (and unresolved for us at the end of the film) so that, along with them, we must deal with the contradictions in a Brechtian way.*

Jacques is a filmmaker who got his start as a screenwriter for the New Wave; now he makes commercials. May 68 changed him. Right after it he was offered a chance to do a David Goodis novel he had always admired, but it no longer mattered. Now he's waiting; he doesn't know what to do ("What is to be done?"). He's an intellectual, and leftist talk about "re-educating the intellectuals" "gives him the willies." He tells us all this standing on a set next to a camera (and we remember "Caméra-oeil"); then he goes back to work directing two go-go girls in red and yellow stockings dancing on a small stage in the black void of the studio (and we remember *Le Gai Savoir*—was that also a dance?). The "noise" of the mindless jingle drowns out Jacques's voice, as the noise of advertising always tends to smother concrete thought.

Susan is a correspondent for the "American Broadcasting System" ("but I correspond to nothing"). She used to cover cultural affairs in France for them. Then she got a reputation as a specialist on leftists. But now, "I work and never get anywhere. . . . The further I go, the less I understand." She tells us this in *her* studio, where sounds are recorded, not images—images belong to Jacques. She is blocked. She can't record anymore. We see her from the point of view of the technician in the control room, twisting knobs, watching dials, while the large red "on-air" light hangs above Susan like an incubus. We also see her in medium shot, facing directly towards the camera (the image is clear); she speaks in English while her words are translated simultaneously in an overdubbed voice (the "noises" of media civilization are complex). Both Jacques and Susan work in media—one mainly in sound, reportage; the other mainly in images, fiction—and their experiences since 1968 are generally representative of those of many French intellectuals.

These two scenes come in the middle of the film. The first four reels are devoted to Susan's and Jacques's experiences of the wildcat strike at the Salumi sausage factory (preceded by an "induction"). This is the heart of the film: the *action* against which Susan and Jacques will have to *re*-act; the conflation of the three noises Godard and Gorin spoke of, of the CP, the bosses, and the "*gauchistes*." The Salumi sequences are a magnificent combination of fiction and Brechtian realism. The union

**Tout va bien* is remarkably similar in many respects with Marin Karmitz's *Coup pour coup* which was made in the summer of 1971 and released while Godard and Gorin were at work on their film. The differences between the two films—matters of style and approach—are equally interesting, and were widely discussed at the time. (For a more detailed comparison, see my article "Working Films: *Coup pour coup*.")

delegate (the CP noise) speaks a monologue taken from *La Vie ouvrière;* the boss speaks in the words of *Vive la société de consommation.* The workers are played not by workers but by extras. There are several "documentary" scenes which quickly describe the inhumanity of the work. But the major sequences take place in a huge cutaway set, showing eight offices on two levels and a two-story staircase. This is Godard/Gorin's homage to the materialist cinema of Jerry Lewis. They make ebullient use of this masterpiece of Hollywood construction, tracking back and forth from the boss's private office on the top floor, left, to the spacious staircase several times. This must have been a great pleasure for Godard, who hadn't really used the facilities of a movie studio since 1960 *(Une Femme est une femme),* but it is also ideologically significant: it forces us to comprehend the situation structurally, rather than linearly, to take the whole into account rather than each of the parts of the strike consecutively. Esthetically, this ideology of the tracking shot also has significance: "For four years," Gorin explains, "we decided to cool down, slow down, to make only stationary shots, make flat films and try to work out the white screen as a blackboard."[24] But the tracking shot is inclusive; it summarizes and allows us the perspective of the long view, which is exactly the function of *Tout va bien* in relation to the Dziga-Vertov films which preceded it.

In terms of movement, these crane shots, like the tracks which complement them later in the supermarket, are "heavy" and "square," the precise opposite in feeling (and meaning) from, say, Max Ophüls's celebrated crane shots. They move relentlessly from one end of a set to another; they don't stop to focus attention on any one aspect of the situation; rather they are inclusive and objective. They call attention to their significance because of their weight.

Within this giant set, Godard and Gorin have placed several scenes which, although they seem to grow naturally and dramatically out of the action, also have a muted heuristic value. A woman calls her husband and explains, "you'll have to heat it yourself. I took care of myself when *you* had *your* strike!" The boss has to use the bathroom. The workers decide to give him the three-minute break *they* are allowed. He doesn't make it, and has to break a window to piss out of. The workers worry if they have treated Susan correctly since she is a journalist. Later, Jacques, for his part, will tell us he didn't know how to act precisely, didn't know what "role" was expected of him. When these simple scenes are set down on paper, one can almost hear the discussion that would follow in a classroom or worker's meeting, but within the film they flow smoothly; this is materialist, Brechtian fiction, but it is also fiction done by professionals who know the tricks of drama. Even the background serves: a worker is quietly painting a wall blue. He works carefully with the roller around a photo of the factory. When he has finished with the wall, he just as carefully rolls the blue paint over the photo. This is not a symbol—it has no specific significance—but it certainly has meaning.

Godard and Gorin know that they will never be able to sell a film about working people in commercial cinema—not even to workers themselves. So they couch what they have to say about the condition of the working class in France in 1972 in a "love story" about two attractive bourgeois. The film's inductive preface situates it in this respect. On the screen, Godard writes crisp new checks and rips them out of the book—so many francs for sound, so many for image, another amount for stars, another for stock. On the soundtrack a man and a woman work through the practical logic of commercial filmmaking:

HE I want to make a film.
SHE You've got to have money to make a film. If we have stars in it, they'll give us money.
HE Good, then we've only got to get stars.
SHE And what are you gonna tell Yves Montand and Jane Fonda? 'Cause actors have gotta have a story before they'll accept.
HE Ah, we need a story?
SHE Yeah, usually it's a love story.
HE There'll be Him and there'll be Her. And they'll have love troubles.[25]

But that's not enough for "Her." Where do they live? What's the period? What do they eat? He replies: "Let's have a country, and in this country, there's this countryside, and in this countryside, there're these towns, and in the towns, there're these houses. . . . Workers working, peasants peasanting, and bourgeois bourgeoising. . . . Gotta add something. For an example, the calm'll be only apparent. Everything's gonna be really stirred up. . . . Every class its own little movement. . . ."

This is the practical situation which leads to the theoretical, fictional, situation of the strike, which is parallel with Jacques's and Susan's own professional crises, expressed in the monologues in the center of the film, which in their turn lead in time and are parallel in structure to their own emotional crisis. The next sequence shows Jacques and Susan at home. She has made the connection between her professional, political dissatisfaction and the situation of her private emotional life. "We meet, we go to the movies, we eat, we sleep, we screw—and every two months we fight." (*"On bouffe et on baise."*) It's necessary to think it through. In the next scene, Jacques thinks it through. He remembers May 1968 and the murder of a student, Gilles Tautin.

Now the film can end. It does so with another magnificent studio tracking shot, and then a postlude. The track shows us a huge supermarket from behind the ranks of twenty-five cash registers, all working. The noise is hypnotic. The shot lasts a full ten minutes. The camera moves from left to right then back to the left, then right again, then ends moving left. Behind the registers are the perpendicular rows of products—everything from soap powders to dress suits. On the first run from left to right we pass, in the middle of the store, a member of the CP who has set up shop with some discount party books. No one pays much attention, least of all the ever-moving camera. When we reach the end of the first run (and *change direction*) a group of kids enters from the right, moving left. We follow them more or less until we reach the CP member, and stop for a moment as Anne Wiazemsky and other leftists challenge him. Susan is watching. Then the group yells "Help yourself, it's free!" (a Maoist tactic of the early seventies) and the melee ensues, the cops come, the shot ends moving left. This completes the description of the *rapports de production* (relationships of production). The film begins with the workers who produce; the middle part is devoted to Susan and Jacques, who work in the media, the "means of distribution"; and the film ends in the temple of the consumers. In each element of the *rapports de production,* "things are stirring." Workers, distributors, consumers, "caught up in it all." The "diagram" of *Tout va bien* is wonderfully balanced, almost classical. Along the horizontal, tracking, axis (in time), the three areas of the *rapports de production;* along the vertical, synchronic axis the levels of social practice—economic, political, and ideological. And all of this in a *movie,* with stars and color and music and money and Jerry Lewis sets!

But the love story hasn't finished yet. The supermarket scene is succeeded by two matched shots: "He" is sitting in a cafe, "she" comes and presses her hand to the window; then "she" is sitting in the same spot and "he" approaches the glass. On the soundtrack: "How do you end a film? They've been through a crisis. . . . The audience feels they'll go through others. . . . But we'll leave them this way. . . . Let's say they're rethinking themselves. . . . Each one of us should be his *own* historian . . . Me, you, us." Then the third tracking shot of the film, in the street, past intersections, then close-up past a long brick wall and beyond. On the soundtrack, a popular song at that time: "The sun is shining all over France/That's all that matters"—the penultimate irony. The ultimate irony: an untranslatable pun, in titles: "Un conte pour ceux qui n'en tiennent aucun" (roughly, "a tale for those who don't hold by them.")

In bourgeois cinema we call this a "tour de force." *Tout va bien* is the first love story of the *rapports de production,* the first comedy of disrealization.

But it's also a movie. In order to explain *Tout va bien* more concretely to its audiences, Gorin and Godard made *Letter to Jane,* a forty-five-minute analysis cum apologia of a still photograph of Jane Fonda in Vietnam which was published in the French magazine *L'Express* at the beginning of August 1972. *Letter to Jane* is a monologue by Godard/Gorin (sometimes one of them stops in the middle of a sentence which is completed by the other) in vaguely accented but wonderfully idiomatic English, accompanied by a complex of still photographs. It is meant as a "detour" which "will enable us to talk more concretely about *Tout va bien*" and the problems that film raised, since the photo of Fonda which is its ostensible subject "asks the same question as the film: what part should intellectuals play in the revolution?" Godard and Gorin used *Letter to Jane* during their tour with *Tout va bien* in the U.S. in the fall of 1972; from all reports, *Letter to Jane* was widely misunderstood. Godard/Gorin spend nearly half the film explaining carefully, logically, and from numerous angles of approach that *Letter to Jane* is not meant to criticize Jane Fonda, but to explain her role as a star and the way her stardom is used by the media ("We aren't asking questions of the actress, but of the photograph . . . we're not aiming at Jane, but at the *function* of Jane"); yet ironically (and instructively), audiences still bridle at the criticism of Fonda they infer.

It might have been expected. Despite the intensity of the film's sound and the "weakness" of its image, audiences are still conditioned by "Hollywood" to pay attention to image, not sound. Since the image of Jane Fonda occupies the screen for most of the time, *Letter to Jane* becomes, de facto, a film about Jane, not about what Godard and Gorin *tell* us it is about: themselves, *Tout va bien,* the function of the intellectual in the revolution, the function of stars in media, the semiology of the journalistic still photograph, and some newly important theories about camera angle ("An angle makes a cut through reality in a certain way,"explain Godard/Gorin).*

If we *listen* to *Letter to Jane,* however (as Godard and Gorin ask us to *listen* to the photograph of her), we discover a witty and well-reasoned *explication de texte* (or *d'image*), not the least of whose qualities is its self-deprecating humor. One could understand the misinterpretations

*For a fine exposition of these last two elements, see Jacob Friedrich Münch's essay, "Jean-Luc Godard, Hans Lucas and mich" in which he develops a theory of the "axiomatic of the concrete" *(der Grundsatz in Wirklichheit).*

of American audiences better if Godard and Gorin had spoken French; then the important information that we get from the *tone* of their voices might be lost. But they speak in good, idiomatic English, and the pleasure they take in the dense reticulation of their cinemarxist logic should come through. It is difficult to indicate the musical quality of the rhetoric in print, but here are a few examples, verbatim.

Godard describes the purpose of *Letter to Jane:*

> We think that it's important and urgent to *really* speak to those who have taken the trouble to come and see our film. "Really" means right where they *are.* And also, right where *we* are. And so we must find a way to enable them to really ask questions if they feel like it—or give answers to the questions that *we* have asked. The spectator must be able to really think—and think first of all about this problem of questions and answers. *We* must be able to be really upset by the spectator's questions—or *an*swers—and to answer—or to ask *ques*tions, other than with readymade *an*swers—or *ques*tions to readymade *ques*tions—or *an*swers! But readymade by *whom? For* whom? *Against* whom?

It's the familiar litany of the Dziga Vertov group. A bit later Gorin rephrases it, shifting the focus slightly:

> For once we will not be alone. The spectator will be there too. He will be a producer at the same time as he is a consumer. And we will be consumers at the same time we are producers.
> GODARD: Perhaps all this seems complicated to you. As Vertov said to Lenin, "The fact is that *truth* is simple, but that it's not *simple* to tell the truth." And Uncle Bertolt had come up with five difficulties for telling the truth, back in his time.

The dialogue between producer of cinema and consumer of cinema is essential; the aim is to break the barriers of communication and create an identity between them; that's the only way we can get at truth, existential truth. But the problem lies not only with languages that we recognize as languages (English, French) but also with languages that we do *not* recognize as languages (the language of the journalistic still photograph). If we have trouble interpreting the very human, conscientious, wisely humorous voice of Godard/Gorin, think how impossible it must be to hear the "tone of voice" of news photos. Godard, again (speaking to Jane):

> We are, as you, submerged in some pretty troubled waters, through which this photograph can help us to see clearly. This is where we have to start from [and now he almost chants]—from you in the U.S.—from us in Paris—from you and us in Paris—from you in Vietnam—from us in Paris *looking* at you in Vietnam—from us going to the U.S.—and from everyone here in the theatre listening to us and looking at you.

All the bases are covered in the first twenty minutes of the film before the analysis proper of the photograph begins. Godard and Gorin know the problem with this approach ("people will say that all this sounds like antiwords"), but they also know it is necessary: this is the global approach, through structural causality, that makes it possible to understand the whole of the problem. Remember the importance of "density"—a warning to the reader of the price he has to pay for genuine thinking. Form counts; it says as much as content. If Godard/Gorin are going to tell us this in regard to a photograph in *L'Express,* they had better also *show* it to us in their own film/letter.

For the filmmaker who made an icon of the face of Karina a decade ago, and who dealt with his own image as star in "Caméra-oeil" (not insignificantly motivated by his inability to make a trip to North Vietnam), this photographic image of the face of Fonda is personally important. It is vital to analyze the picture's "photographic molecular structure" or "social nerve cell" (which Godard/Gorin suggest are two ways to think of the image). In the mid-sixties Godard began to break down printed and written words in order to try to understand their value as (unconscious) signs more fully; this led directly into the experimentation of the Dziga Vertov group with "built images." It was natural that he would eventually try to break down images in the same way.

The analysis proper of the *Express* photograph is broken down into categories which are not meant entirely without irony: "Elements of Elements," "Elementary Elements," "Less Elementary Elements," "Other Elements of Elements," and finally, "Putting Together Some Elements—Or Elements of Elements." These categories subtend a set of contradictions, any one of which could easily provide Godard/Gorin with enough material for a full-length film. First, there is the direct contradiction between what we see—Fonda listening—and what we read in the text below the photo—Fonda "questioning inhabitants of North Vietnam." It is not, of course, a simple mistake; it is prime evidence of the focus of the photo, which is Fonda, not North Vietnam or the Vietnamese. Added to this is the fact that a journalist, Joseph Kraft, took the photo. (If anyone is being criticized, it's he.) The text is right, in a sense, since the "militant" (Godard/Gorin refer to her as the "militant," or the "actress," to avoid what might seem to be personal criticism) is in the foreground of the photo and Vietnam is in the background.

When they examine the construction of the photo in more detail, Godard/Gorin discover a complex of details to support this basic contradiction. The low angle ("emphasized technically and socially by Orson

RETOUR DE HANOI

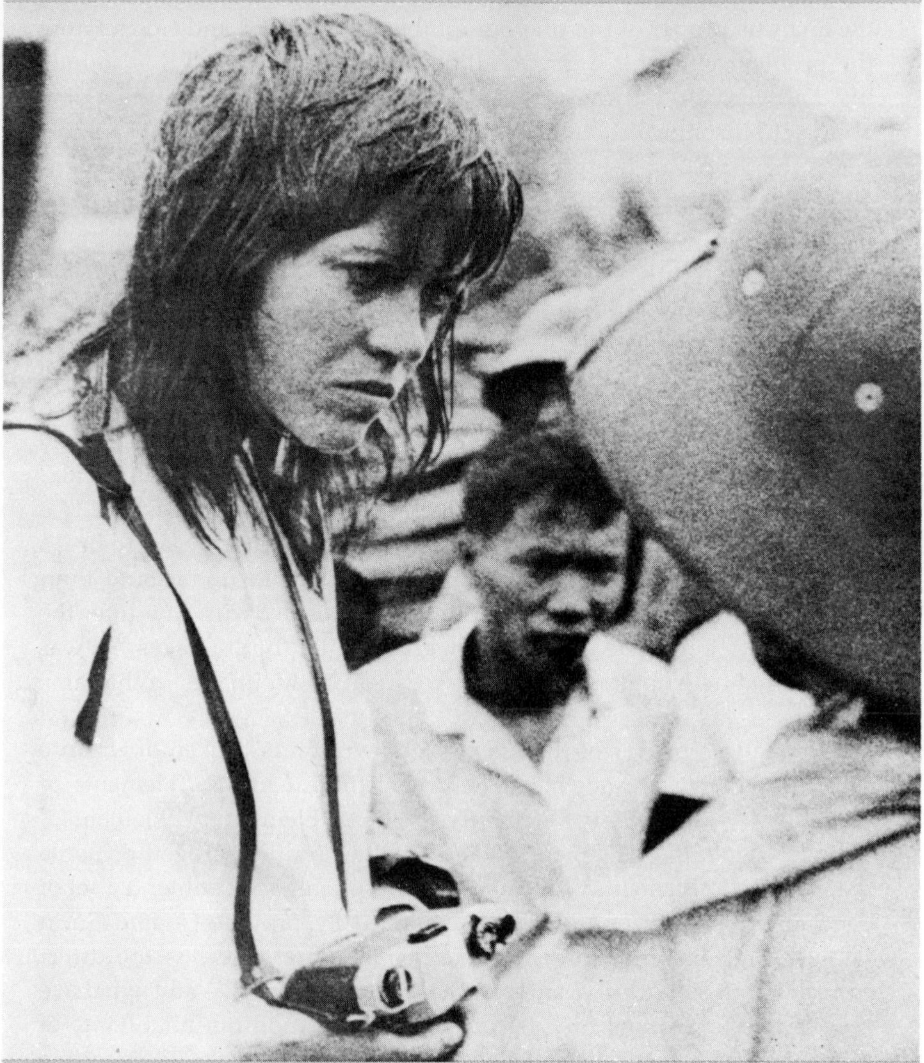

Jane Fonda interrogeant des habitants de Hanoi sur les bombardements américains.

Deux Américains à Hanoi. Deux visions différentes. Le premier, Joseph Kraft, est un des journalistes américains les plus connus et des plus mesurés. L'autre, l'actrice Jane Fonda, est une militante acharnée pour la paix au Vietnam. Joseph Kraft est allé à Hanoi pendant une quinzaine de jours, au début de juillet. Son but : évaluer les chances de paix après les différentes initiatives diplomatiques et militaires du président Nixon. Sa conclusion : une solution politique est possible, mais peu probable. Jane Fonda est restée également une quinzaine de jours à Hanoi, invitée par le Comité pour l'amitié avec le peuple américain. Sa conclusion : les Américains bombardent les digues et la population. C'est un crime inutile, la guerre est perdue. L'Express s'est assuré le témoignage de Joseph Kraft et le reportage photographique de Jane Fonda.

L'EXPRESS · 31 juillet - 6 août 1972

This is not a frame from *Letter to Jane,* but rather the full page which appeared in *L'Express* and from which Godard and Gorin made the images they used.

Brando, Fonda, Fonda, Meir, and Nixon are all sound stars and have therefore learned the same "expression of an expression." But Lillian Gish is a silent star: "I am film therefore I think." (Frame enlargements.)

Welles in his first pictures") is important. The framing is even more significant, "composed for the actress, who is *looking,* rather than for what she is *looking at.*" The American is sharp and clear; the Vietnamese are blurry and unclear, "whereas, in reality it is the American left which is blurry and out of focus, and the Vietnamese left which is exceptionally sharp and clear." These are the "Elementary Elements."

What is most important for Godard/Gorin, however,is not the technical form which the *photographer* brings to the photo, but the form which the *actress* gives it. Most of the analysis of the photo has to do with the iconography of the "actress's expression." "Jane's face gives too much information in too short a time and space," they tell us. In short, it has the intensity of an *acted* expression. It is a codified sign, and as such recalls a whole history of itself. *Letter to Jane,* in its most intriguing sequence, traces the history of that expression backwards in time—through Jane Fonda in *Tout va bien* and *Klute,* back to her father in *Young Mr. Lincoln* and *Grapes of Wrath.* For Godard/Gorin, this sad expression "talks, but only to say how *much* it knows. It says nothing more," that is, about *what* it knows. It is quantitative and emotional rather than qualitative and analytic. There is nothing wrong with that, per se, except that the expression is used—not necessarily by the actress, but by capitalist society—to hide reality, to mask it. It is not so much an expression, Godard tells us, as "an expression of an expression . . . which appeared inevitably by chance with the talkies. It is borrowed, principal and interest, from the free-trade mask of Roosevelt's New Deal." Godard/Gorin offer in evidence of this historical point an elaboration of Kuleshov's experiment: they juxtapose images of Falconetti, Lillian Gish, and Valentino with images of the Vietnamese war.

These stars do not "look" at the war with the same sad expression that the Fondas and John Wayne just did. Silent film, Godard suggests, was materialist. Each actor had his own image. Only with the advent of the talkies did actors begin to "talk" alike. Silent film stars thought, "I am film, therefore I think." Stars of the talkies reversed the proposition: "I *think* that I am an actor, therefore I am filmed." They fit themselves to the role of star they have learned. (*Letter to Jane*, it might be noted, is as Cartesian as it is Barthesian.)

Not only film stars learned this expression of an expression. Moshe Dayan does it as well as Kirk Douglas; Nixon and Golda Meir as well as Che Guevara and Solzhenitzyn. (This is the one part of the film in which it is necessary to look, for the stills Godard has chosen are powerful proof.) The stars (in film), Godard notes, " play a 'heavy' role, as they say, and the real tragedy is that they don't *know* how to play this role." This is the central problem—for Godard, for Jane Fonda, for us all: what part is the intellectual to play in the revolution? But that sentence is shorthand; what it really means is, how can we learn to see better so that we may act more effectively? *Letter to Jane* has no answers; many of the intricate statements it makes about the semiology of the photograph (and related issues) can be contradicted, criticized. But the basic point remains: reality is not understood simply: it is, for us in the twentieth century, both reticulated and mediated: reticulated because linear causality is no longer sufficient; mediated because we comprehend it now not primarily through our own eyes and ears, but through technological media which change reality as they transmit it. In Gorin's words, it is a process of *de*formation as well as *in*formation. We had better take a close look at *form,* the kernel of both those words.

"We are building films—machines—" Gorin said in 1972, "which can produce other films—which are *different* from the ones before. We are beginning to realize we have to quit with the word politics in order to be more political." And Godard adds, "To be more revolutionary is to emphasize the art of listening, in order to be a better speaker."[26] The struggle continues, but on ever-changing fronts.

It may be that the process of struggle and criticism as it is reflected in the politics of film that Godard and Gorin have created will eventually lead from the world of ideas back to the human world; that the filmmakers will at last feel they understand the medium well enough to be free to use it to discover the deductive politics of experience. They have learned how to make political films politically, but they have never learned how to make them deductively: the very existence of the logic of

Marxist esthetics prevented that. Godard's dilemma, in this sense, is archetypally the dilemma of the twentieth-century intellectual, furiously concerned not only to be part of the revolution, but also (having been caught in the fallout from the explosion of theory and logic early in this century) to escape back to the human level, the level of experience. There is something absolutely and inherently hollow about the abstraction of the intellect. Godard has felt it throughout his career; fear of it is the one subtext that runs continuously from *A bout de souffle* to *Letter to Jane*. But he could never quite learn the lesson of 68 in this respect. No one gainsays the value of materialist "disrealization" and the struggle to transform the language of film so that it speaks honestly. But, likewise, we should not overlook the less heroic struggle to understand a little bit more about the politics of our everyday lives through the use of the cinematic language which already exists. There comes a time, after all the truths of esthetics have been admitted, that one has to make a break—ignore them—and return to making cinema not about itself, not about ideas, but about the people who think the ideas.

Truffaut was recently asked by a snide interviewer whether he thought Godard made "tediously political films because he was born rich and so feels a responsibility to make statements." He replied, with more grace than the question deserved,

> No I wouldn't say that. He's very fast-moving by nature. He quickly exhausts what amuses him, what interests him, and movies, which can satisfy someone for his whole life, satisfied him for only a few years. He changed interests, and politics became a stronger interest for him than movies. So he tries to satisfy that passion, staying in movies but with the occasional temptation to get out of them a bit. It's a grave problem, one that I don't have, because movies are an exclusive passion for me.[27]

That "fast-moving" nature is driven by a violent passion to comprehend, not merely how one thing connects with another, but how everything is part of everything else. This makes Godard's films difficult, sometimes inscrutable, often very private, but it also makes of him a poet of cinematic relativity. His thirty-seven films comprise one of the most significant struggles, in any artistic genre, in this century. His sinuous roots twist back to Mozart and Bach, to Picasso, Nietzsche, Hegel, Marx, Dostoevsky, Brecht, Renoir (père et fils), Joyce, Bogart, Mao, Rossellini, Balzac, and Lenin. He has felt and understood the unity of the culture that stretches from Bach to Batman, from Racine to the Rolling Stones, and he has drawn from his study several very real, hard, ineluctable truths:

- that this culture represses and constricts us as much as it expresses our fears and desires,
- that our cities are Alphavillean nightmares,
- that our culture turns women into objects of consumption and men into fearful, paralyzed dreamers, half in love with easeful death,
- that our machines of communication and transportation have overwhelmed us, so that it is they who can be said to "live," not us,
- that our social contract is ludicrously twisted.

More important, he has also tried to indicate several paths by which we can rewrite that social contract, redesign our arts, and redeem ourselves by understanding the true nature of our economic and social structures and learning how to re-create them so that they affirm life rather than deny it. If at times the details of the new social contract seem fuzzy and inexplicit, remember the difficulty of the job.

Remember, too, that throughout his career Godard has been an analyst, not a synthesizer. His job has been to explain, to criticize, to abstract. Perhaps it must be left to others to build, to create. Perhaps it is true that the only way to become a revolutionary intellectual is to cease being an intellectual. Godard's harrowing honesty has already done much to describe just how his own contemplative, analytical nature paralyzes and prevents action.

Yet an analysis such as Godard's, which destroys old patterns of thought and reveals the intimate and direct interconnections between what used to be seen as the separate realms of psyche, society, economics, philosophy, culture, cinema, and logic, must be seen as creative. Godard's art is *consciencieux,* a conflation of conscience and the consciousness of self, an intimate confluence of the personal and the moral, of method and sentiment. It leaves me breathless.

11

CHABROL
Films Noirs in Color

Claude Chabrol was born in Paris in 1930 but spent most of his childhood in the village of Sardent in the Creuse district 150 miles south of the capital, where, at an early age—like most of his future colleagues on *Cahiers du Cinéma*—he was "seized by the demon of cinema." Between the ages of ten and fourteen he ran a film club in a barn in the village. After the war he returned to Paris where, following the wishes of his father, he studied pharmacy. He began to haunt the Cinémathèque in the Avenue Messine and the Ciné-Club du Quartier Latin where he got to know Rohmer, Truffaut, and Godard. He next spent some time in military service (where, he says, he managed to get himself posted as a projectionist in Germany) and apparently during this period also married his first wife, who came from a well-to-do family. Returning from military service, he ran into his old friends again and they insisted he write for their new magazine, *Cahiers.* Like Godard and Truffaut he also wrote for *Arts* magazine during this period, but his most significant contribution as a critic was the study of Hitchcock (1957) which he co-wrote with Eric Rohmer. Chabrol notes modestly that Rohmer was responsible for most of the book. Chabrol did the English period, *Notorious, Stage Fright,* and *Rebecca.*

Chabrol also spent some time as publicity man for 20th Century-Fox in Paris (a job he later turned over to Godard), but when his wife inherited some money, he finally saw his way clear to finance his first film. In December of 1957 he returned to Sardent with a couple of young, unknown actors and a small crew and during the next three months shot *Le Beau Serge (Handsome Serge),* the first film of the New Wave. The film, which cost about $85,000, won a prize at Locarno in 1958 and served as a practical example that the theories of filmmaking that Chabrol, Godard, and the others had been championing in the pages of *Cahiers* would actually work: that personal films could be made well on a limited budget.

For the first few years of the New Wave, Claude Chabrol was its financial angel. Already in 1956 he had raised the money for Rivette's "Le Coup du berger" (for which he also contributed the scenario). Between 1958 and 1960 he also financed Rohmer's "Véronique et son cancre" and *Le Signe du lion* and Philippe de Broca's first feature, *Les Jeux de l'amour.* He helped to finance Rivette's legendary *Paris nous appartient,* which was more than two years in the making, and when Rivette ran out of stock Chabrol came to the rescue with the leftover filmstock from *Les Cousins.* It was the company Chabrol formed at this time, AJYM Films, which served as a nucleus for the early cooperative efforts of the *Cahiers* critics-turned-filmmakers. Although neither the company nor the theory of cooperation survived the early sixties, Chabrol nevertheless deserves more credit than he has so far received for the practical intelligence he applied to the financing of the early New Wave films.

Chabrol has always had the reputation of being the most "commercial" of the New Wave directors. There are various partially valid reasons for this. In the first place, the director himself tends to disparage his own "art." In interviews he conveys a consistently sardonic view of symbols, metaphors, and other such artistic paraphernalia. When asked why there are, so often, literary quotations in his films (Eliot in *La Femme infidèle,* Balzac in *Le Boucher* [*The Butcher*], Racine in *La Rupture*) he replied:

> I'll be truthful. It's to give them substance. I need a degree of critical support for my films to succeed: without that they can fall flat on their faces. So, what do you have to do? You have to help the critics over their notices, right? So I give them a hand. "Try with Eliot and see if you find me there." Or "How do you fancy Racine?" I give them some little things to grasp at. In *Le Boucher* I stuck Balzac there is the middle, and they threw themselves upon it like poverty upon the world. It's good not to leave them

staring at a blank sheet of paper, not knowing how to begin. . . . "This film is definitely Balzacian," and there you are; they're off.[1]

More important, unlike any of his colleagues, Chabrol has consistently concentrated on a single genre of film, and that genre has a notable commercial history. His *films policiers* (which is what, for want of a more precise term, we shall call them for the moment) may be more self-conscious than those of Fritz Lang and Alfred Hitchcock (his paragons), they may be slightly ironic; but, like their predecessors, they have strong story lines which obey certain generalized rules of the genre. The level of discourse has not been raised to a more distanced, objective plane as it has with Godard, Rivette, or even Truffaut. Chabrol must appreciate the fine irony: although one of the basic successes of the *Cahiers* politique during the fifties was in restoring the balance between the personal "fine art" tradition of European film and the popular genre tradition of American film, when Chabrol carried this precept from print into film his critical reputation suffered in comparison with those of his colleagues who forged a union between the two traditions. No wonder he tries to "give the critics a hand."

There is one final reason why Chabrol's reputation is still not what it should be, especially among Anglo-Saxon critics: simply put, he has made more than his share of unsuccessful films. During the mid-sixties when he found it difficult to obtain financing for the films he wanted to make, he retrenched and took several potboilers on assignment; none of the other directors of the New Wave did this. It is necessary to do some weeding in the Chabrolian garden of more than thirty films, not only in the hard-luck period of the mid-sixties but before and after as well. Even when he is in full control of a film, Chabrol makes mistakes. Partly this is the result of his own sardonic attitude to his work (he seems to enjoy the mistakes as well as the successes), and partly a natural consequence of working within genres. Once we've learned to deal with the unevenness of the Chabrol canon, however, his real value appears with striking clarity. He is the craftsman par excellence of the New Wave, and his variations upon a theme give us an understanding of the explicitness and precision of the language of the film that we don't get from the more varied experiments in genre of Truffaut or the more personal, intellectual cinema of Godard.

The basic foundations of Chabrol's cinema reveal themselves in the three major critical documents he produced during his years on the staff of *Cahiers du Cinéma.* "Little Themes" ("Les Petits Sujets") is the shortest and most succinct defense of genre films ever published in those pages. Chabrol sets up two potential scenarios: "The Apocalypse of Our Time," obviously a "Big Theme," and "The Quarrel Between Neighbors," a little one. After having some fun at the expense of the inherent pomposity and vapid pretensions of "Big Themes," he comes straight to the point, which is basically the result of a structural analysis of cinema. As he has set them up, there is no essential structural difference between "The Apocalypse of Our Time" and "The Quarrel Between Neighbors": each offers the same thematic possibilities, but whereas the Big Theme film does so inductively, the Little Theme film proceeds by deduction and is grounded in concrete, experiential reality.[2] Chabrol's films are marked by an insistent—at times obsessive—structural restriction because, as he concludes, "the smaller the theme is, the more one can give it a big treatment."

Underlying this dictum is an attitude—not unlike Godard's (or Truffaut's)—which suggests that it's not what one says but how one says it that really counts: the structure is the message. So Chabrol, very early on, chose his own genre, whose structural rules would provide a haven within which he could work out the details of "the big treatment." With only a few exceptions, all of Chabrol's films have dealt with the structures and materials we usually associate with crime stories. More often than not—especially since 1968—the crime is murder. Chabrol's essay "Evolution du film policier"[3] is the first index of his interest in this genre and, of course, the book on Hitchcock is central. However, while the French term *policier* is broader in meaning than its English equivalent, "detective story," neither of these labels accurately describes Chabrol's own peculiar genre. Whereas the *policier* views events generally from the point of view of the detective, the objective observer, none of Chabrol's films—except for the potboilers of the mid-sixties—takes this perspective. Rather, we are always with those characters who are subjectively involved in the action of the crime, both "victims" and "perpetrators." There are seldom identifiable protagonist/antagonist relationships in Chabrol's films as there always are in detective stories. His world is internal and global rather than dialectical. It is not ratiocination that fascinates Chabrol, but guilt, psychopathy, and violent passion. His films, then, are much closer structurally to the Films Noirs of the late forties and early fifties than to straight detective fiction. They lack the downbeat quality of forties Films Noirs and they do have a sense of humor, so we had best call them "Films Noirs en couleurs."

Chabrol owes a debt to Hitchcock, but there are significant differences between their universes. Chabrol himself in recent interviews has not missed an opportunity to suggest that Fritz Lang's films might be more important referents than Hitchcock's, and with good reason, I think. Central to the classic Hitchcock film is a sense of the tension in the relationship between pursuer and pursued—an element which is not all that important in Chabrol's films, and which he often avoids completely, as in *Juste avant la nuit (Just Before Nightfall).* Hitchcock's films develop a political sense because the detective so often represents the state and because the pursued is often innocent. But everyone is always guilty in Chabrol's films. This is a darker, more Langian guilt than we ever see in Hitchcock where in fact most characters are innocent. Chabrol's people, like Lang's suffer psychological guilt even when the law overlooks their transgressions, while Hitchcock's people don't—even when they are rightly accused. Chabrol, with Eric Rohmer, formed what we might call the Catholic wing of the *Cahiers* group, and this strong sense of guilt has often been interpreted as essentially religious.

However, to concentrate on the moral dimensions of Chabrol's world—whether religious, Hitchcockian, or Langian—is a bit misleading; for Chabrol is more concerned with the structure of his films than with the metaphysics of his characters. In a recent interview, he put it this way:

> It isn't the character which interests me at the start—a character you can always fabricate. . . . not the plot. . . . What interests me is to tease the audience along, to set it chasing off in one direction, and then to turn things inside out.[4]

This—not metaphysics—is Chabrol's most important debt to Hitchcock: a sense of the curious relationship between filmmaker and audience and an understanding of the psychological power of the medium. We may criticize Chabrol's films for their insipid politics, for their cavalier attitude towards their characters, but when he is at his best Chabrol has no peers as a manipulator of the medium.

As his career has developed it has become increasingly difficult to avoid this truth about his work. Molly Haskell, one of the most perceptive critics of Chabrol, put it this way:

> The formal concerns of the early films . . . have become the substance of the later ones, with an accompanying loss of interest in character exploration and psychological development. . . . Theme and plot would be better defined as motifs and movements, forming a kind of symphonic structure which makes [the films] closer to music than movies.[5]

While we might argue over the weight Haskell gives to "character exploration and psychological development" in the early films, there is no doubt that since 1968 Chabrol has focused ever more intently on style. Between 1968 and 1973 he produced ten films with remarkable structural similarities. He was working with the same crew,* and many of the actors made recurrent appearances in this group of films, most notably his wife Stéphane Audran and Michel Bouquet. The result is a group of films which illuminate each other; and therefore the group as a whole is more valuable than the sum of its parts. (The title of the seventh of the series—*La Décade prodigieuse* [*Ten Days' Wonder*]—thus takes on extra significance.)

The elements of Chabrol's "decameron" are easily identified: the materials are thoroughly bourgeois, as is the ambiance. One of the central questions in Chabrol criticism is whether or not (as Robin Wood has put it) "the savage derider of the bourgeoisie has become its elegiac poet." This is not such an easy question to answer as might at first seem. Chabrol reveals a considerable ambivalence towards the bourgeois universe, as we shall see, but it should be emphasized that the subtlety of his films demands a corresponding sense of irony in his audiences. Even when Chabrol is most rhapsodically bourgeois there is still a distancing which gives the films a critical dimension. The problem arises when we place more emphasis on character than Chabrol does and therefore identify with (or infer that Chabrol identifies with) the good businessmen and carefully coiffed and perfumed matrons who people his landscape.

More important, I think, than the bourgeois subject matter of the films is what Chabrol does with it. These are all strongly materialist films in which the qualities of light and texture, the "meanings" of landscape and color, and the way the camera captures, conveys, and modifies these materials take precedence over the données of plot and character. Chabrol is acutely aware of the function of location within a film, and much of his energy during shooting is devoted to capturing the particular qualities of the locale. Paris and its suburbs, Brussels, the village of Trémolat in Périgord, Brittany, and Alsace each have figured prominently in one or more of the recent films. It is within these precise locales and against their particular backgrounds that the characters' elemental passions are displayed.

*Photographer: Jean Rabier; Editor: Jacques Gaillard; Sound: Guy Chichignoud; Music: Pierre Jansen; Designer: Guy Littaye; producer: André Génovès; co-scenarist on six of the films: Paul Gégauff. Chabrol's working relationship with most of these people extends back as far as the late fifties and early sixties.

In the context of these finely observed backgrounds, Chabrol's characters find themselves absorbed, not in the melodramatic events which usually constitute the fabric of a thriller, but in the mundane rituals of everyday life. It has become almost a joke, for example, that meals are an obsession with Chabrol. (It is said that he decided to shoot *La Décade prodigieuse* in Alsace simply because he wanted an opportunity to sample the cuisine of that region.) If there is an emblem for the height of French bourgeois culture, it must be the dinner table. Sex, of course, is important too as a ritual for Chabrol; as pleasurable and meaningful as it is, food is not often the root cause of murder. The arena for both activities is the family which, with very few exceptions, is the central subject—and not always an object of ridicule. "I like the family very much," he has said. "I think it's a much misunderstood thing; very beautiful, and very delicate . . . so I am for it. . . . The bourgeois family is a farce. . . . It doesn't exist. But a *real* family, that is something wonderful."[6] The family, as a political concept, is extended in several of the films to embrace the village—a larger matrix out of which arises, as in *Le Boucher,* occasional aberrant violence. Chabrol's films seldom come to a distinct period; the reason is that the plane of focus is this larger unit (the family or the village), which continues even after the particular story ends. There is an ironic tension between the environment and the passion which is basic to a Chabrol film.

Chabrol organizes all of these structural elements in three dimensions. First, there is the basic excuse of the genre: the *policier* provides the framework within which these elements can be set; the murders are the catalysts which help in our analysis of the structures. Second, Chabrol sets up an elaborate network of conventions—some of which come from the genre, many of which are his alone—which formalize and de-dramatize the proceedings. There is, for example, a recurrent pattern of exchanges of responsibility between characters throughout the films, which some critics have interpreted as signifying Catholic theories of guilt transference. The dialectic between city and country first established in *Le Beau Serge* (and mirrored in *Les Cousins*) is probably the most striking example of this. The pattern extends even to the architecture of the films, the staircase (a device for exchange) being a favorite Chabrol locale. Last, and most important, is the subtle emphasis on point of view which marks Chabrol's films. As we have indicated earlier, mise-en-scène almost always takes precedence over psychology—and the strength of the mise-en-scène forces our consciousness that these events and characters are seen from a precise point of view. This dimension is more abstract than the previous two and not so easily apprehended, but it just may be the key to understanding Claude Chabrol's movies. On the one hand, it is a sign of the formalism of the films; on the other, if we don't have a sense of this filmmaker's irony, not a few of his films degenerate into maudlin exercises in melodrama: this irony is the ultimate rationale for his devotion to "little themes." If we can't sense it, then most of his films have only formal interest for us.

The eight features and one short that Chabrol made between 1958 and 1962 are a curiously mixed group. With the benefit of more than a decade's hindsight we can now discern a quality of febrile experimentation which unites them, but at the time they were first seen they produced in critics a false image of Chabrol's concerns which was not corrected until the early seventies. His first two films, *Le Beau Serge* and *Les Cousins,* were immediate successes—and accurate harbingers of many of the preoccupations of the early New Wave. Yet today we can see that *Le Beau Serge* stands in isolation from the bulk of Chabrol's films and, if *Les Cousins* is still one of his most successful efforts, it may have become popular for the wrong reasons. *A double tour (Leda; Web of Passion),* his third film (1959), was not especially successful—maybe because it clashed with the "mainstream" of the New Wave during that year—*Les Quatre Cents Coups, Hiroshima mon amour,* and *A bout de souffle.* Yet now Chabrol's first color film looms much larger in the canon of his work.

Les Bonnes Femmes (1960) is generally regarded as Chabrol's most important film during this period; *Les Godelureaux,* made the same year, is undoubtedly his worst. Yet both films, in retrospect, are clearly markers along the same path. "Avarice," his contribution to the compilation film *Les Septs Péchés capitaux* (1961), is an unexceptionable piece of work; "Gluttony" would have inspired Chabrol a lot more. In 1962, in quick succession, we were given *L'Oeil du malin (The Evil Eye, The Third Lover),* one of Chabrol's most underrated films; *Ophélia,* one of his worst, and *Landru (Bluebeard),* also unsuccessful at the time, but more appreciated now.

With his customary diffidence, Chabrol describes how he came to make his first film:

> I had come into a little money and it seemed the right time to think about shooting a film—with the actors of my choice, on a subject of my choice—a film capable of supporting the handicap of a limited budget. From the scenarios I was carrying around in my head I chose the one which was a sure thing not to go over budget catastrophically: *Le Beau Serge,* which I

directed, free as the air, in eight weeks in [Sardent], a village in the Creuse. . . .[7]

The film was an immediate success, praised for its novelty and freshness. The location shooting, the use of non-professionals, the "socially conscious theme," the crude but effective black and white photography, all made it seem as if Chabrol were heralding a kind of French neorealism. But of course Claude Chabrol least of all among the New Wave was headed in that direction. The qualities of neorealism were simply the result of practical production decisions. Chabrol's heart lay elsewhere.

The story of a "city cousin," François (Jean-Claude Brialy), who returns home to discover that the "country cousin," Serge (Gérard Blain), has fared poorly during his absence, *Le Beau Serge* immediately sets up a clear pattern of exchange. Serge is ashamed: he has had a mongoloid child and he has turned into a drunkard. The priest can't do anything. (Chabrol considers this film his farewell to Catholicism). François thinks that maybe he can, by providing an example. Serge won't take his advice, but eventually finds his own solution of exchange by going off with Marie (Bernadette Lafont), his wife's half-sister who has been François's lover. A baby is born—healthy—and Serge is relieved of the burden of his guilt. In addition, there is a complex pattern of doublings and recurrences (two old men, two young men who mirror them, two sisters, two scenes in the cemetery, two scenes with Serge's truck, and so forth) which has been well documented by Robin Wood. So what looks like a realist film intent on capturing the details of everyday life and the elemental emotions of country people nevertheless has some of the strict formalism and stylistic distancing that will mark Chabrol's later work.

This structural obsession is even more evident in *Les Cousins*, a film conceived before *Le Beau Serge* which must be read in tandem with it. This time the location is the city, and it is the country cousin who makes the visit. Paul (Gérard Blain) has come to Paris to study law and has moved in with Charles (Jean-Claude Brialy), who lives a life which is a parody of student decadence, replete with Wagnerian parties, redolent of sado-masochism, and seasoned with a touch of fascist sentiment. The basic structure of exchange was established in *Le Beau Serge*, but *Les Cousins* adds several significant elements to the design. In the first film the sexual geometry was quadrilateral—there were two women as well as two men involved in the focal relationship. In *Les Cousins* Chabrol reduces this to the standard triangle: Florence (Juliette

Mayniel) is at the center of the relationship between Paul and Charles. Second, Chabrol has shifted the social locus of the film away from the working class into the bourgeoisie, where it will remain. Most important, the relationship of exchanges has to do now with degeneration and death, rather than salvation as in *Le Beau Serge.* Clovis (Claude Cerval)—one of Chabrol's most malignant characters—has "seduced" Charles in the same way that Charles tempts Paul. (Cerval had played the priest in *Le Beau Serge.*) Murder is a factor now, but the killing occurs only at the end of the film, almost as an afterthought. Gradually, Chabrol will realize that his strongest interest lies in the effects of the murder rather than the events leading up to it. Finally, "Paul" and "Charles" have made their first appearance. They will quickly become types for Chabrol, and although they have not yet been joined by "Hélène," the actress who will play her most often, Stéphane Audran, does make her first appearance in a Chabrol film (in a secondary role).

Les Cousins is also the first film Chabrol co-wrote with Paul Gégauff, which accounts for both its sterner characterizations and a certain lugubrious humor. The films Chabrol has written by himself are, almost without exception, milder in tone, less nasty to their characters, and less distanced. "When I want cruelty," Chabrol has said, "I go off and look for Gégauff. Paul is very good at gingering things up and he can make anyone appear ridiculous. . . . He can make a character absolutely ridiculous and hateful in two seconds flat."[8]

A double tour, Chabrol's second collaboration with Gégauff, was shot mainly on location at Aix-en-Provence during the spring of 1959. The film is notable for its exuberant color photography. Ever since, color has been an important tool for Chabrol, and we can see why here. The formal contrast between the haut bourgeois Marcoux house, full of browns and maroons, and the clear whites and blues of Leda's cottage is striking, as are the occasional punctuation shots—the peacock flaring its tail, or the red field of poppies, for example. *A double tour* also extends the preoccupation with doubling to the structure of the narrative as Chabrol experiments with an architecture of dual flashbacks within the time scheme of a single day. The first flashback parallels the time sequence of the first part of the film, while the second flashback doubles back on the first. The first is narrated by the father, Henri (Jacques Dacqmine), the second by the son, Richard (André Jocelyn); both are stories of Léda (Antonella Lualdi), who is the apex of the triangle of this film (a triangle which is oedipal for the first time). The murder is set in the center of the film this time, as Chabrol begins to discover his interest in the aftermath.

A double tour (the title has a double meaning) is also an unusual film for Chabrol in that its structure offers us a potential alternative perspective. While the main focus of the film is the Marcoux family and the mistress Léda's effect on its members, we are also given a parallel, exterior relationship between Léda and Laszlo Kovacs (Jean-Paul Belmondo) which is altogether healthier. The film *could* have been shot from this point of view, as Chabrol seems to suggest on occasion. The subplot involving the maid Julie (Bernadette Lafont) and the milkman Roger (Mario David) also suggests this alternative. The uncharacteristic extroversion of *A double tour* is also suggested by Chabrol's New Wave in-jokes ("Laszlo Kovacs" is of course Belmondo's alias in *A bout de souffle*.)

In his next film, *Les Bonnes Femmes,* Chabrol returned to a simpler narrative structure. The result is the best of his early films. *Les Bonnes Femmes* is constructed backward from the murder of Jacqueline (Clotilde Joano) which takes place at the end of the film. It is as if the story had been told in detail and then Chabrol and Gégauff had carefully edited out those scenes and other elements which did not pertain to the imminent murder. Jacqueline's long, inviting neck almost begs to be strangled, and she, like the rest of her fellow shopgirls, displays morbid preoccupations whose central symbol is the blood-soaked handkerchief that Mme Louise keeps wrapped up in her handbag—her "mascot" she calls it—which she once dipped in the offal of the guillotining of "Weidman," a convicted sadist and rapist who was executed in 1939. When Mme Louise finally reveals her "secret" (because Jacqueline is in love "and it may bring her luck"!), none of the girls find her obsession in any way distasteful. So André's quiet—almost sacrificial—execution of Jacqueline has an air of inevitability.

This Langian fatality is emphasized by the image we have of the romantic motorcyclist André until just before the murder, when he reveals some psychopathic characteristics—which Jacqueline refuses to see, of course. It is he, after all, who rescues Jacqueline from Albert and his friend who are dunking her in the swimming pool. For most of the film it seems that the girls have more to fear from boredom, and from the boring male partners that Albert and his friends represent, than from violence.

This is one of the few Chabrol films where the emotional geometry is not triangular. The relationship between André and Jacqueline is more a matter of fantasy, and the other characters are not involved directly in it. Jacqueline's co-workers in the eerily empty electric appliance shop each represent a fantasy alternative to death. Rita (Lucile Saint-Simon)

Les Bonnes Femmes: Jane (Bernadette Lafont) and Ginette (Stéphane Audran).

is hoping to marry into the bourgeoisie. Her boyfriend (Claude Berri) gives her nervous lessons in culture just before her first lunch with his parents. Jane (Bernadette Lafont) has an aggressive personality which the others lack and which we sense will stand her in good stead. She enjoys the life of pick-ups and cheap nightclubs. Ginette (Stéphane Audran) is the most sympathetic of the group; she has a secret career as a singer and a sense of her own worth that the others lack.

That *Les Bonnes Femmes* is meant as a generalization is re-emphasized by its closing sequence: in a dance hall a young woman is picked up. She smiles and dances with the man. We never see his face, only hers—and the slowly revolving mirrored ball that hangs from the ceiling. When *Les Bonnes Femmes* was released, it drew the ire of not a few French critics—especially of the left—and we can see why. The film shows little sympathy either with the girls or with their situation. More than any other film, this was the one responsible for Chabrol's early reputation as a cynic. Yet there is much in the film that suggests that Chabrol simply had no idea that the reality behind it could or would be judged by the audience. If *Les Bonnes Femmes* is even today regarded as one of the finest realistic depictions of the Paris of the early New Wave, there is good evidence that that aspect of it was almost beside the point for Chabrol. Robin Wood has analyzed at length the strict formal qualities of *Les Bonnes Femmes*—the contrasts between circles and straight lines, light and dark—which almost overwhelm the film with motifs. More important, perhaps, is its humor. This is the first of

Chabrol's films where we are sure that he actually intended the laughter. If Mme Louise's momento mori is lugubrious, it is also absurd. M. Bertin, who owns the strange shop, takes great pleasure in his conferences with employees who are late for work: "I enjoy reprimanding little girls," he lovingly explains to Jacqueline, as he ogles her through his pince-nez. "It's a privilege of my age." Then he offers her a flower and sings. A bit later the poet enters the shop for his weekly visit. "I've finished two poems!" he declares to the admiring shopgirls: "The Prayer of Priapus, and Sonnet to Saint Peter."

This humor is a strong hint that there is an element of distancing we should consider. There is internal evidence that Chabrol's primary concern is not solely relationships between characters but also the connection through film between auteur and audience. Theaters are an important motif of *Les Bonnes Femmes.* Ginette performs nightly in the role of "a famous Italian singer." André courts Jacqueline by doing crude parlor tricks for her. Most important, however, is the nightclub sequence which begins the film. We are about to observe Dolly Bell's striptease number. The camera fixes on the break in the curtain, a hand extends beguilingly. Just as the curtains are parted Chabrol cuts to a reverse point of view and the audience, rather than the stripteaser, is revealed to us. The meaning of the content of the sequence has been translated into the meaning of its form, and this semiological trick can serve as model for much that is to come in Chabrol.

If *Les Bonnes Femmes* is arguably Chabrol's best film of the early period, *Les Godelureaux,* its successor, is definitely his worst. A reworking of the narrative structures of *Les Cousins,* this film about "fops" reduces Chabrol's growing formalist concern to sterility. He himself dismissed it this way: "It was about uselessness, and its lack of success came from the fact that it too was useless."[9] As in *Les Cousins,* Brialy plays the destructive, decadent character (Ronald). He is joined this time by Charles Belmont as the corruptible innocent (Arthur) and Bernadette Lafont (Ambroisine). Simpler in design than its predecessor (both were written by Gégauff), *Les Godelureaux* dispenses with the figure of Clovis, thus making the destructive relationship between the two central characters more precise and focusing our attention on the function of the woman character as an instrument wielded by Ronald for the corruption of Arthur. Chabrol will do this again—much better—in *Les Biches.*

Around this time Chabrol hit the first dead spot in his career. Aside from his seventeen-minute sketch "Avarice," he was inactive for nearly two years. When he did return to the screen, however, it was with

L'Oeil du malin, one of his most intriguing films. Shooting on location in and around Munich, Chabrol, for the first time since *Le Beau Serge,* worked without Paul Gégauff and the result is a much softer, less distanced, and more compassionate film. It still deals with the geography of the murder genre and the geometry of jealous triangles, but there is a realism to *L'Oeil du malin* which contrasts noticeably with the films Gégauff wrote. It's as if Chabrol had decided to apply the lessons he had learned about the form to a realistic drama. It is the received critical opinion that Chabrol's early films are much more involved with character development and psychological investigation than his later ones, which are more coldly formal. That is a misreading, I think. There is no doubt that *L'Oeil du malin* is a minor masterpiece of character and psychology, but the very contrast that it makes with most of the films that preceded it should show us that this more human, less formal tone is a quality not of the chronological period but rather of the group of films (*Le Beau Serge, La Femme infidèle, Le Boucher,* and *Juste avant la nuit* for example, in addition to *L'Oeil du malin*) which Chabrol wrote without Gégauff.

Albin Mercier (Jacques Charrier) is a journalist sent on assignment to Bavaria who meets Hélène and Andreas Hartman (Stéphane Audran and Walter Reyer) and becomes infatuated with them and profoundly jealous of what he perceives to be their ideal marriage. He photographs Hélène's tryst with her lover and thereby destroys the happiness from which he is isolated. Andreas shoots his wife. Most critics have commented on the classic oedipal situation, and that abstract matrix is certainly responsible for much of the film's power; but what is really interesting about *L'Oeil du malin* is the detail work which makes the drama of jealousy come alive. As with all Chabrol's best films, it is craftsmanship of the highest order—mise-en-scène and montage of great precision and versatility—that gives a classic genre story the pulse beat of felt reality.

There is also a subtext to *L'Oeil du malin,* implied in the title, which cannot be avoided. The film is narrated from Albin's point of view, and at several points Chabrol comments cinematically on our identification with the journalist. In the crucial scene in which Albin photographs Hélène with her lover, Chabrol has him first raise the camera and point it directly at the audience before cutting to a series of shots seen through the lens of the camera. The point is well taken: the camera is l'oeil du malin, the evil eye, and Albin's psychological predicament as a jealous observer is our own. This is one of the key scenes in all of Chabrol, for it explains the relationship between form and content which rationalizes his obsession with film style and film technique and the ways they can be used to manipulate audiences. If Godard was later the one to make the explicit statements of theories of film ethics, Chabrol gave us the best demonstrations of the surreptitious ways in which film manipulates us. Albin's photographs directly cause a murder.

Later in 1962 Chabrol turned to a mythic reinterpretation of the oedipal plot in *Ophélia,* a parody of *Hamlet* whose title is witlessly misleading since the film doesn't give any more attention to the Ophelia figure than did Shakespeare's play. There are a couple of intriguing sequences—such as the opening scene in which we observe the closing of a casket from the point of view of the corpse. We watch as the casket enters the church while the camera remains outside. Then the doors open and a wedding party bursts forth: a perfect cinematic translation of "the funeral baked meats/Did coldly furnish forth the marriage tables." Yet most of *Ophélia* is weary, stale, flat, and unprofitable stuff, mainly due to the nearly total disaster of André Jocelyn in the role of Hamlet. It is worth noting, however, that Hamlet catches the conscience of the king with a film—called "The Mousetrap," of course. The central conceit of *L'Oeil du malin* is still important for Chabrol.

Landru (also 1962) was written by Françoise Sagan and is, for that reason and others, altogether one of the most curious of Chabrol's films. Any concern with the psychology of murder in previous films disappears here in Chabrol's droll recounting of the workaday atmosphere surrounding Landru's numerous crimes. As *L'Oeil du malin* is the realist pole of Chabrol's early work, so *Landru* is the formalist pole. As played by Charles Denner, the conscientious mass murderer is a rather nice fellow—certainly more at ease with himself and more assured than the tormented heroes of earlier films. He accepts his role as a scourge of bourgeois womanhood with equanimity and takes pleasure in the craftsmanship of his work. There is a kind of humor here which is vital to Chabrol. And it is probably most strikingly expressed in the color scheme of the film: an extraordinary, controlled palette of flat pastels which is the perfect language with which to express the droll insipidity of Landru's magnificent obsession. It's clear from *Landru* that mise-en-scène has taken the ascendency for Chabrol over psychology.

Chabrol's last personal film before the drought set in, in 1964, was "La Muette" ("The Mute"), his contribution to *Paris vue par . . . (Six in Paris).* It is a small gem of a film, a summary in twenty minutes of the basic elements that Chabrol would four years later begin weaving together into his "decameron." Stéphane Audran plays a bourgeois

Parisian matron with a notably sharp tongue, and Chabrol himself plays her husband, who has little interest in his family or his home except when it comes to mealtimes or a roll in the hay with the maid. Through this comic middle-class ménage (or menagerie) wanders their son (Gilles Chusseau), a young man who occasionally shows flashes of his parents' malign and febrile nastiness, as when he puts out the eyes of a photograph. His parents' constant inane chatter and bickering annoys him greatly until one day he hits upon a wonderfully simple solution: earplugs. Bliss! He can now sit through a dinner without having to listen to the high-volume (and very funny) arguments that pass for conversation with his parents. (We "hear" most of the film from his point of view.)

One day his mother trips and falls down the stairs. She screams, but her son can no longer hear her. She dies ludicrously and loudly at the bottom of the staircase. The boy leaves the house, happily unaware, and wanders out into the freedom of the streets of Paris. The death is a fine absurdity; the sketch of bourgeois home life and mealtime is classic Chabrol; and the violence that runs beneath the deceptively calm surface of middle-class existence is perfectly caught. But it will be four years and more before Chabrol will be able to exploit these elements in a full-length film.

"Vital To Keep Making Pictures, and What Sort Not Relevant; Chabrol No 'Doctrinaire' Type," declared a *Variety* headline of the late sixties. From 1964 through 1967 Chabrol took on a succession of commercial assignments, including four spoofs of the contemporary spy genre *(Le Tigre aime la chair fraîche* [*The Tiger Likes Fresh Blood*], 1964; *Marie-Chantal contre le Docteur Khâ* [*The Blue Panther*], 1965; *Le Tigre se parfume à la dynamite* [*An Orchid for the Tiger*], 1965; and *La Route de Corinth* [*The Road to Corinth*], 1967); a self-parody in both English and French versions with international English-speaking stars—*Le Scandale* (*The Champagne Murders,* 1966); and a historical film about the Occupation, written by an aging colonel whom Chabrol cautiously described as "a man of the right" (*La Ligne de démarcation,* 1966).

There are occasional flashes of wit in each of these films, most of which, if they were distributed at all in England or America, appeared in crudely truncated, dubbed versions; and there are sequences of real appeal—the portrayal of village life in *La Ligne de démarcation,* for example. But Chabrol described his attitude towards the spy films this way:

> I like to get to the absolute limit of principles. . . . in drivel like the Tiger series I really wanted to get the full extent of the drivel. They were drivel, so O.K. let's get into it up to our necks and even beyond if necessary, but let's not do things by halves. In the spy stories the silliness was more important than the spying, so they had to fall into the genre of drivel, rather than the spy genre. *La Route de Corinthe,* which was the most foolish, is the most successful of those films, but it is completely empty.[10]

Enough said.

Le Scandale, with Tony Perkins and Henry Jones joining a basically French cast, and shot in simultaneous English and French versions, may be more interesting in French than in English but even so, as with the later *La Décade prodigieuse,* Chabrol seems to lose control when working in a language not his own. There is a considerable quotient of verbal wit in his best films which simply isn't translated in either of these American co-productions. The film serves best as a parody of Chabrol's own best work—and not a very loving one.

As for *La Ligne de démarcation,* generally regarded as the best film of this period, Chabrol explains:

> Colonel Rémy [the former resistance fighter who wrote the script] is one of the most appalling characters I know. The only effort I had to make was to stop the film turning into German propaganda. Because the good Colonel, who is a man of the right, had a pet theory that the heavies were the Gestapo, while the Wehrmacht was very fair.[11]

The redoubtable Colonel Rémy was a regular visitor to the set, full of insistent suggestions for scenes that would serve this "pet theory" and others like it. To moderate the script, and mollify him, Chabrol sometimes shot the scenes he suggested—without film in the camera. Rémy was satisfied; Chabrol survived.

The ten films Chabrol made between 1968 and 1973 are an unusual achievement. They are simpler in design than the films he made a decade earlier, and that simplicity gives them a sharper focus. With the exception of *Nada (The Nada Gang),* the last one, each of them concentrates on the finely tuned sensibilities of the bourgeois characters Chabrol knows best. Whereas the earlier films had been populated for the most part by young people, this group deals almost exclusively with middle-aged characters. *Nada* is a blow for independence from that middle-aged, middle-class milieu; but this time Chabrol is a stranger in the city of youth.

There is less psychologizing now, but paradoxically a greater depth of character. There is a much more controlled formalism, but—again paradoxically—less distance felt between us and the characters. Our sense of these changes is communicated through the increasingly masterful mise-en-scène, now more restrained, almost rigid at times. What strikes us first about these films is their stunning craftsmanship. There isn't one that doesn't offer at least three or four sequences that are breathtaking tours de force. It's a curious fact that the parts of Chabrol's films are often more impressive than the wholes—and conversely, each of his films has more meaning when seen in context with its neighbors than it does when it stands alone.

This loosely linked series began in 1968 with *Les Biches (The Does, The Girlfriends)*, a film which, as we have already noted, has a structure that is congruent with both *Les Cousins* and *Les Godelureaux:* the classic triangle of sexual jealousy. *Les Biches*, however, has a symmetry which was lacking in the earlier films. It is still a story of initiation, of an innocent corrupted, but Chabrol now gives equal weight to each side of the figure: Frédérique (Stéphane Audran) first seduces Why (Jacqueline Sassard); then Paul (Jean-Louis Trintignant) is introduced into the equation. He first makes a bond with Why, then switches to Frédérique, which is the direct motive for Why's eventual murder of Frédérique. But within this simplified plot, Chabrol sketches all possible permutations: Why is clearly bisexual, so that her murder of Frédérique is an act both of love and of hate: it isn't clear whether she has killed the love object who has betrayed her, or the rival who has stolen the love object away. Paul, in this film, acts a neutral role (Chabrol called him a "man-object"); he is a conduit for the expression of the women's complex emotions. Likewise, it isn't clear whether Paul first seduces Why because he is interested in her, or because he sees a way to get to Frédérique through her. The genius of the film lies in this highly subtle symmetry, a system of balances which gives it an illusive shimmer.

It goes without saying that the *frissons* of these acute emotional bonds are conveyed to us through mise-en-scène. The sad-eyed does that Why is fond of painting tell us more about her pre-adolescent emotional state than any dialogue. The sharp pain she suffers is conveyed in the scene in which she stands outside the bedroom door as Frédérique and Paul make love inside. There is no high drama here; only the restrained construction of the shot lets us share her feelings. A bit earlier, the trio has been walking arm-in-arm on the patio. Why makes a point of moving from Paul's side to Frédérique's. The motion tells us more than dialogue. *Les Biches* has often been criticized for the apparent lack of

Why caresses the door handle as Frédérique and Paul make love on the other side.

motivation of its characters—Chabrol has been charged with imposing the geometry on them. To a certain extent, that is true. No doubt the abstract design came before the concrete working out of it.

As in all Chabrol's best films the closely worked details of the relationships are the key. It is through them that he achieves the aura of violent, fatal complicity which links all his characters and which makes the films, finally, not case histories of aberrant *others,* but memories of ourselves. The murder plots, more and more obviously, are cinematic conventions which serve mainly to heighten strong, wide currents of passion—emotions which envelop and represent repressed bourgeois society. The trip towards the politics of *Nada* is a long one, but *Nada* is always the destination on the horizon.

Almost all of the early films had had a dramatic structure which contrasted innocence with experience, or youth with age in some way. This generational conflict was summarized succinctly in "La Muette" and also informs *Les Biches,* where it is handled with greater finality and more assurance. But Chabrol was not to return to it for four years (until *La Décade prodigieuse* and, later, *Nada*). From *La Femme infidèle*

(1968) onwards he is mainly concerned with marriages—relationships between individuals who share a certain level of sexual and psychological maturity—although the signs of innocence are always to be found in the background, as a reminder: for example, the child Michel in both *La Femme infidèle* and *Que la bête meure*. From *La Femme infidèle* onwards bourgeois married life becomes progressively more absurd until it explodes, cinematically, in the black comedies of *Docteur Popaul* and *Les Noces rouges (Red Wedding, Wedding in Blood)*. The three films Chabrol wrote without Gégauff during this period (*La Femme infidèle, Le Boucher*, and *Juste avant la nuit*) are especially useful markers since they all (unlike the Gégauff-Chabrol collaborations) focus our interest intensely on complicity.

La Femme infidèle would, at first glance, seem to be the most mundane of murder stories; it is the crudest triangle of jealousy. Chabrol finds the commonplace cinematically useful: surely the centerpiece of the film is the extended sequence in which poor Charles Desvallées (Michel Bouquet) methodically if clumsily disposes of the evidence of his murder of his wife's lover Pégala (Maurice Ronet). There is so much blood to wash up, and the body is so bulky and awkward. We have had a hint of this sublime mundaneness in the opening shots of the film, which reveal what the script calls "a maniacally well-kept garden" in which Hélène (Stéphane Audran) and her mother-in-law are having an exquisitely dainty tea. We are never very far from Ionesco's clown shows in Chabrol.

But humor isn't the only aim of the flat-footed plot. In effect, the ordinariness of the story de-dramatizes it so that Chabrol can concentrate on subtle shifts of meaning between his characters. Charles is not demoniacally possessed. It isn't certain that he has visited Pégala with the intention of killing him. In fact, the last straw is Pégala's comment: "Good God! You've got a dumb mug!" Charles can hold it in no longer and smashes Pégala's head with a statuette. "Yes, I know," he says.[12] Like all victims in Chabrol, Pégala shares responsibility, if not legal culpability, with his murderer. The victims, literally or figuratively, ask for it. Just before he performs his clumsy killing, Charles has seen the huge zippo lighter that Hélène had given Pégala. He becomes ill; he has to leave the room—with Pégala's help, of course. The lighter is a droll symbol of the spiritual flame (as in *Le Boucher*); but more to the point, it is also a gross, absurd exaggeration of the crass materialism of their lives.

La Femme infidèle is a summer film—languid, relaxed, and a little dreamy—so it is no surprise that the murder, in the exact middle of the film, does not have particularly violent consequences. If Charles has driven Hélène to take a lover (there is evidence of this), then Hélène learns to accept the consequences. The last sequence—one of the most striking in all of Chabrol—sums this up. Hélène burns a photograph of Pégala, as if to show her solidarity with her husband. Everyone (Michel included) tells everyone else "I love you." The police come to take Charles away. The last shot, a very slow tracking shot backwards with a concurrent zoom in, shows us the woman and child from Charles's point of view as he is led away: the shot tells us that he is leaving them but that he is closer to them than ever before.

With his next film, *Que la bête meure (This Man Must Die, Killer!)* Chabrol moves from jealousy to revenge—or does he? Charles Thénier (Michel Duchaussoy) is plotting to revenge the death of his son. Michel Thénier (Stéphane di Napoli) has been killed in an efficient and gripping pre-credit sequence, hit by a car driven by Paul Decourt (Jean Yanne), an eminently nasty man, as his entire family will attest. Charles makes elaborate plans for the murder of Paul, but it is not clear at the end of the film whether he has actually done so, or whether he has simply taken the blame for an act committed by Paul's son Philippe. (played by Marc di Napoli, evidently the brother of the boy who played Charles's son). After the film was made Chabrol was quoted as saying, "you'll never see a Charles kill a Paul. Never,"[13] so that if we want to incorporate external evidence we can be sure that Philippe is the one responsible for the murder of his father and Charles has sacrificed himself for Philippe. The symmetry is intriguing: what looks like a revenge drama gradually and inexorably turns into a story of jealousy and envy as Charles becomes less and less interested in avenging his own son's death and grows fonder of Philippe, the murderer's son. If *Que la bête meure* is not a homosexual triangle it is nevertheless certainly a film of paternal and platonic love. There is no mention of Charles's wife (he did have one: we see her in his home movies), but he did love his son, and he learns to love Paul's son and hate Paul, supposedly for his bestiality. The scenes between Philippe and Charles are cluttered with clues as to the nature of their relationship: they have a long talk about the Greeks and *The Iliad,* phallic symbols abound—a cigarette on an ashtray, the image in *The Iliad* of a spear through the back of a head, then through the mouth ("a beautiful image, don't you think?" says Charles).

All this is set against a superb background of Brittany in winter and early spring. As with the best of Chabrol, the texture of the landscape is an element in the drama, and we learn more about Charles, Paul, and

Philippe from their environment than from much of the dialogue. The milieu is one of extraordinary repression (in contrast with the wild scenery). Every character in the film—except Paul—is a bit precious, too fastidious, queerly repressed. This makes Paul seem all the more alive and healthy, despite his nastiness. Once again, Chabrol carefully balances the equation of characters. Yet the balance means that Charles's obsession is going to disintegrate under its own overblown weight. The terror that breaks through the calm surface of bourgeois existence in the first sequence of the film is never fully resolved. It cannot be, since there is no particular character who is individually responsible for it and because the dramatic relationships quickly become so complex. This is why *Que la bête meure,* like most of Chabrol's films is, as a unit, ethically unsatisfying. We never break through to new ground. There is no catharsis, nor anything like it. At the end we have come full circle; there is a sense of suffocation.

Several critics of Chabrol—Robin Wood probably chief among them—like to point to the recurrent "id" figures in his films: Clovis, Laszlo Kovacs, André the motorcyclist, Albin, Landru. *Le Boucher* (1969) gives us the culmination of these id characters in Jean Yanne's portrayal of the butcher Popaul. Despite the fact that there are four deaths in the film—the last of them Popaul's, the first three of girls whom he murders—the film is mainly a love story. That he is a murderer is a fact we accept as we would the information that he was suffering from terminal cancer, or that he was a hemophiliac. Mlle Hélène (Stéphane Audran) seems to take the news the same way when she finally discovers the truth about her lover. He comes to her at the end with a knife in his hand, but full of shame, and says quietly: "I know that I make you frightened, and I can't stand that." But Hélène can't grasp immediately the figure of the victim within the image of the monster, and by the time she recovers, it is too late. The butcher has butchered himself.

The romance is over. Chabrol locates the story in the village of Trémolat in Périgord close to the site of some prehistoric cave paintings. He opens the film with a series of shots of those reminders of art in the midst of a more brutal world. He comes back to them at least once more in a shot which contrasts them with the superficial civilized atmosphere of the Louis XIV pageant in the middle of the film. Popaul, a modern version of one of the characters in the cave paintings, has returned from fifteen years in the army, where his psychopathic talents were highly regarded and much in demand. Personal, individualized guilt is not the theme of *Le Boucher;* collective, social guilt is—from prehistory to the present. Like a Saint out of Genet, Popaul sacrifices himself for us all, living out our own collective madness for us and making it concrete.

As always in Chabrol's "decade," the formal dialectics are a matter of contrast between the seductive, peaceful, effulgent surface of bourgeois life and the searing, abrupt violence which every once in a while unpredictably rips through it. This time, however, the element of satire is all but missing. *Le Boucher* is one of Chabrol's most compassionate and serious films, and the bourgeoisie is not the proper stage for it. Hélène is a schoolteacher, Popaul a butcher; neither character has very strong roots in the social milieux of the previous films. The family structure, so important in *La Femme infidèle* and *Que la bête meure,* has been enlarged and extended thematically: there is no nuclear family in *Le Boucher,* but the life of the village and Mlle Hélène's class of schoolchildren take its place. To strengthen the sympathy between audience and characters Chabrol used only three professional actors in the film. The village people are played by themselves, and Chabrol explains that he chose Trémolat because he felt it did exist in splendid isolation as a community that still worked satisfactorily. He makes much of this in the mise-en-scène. Popaul's mordant obsession is a small element in the mosaic of village life, but an unavoidably intractable one—just like the tiny drops of blood that drip slowly on the sandwich of the schoolgirl on an autumnal picnic with her teacher Hélène. Because there is no triangle of jealousy, because the background is so affirmative (the film begins with the celebration of a wedding), because Chabrol for once treats his characters with unguarded compassion, *Le Boucher* is an eloquent statement of pity for all of us who can't escape the terrors of the id, even if we don't always express them in murder.

La Rupture (1970) continues Chabrol's interest in psychopathic, rather than neurotic, murder, It opens with one of his most stunning and effective sequences. The first shot is of the suburban house in which Hélène (Stéphane Audran), Charles (Jean-Claude Drouot), and their son live. The shot begins focused on the rough bark of a large tree in front of the house. There is one ominous chord, a quick pan to reveal the house, and then a cut to the inside. In the warmly lit kitchen, Hélène is feeding her young son breakfast, talking with him in a natural, relaxed, and intimate way. Whatever tensions were raised by the first shot—the rough grey bark, the overcast sky, the ominous chord—are immediately dissipated. Then Charles lurches forth from the bathroom. He is a sepulchral figure in the first place and has a day's growth of beard, which makes him look even more ominous. It

Charles Régnier (Drouot) hurls his son across the brightly lit kitchen.

becomes clear quickly that he is drugged and unhearing. As the child comes over, obviously upset about his father's condition, Charles picks him up with one hand and flings him across the room where he smashes into the edge of a cabinet. Hélène, enraged and terrified, grabs an iron frying pan and beats Charles down, each of the many blows clanging as he sinks slowly.

The rest of the film is a long circle back to the beginning. Charles, very ill, is in few of the scenes. We follow Hélène instead as she moves into a boarding house near the hospital in which her son is recuperating and tries to put her life back together. If *Le Boucher* was about the coming together of psychopath and woman, *La Rupture* is the opposite: their splitting apart. Consequently, there is no pattern of exchange of guilt in this film, unless it is between Charles and his parents. It is his father (Michel Bouquet) who hired Paul (Jean-Pierre Cassel) to "get the goods" on Hélène. His parents have always hated her. Charles atones in a way for the antagonism between his parents and his wife by carelessly throwing his mother down the stairs just as he leaves his sickroom in search of Hélène. The difficulty with the film is in Hélène's incorrigible goodness. She is one of the most isolated of Chabrol's characters—a former stripper who has married into a wealthy family who hate her and who has managed to raise a child and take care of a sick husband all on her own. She is sealed off from any exchange with the other characters until the very end, when Paul's LSD-spiked orange juice sends her on a journey which requires the aid of three old ladies who inhabit the rooming house. In addition, Paul—one of the most likeable "villains" in Chabrol—is haunting Hélène solely for the money. He doesn't really want to do it, and in fact learns to admire her courage and tenacity.

So *La Rupture* is a disconnected film and something of an anomaly for Chabrol. Yet there is one extended sequence in the middle which gives us a clue to its possibilities. Hélène is riding on a tram with the sympathetic lawyer who will handle her divorce. The tramline is straight and true and cuts a path through a neat wooded park. There is no other traffic. It is an afternoon in late winter, and as the grey Belgian light yellows and the sun lowers in the sky, Hélène tells the lawyer the story of her life. The tramway, the light, the woods, the sound of the wheels on rails are all hypnotic, and it looks for a while (in this homage to Murnau's *Sunrise*) as if Hélène—and Chabrol—are going to break out of the fatal circular pattern of this film. But Chabrol is not yet finished investigating bourgeois crime.

His next film, *Juste avant la nuit* (1971), is an important step out of the woods, however. Here murder begins the story. Charles Masson (Michel Bouquet) accidentally kills his mistress, who also happens to be his best friend's wife. The murder may have been an act of love, in a way. Charles later explains that his mistress "took pleasure in seeing me suffer when she made me beat her." He soon confesses his crime to his wife Hélène (Audran as usual) and to his victim's husband François (François Perrier). He wants not forgiveness but condemnation from them. In a neat reversal of the structure of guilt and exchange that has applied until now, both of them immediately excuse him of culpability. They understand, they accept, they try to help Charles pick up the pieces and learn to live again. But he sinks deeper and deeper into his self-imposed guilt. The police refuse to accept the clues he offers them; he is haunted by reminders on all sides—including a detergent named "Culpa." The film ends with a long night of the soul. Charles and Hélène talk in their egregiously modern suburban villa—all marble, cold glass, concrete, and steel illuminated by lights that reflect off copper sheets. Hélène tries to convince him that "giving yourself up has no moral value." She calls his attitude sheer perversion.

Charles Masson (Michel Bouquet) deep in thought after having accidentally murdered his mistress who is also his best friend's wife. One of several nude-on-bed studies in later Chabrol.

But he is now determined to turn himself in in the morning. He asks for something to make him sleep. The camera pans to follow her into the bathroom. They are separated in the frame, his head on one side, hers on the other with the brown expanse of the walls between them. Then a reverse shot of Charles from the bathroom. The camera pans slightly to reveal Hélène's image in the mirror as she puts drops of laudanum into a glass of water. They are united in the reversed mirror image now. The camera pans again to a direct shot of Hélène alone as she adds first one drop, then two, then three. Plink. Plink, plink. Then the entire drop-perful, as the camera pans away from her. She goes back into the bedroom with the lethal drink, gives it to Charles, and sits down on her bed opposite him. Each time he takes a fatal swallow, she jumps back a bit, withdrawing into her own bed. "Faire la nuit," she tells him, and shuts the lights.

I haven't described it in sufficient detail, but this meticulously planned and orchestrated sequence is breathtaking. It speaks volumes about guilt and exchange, murder and death and love. In a way it frees Chabrol, and his audiences, from the obsession with guilt that has marked his films until now. His next films move rapidly away from identification with this middle-class world, towards a more objective and cooler view.

From the frigid and duplicitous clarity of the glass house in *Juste avant la nuit* Chabrol shifted to the dim, baroque—and equally duplicitous—country house of *La Décade prodigieuse* (1972). This adaptation of an Ellery Queen novel is a better film than it appears to be, partly because the English-language version suffers not only from sloppy, crude dubbing but also from poor visual technical quality. Although *La Décade prodigieuse* neatly provides us with a label for this period of Chabrol's work, it is the least characteristic film of these five years. Unlike its companions it is a very busy film, both technically and thematically; and it reverts to the oedipal universe of Chabrol's early period—the family as seen from the point of view of the victimized child. In addition, it comes closest of all Chabrol's films to abandoning his commitment to "little themes," as it throws itself deliriously into the thickets of classical and Judeo-Christian symbology: the "decade" of the title represents Charles's subconscious but methodical contravention, one by one, of the commandments of the decalogue. As Jan Dawson, one of Chabrol's most perceptive critics, has pointed out, Chabrol has expanded the basic device of the Ellery Queen novel to support an essay on comparative religion. If this isn't a big theme, it's as close as Chabrol will ever get to one.

The successes of *La Décade prodigieuse* therefore are more thematic than technical. Compared with the film which immediately precedes it, it is fairly uninteresting visually. But it is an interesting summation of some Chabrol obsessions. As in *Le Boucher* and *La Rupture,* the key is psychopathy, but this time the psychosis is also a matter of jealousy, so the twin motives of this decade of films are united for once. Charles (Anthony Perkins) is the stepson of Théo (Orson Welles). Hélène (Marlène Jobert this time, although she is made up to look a caricature of Stéphane Audran) is Théo's wife—and his former stepdaughter. The basic motive for Charles's fits of amnesia, and for his working out of the ten cardinal sins, day by day, is his unacknowledged love of his stepmother. But Chabrol complicates this triangle. Charles has not only a real father in addition to his stepfather but Paul (Michel Piccoli), who is his spiritual godfather. Paul is a philosophy professor, at work on a thesis in inductive reasoning. When we add Charles's own mad mother, we come to a total of five parental figures.

That neither Charles, nor Théo, nor Hélène has any blood relationship with each other extends the oedipal paradigm past the level of the family. In addition, Charles's stepfather has "created" him as he has created not only his wife but also the time in which he lives (he chooses, with his vast wealth, to live in the past, like Pirandello's Henry

IV). Finally, Paul, the spiritual godfather, has "taken Charles's God away from him." The whole incestuous pattern is redolent with artifice which makes us immediately recall the earlier *Ophélia*. Like that earlier film, *La Décade prodigieuse* tends to suffocate in symbological miasmas. Chabrol seems to know this: he perversely litters the landscape with all sorts of red herrings which further increase the confusion. It is almost as if he himself is becoming impatient with the variations on a theme now that there have been seven in four years.

Docteur Popaul (also 1972), which at this writing has not yet been seen in English-speaking countries, seems to have been a further attempt at breaking out of the pattern which had come to such magnificent fruition with *Juste avant la nuit*. Uniquely in *La Décade prodigieuse* there was a detective (Paul, who played the Ellery Queen role) who fit into the geometry of the characters. In *Docteur Popaul* Chabrol turns this newly discovered interest in ratiocination back on itself. Popaul (Jean-Paul Belmondo) indulges himself in a black-comic chain of murders. There is no *crise de conscience* as a consequence; rather, as Jacques Siclier has noted, "the *novelty* of *Docteur Popaul* comes from the offhandedness with which the the criminal history is treated. . . ."[14]

Popaul is lying in a hospital bed after an accident, convinced that he will be paralyzed from now on. He remembers earlier episodes of his life: his fondness for ugly women, which led him to marry his wife Christine (Mia Farrow); his discovery of the pleasures of beauty, which led him to lust after his sister-in-law Martine (Laura Antonelli); and his ingenious murders of Martine's three husbands so that he can become her lover. Just as he is about to commit suicide he realizes that Christine has been equally ingenious and has maneuvered him deftly to the brink of self-destruction. So it is now the murderer who has turned detective in order to prevent his own murder, one which he is about to commit himself.

The pathos which attached to the earlier Popaul's ritual murders of women (in *Le Boucher*) is completely reversed in the present Popaul's comic elimination of rivals. There is a stronger element of satiric distancing in *Docteur Popaul* than in any of Chabrol's previous films except "La Muette"; another step away from the bourgeois universe of the films of the late sixties. The triangle remains, the psychopathic element remains, the milieu is the same, but all are now treated with impatient irony.

Les Noces rouges (1973) continues along this line, although it is both more subtle and more meaningful than either *Docteur Popaul* or *La Décade prodigieuse*. For the first time politics becomes a significant part of the structure of a Chabrol film. *Les Noces rouges* is based loosely on newspaper accounts of similar murders in the town of Bourganeuf (although it also owes something to James M. Cain's *The Postman Always Rings Twice*). In the spring of 1973 the French censor forbade screenings of the film for more than a month, ostensibly because it might have influenced jurors in the Bourganeuf case which was then on trial; but Chabrol made it quite clear in a series of statements at that time—and the film bears him out—that the real motive was the coming election in April of that year. *Les Noces rouges* gives us a triangle as classic as any in Chabrol: Pierre (Michel Piccoli) loves Lucienne (Stéphane Audran), who is married to Paul (Claude Pieplu), the Gaullist mayor of their provincial town. Pierre disposes of his invalid wife Clotilde and then, with Lucienne, arranges the death of her husband. But the obligatory guilt this time becomes a matter of public concern, for Paul was involved in a venal scheme to make a quick killing on some public land and had inveigled Pierre (who is portrayed as vaguely left of center) into fronting for him. It's clear that Paul's death is suspicious, but on orders from "M. le Président" himself the police are enjoined from investigating further.

Lucienne and Pierre's affair, in the foreground of the film, has the kind of gleaming, mad, ridiculous passion that has its roots in "La Muette." They rush at each other in their precious moments together with egregious and greedy abandon. They seem particularly to enjoy making love in the room where Pierre murdered his wife, and their salacious kiss at the site of the "accident" in which Paul is killed is a perfect comic emblem for the film. Paul, by the way, is extraordinarily pleased to discover his wife's infidelity. He has been impotent for a long time, and it will only help him secure Pierre's help in the land scheme. The satire is scathing, and reminds us of the best of Buñuel. *Les Noces rouges* is a necessary film in Chabrol's canon, for it makes explicit what has only been implied before: that Chabrol's masterful series of Balzacian melodramas may have a practical political dimension. *Les Noces rouges* interweaves the political, sexual, and criminal strands into a tight fabric.

Pierre and Lucienne are finally brought to justice not through their own mistakes, not through any vigilance on the part of the authorities, but because Lucienne has betrayed the compact she made with her daughter Hélène (Eliana de Santis), who is clearly cast in the same tough mold as her mother. For years Lucienne and Hélène had taken private pleasure in their shared ridicule of Hélène's stepfather. They were united against him; but now Lucienne has failed to take her daughter into her confidence. So, in a neat reversal Hélène turns them in. The police ask Pierre and Lucienne why they simply hadn't left the town. "Leave? It never occurred to us!" They are caught in the discreet bourgeois trap that Buñuel has described so often and so well. But Claude Chabrol is beginning to break free.

Nada (also 1973) is closely based on a *série noire* novel by Jean-Patrick Manchette. It is Chabrol's first venture outside the safe confines of the charmed bourgeois lifestyle. It elicits a complex response, for the salient characteristic of the film is its ambivalent tone. The irony with which Chabrol treats the bourgeois power structure is lethal, as we might expect, but the attitude the film takes towards the varied crew of militants who comprise the Nada group is at times self-conscious and tendentious. Chabrol is not nearly so familiar with these people as he is with their natural enemies. And he seems to find it necessary to excuse the serious nature of his subject by injecting the exaggerated flavor of a cheap thriller, mainly through the soundtrack (loud, insistent "chase" music and military themes) but also in the mise-en-scène. *Nada* reveals very little of the visual sophistication we have come to expect from Chabrol. It is filmed in a straightforward style which betrays his uneasiness with the subject matter.

The Nada group itself is carefully designed to represent a spectrum of the political left: Diaz (Fabio Testi), the romantic revolutionary desperado, is decked out in a black turtleneck and broad-brimmed black hat straight out of *Antonio Das Mortes* by way of spaghetti Westerns. Epaulard (Maurice Garrel) is the aging cynic of the group, combining, as Andrew Sarris has pointed out, the "wrinkled fatalism" of Bogart's myth with the "wistful patience" of Montand's.[15] André (Lou Castel) is a properly righteous descendant of the bourgeoisie; and D'Arey (Didier Kaminka)—a vaguely drawn character—is a waiter, working class, with a touch of the hippie about him and a psychotic wife at home. And the girl—there's always a girl: Véronique Cash (Mariangela Melato) goes by her last name, has a brief affair with the unlikeliest of the men (Epaulard), and properly provides them with a hide-out. It's clear that Chabrol is most comfortable handling these alien characters by way of cinematic stereotypes with which he is more familiar: the echoes of Westerns—specifically those by Sergio Leone—repeatedly punctuate the action. Also, as always when Chabrol is working with foreigners in the cast, the dialogue tends to be both overwritten and crudely delivered.

The last of the group is Truffais (Michel Duchaussoy). We know from both his name (does he have an alter ego "Resnaut"?) and the fact that the actor who plays him is a regular colleague of Chabrol that he will be something of a *raissonneur* in *Nada.* He is. A philosophy professor trapped in an antagonistic relationship with his snotty, blue-jeaned middle-class students, he is the one member of the group who chooses not to go through with the plot. He calls himself a "libertarian communist" and has written that "left terrorism and state terrorism are parts of the same jaw." Truffais is the intellectual, and therefore closest to Chabrol's own point of view. (We know little of Chabrol's politics, but he was apparently deeply involved with the most radical scheme of the Etats-Généraux du Cinéma in the summer of 1968.) At the end of the film, after the rest of the group has been thoroughly and mercilessly massacred, Diaz alone will stagger back to tape a manifesto, repeating Truffais's words: "The desperado assassin becomes a consumable of society. The two are jaws of the same trap." The "teacher" has been vindicated; the "students" have failed, however valiantly.

So *Nada* deals from a stacked deck. There is no doubt that Truffais is correct: the romantic but essentially futile gestures of a score of Nada groups have proved that during the last five or ten years. But Truffais's truth is only a partial one. Existentially, the actions of the Nada group justify themselves. The point is that the question of terrorism is a serious dilemma for the left; it has not yet been resolved, it never was resolved in earlier eras, it probably won't be resolved in our own. By rephrasing it Chabrol answers the question, but avoids the dilemma. The solution is semantic, not practical. Diaz also says that "criticizing terrorism is not to be construed as criticizing civil war." I doubt whether there are many serious people on the left who have taken that road who don't think of their actions as battles in a civil war. We could, nevertheless, read into *Nada* an understanding of the excruciating nature of that dilemma were it not for the ambivalent mise-en-scène of the scenes with the Nada group. With the bourgoisie Chabrol is more at home, as in the scenes devoted to the actions of the Minister of the Interior (who sleeps under a glowing portrait of Pompidou and enters the fray in his own personal helicopter as his wife waves goodbye from the steps of their floodlit chateau), and to the chief of police and the various operatives of intelligence and counterintelligence who are at war with each other while they are battling Nada. The Nada people have the good sense to capture their hostage, the American ambassador, during his weekly Friday-night visit to a chic bordello. This gives Chabrol an opportunity to inject a little sex and shoot his by now obligatory scene of a young woman sprawled naked on a bed. (One of the militants chastely drapes her crotch before they leave, as if criticizing Chabrol.) There is considerable humor in these scenes, which contrast sharply with the scenes of the group alone.

It is doubtful that Chabrol will every be able to get any closer to the people of Nada; but with all its problems the film is a refreshing attempt to move out of the constricting circles of bourgeois guilt into psychological as well as political liberation. As Tom Milne has noted, in *this* film "the transference of guilt is to the spectator forced to take sides by the events themselves."[16]

Chabrol's prolific career presents a special problem to those who write about his films. Like all the directors covered in this volume, he of course deserves a book of his own. Within the confines of this study I have been able only to suggest some of the major aspects of his cinema. Next to nothing has been said about his films in comparison with those of Buñuel, which they complement nicely. Balzac has been mentioned once or twice, but an extended comparison of the nineteenth-century novelist's *comédie humaine* with that of the twentieth-century filmmaker would be more than instructive. We have examined quickly only a few examples of Chabrol's superb technical mastery; there are dozens more in most of his films, but the best way to discover his craftsmanship is to observe it. Tom Milne speaks aptly of *Nada* as being "done with Chabrol's derision at full stretch." More needs to be said about the special problems which that derision creates at various periods in Chabrol's career.

Moreover, since *Nada* (the most recent of Chabrol's films to be commercially released in the United States) he has completed five other feature films: *La Partie de plaisir* (1974), which appears to be the ultimate Gégauff film since it was not only written by Paul Gégauff but stars him, his ex-wife, and his daughter; *Les Innocents au mains sales* (also 1974); and *Initiation à la mort, Le Malheur fou,* and Dashiell Hammett's *The Dain Curse* (his first film in the U.S.), all in 1975. He has also completed two television films based on stories by Henry James (it was inevitable that he would turn to James sooner or later): *DeGrey* and *The Bench of Desolation.* The latter, based on a single viewing, seems to be a straightforward adaptation of James to the screen. In addition, in 1974 Chabrol organized a television series of six "Histoires insolites" ("Unusual Stories"), four of which he directed himself.

This furious schedule of production is a sign of Chabrol's most important contribution to the New Wave. Truffaut may have investigated genres with greater intelligence. Godard condemned them in order to begin again. Resnais and Rivette have worked slowly, exploring the crucial dimension of time. Rohmer has made the connection between cinema and literature. But only Claude Chabrol has thrown himself completely into the role of entertainer-filmmaker which, when it was played by the great American directors of the thirties and forties, first inspired the group as a whole.

12

ROHMER
Moral Tales: The Art of Courtly Love

A decade older than Godard, Truffaut, and Chabrol, Eric Rohmer is almost obsessively secretive about his personal life. During the last few years he has agreed to give several interviews for various magazines, but he seldom gives the same information twice. He was born at Nancy on 4 April 1923 . . . or on 1 December 1920 . . . or on 4 April. He is married and has two children, but maintains that his family life is strictly separate from his career—in direct contrast to Godard and Chabrol, whose marriages have been professional partnerships, and Truffaut, who named his children after films. As a child, Rohmer says, he wasn't much interested in film, coming to it rather late when he discovered the Cinémathèque as a student. During the Occupation he wrote a novel, variously called *Elizabeth* and *Les Vacances,* and after the war he began to write for film magazines. His real name is Jean-Marie Maurice Schérer, but he used the pseudonym "Gilbert Cordier" for the novel, shifting to "Eric Rohmer" when he began to write for film magazines.

In the early fifties Rohmer joined his friends Truffaut, Godard, Chabrol, and Rivette writing for the newly founded *Cahiers du Cinéma* under the direction of André Bazin. He wrote for that magazine for more than ten years and was its editor from 1957 until 1963. During the fifties Rohmer also completed half a dozen short films, ranging in length from ten to sixty minutes—"Journal d'un scélérat" (1950), "Présentation, ou Charlotte et son steak" (1951–61), "Bérénice" (1954), "La Sonate à Kreutzer" (1956), "Véronique et son cancre" (1958)—and in 1959, that watershed year in French cinema, he made his first feature film, *Le Signe du lion*, for Claude Chabrol's new production company.* The film was recut and rescored when Chabrol was forced to sell the company and generated only minor interest when it was released. While Godard, Truffaut, and Chabrol had enormous successes with their first features, Eric Rohmer, like Jacques Rivette, was caught in the backwash of the New Wave. Already near the age of forty, Rohmer must not have found the experience pleasant. Continuing to edit *Cahiers*, he retrenched, realizing that the only economically viable way he could continue to make personal films was to do shorts in 16 mm.

The first two of his series of Contes moraux, *La Boulangère de Monceau* (1962, 26 min) and *La Carrière de Suzanne* (1963, 60 min), were filmed this way, as were "Nadja à Paris" (1964, 13 min), "Place de l'Etoile" (1965, 15 min), "Une Etudiante d'aujourd-hui" (1966, 13 min), and "Fermière à Montfauçon" (1968, 13 min). All of these films, as well as all four features which complete the cycle of Moral Tales, were produced by Barbet Schroeder, with whom Rohmer formed the production company Les Films du Losange in 1962; in the late sixties Schroeder was joined by Pierre Cottrell. It is clear that Les Films du Losange has provided vital protection and support for Rohmer's delicate career.

After he left *Cahiers du Cinéma* Rohmer turned to television, directing fourteen films on a wide range of topics for both O.R.T.F. and Télévision Scolaire between 1964 and 1966.† In 1965, as their first venture into features, Films du Losange produced the six-part compilation film in 16mm, *Paris vue par . . .* ; Rohmer's contribution was the sketch "Place de l'Etoile." By 1967, Rohmer could afford to return to 35 mm for the next episode of his projected cycle of Moral Tales, *Ma nuit chez Maud (My Night at Maud's).* But Jean-Louis Trintignant was not available for nearly a year, so production of this film, which was to

*During this period Rohmer also completed (with Claude Chabrol) his respected critical study of the films of Alfred Hitchcock, a filmmaker whom we would never expect to have been an influence on this gentle spinner of moral tales, were it not for the existence of the book.

†"Les Cabinets du physique" *(La Vie de société du XVIIIe siècle);* "Métamorphose du paysage" (*L'Ere industrielle*); "Perceval ou le conte du Graal"; "Don Quichotte"; Les Histoires extraordinaires d'Edgar Poe" (extracts from films); "Les Caractères de La Bruyère"; "Pascal"; "Victor Hugo: Les Contemplations"; "Mallarmé"; "Hugo Architecte"; "Louis Lumière"; "La Béton"—all for educational television. For O.R.T.F., two episodes in the series *Cinéastes de notre temps: Carl Dreyer* and *Le Celluloid et le marbre.*

solidify Rohmer's reputation and give him for the first time some sense of security as a filmmaker, had to be postponed. Instead, Schroeder and Rohmer sold television rights to two of the short films they had made and used the small sum they received to film *La Collectionneuse,* the fourth Moral Tale, with a cast of nonprofessionals. Their only expenses that summer were for film stock and rent for the house in Saint-Tropez which was the set and which also housed cast and crew. There was also a small budget line for the salary of the cook who, the stories go, cooked nothing but minestrone during the entire shooting schedule. She also appeared in the film. The cast and crew worked for percentages. The film had some *succès d'estime,* but it was not until *Ma nuit chez Maud* premiered at the Cannes Festival nearly two years later that Rohmer, approaching his fiftieth birthday, appeared to have a safe future as a filmmaker. He followed quickly with the last two Moral Tales—*Le Genou de Claire (Claire's Knee,* 1969) and *L'Amour, l'après-midi (Chloë in the Afternoon,* 1972). It was more than three years before he began work on his first post–Moral Tale, an adaptation of Heinrich von Kleist's *Die Marquise von O* (1975). It appears from statements Rohmer has made, that he will concentrate in future on such historical films, a genre with which he has some acquaintance from his work in educational television in the mid-sixties.

In a career as a filmmaker that spans more than twenty years, then, Rohmer has made only six features, four of them in the space of a relatively intense five-year period. One is impressed with the extraordinary difficulties Rohmer faced during that long period, despite the help of Schroeder and Les Films du Losange. The length of his journeymanship has made the recently produced features all the more intense and finely wrought. Of necessity, we will focus on those last four films. Yet his earlier films are not without interest, especially seen in retrospect.

Le Signe du lion is a simple Renoiresque story that looks a lot more interesting now that we know Rohmer's later films than it must have in 1959. It is not, like *Les Quatre Cents Coups, A bout de souffle,* and *Les Cousins* which were its contemporaries, a film which announces with every frame that it intends to change the course of the cinema. Indeed, Rohmer often separates himself esthetically from his former colleagues of *Cahiers* and the early New Wave by making clear the difference between *their* films, which are always highly conscious of their own cinematic natures and ever aware of the esthetic and historical traditions that stretch behind them, and *his* films, in which "art," especially "film art," is assiduously avoided except as it is useful to convey Rohmer's own fascination with character, place and time. *Le Signe du lion,* now clearly a Rohmer film and therefore quiet, artless, intently concerned with the people he is photographing, the place in which they live, and the time of year, is almost directly contradictory to everything we know about the early films of Godard, Truffaut, Chabrol.

The title gives us the time of year, the month of August, in which Rohmer quietly recounts a simple story. Pierre Wesselrin (Jess Hahn) is a Dutch violinist who lives in Paris. He is awaiting an inheritance and, at the beginning of the film, is surrounded by friends and acquaintances and very much a part of the kind of good-humored social milieu that marks most of Rohmer's films. As the summer progresses and his friends leave for vacations, Pierre runs out of money, loses his flat, and eventually winds up thoroughly alone and isolated in a deserted city, awash in the bright heat of mid- and late summer. He meets and befriends a tramp on the banks of the Seine, and the two of them work up a musical act which they perform for tourists in the cafes. As the tempo of life begins to pick up again in early September, Pierre is rediscovered by his old friends returned from vacation and finally receives the inheritance he has been waiting for. The film ends. What obviously excited Rohmer about this slim plot was the opportunity it afforded to capture the light, the moods, the atmosphere of Paris in August. Against this liquescent, subtle background he has sketched a couple of Renoiresque characters, Pierre and the tramp (Jean le Poulain), who would not find themselves out of place in the world of Boudu. All the hallmarks of Rohmer's later, more mature work are evident here: the acute sensitivity to the light and the mood of a specific city; the open, compassionate, yet intellectually ironic discourse on the central humanity of the characters; the fascination with the self-analysis to which intellectuals are partial; the display of quotidian details; and the poet's love of the subtle but sharp colors and forms of well-spoken language.

It would have taken, however, a critic of unusual perspicacity to divine all this in 1959, for Rohmer's first film, like all that would follow, owes its power more to literary than to cinematic traditions, especially the ones in vogue during the period of the early New Wave. It was only later, with the support of the invented structure of Moral Tales, that most viewers found it easy to understand the provenance of Rohmer's iconoclastic film style. The film was not a success when it was released, and Rohmer turned back to the job of editing *Cahiers du Cinéma* and began to formulate the project of the Contes moraux, which would take him ten years to complete. He continued to make shorts throughout the sixties, but only one of them is generally available outside France. Since we have so little of Rohmer's work other than the Contes moraux by which to measure him, it is worth a little time to discuss "Place de l'Etoile." Other young directors contributed to *Paris vue par . . .*, but it is evident that the governing idea of the film—stories of Parisians organized according to neighborhood—is Rohmer's. On the whole, the film is surprisingly successful, considering that it is the sum of the joint efforts of six filmmakers, and Rohmer's episode, like its locale, is geographically central. A fastidious clerk, who works in a shirt store in the Place de l'Etoile, walks to work from the Métro exit by the same precise circuit each day, being forced to cross five or six of the twelve avenues that meet at the Place de l'Etoile. The structuralist irony is intended: the clerk's limited, introspective character is directly contrasted with the open, expansive, centrifugal nature of the Place de l'Etoile, and probably has been formed by it. One day the clerk has the kind of minor altercation with a man on the street that further emphasizes the obstacles in the path of his daily life. He knocks him down—by accident—and, frightened that he has killed him, runs away. He spends the next week or so in terror that the man has died. The guilt he imposes upon himself is almost unbearable, although the tone of the sketch is comic. He searches the newspapers for news of the death. There is none. Finally, the sketch ends abruptly when the clerk sees his victim on the Métro—alive, well, and displaying the same obstreperous belligerence he'd met before.

The sketch introduces us to some elements of Rohmer's world that were not present in *Le Signe du lion:* the structuralist quality of the mise-en-scène is one of the most important, and least noticed, of them. The "moral" conception of guilt is another. And the details of everyday life, materials for all of Rohmer's films, are really the abstract subject of this short film.

As one would expect, Rohmer has some very specific views about the medium of television, and he makes it clear in interviews that he considers the work he has done for educational television important. Although he has made a couple of programs for the O.R.T.F. in the Cinéastes de Notre Temps series which he considers simply an extension of his work as a critic, the major part of his TV work has been for educational television and he has made some documentaries for that sub-medium which, he says, "were real films and which I like a lot. Or, rather, I like them as much as the work I have done elsewhere."[1] The difference between general and educational TV is once again a matter of audiences: with educational TV, Rohmer was assured of the (exceptionally) restricted audiences he knew he had to seek. His television films covered a broad range of subjects—the Parsifal legend, the industrial revolution, girl students in Paris, Louis Lumière, Pascal (of course)—

and it is significant that so many of them dealt with *ideas,* which did not lend themselves very well to the medium of film. The opportunities for experimentation were great, and he availed himself of the freedom, yet one feels he thought TV was constricting:

> When you show a film on TV, the framing goes to pieces, straight lines are warped, the decor no longer looks solid and three-dimensional. As for the feeling of "immediate time," which is central to a film like *La Collectionneuse,* that goes completely. . . . the way people stand and walk and move, the whole physical dimension . . . all that is lost. Personally I don't feel that television is an intimate medium.[2]

Nevertheless he admits that television, because of its limitations, taught him to produce "readable" images.

The first two Contes moraux (*La Boulangère de Monceau* and *La Carrière de Suzanne*) were short films, shot in 16-mm black and white, the technical quality of which apparently embarrasses Rohmer. Both films are little more than introductions to the themes of the last four films, which by then, were worked out in profuse detail. In each of the six films Rohmer had planned the basic structure was this: a man who has a commitment to one woman meets another and is attracted to her but avoids making love with her and finally returns to the first woman. The structure is very clear in the first of the six tales, which is about a boy who sees a girl in the street and falls in love with her but doesn't know how to get in touch with her. He decides to make a systematic search for her in the area in which he's seen her, which he does, with no results. In the course of his daily searches he develops the habit of going into a bakery to buy some cakes to eat. He notices that the shop assistant is getting interested in him and, as he's getting a bit bored, he starts flirting with her. As the memory and the hope of the first girl begins to fade he makes a date with the *boulangère,* but just as he's about to meet her he rediscovers the first girl and the fliration with the *boulangère* stops cold.

La Carrière de Suzanne is longer and more complex: a young boy who has a great admiration for an older friend of his who is a student, nevertheless doesn't think much of his choice of women. The older boy, for example, is going out with a girl the younger one doesn't like very much because she's not even a student. The older boy isn't too happy with the arrangement either, however, so he disengages himself from the girl who promptly begins flirting with the younger boy even though she is in love with the older boy, mainly because of his closeness to the older boy. The younger boy doesn't like this, but he is afraid to displease his older friend and he goes along with the game. There is another young woman in the film, whom the younger boy is a little bit in love with, but she is older than he is and isn't interested in him so, as Rohmer says, "There's really nothing but failure in the film."[3]

While each of these films fits the basic form of the Contes moraux, neither exhibits the more elaborate qualities of the four later films that have given Rohmer his reputation. Since those four films are so closely interrelated, it may be best to treat them together, as they were intended, as variations on a single theme. Rohmer's films, even more than Godard's, cry out to be analyzed and divided into parts and "aspects," each labeled and categorized. The Cartesian logic which informs the whole group almost insists that they be discussed not as discrete and separate entities, but as various facets of the larger edifice. Not that any of them is disjointed. The seams never show in Rohmer's films; the fabric is so tightly woven that some people feel there is less there than meets the eye. Not true. The last four Moral Tales involve questions of language and logic, character and locale, light and mise-en-scène, cinema and literature, sex and love, daily life and ideals, rationality and rationales, action and thought. Whatever else they may be, they are certainly films with complex, harmonic resonances.

The rubric which covers all six films has caused some problems, especially for English-speaking audiences. The adjective "moral" means something quite different for Rohmer from what it usually means in English and, since he explains it so well, it is worth quoting him at length:

> In French there is a word *moraliste* that I don't think has any equivalent in English. It doesn't really have much connection with the word "moral." A *moraliste* is someone who is interested in the description of what goes on inside man. He's concerned with states of mind and feelings. For example, in the eighteenth century Pascal was a *moraliste,* and a *moraliste* is a particularly French kind of writer like La Bruyère or La Rochefoucauld, and you could also call Stendhal a *moraliste* because he describes what people feel and think. So *Contes Moraux* doesn't really mean that there's a moral contained in them, even though there might be one and all the characters in these films act according to certain moral ideas that are fairly clearly worked out. In *Ma Nuit Chez Maud* these ideas are very precise; for all the characters in the other films they are rather more vague, and morality is a very personal matter. But they try to justify everything in their behavior and that fits the word "moral" in its narrowest sense. But "moral" can also mean that they are people who like to bring their motives, the reasons for their actions, into the open. They try to analyze; they are not people who act without thinking about what they are doing. What matters is what they *think* about their behavior, rather than their behavior itself. They aren't films of action, they aren't films in which physical action takes place, they aren't films in which there is anything very dramatic, they are films in

> which a particular feeling is analyzed and where even the characters themselves analyze their feelings and are very introspective. That's what *Conte Moral* means.[4]

In English we would tend to use the rather broad adjective "intellectual" for the French *moral.* Even the French noun *morale* has more to do with ethics than with morality or "morals." It becomes clear from Rohmer's succinct statement of purpose that his films situate themselves in a long and honored intellectual tradition, one which has been mainly literary. This is the prime antinomy that Rohmer's films set up: they are evidently highly cinematic works, yet the tradition they draw upon is highly literary.

Rohmer's description of the *moraliste* as someone who is concerned with states of mind—in other words, the psychology of reason—makes it seem as if an Anglo-American author, Henry James, would be as good a literary paradigm as most French authors. If most of us have to spend some time developing a taste for James's psychological realism before we can thoroughly enjoy it, the same is true for Rohmer's films. I can think of no filmmaker who has ventured into this territory before; and even Henry James's disappointing experiences with the stage prove that it is exceedingly difficult to translate this kind of subtle investigation into dramatic or filmic terms. Yet Rohmer has a better chance of success, for film has several important advantages over the stage, especially in the development of atmosphere or milieu. It is no accident that all four major Moral Tales are narrated films: the voice of the narrator and the latitude which that affords the filmmaker to express simply ideas that could never be translated into images or sounds is an important aspect of his work and an advantage which James would have liked to have for his stage works.

If Proust seems a more striking literary antecedent for *Le Genou de Claire;* Choderlos de Laclos for *La Collectionneuse;* Pascal for *Ma nuit chez Maud;* and, possibly, Balzac for *L'Amour, l'après-midi,* nevertheless the novelist who most closely parallels Rohmer throughout the series is still James. And Max Beerbohm's immortal caricature of James peering through the keyhole would be doubly meaningful if the passive novelist were joined by the equally reticent and reclusive man with a movie camera, Eric Rohmer. They are each devoted *moralistes,* enthralled not by what we do but with how we think about what we might do. Rohmer's career is separated from James's, however, by a vast seventy years and also by a wide Channel. Despite the anachronism journalists have ascribed to Rohmer, he is very much a modern thinker, at least as compared with the Henry James of the turn of the century. Rohmer takes things much less seriously. His characters never invest their relatively sardonic, worldly wise musings with anything like the significance or drama which turns on every sentence in James. There is an existential irony present in Rohmer's films that prefers not to reveal itself until we compare those tales with the yarns spun by the much more stern James. And Rohmer is utterly French in this respect as well, drawing on the more distanced, less puritanical humors of Marivaux, La Bruyère, or La Rochefoucauld.

The psychological realism of his *moralistes* reveals its French roots in another way as well. Rohmer has so far chosen, for various reasons, to limit the boundaries of his characters' intellects to the pleasant but well-defined territory of *amour.* John Simon has dismissed Rohmer's constant subject as *amours de tête;* other critics have explained his heroes' continual rationalizations as the product of an overbearing *amour propre* or "self-love"; Carlos Clarens thinks highly of what he calls Rohmer's *amour sage;* while Rohmer himself often speaks, with both modesty and more precision of *l'amour par désoeuvrement,* love from idleness. Regarded in this way the materials of the Contes moraux are not simply to be dismissed as exercises in Marivaudage (as they have been by Simon), but rather as the faintly glowing embers of the quaint but epochal 800-year-old tradition of *amours courtoises* first celebrated by the troubadours of Provence. Andreas Capellanus distilled a definition of "courtly love" in 1174 as "a certain inborn suffering derived from the sight of and excessive meditation upon the beauty of the opposite sex, which causes each one to wish above all things the embraces of the other and by common desire to carry out all of love's precepts in the other's embrace."[5] The necessary changes being made for the attenuations of eight centuries, what better description could there be for Jérôme's obsession with Claire's knee, Frédéric's fascination with Chloé, or Adrien's anger at Haydée? Brother Andreas knew then that the pleasures of this pastime—the love that comes from idleness—are as much intellectual as physical.

Courtly love is moribund, but the memories of it and the literary traditions that lasted for centuries are the subject matter of Rohmer's films. If Andreas warned us that "marriage is no real excuse for not loving," Rohmer shows us that the converse in the twentieth century is even more true: loving is no excuse for not marrying. Each of his protagonists finally decides in favor of marriage. As the troubadours knew well, the affectionate state of marriage has little to do with the "inborn suffering" of courtly love.

Behind the intricate structures of Rohmer's intellectual universe, underneath the richly humorous stuff of *les amours par désoeuvrement* which fills his films, lies a classic philosophical problem: the ethics of choice. Like most intellectuals, Rohmer's men choose not to choose, but this essential paralysis is moot since they prefer to emphasize the possibility of choice rather than the activity of it. It is in this sense that the tales are moral in the *English* sense—there is a morality as well as a love based in idleness, and part of Rohmer's comic genius is that he makes us understand the humor of our rationalizations and excuses. None of his male characters really have the strength to choose; they do have, however, a finely tuned intellectual apparatus which gives them the power to recreate the world surrounding them so that, by an elaborate and eloquent logical maneuver, their inaction is redefined as action. That is why the endings of Rohmer's films are all a bit sad. As Rohmer explains it:

> They are not what one is expecting to happen, they are to some extent *against* the person concerned. . . . The character has made a mistake. He realizes he has created an illusion for himself. He had created a kind of world for himself, with himself at the center and it all seemed perfectly logical that he should be the ruler or the god of this world. Everything seemed very simple and all my characters are a bit obsessed with logic. They have a system and principles, and they build up a world that can be explained by this system. . . . It's not exactly happy, but that's what the films are all about.[6]

In the world of the Contes moraux the fascination is with the psychology of the *moraliste,* the subject matter is the tradition of courtly love, still faintly distinguishable in twentieth-century garb, but the profound emotion is that sense of sadness we all pass through periodically as we rediscover that we are not in control of the choices which mold our lives.

Since Rohmer has made so much of the concept of the cycle which relates the six films to each other, one looks immediately for some pattern of development in the Contes moraux. Rohmer explains that, in addition to a desire to treat the same subject in six variations, he was also motivated by the hope that his somewhat esoteric subject might eventually *appeal* to an audience, if only because of the repetition. "I was determined," he explains, "to be inflexible and intractable, because if you persist in an idea it seems to me that in the end you do secure a following. Even with a distributor . . . it's much more difficult for him to put up arguments and criticisms about a scenario which is part of a group of six than about an isolated script."[7] Nevertheless, there is a larger logic to the series.

As we have already noted, the first two films present the bare skeleton of the common approach. *La Collectionneuse* advances the ages of the characters involved in the triangle by a bit and gives us a relationship between an older man and a younger woman, an arrangement which will be repeated in greater detail in the fifth film, *Le Genou de Claire*. If the students of the first two films knew little of women, Adrien (Patrick Bauchau) of *La Collectionneuse* has had some experience, but he is profoundly puzzled and disturbed by Haydée (Haydée Politoff), who is presented as a kind of proto-hippie. The generational conflict is central, and it doesn't really matter that Adrien is not that much older than Haydée—the important difference is a matter of style and attitude. All of the six films (if we take the liberty of using the English title for the last), announce in their titles that the central, active character is the woman, not the man, and *La Collectionneuse* gives the pivotal female character more power and more control than any of the other films, even though Haydée may be the least understood and least appreciated of all the Rohmer women. This is very much a summer film, and the relationship between Adrien and Haydée is therefore more idle and more isolated than the relationships of the other films. In addition, *La Collectionneuse,* unlike the films which follow it, is composed of a triangle with two men and one woman (Adrien's friend, the painter Daniel [Pommereulle], is the third party), and this puts greater emphasis on the simplest aspect of the *moraliste*'s dilemma—jealousy. Jealousy will be part of the fabric of *Claire* as well, but it is a much more complicated phenomenon there and Claire herself is a less forceful character than Haydée.

Ma nuit chez Maud is clearly the centerpiece of the series. The characters are older here than they are elsewhere and the narrator, Jean-Louis Trintignant, spends much more time and energy in thought than the other men of the series. This is the only film to take place in winter, and its characters are more involved in their careers than in any of Rohmer's other films, with the possible exception of the last. The simple triangle has been discarded, and the relationship between the narrator and Maud (Françoise Fabian) is more open, direct, and intellectual than anywhere else. One gets the feeling that Rohmer might find himself closest to this film, a judgment which is strengthened by the knowledge that only in *Maud* is the male narrator never given a proper name, but always referred to in the script as "I." *Maud* is the coolest of the six films and the first in which the protagonist views himself from an angle which is distinctly different from ours. It's clear here for the first time that the woman is both more honest and more emotionally intelligent than the man, a situation which will be developed further in the later films. This is the only Tale, as well, in which the relationships proceed in such purely reasonable terms, and the presence of the narrator's

Haydée Politoff collecting a specimen on the beach.

Marxist friend Vidal (Antoine Vitez) makes that rationality even more pointed. The debate between Vidal and the narrator on the Marxist and Catholic interpretations of Pascal's wager which is the theoretical centerpiece of the film focuses attention on the significance of "le pari" (the bet), which will hold for the rest of the series. Here, for the first time, the focus is clearly set on the ethical and existential question of choice. If it isn't clear within *Maud* who actually is making the wager and whether or not they win or lose, that only enlarges the idea of "le pari" into the encompassing metaphor that Rohmer wants for the entire series. Yet, despite all the talk and thought, the narrator of *Maud* is not as "wise" as Jérôme and Frédéric who will follow, and his marrying the girl he saw in church, Françoise (Marie-Christine Barrault), makes the film a little more mundane than its successors.

The first two films deal with students. *La Collectionneuse* has a woman student but an older man, who nevertheless is not thinking much of marriage. *Ma nuit chez Maud* continues the progression: the woman is divorced, the man is about to get married—an existential decision. *Le Genou de Claire* has a man in exactly the same position as the narrator of *Maud,* but he is now absorbed with two schoolgirls and the intellectual companion is an older woman novelist, not the relatively cool Marxist of *Maud.* The last film gives us our only married couple, and the progression from adolescence to marriage is complete. *Claire,* like *La Collectionneuse,* is a summer film, and the discussions which form its warp and woof are altogether warmer, more emotional, and more human than any we have seen previously. It is also the most complex in structure, since Jérôme (Jean-Claude Brialy) is surrounded by five women rather than one or two. The companion, and in the metaphor of the film the weaver of the tale, is Aurora Cornù, the Rumanian novelist (who plays herself)—an old friend of Rohmer's whom he had always wanted to use in a film. Jérôme is planning to marry Lucinde (whom we never meet) and, although his reasons for marrying are relatively more sophisticated than those of the narrator in *Maud,* the decision is again existential. It's still a bet with fate. The situation in which he finds himself is almost the direct reversal of *Maud,* for he is confronted not with a successful, mature woman but rather with two schoolgirls, Claire (Laurence de Monaghan) and Laura (Béatrice Romand), the latter having a crush on him, the former being a cool unknown quantity whose knee, oddly enough, is the sublime focus of his passion. Their mother is a minor factor in this complex equation, as is Claire's boyfriend Gilles. The perspective from which we see *Le Genou de Claire* differs even more from the narrator's than in *Maud,* since Jérôme's passion is not only momentary but also slightly absurd and certainly abstract. Yet Claire's knee is more than a simple symbol for lost youth; when Jérôme finally does achieve his objective and touches the knee, the terms of the game he has set for himself have been wiped out and he has been forced into a more human, less abstract relationship with the girl, which the ambiguity of the ending only fortifies. Jérôme has as little control over the events and people of his life as any of Rohmer's other characters, only he knows it and they don't, and that makes *Claire* a much sadder film. This is Rohmer's most idyllic film, but it marks a trend away from the fullness and breadth which characterized Maud; the wise woman is still here, but now she is the friend rather than the object of desire and that doesn't bode well for Rohmer's men.

The last of the Contes moraux, *L'Amour, l'après-midi,* is built around the most complex relationship of the series. In the first place, Frédéric (Bernard Verley) and Hélène (Françoise Verley) are married. There are children, living bonds of commitment. And it is clear that Hélène has a life of her own. Frédéric's liaison with the "other" woman, Chloé (Zouzou), is mirrored by Hélène's own attempt at an affair (even if we don't see much of it since the point of view of the film is still strictly male). We barely met Adrien's woman in *La Collectionneuse;* Françoise was little more than a cipher in *Ma nuit chez Maud;* Lucinde, Jérôme's fiancée, appeared only in photographs in *Le Genou de Claire;* but Hélène is real and very much present in *L'Amour, l'après-midi.* Second, the distance between the narrator, Frédéric, and the other woman, Chloé, has increased. Like Claire and Haydée before her she is seen—from the

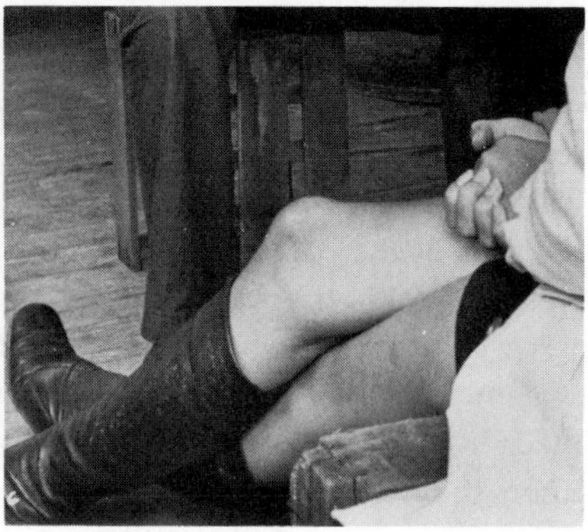

The structure of *Le Genou de Claire:* in the gazebo during the rainstorm Jérôme gazes at Claire's knee, which he is about to touch.

narrator's point of view—as a stereotype. Once again woman is mystery—a bit wild, not as intellectually attractive as Maud or Aurora, more passionate and physical. These two factors mutually reinforce one another: because the figure of the woman to whom the commitment has been made looms larger here, the relationship between the narrator and the other woman must recede in importance. Throughout the first five films Rohmer's men seemed to be moving towards a greater maturity and the wisdom that comes with it. In *Claire* that progression slowed a bit; in *Chloë* it comes to a halt; the development of a moral sensitivity is complete: Frédéric and Hélène have established a balance at the end of the film the likes of which we have not seen earlier. *L'Amour, l'après-midi* begins with a prologue, a reprise in fantasy of the amours par désoeuvrement of the earlier films (signaled by the appearance of the actresses). Frédéric dreams of a magic amulet that will annihilate a woman's will. It is a joke, but it has significance. By the end of the film these male fantasies themselves are annihilated: by Chloé's own strong will and by Hélène's parallel adventure. Frédéric, the last of the narrators of Contes moraux, is brought back to reality with finality as the roles are switched and he is made to see the situation from Hélène's point of view.

Point of view is most important here. Rohmer explains:

> My intention was not to film raw events, but the *narrative* that someone makes of them. The story, the choice of facts, their organization . . . not the treatment that I could have made them submit to. One of the reasons that these Tales are called "Moral" is that physical actions are almost completely absent: everything happens in the head of the narrator.[8]

For Rohmer, as for all his colleagues of the New Wave, the relationship between events and the structure of narrative is important.

The Contes moraux may seem to be about men and other women—Haydée, Maud, Claire, and Chloé—but they are not. In the truest sense their subject is the way Adrien, *Maud*'s narrator, Jérôme, and Frédéric perceive their involvement with these women—and the way they explain it to us. And these narratives are subtly but effectively modulated by the narrators' original commitments to woman who, even when they don't appear on screen, must nevertheless be considered major presences in all the films.

Once they are allowed into the frame of the Contes moraux—in the person of Hélène—the series must reach its conclusion and the fantasies of the narrators, reprised in the harem sequence, evaporate. Structurally, the story ends not when Frédéric comes to certain conclusions about his own feelings but rather when the force of another point of view—Hélène's—rivals his own. *L'Amour, l'après-midi* is then no longer his story alone. What-might-have-been yields to what-is, "the narrative that someone makes of them" is overpowered by the "raw events": only the bond of marriage remains.

Everything we have discussed so far about Eric Rohmer's films—their characters, their plots, and the themes Rohmer weaves with them—all of this is a matter of *narrative* art. We could speak in precisely the same terms if Rohmer were a novelist. But cinema is an art which always operates from two matrices and Rohmer's films are just as rich in images as as in narrative structure. Rohmer has said: "I wanted to portray in film what seemed most alien" to it. In this respect, surprisingly, he has allied himself with contemporary film theorists like Straub, Fassbinder, Rossellini, and of course Godard, who have sought to extend the boundaries of the permissible in film language. What is most exciting about Rohmer's films is not so much their vaunted literacy, but rather his considerable success in finding cinematic images for what are notably uncinematic subjects.

It is not as if he had perversely decided to do a job that was not only difficult but which shouldn't have been done at all. Rather, he has given us prime evidence that film is an art that can grow organically out of the art of the novel. Imagistic structure and narrative structure are not antagonistic; there is a continuum stretching between them, which begins with the allusive nature of the scripts. Godard quotes books, Truffaut filmed a paean to them, but for them books are always objective and discrete. For Rohmer, the object is not so important as the mood to which it alludes. The allusions, except for Pascal in *Maud*, are usually light touches, washes that subtly color the milieux of the films:

The courtship of Maud and the narrator is a matter of conversation, coffee cups, and ashtrays.

Choderlos de Laclos in *La Collectionneuse,* as well as Rousseau and "German Romanticism" which the characters are reading; a bit of Proust in *Le Genou de Claire,* and a touch of Rousseau as well (Rousseau lived in Annecy and told a story of a cherry tree which is comparable to Rohmer's tale); Bougainville's *Voyage Around the World* in *Chloë,* which Frédéric is reading on the commuter train between Saint-Cloud and Paris (Rohmer finds this immensely comic) and which discusses polygamy in Tahiti, a practice which Frédéric will find as foreign as he does the book. These are all minor but well-conceived touches which help set the mood.

Like Godard and Chabrol, Rohmer has a fine eye for the details of everyday life, and these punctuate his films: the incessant smoking in *Maud* (Trintignant thought Rohmer paid more attention to the ashtray than to him), the story of the sunglasses in *La Collectionneuse,* commuting in *Chloë,* the diary structure of *Claire,* numberless small meals, cups of coffee in all the films. They are mosaics of these mundane details, if only because Rohmer's people must have something to do while they talk. Yet this is what we all spend most of our time doing, and Rohmer manages to invest *la vie quotidienne* with some meaningful rhythms: this is the real structure of our lives.

His actors are chosen with the same eye for a combination of ordinariness and freshness. Except for *Maud,* he has used only one professional actor in the Moral Tales—Jean-Claude Brialy—and he used him mainly because he had always thought Brialy was capable of doing a character quite different from his "type." The nonprofessionals add what Rohmer believes is an essential quiet reality to the mood of the films. Nonprofessionals never "project" personality as well as professionals, and this is precisely the quality Rohmer (like Robert Bresson) wants. The quietness and the truth of these characterizations, if such natural performances can be called that, is the background that makes all the rationalization and intellectual sparring believable and gripping. If, for example, a schoolgirl's knee is needed and it must be an emotionally cold and perfect object for the fantasies of Jérôme, no actress could perform the role; the natural aggrandizements of ego would make it nearly impossible. Yet Laurence de Monaghan, a schoolgirl herself, finds the right note of isolation and distance without trying. The nonprofessional is not limited to self-effacing roles only, however, as Béatrice Romand demonstrates in the same film. She has a naturally strong personality that, because of its uniqueness, has given her a career as a professional actress since the film was released.

The necessary value of nonprofessionals for Rohmer's films is probably demonstrated most clearly in *L'Amour, l'après-midi,* which has a kind of natural intensity that professionals can seldom achieve. Zouzou gives Chloé's personality a brash, rough, public, but vulnerable quality that is vital to the success of the film. The husband and wife (Bernard and Françoise Verley) who are married as they say, in "real life," show even more clearly what Rohmer is after: that moment "when the actors forget they are actors and I forget that they are actors too." He describes that moment in *Chloë:*

> In that last scene . . . when the wife comes in, I have the impression that the two actors did more than just merely play a part . . . that's what they told me. When we shot that scene I was almost embarrassed to sit through it even though I knew they were acting out. It was a scene we did only one take of and it would have been absolutely impossible to have done it over. I like when in my films something happens that I am not forcing—that happens and I just have to film.[9]

Not only are the visual images of the characters, which depend on the nonprofessionalism of Rohmer's actors, important to him; so is the quality of their voices. Rohmer has used no music in his films since *Le Signe du lion,* and that means the dialogue must have something of the presence and emotional precision that music usually gives to a film. The filmmaker is acutely sensitive not only to the tenor and intonation of the voices of his characters but also, naturally, to their vocabulary and verbal style. Although the dialogue for all his films is written out in advance, seldom improvised, Rohmer has developed techniques which enable him to capture those precise verbal styles with considerable accuracy. He is able to write lines that fit the characters by spending countless hours in conversation with the actors, all of it tape-recorded. This is less true for *Maud,* whose people are all much closer in style to Rohmer than the characters of the other films, yet even here he worked out Antoine Vitez's Marxist speech in concert with Vitez. Rohmer says that in *La Collectionneuse* the argot was so rich that there are lines he wrote which *he* still doesn't understand. Of course the girls in *Claire* contributed much to the tone of their dialogue, which is why it amuses Rohmer to be criticized for putting big words in Laura's mouth. He has no rigid rule against improvisation, however, and the scene in *Le Genou de Claire* of the quarrel with the lifeguard at the campsite is a good example of conditions in which improvisation is necessary. "I was very anxious that this should retain an authentic slightly incoherent quality which a written script would have eliminated. As it was, there was some tension while the scene was being shot."[10]

This quiet obsession with verisimilitude extends even to the shooting schedule. The story of *Ma nuit chez Maud* begins on Christmas Eve; therefore, shooting had to begin on Christmas Eve; but Trintignant couldn't be there precisely at that time so the film was postponed a whole year. Rohmer's films are very much products of their places and their seasons. Like Chabrol he knows that there are certain stories that can be told on film only in Annecy, or Clermont-Ferrand. Like Ozu, he knows that some narratives belong to early autumn and others specifically to late June. All this may seem meticulous, even finicky, yet each of Rohmer's films is the sum of thousands of these details. If the main aim is to create an atmosphere, a finely tuned mood, the details can be overlooked only at the peril of weakening the verisimilitude. It comes as no surprise that Rohmer has very strong feelings about black and white and color photography, and his attitude is instructive. He never uses color, or black and white for that matter, as a dramatic element. Let me quote him on *La Collectionneuse* and *Le Genou de Claire:*

> I think that in *La Collectionneuse* color above all heightens the sense of reality and increases the immediacy of the settings. In this film color acts in an indirect way; it's not direct and there aren't any color effects. . . . I've never tried for dramatic effects of this kind, but, for example, the sense of time—evening, morning, and so on—can be rendered in a much more precise way through color. Color can also give a stronger sense of warmth, of heat, for when the film is in black and white you get less of a feeling of the different moments of the day, and there is less of what you might call a tactile impression about it. In *La Genou de Claire* I think it works in the same way: the presence of the lake and the mountains is stronger in color

> than in black-and-white. It's a film I couldn't imagine in black-and-white. The color green seems to me essential in that film. I couldn't imagine it without green in it. And the blue too—the cold color as a whole. This film would have no value for me in black-and-white. It's a very difficult thing to explain. It's more a feeling I have that can't be reasoned out logically.[11]

So Eric Rohmer is a realist. He may very well be open to charges that his narrative is precious, that his subjects are irrelevant, that his characters—especially his men—are narrow and limited to a thin stratum of society:* all this is valid criticism. Yet his fascination with the intellect of the *moraliste* is not the result of an inductive process by means of which he has imposed a complex intelligence upon his characters; rather it is the product of deductive reasoning and observation and the perceptions he has gained from it. This is what makes his films strong and valid. Like the painters he most admires—Rembrandt, Turner, Cézanne—he is concerned foremost with character and the quality of light and the way we perceive character through light and sound.

In the end, it is not the fine details of the structure that are most intriguing, nor the precision of the moralizing: it is the source for both of them that impresses us: the people Rohmer knows and observes. If his scope is narrow, it achieves intensity; if he focuses on middle-class intellectuals exclusively, those are the people, for better or worse, that he knows. The vitality of Rohmer's films comes from the people who inhabit them. The irony comes from his vision of them: it is always sharp, but it is also ambiguous. "When you find an explanation," he says, "—and you always can—there is always another explanation behind the first one. I never really manage to finish my stories, since the endings I find all have multiple repercussions. Like an echo."[13] And the films themselves are, in turn, echoes of something tangible and concrete that came before them. It's this balance between what has been done and what is thought, between the people and their environments, between the materials of the films and Rohmer's thoughts and feelings about them, that makes his films valuable.

The device of the echo is something he has used in all his Contes moraux, "but it is also an essential part of the theme, or the chemical ingredients that go to make up the theme: this way of ending on an echo."

*But never, please, identify Rohmer with his men: "You should never think of me as an apologist for my male character, even (or especially) when he is being his own apologist. On the contrary; the men in my films are not meant to be particularly sympathetic characters."[12]

13

RIVETTE
The Process of Narrative

Jacques Rivette, the son of a pharmacist, was born in Rouen in 1928. At the age of twenty he arrived in Paris, entered the Cinémathèque, and stayed there, glued to the screen, for years. Of all the members of the New Wave, he is still the greatest cinéphile and the only one who can still regularly be found in attendance at Cinémathèque screenings. During the fifties he wrote for *Cahiers du Cinéma,* where he displayed an eclectic taste, and also received a more practical training than his critical colleagues, acting as assistant director to Jean Renoir and Jacques Becker on several films.

His cinema reveals these roots, which were both practical and theoretical: on the one hand, it is much simpler and less global than Godard's; on the other, it is more direct and less "popular" than Truffaut's. If Truffaut is the practical historian of the group, and Godard the theoretical, semiological politician, then Rivette has become the experimenter, describing the geometry of the relationships among the elements of film art by amassing the sheer weight of the experience of it. With Truffaut, we concentrated on the end product of the films themselves and worked backwards to the process by which they were made, and then to the theory that we found inherent in the product and the process. With Godard, the focus shifted so that the theory came first, then the product, which itself led us to a study of the idealized and theoretical *pratique* which is the channel between the two. Now, with Rivette, we are concerned primarily neither with product nor theory, but with the concrete practice of filmmaking. It is this that fascinates Rivette above all else, and whatever theories he has developed about the art seem to have been worked out experientially. He is not so interested in the film that eventually results from those labors, he explains, as with the process of work through which he and his co-workers pass.

It is no surprise to discover, then, that Jacques Rivette's films depend on duration for their effect (they range in length from slightly more than two hours to the legendary 12 hours, 40 minutes of the first version of *Out One)* and that three of his five features organize themselves around theatrical troupes in rehearsal. The other two films, as we shall see, call attention to the primary importance of process in more subtle ways. Obviously, this is not the kind of filmmaking that draws popular audiences. It is experimental in exactly the same way that theatre (Robert Wilson, Peter Brook, Jerzy Grotowski) and the novel (Alain Robbe-Grillet, Michel Butor, William Burroughs) have been experimental during the last decade or two: as a clinical, unrelenting analysis of narrative structure. In this sense Rivette is a "filmmaker's filmmaker": it is necessary to care about the art of film to appreciate his films.

Understandably, Rivette is the last of the group of *Cahiers* filmmakers to come to maturity. Although he had made his first short film as early as 1950 (only a few months after the aspiring cinéastes had met in the darkness of the Cinémathèque), it was not until well after 1968 and the revelations of *L'Amour fou* that his objectives were well understood. He began shooting his first full-length film, *Paris nous appartient (Paris Belongs to Us),* in 1957, but because of financial and organizational difficulties shooting was not completed for more than two years and it was late in 1961 before the film finally premiered. Rivette then turned to the project of *La Religieuse (The Nun),* which he had first directed as a play in 1963 at the Studio Champs-Elysées. The film version of *La Religieuse* was not completed until 1965, at which time it was banned by the government censor, even though it represented the country at the Cannes festival in 1966; Rivette was occupied for a good part of a year defending the film's right to be shown. When the ban was finally lifted, *La Religieuse* became his only solid financial success.

Thus a good part of the decade of the sixties was taken up with one arduous project which, although it was a *succès de scandale,* was not really crucial to Rivette's development as a filmmaker. In 1966 he shot

Jean Renoir, le patron, three programs for the television series Cinéastes de Notre Temps, and then in 1968 *L'Amour fou* which, a decade after he had begun his work in earnest, finally solidified his reputation. In May and June of 1970 he shot the nearly thirteen hours of *Out One,* a film which he originally intended as a television serial. The editing of that extensive project took considerably longer than the shooting (Rivette recalls that he had between twenty-five and thirty hours of footage to shape); not surprisingly, Rivette could not convince the O.R.T.F. to take it on. There was not even enough money to make a projection print, and so the original version of *Out One* has been seen publicly only once, at a special screening in Le Havre on the ninth and tenth of September 1971.

Rivette then spent nearly a full year reworking the materials of the original *Out One* into a shorter, more commercially viable film which he calls *Out One/Spectre* and which runs 255 minutes—about a third the length of the original 760-minute cut. This film was released in the spring of 1974, four years after it had been shot. It was quickly followed by *Céline et Julie vont en bateau,* which had been made during the summer of 1973.* Rivette's career, like his films, depends for its effect on our sense of its *durée.* Godard once said, "Someone like Rivette who knows cinema so much better than I shoots seldom, so that people don't speak of him. . . . If he had made ten films, he would have gone much further than I."[1]

So of all the New Wave directors, Jacques Rivette clearly best fits the image of the "experimental" or "underground" filmmaker which we have come to associate with the idea of the avant-garde. Yet as *La Religieuse* and *Céline et Julie* both demonstrate, he is evidently capable of making films which are accessible to general audiences. The problem with his films is thus not that they are avant-garde or difficult, but that the narrow focus of his inquiries insists that audiences have an understanding of the *premises* of his work—and it has taken more than a decade for those premises to become clear. Even Godard allows us multiple entrances into his fictional universe (is not *Tout va bien* a love story, among other things?); but there is generally only one proper entrance into what Jonathan Rosenbaum (who has written well about his work) calls Rivette's "House of Fiction."

Our approach to the Rivette domain is complicated by the close-knit

*In the early seventies, Rivette also spent time on the unrealized project called *Phénix,* a film set in the milieu of Parisian theaters around the turn of the century which was to star Jeanne Moreau. The high cost of period drama evidently doomed the project.

matrix of intellectual traditions which nourishes his films. Although Rivette is perhaps the most confirmed cinéphile of the New Wave, we might better look towards literature for the philosophical foundations of his cinema. Indeed, at the time of *Paris nous appartient* it appeared that, of all the young filmmakers of the New Wave, Rivette might have been the least "cinematic," the most literary in approach. That film looked, and still looks, like an attempt to translate some of the narrative modes of recent fiction into cinematic terms. Even the existential aura that surrounded that film seems more appropriate to a novel of the fifties than to a film of the sixties. It had a certain dry, literary didacticism which set Rivette distinctly apart from his colleagues, all of whose films were informed by the vitality of movies and avoided the modes of contemporary avant-garde literary fiction. *Paris nous appartient* seemed to be exactly the kind of film one would expect a critic to make, full of what seemed like forced, false intellectual mystery: thin, monotonous, and lacking resonance. The elaborate literary history of *La Religieuse* did nothing to dispel this first impression. Diderot's eighteenth-century prose narrative was first reworked by Rivette and Jean Gruault into a theater piece and only then filmed, almost as a record of the stage work. By the time it reached the screen it had achieved a highly "written" texture (Rivette's own phrase) which seemed to distance it from the proper realm of cinema.

For a long time, then, it seemed as if Jacques Rivette was to fill the role of poor literary cousin of the New Wave. It was not until *L'Amour fou, Out One,* and *Céline et Julie* that he effectively applied literary theories of narrative to cinema and confirmed the usefulness of his approach. "Sometimes it is necessary to go a very long distance out of your way in order to come back a short distance correctly." The experience of the earlier films was a prerequisite to the success of the later ones. Rivette seems to indicate that this was true emotionally as well, when he explains that he didn't feel really comfortable with his work until *L'Amour fou.*

Yet to think of Rivette as highly literary is a mistake. A book by Borges appears on a table in the opening shot of *Paris nous appartient,* for instance, but Rivette explains that this happened only because "Suzanne Schiffman happened to be reading it." Despite critics' comparisons of the film with the work of the Argentinian author, Rivette did not begin to read Borges until after the film was completed, when he "of course, found him magnificent." Rivette has often availed himself of literary *materials*—Henry James, Lewis Carroll, Bioy Casarès, and Balzac among the most prominent sources—but he has arrived at his current position not by adapting literary theory to cinema, but rather by discovering *within* cinema some truths that, for the outsider, are more easily understood in terms of literature.

More important to Rivette's historical evolution than Borges or Lewis Carroll are Louis Feuillade and the traditions of the film serial and the film of the fantastic in which he pioneered. Above all, for Rivette, film is a matter of fiction, and he seldom if ever strays very far from the comforts of the "House of Fiction," which for him, is an enclosure, a structure which can never be ignored for long. We may think we are watching events or people within this "house," but inevitably our attention returns to the setting, the architecture of the fictional environment. If any common interest unites the filmmakers of the New Wave, it is certainly an obsessive concern for techniques of narrative, for fictional modes of discourse. Yet while Truffaut, Godard and the others are absorbed by the problems of narrative because they want to use cinema to certain ends, Rivette is almost entirely concerned with fiction as an end in itself. Whatever else we learn about the world outside the House of Fiction from Rivette's films more often than not comes from an examination of what they tell us about the problems of narrative.

What are these problems of narrative fiction, precisely? Rivette's films seem to indicate three foci around which his investigations revolve: first, the function of the narrator; second, theories of invention and mystery; third, the phenomenology of duration. What he is after, to generalize, is a theory of the psychology of fiction. The practical result (*Out One* is the prime example) is a kind of "cinema degree zero" in which invention and mystery, the stuff of fiction, have become abstract and arbitrary, so that they no longer have the traditional affective qualities, and in which the narrator, who determines the duration of the fiction, its size and shape, strives for neutrality. Godard and Pirandello come to mind as referents. Was not Godard after much the same thing in his attempt to return to zero? Yes, but Godard put himself in the center of the fictional universe, whereas Rivette tries to mute his own presence. Pirandello's experiments with theatrical structure seem comparable, but although Rivette's films are suffused with Pirandellian ironies, he never, so far as I can remember, refers directly to Pirandello's work. Godard and Pirandello wrote essays in the languages of theatre and film about the problems of theatre and film. Rivette senses the same constellation of problems, but he gives us examples instead—experiments, not narrations of the results of experiments. His attention is on the experience of the process, not the postulates which led to the process, nor the conclusions that can be drawn from it. There is a connection between the process and the end result, but it is more existential than logical: "I would hope that the result is dominated by the process," he explains, "and that when the film is finished and then given to the audience, they experience some of the same feelings that we the crew did in making the film."[2]

• *The function of the narrator:* It is the narrator (the author) who controls the fiction and who therefore uses the power inherent in fiction to his own ends. Like Godard, Rivette rebels against this tyranny and wants to restructure the politics of filmmaking. But unlike Godard, he comes to this position through the experience of film rather than through the application of political theory to it, especially during the lengthy project of *La Religieuse:*

> The shooting of *La Religieuse* was difficult. . . . I was troubled because we had done the piece before as a play with the sentiments, rehearsals, etc. and I realized when I shot the film that since the people were doing the same text, the same words, my mind was wandering and I was no longer listening to the words.

Out of this experience came the shift towards improvisation, because "with improvisation, you automatically listen," and a conception of the director of a film as less an author than an "analyst, a person who must listen to what the people say—*all* words are important. You must listen to all and not have any preconceived ideas as a director." So Rivette became an anti-auteurist, and succeeded in his later films, far better than Godard ever did, in creating communal films. The actors in *L'Amour fou* and the films that follow it were involved in the projects from the beginning. In *Out One,* they even created their roles separately; Rivette's job was then to discover links which would allow the roles to be woven together into a fiction with some coherence.

• *Invention and mystery:* Practically, then, as well as theoretically, the real weight of creation shifted from the director of the film to the actors; they become the true narrators. This seems simple enough; we have heard enough about improvisation in theatre and film in recent years not to be surprised. But for Rivette it has a much deeper significance. It is not just a new method of operation; it destroys the way we have been accustomed to apprehending films. We are now no longer presented with a *fait* (or *fiction) accompli,* but with material which has been only slightly edited for our convenience and which we must work to interpret. Naturally, there will be false leads, dead spaces, and arhythmic developments. All the better. The intention is not to "offend the audience," to borrow a phrase from Peter Handke, but to open up new areas in which the audience can exercise its intelligence. The natural form for this is mystery, the root of all fictional narrative, in which the audience is always placed in the position of asking the continual question: "and *then* what happens?" All of Rivette's films, with the exception of *La Religieuse*, perhaps, revolve around mysteries. None of them are ever really solved; that's not the point. Like the candies of *Céline et Julie* they exist to draw us into the fictional milieu. Hitchcock called them MacGuffins; he also knew that it was not necessary to solve them, that the audience was more interested in the experience than the solution.

If we make the metaphorical jump, Rivette's films become, not mysteries, but studies of the phenomenon of mystery—especially the general mystery of fiction: *how* do we interpret the data a novelist or filmmaker gives us? *Why* do we want to interpret it? Rivette's "characters" are more often than not actors, involved in the work of interpretation of texts and therefore surrogates for the audience who must also interpret. The films thus mirror their own fiction and duplicate our response to its mystery.

• *Duration:* Jacques Rivette has never made a short film. The average length of his seven films (five features, the second version of *Out One*, and the television programs on Renoir) is more than four hours. Such a length is not unknown in film history (Gance's *Napoleon* and Stroheim's *Greed* come immediately to mind), but previously the abnormal length of a film was an index of its epic scope; it was long because it had to be to cover the wealth of incident out of which it was woven. The converse is true with Rivette: his films are long not because so *much* "happens," but because so little does. If the narrator is not to intervene on our behalf to edit the proceedings, if we are going to be given the freedom to work out the mystery for ourselves, then length is a necessity. Psychologically, it operates in three distinct ways on an audience. First, the *durée* works to break down our resistance to the world of Rivette's characters. There comes a point after a couple of hours of film time when we cease reacting to the logic of the film and begin to flow with it. This is a phenomenon which seems to me unique to the medium of film, although there might be correlatives in music (the attitude necessary for a full appreciation of a Wagnerian opera, for example, or the structures of the more elaborate Indian ragas). It does not happen on stage where, even during a twelve-hour performance of a Robert Wilson piece, to take one example, we still maintain a psychological distance from the action (or inaction). It certainly does not happen in written fiction, where the reader controls the time scheme of the experience.

Those long sessions in the Cinémathèque must have demonstrated to Rivette the psychological power of this technique, but there are more pointed reasons for it, as well. In most of his films Rivette concentrates on two basic rhythms of action: the first is that of the theatrical rehearsal, repetitious, ritualistic, cyclical. (Compare Resnais's experiments with this mode in *Je t'aime, je t'aime.*) It attempts to dominate the reality of character and event and to make them exoteric by the force of its innate structuring capacity. The second rhythm, which we might call veristic, is evident, for example, in the long scene in the apartment in *L'Amour fou* or the shorter scenes in the boutique in *Out One.* Rivette allows a dramatic relationship between two characters to build at a natural rate—one which is often slow and erratic. It is vaguely reminiscent of Japanese cinema (Rivette talks of Mizoguchi; Ozu's empty spaces fit too). Its importance lies not so much in its aleatory nature as in the power that subtly builds while our defenses are down. The agony of the end of the apartment scene in *L'Amour fou* demonstrates that power forcefully.

So the *durée* of Rivette's films is not so arbitrary as it seems.* If the rigid conventions of cinematic narrative are to be broken down, something like the phenomenon of duration will have to be employed. The audience's learned sensibility must be attacked. There are two basic ways to do this, as Brecht and Artaud showed years ago: to distance the audience intellectually (Brecht); or to exaggerate the metaphorical danger of the experience (Artaud). If Godard is the New Wave's Brecht, Rivette is its Artaud. If he is to convey the essential experience of his actors and characters, Rivette is going to have to give us long chunks of it. We'll never really get into it, otherwise.

Finally, these experiments in duration, narrative, and the mystery of fictional invention have value for us (if we accept their premises and suspend judgment) because, as we learn how better to deal with fictions, we also learn how to interpret what we like to call reality more precisely. It is the Pirandellian rationale. As the Father (a "character") explains in *Six Characters in Search of an Author:*

> The drama lies all in this—in the conscience [*coscienza*] that I have, that each one of us has. We believe this conscience to be a single thing but is is many-sided. There is one for this person, another for that. Diverse consciences. So we have this illusion of being one person for all, of having a personality that is unique in all our acts. But it isn't true.[3]

This is the Special Theory of Relativity of human relations upon which so much of contemporary metaphysics is based. There is no better way

*Although I should note that there is also a much simpler reason. Rivette, bluntly, suffers from a good case of logorrhea. Even if he had none of these rationales, he would still make long films. In interviews he speaks in endless, ebullient sentences that surround their subjects like spider's webs and sometimes suffocate them.

to study the phenomenon of the ever-changing *coscienza* (consciousness of self, as well as "conscience") than to examine the frozen laboratory sections of it we find in fiction—and then to investigate the epistemology of fiction and describe the sociology of the people who make it. This is what Jacques Rivette is trying to do. "If cinema has a social function," he explains, "it's really to make people confront other systems of thought, or other systems of living than the ones they habitually know."[4]

Rivette was the first of the *Cahiers* group to make a film. In 1950, barely a year after he had arrived in Paris from Rouen, he directed two shorts, "Aux quatre coins" and "Quadrille" (in which Godard was the principal actor). "Le Divertissement," his third 16-mm short, dates from 1952. None of these early efforts seems to have survived, but Tom Milne has given us an account of his own experience of one of them, "Quadrille," which he remembers from a program of experimental shorts he happened upon in Paris one evening late in 1950:

> One film had something: a certain hypnotic, obsessional quality as, for some forty minutes, it attempted to show what happens when nothing happens by observing, in strict objectivity, behavior in a dentist's waiting room. No plot, no dialogue; simply the play of silence, covert glances, magazines nervously skimmed, cigarettes furtively lit, as strangers casually thrown together try to come to terms with each other with nothing to come to terms about.[5]

As Milne describes it, "Quadrille" must have been a good emblem for Rivette and a pointed introduction to what was to come. In the mid-fifties he worked as an assistant to Becker and Renoir, acted as cameraman for Truffaut's "La Visite" and Eric Rohmer's "Bérénice," and completed one more short film of his own, this time in 35 mm with commercial backing. "Le Coup du berger" (1956) is a distanced, stylized description of the sexual geometry of four young people—a woman, her husband, sister, and lover,—accompanied by the music of Couperin and couched in chess metaphors.

Shortly thereafter Rivette began work on the scenario for his first feature. *Paris nous appartient* and Chabrol's *Le Beau Serge* were the first feature films of the New Wave to go into production. During the course of the shooting and editing *Paris nous appartient* achieved a legendary reputation, but by the time the film was seen by the public its potential effect was considerably blunted by the precedents of *Les Quatre Cents Coups* and *A bout de souffle* and *Hiroshima mon amour*. With the benefit of hindsight we can fit it neatly into the pattern of Rivette's development, but on its own in the early sixties the film met with a confused response. It was not so clearly a blow at the old forms of narrative as the three films which had been released during its lengthy production. On the one hand, *Paris nous appartient* seemed to be vaguely avant-garde, but nevertheless within the traditions: it is suffused with existential angst. Jeander, the critic for *Liberation,* was thus able neatly to categorize it as showing "perfectly the moral and intellectual confusion of these young people who are repressed by their epoch far more than their elders were. . . ."[6] On the other hand, there was at least some indication that Rivette was also able to describe the essentially literary existential situation of his characters with a cinematic grammar that could be compared with Bresson's (the only useful cinematic referent for Rivette). Writing in *Combat,* Pierre Marcabru noted:

> The life of Paris, in a cinematic sense, is put in a new light. For the first time, the stones and the streets have a secret grace which is that of the imaginary. . . . Except with Bresson, the connection between image and sound has never been so striking, evocative, or necessary.[7]

Paris nous appartient very much needs perceptive criticism of this kind, for it is not a film that describes itself well. Even more than the films which follow it, it seems to require a preface, where the author can explain intentions and connections. It has a hermetic quality which made it easy to dismiss the film as just that kind of deadly cinema one might have expected a critic, weaned on the existential literary atmosphere of Paris in the fifties, to make.

Yet all the basic elements of Rivette's art can be found in embryo here. *Paris nous appartient* is essentially the story of a young woman, Anne Goupil (Betty Schneider), who finds herself involved in, first, rehearsals for a production of Shakespeare's *Pericles** which will never come off; and second, a sinister and vaguely political conspiracy which will turn out to be, in the end, a fiction invented by a paranoid American novelist, Philip Kaufman (Daniel Crohem), even though it results in several deaths—real ones. The tone of the film is strictly controlled—limited and attenuated—and the action proceeds mainly through dialogue. Rehearsals take up less time than they will in later films, but they still interrupt the rhythms of the film abruptly and pointedly. The film lasts 135 minutes, which is long enough to call attention to its duration, and there is the same sense of futility in the "mystery" which we get in the later films. What is missing here, however, is the irony and humor of *Out One,* or even *L'Amour fou.*

*A perfect choice for Rivette—that sprawling, static romance that stretches over five cities and twenty years.

If *Paris nous appartient* pales in comparison with later Rivette films, it is because Rivette is still dominated by the feeling that he has to control this fiction as rigidly as any mythical auteur. He hasn't yet learned how to let go; but the experience is not wasted. Although *La Religieuse* is just as tightly dominated by its director, by 1963 Rivette was already speaking against the "myth of the auteur" in interviews:

> Obviously we—the *Cahiers* team, with Truffaut as chief spokesman—were responsible for this myth, but we were writing at a time when polemics, shock statements like "anyone can make a film," were a necessary reaction against the rigid stratification which was then strangling cinema. . . . Since 1959 and the birth of the New Wave, all these attitudes have been taken much too literally.[8]

In *Paris nous appartient* he has organized his materials, but he has not yet discovered the proper approach to them. He treats them as if they were the ordinary materials of cinema, when of course they are not. His real success came after *La Religieuse*, when he found a new approach for the new materials, and eventually he saw that the materials don't matter much: process is all.

Since his first film has a value that is more evident in theory than in practice, it may be best to let Rivette explain that theoretical motivation for *Paris nous appartient* in his own words:

> If I try to summarize the experience of *Paris nous appartient*, I couldn't do better than this: an experience—an adventure, unachieved, aborted, perhaps, but isn't that the risk of experience? Experience of what? Of an idea, of a hypothesis, by turns proposed, isolated, taken up again, deformed, refused, deprecated—consumed, finally, by having everything that it suggests brought back again to it. A film is, in general, a story *built* upon an idea: I tried to tell the *story* of an idea, with the aid of the detective story form; that is to say that instead of *unveiling* primary intentions at the end of the story, the denouement can't do anything but *abolish* them: "Nothing took place but the place."[9]

Rivette began work on the *Religieuse* project early in 1962. During the editing of *Paris nous appartient*, Jean Gruault (who was to become one of the most valued screenwriters of the New Wave) brought Rivette the first draft of a stage adaptation of the novel by Denis Diderot. It had been written in 1760, only a few years after Diderot had completed his two major plays, *Le Père de famille* and *Le Fils naturel*, and both Rivette and Gruault were attracted to the text because it was "highly wrought" and very theatrical. Ironically, Rivette notes, the film that was eventually to emerge became his most theatrical work, even though it is the only one of his feature films that does not directly or obliquely concern actors and their problems. Rather, with *La Religieuse,* the theatrical metaphor exists just off the edge of the screen. *La Religieuse*

> is the one of my films which is most willingly about theatre, for several reasons: because it is "extremely written" (*extrêment écrit*), because it came out of the experience of working on the stage, and finally because the subject deals with Catholicism which is the absolute peak of theatre. This was the reason why I wanted to do the film.

Rivette had hoped for an even more ebullient theatrical quality than he was able to achieve, but despite the relatively popular nature of his second project there were nevertheless money problems which limited him. (Anna Karina was not a star when the project began; she had done only a few films for Godard and had a rather thick Danish accent, which scared the producers.)

> I couldn't show the ceremonies, the paraphernalia of the offices. The *rapport* of *La Religieuse* is regulated by the entrances and exits; the mise-en-scène depends on the ritual of actors. So, in this manner I did try to be extremely theatrical even though I didn't completely succeed because one thinks of the things that are missing. I call it *cinéma manqué.*

The stage version of *La Religieuse,* produced in 1963, ran more than three hours; only lack of money kept the film down to 130 minutes. Yet these restrictions were probably more salutary than not. *La Religieuse* is the simplest and most direct of Rivette's films and has a clarity which is not always present in the later ones. From Diderot to Gruault to the stage production and finally to film, the project was a process of condensation: only the distilled essence of *La Religieuse* remains.

Because it was based on a novel and because it went through this process of concentration, the film is structurally anomalous, as well. This is the only time so far that Rivette has allowed a story to carry only its own interior meaning without forcing it to become an element in a symbolic or indexical system of theory, most of which lies outside the boundaries of the film. We can talk about the story as *story* here, in the old, simple sense of the word. Consequently, *La Religieuse* has been Rivette's most popular film to date, even if we can assume that some of that success was due to its being banned.* Materially, it is a rich film, eloquent with subdued period detail, which contrasts sharply with the controlled barrenness of *Paris nous appartient.* The story itself has an

*The ban was lifted when the title was changed to *Suzanne Simonin, la religieuse de Diderot.* As with Godard's *La Femme mariée,* the censor was acutely sensitive to the grammatical manifestations, not the substance.

inexorable, classical dramatic logic which audiences can easily relate to and a mythic dimension of some power. The complexity of the narrator's situation, ironically, is derived this time from the source of the story, Diderot. *La Religieuse* began as an elaborate practical joke on Diderot's friend the Marquis de Croismare. Diderot wrote a series of letters to the Marquis in which he represented himself as Suzanne Simonin, a young woman whom the Marquis had earlier assisted in an unsuccessful attempt to revoke her vows. He also composed a journal supposedly kept by Simonin. These were the origins of the novel, but Rivette meticulously avoided any kind of similar distancing in his film, staging it austerely and a bit abstractly, but nevertheless straightforwardly. *La Religieuse* does display the typical slow rhythms of a Rivette film, but they are counterbalanced by the elaborate decors and, since they are applied to a calculated dramatic story, they build inexorably to the tragic conclusion.

The structure of the film is similarly spare and solid. Simonin spends most of the first half in one convent—austere, dark, prisonlike, and devoted to mortification—and most of the second half in another, the logical converse of the first—ebullient, light, frivolous, and sybaritic. While the relief she feels at moving from the first to the second is apparent, it is nevertheless the second which kills her, since, under the guidance of Diderot, Gruault, and Rivette, she understands her situation in terms of pure liberty—and its absence. Indeed, she seems to adapt best to the medieval repression of the first convent, so long as it is tempered by the truly religious love the first mother superior shows her. When that woman dies, however, it becomes unbearable. What makes the second convent finally fatal for her is the complementary sexual passion which the mother superior there evinces for Suzanne. There are two much briefer sequences which show us Simonin in the world outside the walls, the first in the more relaxed prison of her family, where as a younger daughter she must expect to be sent to a convent, the second after she has escaped from the second convent only to discover that there was some justice—or at least logic—in the actions of her parents: she is unequipped to deal with the outside world. More precisely, the world is not constructed in such a way that a woman like her will be *permitted* to survive.

Here we have the kernel of *La Religieuse:* a vivid and direct essay on the politics of personal liberty, especially as regards woman in society—a lesson direct from the eighteenth century which Rivette and Anna Karina have described with quiet passion. Molly Haskell has written cogently about this aspect of the film:

> Diderot's nun, like very few women in life and fewer in literature (some of Ibsen and Shaw's heroines maybe) desires freedom, not for love of a man or for God, but for its own sake. She is capable of disinterested desire, of passion for a principle, and she seeks liberty rather than romance or security or rest or the other pragmatic goals which are considered to be the instinctive aspirations of women. Under Rivette's direction, Anna Karina gives us just such a nun, serious, intelligent, innocent, her life and her purity seen finally as one continuous impulse towards freedom. She is, to use Simone de Beauvoir's distinction, transcendental rather than immanent, but she is also feminine.[10]

This is the real achievement of *La Religieuse,* and we can recognize its value all the more distinctly when we compare Karina's incisive portrait here with her work with Godard. That Rivette can allow such a woman to exist in his cinema gives it a value that we never find in Godard's films—and seldom in Truffaut's.

Of course, the respect that Rivette evinces here for women also extends to the men of his films; his attitude towards Suzanne Simonin is emblematic of his judicious and liberal feeling for all the characters in the films to come—and more important, for the actors whom he allows to create them. This respect and reverence for the *conscience* of others may be one of Rivette's most valuable qualities as a filmmaker, and *La Religieuse* gives us a chance to examine it without the sometimes confusing interference of concurrent experiments with narrative forms of the later films. It's important to recognize that Rivette's obsession with formal matters has at least a provenance in simple human politics. He shows his solidarity with Truffaut, Godard, and Resnais in finding a vital parallel between psychological and political repression and his own esthetic repression by forms. Whereas the other filmmakers work out this geometry theoretically, with paper and pencil, and use films to illustrate their findings, Rivette goes directly to the experience itself, the act of filmmaking.

L'Amour fou, shot in the fall of 1968, is—like *La Religieuse*—an essay in the psychological aspects of individual freedom. But whereas Suzanne Simonin existed in splendid isolation, Claire and Sébastien, the condemned couple of *L'Amour fou,* are inextricably and very nearly fatally linked to each other, as the title indicates. Moreover, *L'Amour fou* has a much more complex narrative than its predecessor. The interrelationships of dramatic modes, which had been hidden in *La Religieuse,* are now directly evident, as they will be from now on; yet *L'Amour fou* is different from the films which succeed it in that its psychology is simpler and more direct. This film has none of the fictive mystery that characterizes *Out One* and *Céline et Julie:* there is instead a straightforward progression into madness which requires no interpretation whatsoever on the part of the audience even though it is paralleled and aided by the geometry of narrative modes that Rivette sets up alongside it. This makes *L'Amour fou* Rivette's most easily accessible film and possibly his most powerful.

By this time Rivette had completely rejected the concept of filmmaking which divided it into three distinct motions—scriptwriting, production and shooting, and montage. "In my idea of cinema," he explained,

> all the stages should be totally interacting. I want to return, though with quite different methods, aims and end-products, to the old Dziga Vertov idea: that the montage should be conceived with the project and not merely with the exposed film. This may sound like a conceit, but you could say that the script is written in the montage, and that the montage is established before shooting. . . . I reject the word "script" entirely—at any rate in the usual sense. I prefer the old usage—usually scenario—which it had in the Commedia dell'Arte, meaning an outline or scheme: it implies a dynamism, a number of ideas and principles from which one can set out to find the best possible approach to filming.[11]

To this end, Rivette approached Jean-Pierre Kalfon with the idea of forming a group to rehearse Racine's *Andromaque,* scenes of which would form the foundation of the film. Kalfon actually directed the group in rehearsals (as did Lonsdale and Moretti in *Out One),* so that there is a cinéma-vérité sense of the progression of that kind of project from the first exhilarating hopes through the depression that comes with repetitious and usually half-successful work to the climax of opening night. Significantly, the film ends with the bare stage—which looks like a modified boxing arena—just previous to the first public performance. As with *One Plus One* it is important that we *don't* see the completed work of art—only the meticulous process of construction.

This was the first element of *L'Amour fou,* to which Rivette added two others: first, the direct cinematic drama of the breakdown of the relationship between Sébastien (Kalfon) and his wife Claire (Bulle Ogier); second, the idea that the rehearsals would be shot by a television crew preparing a documentary. For this Rivette set up a separate camera crew to work in 16 mm. André S. Labarthe, the critic and filmmaker, acts the "role" of the TV director/interviewer, and we can assume that he was at least in part responsible for directing that separate crew. The result is that the dialectical tensions between the various combinations of cinema, stage, and television are vividly clear in *L'Amour fou,* whereas the comparable oppositions in *Paris nous appartient* were muddy and indistinct, and those in *La Religieuse* were only implied. As Tom Milne has

The blank, spare, solid space of the stage in *l'Amour fou:* Claire (Bulle Ogier) rehearses tensely in this early shot; the 16-mm crew is at left.

pointed out, the interplay between the 35-mm and 16-mm sequences reinforces "with superb economy" the conflict between the two worlds of "fictional" theatre and "real" life, and it does so both texturally and stylistically: the slightly muzzy quality of the 16-mm photography gives the theater a haunting quality which directly opposes the harsh, brightly lit reality of Sébastien's life with Claire; and the mobility of the 16-mm camera is in sharp contrast to the stolidity of the 35-mm Mitchell which "impassively watches Claire and Sébastien thresh about in the grip of their inflexible decline."[12]

As for the psychodrama of the relationship between Claire and Sébastien, which is after all the heart of the film, this too is connected in ingenious but not obtrusive ways to the contrasts between the fictive modes. We might expect the play in rehearsal to have some commentative relationship to the private drama, and it does, but although Rivette indulges himself in a few meaningful match cuts between 16- and 35-mm footage, he also warns us against taking this business too seriously: the relationship between the dramatic rehearsals and the private drama "is never rigid. The play serves mainly as a text, a base." Rivette decided on *Andromaque* mainly because it would not intrude upon the central action of the film. It is well known and therefore makes fewer demands on the audience's attention. He was intrigued at first by the idea of using something by Ford or Dekker, but the English Stuart theatre would have been too unfamiliar to his audience, even though the substance of those plays fits strikingly with the private drama.

The mad love of Sébastien and Claire is also rooted in the theatrical experience by simple plot devices, since it is Claire's decision to quit the project that sets off the series of events which lead to the breakdown. But the most ingenious and intriguing bond between the 16- and 35-mm worlds develops out of Claire's own actions in isolation from the troupe she has just left. Shots of Claire at home are intercut with shots of the rehearsal as Claire's story parallels the progression of the theatrical action. She works with a tape recorder which becomes a symbol of the unity between audience and actor (it listens to her, then it talks back to her), between author and interpreter, producer and consumer. At the same time it mockingly reminds her of her own self-imposed alienation from the troupe which is going to lead to the Strindbergian logic of self-destruction. Like Strindberg's Father or Miss Julie, Claire has boxed herself into a psychological corner from which she can't escape. Indeed, the hour-long scene in the apartment at the end of the film, in which Claire and Sébastien methodically destroy their environment in an orgy of *amour fou* and self-contempt, has thematic echoes from later Strindberg—*The Ghost Sonata,* for example.

Not surprisingly, Claire in her fury is able to condense the purer meaning from *Andromaque,* and several of the passages she records provide direct commentary, especially these lines—the Racinian root of *L'Amour fou:*

> Où suis-je? Qu'ai-je fait? Que dois-je faire encore?
> Quel transport me saisit? Quel chagrin me dévore?
> Errante, et sans dessein, je cours dans ce palais.
> Ah! ne puis-je savoir si j'aime ou si je haïs.*

These lines are so appropriate that they remind us that the sentiments with which the film deals are not the exclusive province of pop existentialism. If *Pierrot le fou* comes immediately to mind as correlative (remember Marianne's lines on the beach), so does the sexual nausea of Ford, Dekker, and Shakespeare. *La Religieuse* had an eighteenth-century provenance; *L'Amour fou* has roots in the seventeenth.

What this loose structure (this "commedia dell' arte scenario," to use

*Where am I? What's to do? What must I still do?/ What fury has seized me? What sorrow devours me?/ Wild, without design, I run through this palace./ Ah! Nor can I know if I love or if I hate.

his own words) gives Rivette is a matrix which will make the cinéma-vérité development of the Claire-Sébastien breakdown mythically effective. Milne calls this "cinéma-vérité for once organized, controlled, and chiseled into shape." The temps morts, the aleatoric rhythms, the repetitions and cinematic fatigue give the audience the chance to enter into the film, to reflect, to examine, and therefore to take an emotional part in the drama—not as spectators usually do, manipulated into feeling, but as we do outside the theatre, outside the cinema in the haphazard fiction of our own lives, when, as we are thrust into situations like these, we often repress direct emotional responses. The true test of the success of *L'Amour fou* might just be in the quality of our response to this story, not while we are watching it, but a day—a week—later.

This cinematic encounter experience absolutely requires the duration of *L'Amour fou* (252 minutes). Interestingly, an unintentional experiment proved this point: the producer released a two-hour version of the film which for a while was playing simultaneously with Rivette's original four-and-a-quarter-hour version. The original version was more popular than the producer's reduction. There is a feeling of exhilaration and liberation in the full duration of *L'Amour fou*—almost as if Rivette had always known that this was the way he had to make films but hadn't, until now, had the courage to try. This was his first film edited by Nicole Lubtchansky (she cut the next two, as well), and he seems to have found a collaborator who understands these long, periodic rhythms. Many references in the film show a concern with rhythm—drums, rehearsal exercises, and so on—and it is clear that Rivette is thinking in quasi-musical terms. Yet his audiences, accustomed to simplistic western rhythms of two, three, and four beats may be lost in a film which is best compared, rhythmically, to Indian tals—long, enormously complex rhythmic structures of as much as thirty-two beats. (In *Paris nous appartient,* some of the characters are discovered listening to Indian music—long before the Beatles. A clue?) In short, it is clear finally that Rivette has found the mode in which he can make the most substantial contribution. Despite the dark tone of *L'Amour fou,* Rivette remembers the shooting as a happy time. There was a sense of accomplishment among cast and crew. The *amour fou* Rivette had had for fifteen years with cinema was at last being requited.

Out One, which was shot during a period of only six weeks in April and May of 1970, entirely in 16 mm is a sprawling giant of a film—a cinematic plaza on which all of Rivette's various interests and obsessions can meet and exchange views. Since there is as yet not enough money to make a projection print of the original twelve-hour, forty-minute version and it has only been screened once, it is also a contemporary cinematic legend. The very fact of its length has superseded all other considerations. Rivette was motivated by a desire to extend the experimental lines of development that had been established in *L'Amour fou* while at the same time avoiding a duplication of that film. For some months before the actual shooting began he discussed the project "in a rather vague way" with the actors who were to take central roles (Michael Lonsdale, Juliet Berto, Bulle Ogier, Michèle Moretti, and Jean-Pierre Léaud), but it was not until a week before the scheduled starting date that any kind of detailed scenario was worked out, and only then because in order to shoot the maximum amount of footage in a minimum amount of time some plan would be necessary.

Each of the actors had developed his or her own character in some detail. Lonsdale had been working with his own loosely knit theatre group with Peter Brook in Paris in the months previous to the spring of 1970—on a project called "Balls," based on the *The Tempest*—and was interested in continuing along Brookian lines. Michèle Moretti decided that she wanted to use *Seven Against Thebes* because, of all of Aeschylus' plays, Rivette reports, "it was distant from us, a play practically unplayable, because practically all that is said in the text does not concern us, so it was purely a text with which to do vocal exercises, movements, and so on." Berto developed a character in direct contrast to the ones she had so far played for Godard and other filmmakers, a down-and-out hustler who would exist in the margin of the film and eventually die. Léaud had a similar character in mind: he began with the conception of playing the first several scenes of the film as a deaf-mute, simply for the effect of the eventual scene in which the audience would discover that he was a fake. Bulle Ogier's character—who goes by two names, Pauline and Emilie—was the least well-defined element of the film, largely because she was working on another project at the same time. Confronted with these disparate plots, Rivette had to come up with a device to unite them in some way. Shortly before shooting began he hit upon the Balzac trilogy, *Histoire des Treize*. Ironically, this choice meant that Léaud, who had been most marginally involved in the pre-production discussions, would become the central character—if not the *raisonneur*, at least the *policier*—and the audience's surrogate in the midst of this narrative web of mysteries.

If we accept Rivette's premise that the answers to these mysteries are unimportant, that the mysteries have ultimate value in and for themselves, then *Out One* is proof of the success of the collaboration between actors and director. In terms of narrative structure, it is as resonant as any more pedestrian detective story which bothers to solve its mysteries. Let me outline the structure of the film and at the same time summarize what in other circumstances would be called its plot.*

Michael Lonsdale and a troupe of actors are rehearsing a production of *Prometheus Bound*. They fully expect to put the play before the public eventually, but most of the scenes devoted to their rehearsals deal with elementary exercises in the manner of Peter Brook. Michèle Moretti and a second group, meanwhile, are performing another set of exercises based on *Seven Against Thebes*. Moretti's group tends more towards the methods of Jerzy Grotowski's Laboratory Theatre and couldn't care less about eventual public presentation. (Lonsdale, by the way, is called "Thomas," while Moretti plays "Lili," but separate names for the characters are almost superfluous.)

Meanwhile, Frédérique (Juliet Berto) hustles in cafes and is also something of an artist, and Colin (Jean-Pierre Léaud) plies his trade in bistros, acting the deaf-mute and selling cards which declare "the Message of Destiny." To announce his presence, he often whips out a harmonica and riffles through a few discordant notes. He soon becomes the focus of the film, as he is handed strange messages which speak incoherently of Balzac's *Histoire des Treize* and Lewis Carroll's *Hunting of the Snark*. He becomes obsessed with explicating these inscrutable texts and returns to his room to work them out on a blackboard. The poem he writes there seems susceptible of crossword and anagram interpretation and most certainly contains hidden clues (although they are never quite fully worked out), but Colin learns enough to surmise the existence of a utopian political group based on the Thirteen *(treize)*. The messages seem to be an attempt on their part to draw him within their orbit.

He discovers in code an address—2 Place Saint-Opportune—and when he goes there finds a hippie boutique called "L'Angle du hasard," the name of which might be useful to *us* as well, since it is a good description of the fictional geometry of the story of *Out One:* instead of following the straight line of the story, we take off at various points on "chance angles." It is here that we meet the fourth group of characters, centered around Bulle Ogier's Pauline/Emilie. The boutique is a front for an underground newspaper which itself may be a front for the Thirteen.

But now Thomas (Lonsdale) is running into trouble in rehearsals. He visits Sarah (Bernadette Lafont), a novelist who lives at the seashore, to ask for help. Sarah, like Lucie (Françoise Fabian), a lawyer, is one of the

*Unless otherwise noted, I am referring to the 4¼-hour version of the film.

Colin says goodbye to Pauline outside l'Angle du hasard, the boutique which supplies the geographic focal point of the first half of *Out One*.

marginal characters whose function is to provide a background for the four central groups of characters. Colin is becoming involved with Pauline/Emilie. Just as Colin is leaving L'Angle du hasard for the last time, he passes Frédérique, who is coming in. They do not acknowledge one another. This is the exact middle of the film (in both versions), and the rationale for this seemingly insignificant scene is exemplary. Rivette explains that the meetings between various pairs of characters had been worked out far in advance of the story, not on the basis of plot or character, but because of the previous experiences of the actors involved. "This was the diagram," Rivette explains. "For example, a sequence was decided upon for Lonsdale and Léaud because of the work each had done in previous films. We thought it would be amusing. It was only *after* that we searched for the reasons why, which were very arbitrary." Since Berto and Léaud had worked together in two films by Godard, "it was hardly worthwhile for *them* to meet." To emphasize their ignorance of each other, then, their paths cross in the exact middle of the film. "It is this scene which pulls, in fact, the rest of the film"—the knot where all the threads meet.

By this time (I have left out a great many details) tenuous connections have been made among all the various elements of the cast. Likewise, the set of themes has been established: the mystery (carried by Léaud and Berto), the rehearsal (Lonsdale and Moretti), the utopia of the thirteen (Ogier, Fabian, Lonsdale, and Lafont). We have also been introduced to two spectral presences in the evanescent plot of the Thirteen—Pierre and Igor, who never appear, but who seem to carry the motivation of the plot. At the end of the fourth hour, the various groups and individuals mesh in a series of scenes in Sarah's house (Aubade), the silent House of Fiction. But nothing happens. They disperse. And the last few minutes of the film show them separate and isolated. Emilie is still at the house and has found a key to the locked room. Juliet is back in the cafe, hustling once again and contemplating her death. Léaud, in the last scene, stands alone, swinging a model of the Eiffel tower and counting loudly to thirteen. "It didn't work," he says. The end of the film. Could the mystery have been false? Colin replies when this is suggested: "In that case the magic world I live in would suddenly grow dim!" No, the mystery is real, but we will never have enough information to solve it. The meetings of the characters were designed arbitrarily just to prevent any sense of order from creeping in. Balzac and Lewis Carroll will not mix. The film is a collection of tangents *à l'angle du hasard.* Intercut with the last set of scenes of *Out One* are some haunting shots of the Place d'Italie, empty save for a few automobiles. They punctuate the mystery: shots of people—characters with pasts and stories—have dissolved into empty, directionless streetscapes. The void, the nightmare of *Out One.*

This shorter version of the film, titled *Out One/Spectre** to indicate that it is but a ghost of its former self, was meant not as a summary of the original version (which was ironically subtitled "Noli Me Tangere"), but as a different film entirely. Nicole Lubtchansky edited the original film, but Rivette worked with Denise de Capabianca (who had edited his earlier films) for nearly a year to reshape the thirteen hours of the original into *Spectre,* with "its own rhythm and its own inner design." Juliet Berto calls the original "a clinical analysis of the sickness of the actor," and it is clear from reports that the major difference between the two versions lies in the amount of time and space devoted to the acting troupes. The earlier film had been roughly divided into eight episodes with the intention of selling it as a television serial, some less than an hour long, others almost two. In the original, for example, Colin doesn't receive his first message from the Thirteen until nearly

*The title *Out One,* by the way, has something to do with "out-takes." Rivette doesn't quite know what.

four hours have elapsed. (In *Spectre,* the message comes after twenty minutes.) Most of that time was taken up with a great deal more attention to the acting groups—to reportage, "both true and false." So the concept of rehearsals looms much larger in the original, while in *Spectre* we discover that that metaphor is being replaced by the much more intriguing dream of the House of Fiction—relatively empty here, but soon to be filled with the crotchety story of *Céline et Julie.*

There was also a subplot, very little of which remains, in which a boy wins the *tiercé* (a French lottery) and has the money stolen. It isn't clear how this was connected to the rest of *Out One.* The most striking omission in the shorter version is the death of Frédérique, but from Rivette's point of view the most significant difference is a matter not of plot but of rhythms.

> In the thirteen-hour version there were very long sequences of pure reportage about the two groups of actors, and also moments of "letting go," particularly where the camera was concerned: ten-minute takes of the actors left entirely to themselves and cracking up rather spectacularly. It became something of a psychodrama.[13]

We can see the relevance of Berto's description of the film as a "clinical analysis." One of the major impulses lay in Rivette's experience with the legendary nine-hour screening of the rough cut of Jean Rouch's *Petit à petit* (or *Jaguar,* as it was then called). The film was later cut to four hours, then to an hour and a half, which is the version now in release, but Rivette was extraordinarily impressed with that single screening of the "whole" film. ("Nine hours from end to end of Jean Rouch is just fabulous.") And he wanted to capture the same feeling of the truth of acted cinéma vérité that Rouch had caught. There is not very much of this quality remaining in *Spectre* which, in fact, is all too short a film even at four and a quarter hours for what it wants to do. *Spectre* is both less ethnological and less political than its parent film; it shifts attention back towards the questions of mystery and fiction and away from "the problem of actors and the problem of what to do after 1968 and how,"[14] which is the way Juliet Berto describes the theme of the original.*

> What we are left with is [as Rivette describes it] not a digest of the long version, but another film having its own logic: closer to a puzzle or a crossword game, playing less on affectivity and more on rhymes or oppositions, ruptures or connections, caesuras or censorships.[15]

*For an interesting account of the screening of the original *Out One* in September 1971 at Le Havre, see Martin Even's reportage in *Le Monde,* September 18, 1971.

Pauline/Emilie doubled and redoubled in the house of fiction.

The key to the puzzle lies in the subtitle, *Spectre,* a half-intelligible hint that the hypothesis of the film is the *location* of the story; that the location is "Paris and Its Double"; and that the time of the story, April and May 1970, is, concretely, its "meaning." Within the film itself, as it now stands, our attention is led inexorably, not to the solution of the plot of the Thirteen, but to the geographical location to which most of the aura of that conspiracy attaches—the House of Fiction, in which the novelist Sarah has difficulty writing, and in which the split character Pauline/Emilie will eventually find the empty room of mirrors which re-echoes her image to infinity. Finally we will be left in the empty Place d'Italie—where "nothing takes place but the place"—Paris and its Double. A wealth of evidence. And no solution. The mystery is still alive.

When an interviewer once confronted Rivette with the blunt, standard question: "Do you believe, as an artist, in messages?" he replied with good humor: "If you mean the messages that Jean-Pierre receives—Yes!" and laughed heartily.[16]

Céline et Julie vont en bateau is Rivette's most relaxed and assured film; as a result, it has the potential to be his most popular as well. It is a summary of some of the discoveries of the earlier films—especially *Out One;* but in its own quiet and humorous way it is also another step in the progression. The metaphor of the House of Fiction dominates now. Political plots and conspircies have been replaced by the primal experience of childhood fantasy. The empty house of mirrors at the end of *Out One* is now filled with fiction, and what was abstract in the earlier films—the elements of mystery, denouement (or *re*nouement), and the relationship between the observer and the event—has now been made concrete. Rivette explains the original motivation for the film:

> Simply the desire to make a film. To get out of the dumps that we all felt we were in, make a film for as little money as possible, and, we hoped, amuse people. Because the adventure of *Out* didn't turn out very well, from the point of view of public reception—there *was* no reception. It was almost impossible to show the film. Meanwhile, there had been another project [*Phénix,* based loosely on *Fantôme de l'Opéra*] which we couldn't do because it was too expensive, which Juliet Berto was also involved in. When we realized [in the spring of 1973] that we couldn't bring this project to fruition, I spoke to Juliet one evening and we decided to do something else. Something which would be on the contrary very cheap, as easy to make as possible, and fun to do. The first idea was to bring together Juliet and Dominique [Labourier], who were already friends. . . .[17]

After a couple of hours of conversation with the two actresses about the roles they wanted to play, the first concrete decision was the choice of their characters' names. Rivette put a calendar of saint's days in front of them; Berto chose "Céline," because she was surprised to discover it was a first name (as well as the name of the writer), and Labourier chose "Julie." It was only a year and a half later, after the film had opened, that an interviewer told Rivette that "Céline" and "Julie" were the names of Henry James's two favorite actresses when he was a young man.* (Two Henry James stories form the basis for the fiction within the House in the film.) Rivette took the information as delightful proof of the rightness of his theories regarding the mystery of fiction.

After the characters had been outlined, Eduardo de Gregorio joined the group to help develop a story line. Rivette knew from the beginning that he wanted a second story "both in opposition and relation to the first," but he also knew that it was time to leave the metaphor of theatre behind. Gregorio came up with the Henry James stories, "The Other House" and "A Romance of Certain Old Clothes," from which the group would draw the materials for the fiction within the House. Last

*Fred Barron identifies the actresses as Celine Celeste and Julia Bennet. They appeared together in *The Green Bushes,* by J. B. Buxton.

came the invention of a mechanism for relating the two parallel worlds of the film: the visits to the "haunted" House that the girls make and the candies they come away with which enable them to relive the experiences they have within the House, which they never remember without the help of the sweets. Rivette's first impulse was to make Céline and Julie film editors, but it was felt that this was too mechanical a solution.

The story of *Céline et Julie vont en bateau,** or "Phantom Ladies over Paris," as the subtitle has it, is deceptively simple. Sitting on a park bench on a summer's day, Julie, a librarian with an interest in the occult, watches as a strangely dressed young lady hurries by, tripping and stumbling and dropping her glasses in the process. Julie follows her and discovers that Céline is a magician who entertains in a small theater in Montmartre. The two meet and quickly discover an affinity between them that extends as far as ESP. They begin taking turns paying visits to a house at "7 bis rue du Nadir des Pommes," from which they emerge stunned and remembering nothing. The only evidence of the experience is a piece of candy which, when they eat it, later allows them to relive in starts and spurts pieces of the fiction within the House. That story, as it is revealed to them and to us shard by shard, with repetitions and revisions, is a Victorian melodrama about a little girl named Madlyn, her widowed father Olivier (played by Barbet Schroeder, the film's producer), and his relationships with two strange ladies named Camille (Bulle Ogier) and Sophie (Marie-France Pisier). "Miss Angèle Terre," Madlyn's nurse, is alternately played by Céline or Julie *(les deux Angèle-Terres?)*. Eventually it becomes clear that Camille is planning to murder Madlyn (in fact we see her smother the child).

Céline and Julie to the rescue! Protected by an occult potion they have concocted, for the first time they both enter the house at the same time, derail the cyclical fiction of the inhabitants (who, like Pirandello's characters in search of an author, are condemned to live in the eternal moment), and rescue little Madlyn. They swallow candies and wake up back in their room, but a piece of the fiction has "stuck" to them: Madlyn is with them now in reality. They take her for the boat ride of the title and pass another boat which carries the spectral, motionless characters they have left in the house. The last scene shows us Céline dozing on the park bench as Julie rushes by, dropping her book. The roles are reversed.

*The title is a pun: *monter en bateau quelqu'un* means to put someone on. Rivette also meant to allude to the titles of old cartoons, such as "Mickey and Minnie Go to the Circus."

Céline (Juliet Berto) and Julie (Dominique Labourier): their new friendship is sealed with a bandage.

Although Barbet Schroeder had been able to raise the money for the film only on the condition that it be less than two hours in length, Rivette was either unwilling or unable to control the duration of *Céline et Julie,* and the film wanders pleasantly through three hours and a quarter. Nevertheless, it is structurally different from the two previous films, which had depended absolutely on duration for their effect. Like *La Religieuse, Céline et Julie* is a highly "written" film, but much more cinematic and less theatrical and literary. On one level we see this in the nature of its allusions. From the very first title, *Céline et Julie* constantly refers us back to other films and works of literature: *Alice in Wonderland* (the first scene); the serials of Louis Feuillade (the subtitle, the repeated intertitle: "But, the next morning . . .," and a scene with the girls dressed in black tights); Frank Tashlin's *Artists and Models;* Cocteau; Pirandello; Henry James; Bioy Casarès (the structure is reminiscent of *El Perjurio de la nieve);* cartoons; Hitchcock; Mizoguchi . . . and many others. More important, perhaps, if not so obvious, is the fact that the film is strongly edited (by Nicole Lubtchansky again). Unlike *L'Amour fou* and *Out One,* whose narratives proceeded in straight lines—even if the lines were sometimes perpendicular to our expectations—*Céline et*

Julie is layered and helical; it therefore has greater resonance than its predecessors. The analogue here is commedia dell' arte rather than cinéma vérité. In *Spectre* Rivette had used some black and white still photos that were originally planned to serve under the credits of the episodes of *Out One* as punctuation marks. Accompanied by a loud buzz on the soundtrack, they came along every once in a while to remind us of our separation from the film and to echo scenes which had already taken place or foreshadow those that were to come. It was a useful device and a crude attempt at the layering of cinematic reality which forms one of the motifs of *Céline et Julie*. The House of Fiction at 7 bis rue du Nadir des Pommes is a kind of magic box very much like the time machine of Resnais's *Je T'aime, je t'aime* which allows Rivette to reveal to us the secrets of time that appear to filmmakers on the editing table. As we go back repeatedly to the same scene viewed from different angles, the compressed reality we get is in direct opposition to the elongated exaggerations of the previous films.

So *Céline et Julie vont en bateau* is a pleasant, colorful fable; children would like it—and it is also an experiment in montage à la Resnais and Hitchcock. But the simple story also works as an isolated code in which the signifiers are susceptible to a number of interpretations. We see this film from Julie's point of view. Her life is rooted in reality; she has a past and she works in a library where her job of course is to catalogue, organize—control—fiction. Into this situation comes Céline, tripping like the White Rabbit to upset the balance of fiction and nonfiction. She is the fantastic doppelganger of the realistic Julie. Her first job is to draw Julie out of the ordered world of the library; her second to cut her off from her past, which she does by masquerading as Julie in a meeting with an old boyfriend, teasing him until he calls her "an unspeakable monster of vulgarity" and swears he's going to become a monk. Now that Julie is cut off temporally and spatially, she is ready for her adventures in the House of Fiction, which accrete slowly, like found bits and pieces of an old movie, in which she literally plays nurse to the child of the House. When the girls rescue the aptly named Madlyn, they are also saving the fictionally magic biscuit that allows us to transmute our experience into art. While the scenes in the House look real enough throughout most of the film, in the final sequence when the girls move in to rescue the little girl, the daylight has disappeared, the actors of the House are made up in lugubrious white and gray tones, and everything is shot from strange angles. The fictional control of the author of the House is breaking down. When the child leaves, so do the adults. Fiction has been liberated into life. A perfectly Rivetting adventure, and a summary of what he has been trying to do, in various ways, throughout his career: rescue the madeleine from the prison of fiction and transmute it into an ethical and moral tool.

No more detailed explication of narration, invention, and the fictive experience here—only a charmed fable. We have moved from one kind of plot, through another; from *complot* and *trame,* through *l'intrigue*—and out again into the sunshine. Céline and Julie fall into fiction and then out of it and liberate us, in the process, from the plottings of tyrannical authors.

NOTES

1. INTRODUCTION: The Camera Writes

1. James Monaco. Interview, October 1974.
2. "The Birth of a New Avant-Garde: La Caméra-Stylo," in *The New Wave,* ed. Peter Graham. Trans. from *Ecran Français* 144, 30 March 1948.
3. See Penelope Gilliatt. "The Decoy Fanatic," *New Yorker,* 24 March 1975.
4. Quoted in C. G. Crisp. *François Truffaut,* p. 57.
5. "The Birth of a New Avant-Garde: La Caméra-Stylo."
6. "The Evolution of the Language of Cinema," in *What Is Cinema?* vol. 1. Trans. and ed. Hugh Gray, p. 35.
7. "La Politique des auteurs," in *The New Wave,* ed. Peter Graham. Trans. from *Cahiers du Cinéma* 70, 1957.
8. *Writing Degree Zero,* trans. Annette Lavers, Colin Smith, p. 14.

2. TRUFFAUT: The Antoine Doinel Cycle

1. Michèle Manceaux. Interview, *L'Express,* 23 April 1959.
2. Manceaux.
3. Manceaux.
4. Manceaux.
5. Manceaux.
6. *New Yorker,* 20 February 1960.
7. *Arts,* 26 September 1956.
8. *New Yorker.*

9. Truffaut. "Introduction: Who Is Antoine Doinel?" *The Adventures of Antoine Doinel,* trans. Helen G. Scott.
10. Truffaut.
11. Quoted in André Parinaud. Interview. *Arts,* 29 April-5 May 1959.
12. *New Yorker,* 8 March 1969.
13. Truffaut.
14. Truffaut.
15. Truffaut.
16. *Stolen Kisses, The Adventures of Antoine Doinel,* p. 177.
17. *Stolen Kisses,* p. 198.
18. *Bed and Board, The Adventures of Antoine Doinel,* p. 308.
19. *Bed and Board,* p. 311.
20. *Bed and Board,* p. 312.
21. Truffaut.
22. *Bed and Board,* p. 309.
23. *Cahiers du Cinéma,* May 1959.

3. TRUFFAUT: The Statement of Genres

1. "Questions à l'auteur," *Cinema 61,* January 1961.
2. "Questions à l'auteur."
3. "Questions à l'auteur."
4. *New York Times,* 24 July 1962.
5. Quoted in Sanche de Gramont. "Life Style of Homo Cinematicus—François Truffaut," *New York Times Magazine,* 15 June 1969.
6. "Aznavour donne le 'la'," *Cinémonde,* 5 May 1960.
7. Karel Reisz, Gavin Millar. *The Technique of Film Editing,* 2nd rev. ed., p. 333.
8. Dan A. Cukier, Jo Gryn. "Entretien avec François Truffaut," *Script 5,* April 1962.
9. Introduction to Henri-Pierre Roché. *Jules and Jim.*
10. Marshall Lewis, R. M. Franchi. "Conversations with François Truffaut," *N.Y. Film Bulletin,* 1962.
11. *Cahiers du Cinéma,* March 1962.
12. *Sight and Sound,* Spring 1963.
13. *Jules and Jim,* trans. Nicholas Fry, p. 11.
14. *Jules and Jim,* p. 92.
15. *Jules and Jim,* p. 74.

4. TRUFFAUT: The Explosion of Genres

1. *New Yorker,* 31 October 1964.
2. Louis Marcorelles. "Interview with Truffaut," *Sight and Sound,* Winter 1962.
3. *New Yorker.*
4. Review, *Sight and Sound,* Autumn 1964.
5. Quoted in C. G. Crisp. *François Truffaut,* p. 46.
6. Quoted in Sanche de Gramont. "Life Style of Homo Cinematicus—François Truffaut," *New York Times Magazine,* 15 June 1969.
7. *Journal of Fahrenheit 451.*
8. *Journal of Fahrenheit 451.*
9. Quoted in Crisp, p. 98.
10. *New York Times,* 11 April 1970.
11. Quoted in Crisp, p. 120.
12. Quoted in Crisp, p. 120.

13. Quoted in Gramont.
14. Quoted in Crisp, p. 118.
15. Quoted in Gramont.
16. Quoted in Gramont.

5. TRUFFAUT: Intimate Politics

1. Victor Bockris, Andrew Wylie. "Conversation with François Truffaut," *Oui*, September 1974.
2. *New Yorker*, 31 October 1964.
3. *New Yorker*.
4. Quoted in United Artists press release.
5. Guy Flatley. "So Truffaut Decided To Work His Own Miracle," *New York Times*, Section 2, 27 September 1970.
6. "How I Made *The Wild Child*," Introduction to *The Wild Child*, trans. Linda Lewis, Christine Lémery.
7. *The Wild Child*, p. 131.
8. *The Wild Child*, p. 154.
9. *The Wild Child*, p. 170.
10. *The Wild Child*, p. 15.
11. *The Wild Child*, p. 17.
12. *New Yorker*, 17 October 1970.
13. Quoted in Yvonne Baby. "A Physical Film About Love," *Atlas*, February 1971. Reprinted from *Le Monde*.
14. Baby.
15. "Why *Les Deux Anglaises?*" Janus Film press release. Trans. Danielle Gardner.
16. "Truffaut: Tale of Two Brontes?" *Village Voice*, 14 December 1972.
17. Quoted in Warner Bros. press release. "Day For Night," 15 August 1973.

6. GODARD: Women and the Outsider

1. "Godard," *Styles of Radical Will*.
2. *Godard on Godard*, ed. Jean Narboni, Tom Milne. Trans. Tom Milne. p. 171. (Hereafter referred to as "Milne.")
3. *Jean-Luc Godard*, p. 7.
4. *Private Screenings*, p. 307.
5. *Cahiers du Cinéma*, December 1962; in Milne, p. 192.
6. *Cahiers du Cinéma*, March 1952; in Milne.
7. *Cahiers du Cinéma*, June 1957; in Milne.
8. Quoted in *Le Petit Soldat*, ed. and trans. Nicholas Garnham, p. 9.
9. Quoted in Richard Roud. *Jean-Luc Godard*, p. 39.
10. *Cahiers du Cinéma*, December 1962; in Milne, p. 178.
11. *Cahiers du Cinéma*, July 1960; in Milne, p. 164.
12. *Cahiers du Cinéma*, December 1962; in Milne, p. 177.
13. *Le Petit Soldat*, pp. 38–39.
14. *Le Petit Soldat*, p. 46.
15. *Cahiers du Cinéma*, December 1962; in Milne, p. 179.
16. *Cahiers du Cinéma*, December 1962; in Milne, p. 185.
17. *Cahiers du Cinéma*, December 1962; in Milne, p. 182.
18. Milne, pp. 166–67.
19. *Cahiers du Cinéma*, December 1962; in Milne, p. 182.
20. Milne, p. 166.

21. *Cahiers du Cinéma,* December 1962; in Milne, p. 186.
22. *Cahiers du Cinéma,* December 1962; in Milne, p. 187.
23. Quoted in Jean Collet. *Jean-Luc Godard: An Investigation into His Films and Philosophy,* p. 175.

7. GODARD: Modes of Discourse

1. "On the Impression of Reality in the Cinema," *Film Language: A Semiotics of the Cinema,* p. 13.
2. "The Cinema: Language or Language System?" *Film Language,* p. 31.
3. "The Cinema: Language or Language System?" p. 69.
4. *What Is Cinema?* p. 26.
5. *Brecht on Theatre,* ed. John Willett, p. 125.
6. "Notes Toward a Phenomenology of the Narrative," *Film Language,* p. 20.
7. *Cahiers du Cinéma,* August 1963; in Milne, p. 198.
8. Milne, p. 197.
9. *Cahiers du Cinéma,* December 1962; in Milne, p. 190.
10. Quoted in Herbert Lottman. "Cinéma Vérité: Jean-Luc Godard," *Columbia University Forum,* Spring 1968.
11. *Cahiers du Cinéma,* August 1963; in Milne, p. 200.
12. Milne, p. 201.
13. Milne, p. 201.
14. Milne, p. 201.
15. *Cahiers du Cinéma,* October 1965; in Milne, p. 211.
16. Milne, p. 211.
17. Milne, p. 212.
18. *Cahiers du Cinéma,* December 1962; in Milne, p. 188.
19. *The Films of Jean-Luc Godard,* ed. Ian Cameron, p. 62.
20. *Une Femme mariée, L'Avant-Scène du Cinéma,* March 1965, p. 15.
21. *Cahiers du Cinéma,* October 1964; in Milne, p. 208.
22. *Sight and Sound,* Summer 1965.
23. *Une Femme mariée,* p. 17.
24. *Une Femme mariée,* p. 17.
25. *Une Femme mariée,* p. 18.
26. *Une Femme mariée,* p. 22.
27. *Une Femme mariée,* p. 27.
28. *Une Femme mariée,* p. 27.
29. *Sight and Sound,* Summer 1965.
30. *Une Femme mariée,* p. 20.

8. GODARD: A Season in Hell: Icy Poetry

1. *Mid-Century French Poets,* ed. and trans. Wallace Fowlie, p. 121.
2. *Mid-Century French Poets,* p. 121.
3. *Mid-Century French Poets,* p. 123.
4. *Alphaville,* ed. and trans. Peter Whitehead, p. 39.
5. *Alphaville,* p. 70.
6. *Alphaville,* p. 74.
7. *Alphaville,* p. 66.
8. *Cahiers du Cinéma,* October 1965; in Milne, p. 218.
9. Milne, p. 214.
10. Milne, p. 215.

11. *Alphaville,* p. 59.
12. *Alphaville,* p. 63.
13. Milne, p. 221.
14. *Pierrot Le Fou,* ed. and trans. Peter Whitehead, p. 82.
15. *Pierrot Le Fou,* p. 83.
16. *Pierrot Le Fou,* p. 90.
17. *Pierrot Le Fou,* p. 23.
18. Milne, p. 234.
19. *Masculine Feminine,* ed. Robert Hughes, Pierre Billard, p. 44.
20. Milne, p. 225.
21. *Masculine Feminine,* p. 30.
22. *Masculine Feminine,* pp. 90–91.
23. *Masculine Feminine,* pp. 174–77.
24. *Masculine Feminine,* pp. 138–43.
25. "Modern Life," *Take One,* February 1967. (From *Le Nouvel Observateur.*)
26. *Mythologies,* p. 56.
27. "Modern Life."
28. "Modern Life."
29. *Made in U.S.A.,* ed. and trans. Lorrimer Publishing, Ltd., p. 36.
30. *Made in U.S.A.,* p. 37.
31. *Made in U.S.A.,* p. 38.
32. *Made in U.S.A.,* p. 26.
33. *Made in U.S.A.,* p. 33.
34. *Mythologies,* p. 9.
35. *Made in U.S.A.,* pp. 39–40.
36. *Made in U.S.A.,* p. 75.
37. *Made in U.S.A.,* p. 76.
38. "Délires II: Alchimie du verbe," *Une Saison en enfer.* English translation: Louise Varèse, *A Season in Hell.*
39. Quoted in Richard Roud. *Jean-Luc Godard,* p. 118.
40. *L'Avant-Scène du Cinéma,* May 1967; in Milne, p. 239.
41. Milne, p. 242.
42. *2 ou 3 Choses que je sais d'elle,* Editions du Seuil, pp. 49–51.
43. *2 ou 3 Choses que je sais d'elle,* p. 69.
44. *2 ou 3 Choses que je sais d'elle,* p. 86.
45. *2 ou 3 Choses que je sais d'elle,* pp. 110–11.
46. *Le parti pris des choses,* p. 37.
47. Quoted in Herbert R. Lottman. "Cinéma Vérité: Jean-Luc Godard," *Columbia University Forum,* Spring 1968.

9. GODARD: Returning to Zero (Picture and Act)

1. *La Chinoise, l'Avant-Scène du Cinéma,* May 1971, p. 14.
2. *Quotations from Chairman Mao Tse-Tung,* p. 89.
3. Jacques Bontemps et al. "Lutter sur deux fronts," *Cahiers du Cinéma,* October 1967. Trans. *Film Quarterly,* Winter 1968–69.
4. *La Chinoise,* p. 24.
5. Bontemps et al.
6. *La Chinoise,* p. 19.
7. Bontemps et al.
8. *La Chinoise,* p. 38.
9. *Weekend/Wind from the East,* ed. and trans. Lorrimer Publishing, Ltd., pp. 104–5.
10. *Weekend/Wind from the East,* p. 61.

11. *Weekend/Wind from the East,* p. 17.
12. *Weekend/Wind from the East,* p. 66.
13. *Weekend/Wind from the East,* p. 63.
14. "Godard and Weekend," *Movie,* Winter 1968–69.
15. *Weekend/Wind from the East,* p. 103.
16. Richard Roud. *Jean-Luc Godard,* p. 143.
17. Roud, p. 146.
18. *Reading Capital,* pp. 317–18.
19. *Marxism and Form,* p. xiii.
20. Quoted in Roud, p. 146.

10. GODARD: Theory and Practice: The Dziga-Vertov Period

1. Christian Braad Thomsen. "Filmmaking and History: Jean-Pierre Gorin Interview," *Jump Cut,* September-October 1974.
2. "Jean-Luc Godard," *International Film Guide 1974.*
3. Michael Goodwin, Tom Luddy, Naomi Wise. "The Dziga Vertov Film Group in America—An Interview with Jean-Luc Godard and Jean-Pierre Gorin," *Take One,* March 1971.
4. Thomsen.
5. *Quotations from Chairman Mao Tse-Tung,* p. 385.
6. Goodwin et al.
7. *Cinéthique,* September-October 1969.
8. *Cinéthique.*
9. Kent Carroll. "Film and Revolution: Interview with the Dziga-Vertov Group," *Evergreen Review,* October 1970.
10. See his comments in Goodwin et al.
11. Review. *Take One,* June 1971.
12. Carroll.
13. *Weekend/Wind from the East,* ed. and trans. Lorrimer Publishing, Ltd., p. 121.
14. *Weekend/Wind from the East,* p. 124.
15. *Weekend/Wind from the East,* p. 159.
16. *Weekend/Wind from the East,* p. 186.
17. Goodwin et al.
18. *Weekend/Wind from the East,* p. 160.
19. Goodwin et al.
20. Thomsen.
21. Press release for *Tout va bien,* trans. in *Cinema Rising,* May 1972.
22. Quoted in Michael Goodwin, Naomi Wise. "Raymond Chandler, Mao Tse-Tung and Tout va bien," *Take One,* October 1972.
23. Robert Philip Kolker. "Angle and Reality: Godard and Gorin in America," *Sight and Sound,* Summer 1973.
24. Kolker.
25. Trans. Tony Rayns. *Cinema Rising,* May 1972.
26. Press conference, New York Film Festival, October 1972.
27. Victor Bockris, Andrew Wylie. "Conversation with François Truffaut," *Oui,* September 1974.

11. CHABROL: Films Noirs in Color

1. Rui Nogueira, Nicoletta Zalaffi. "Conversations with Chabrol," *Sight and Sound,* Winter 1970–71.

2. *Cahiers du Cinéma,* October 1959.
3. *Cahiers du Cinéma,* December 1955.
4. Nogueira, Zalaffi.
5. *Village Voice,* 12 November 1970.
6. Nogueira, Zalaffi.
7. Quoted in Unifrance Film press release, May 1973.
8. Michel Ciment, Gérard Legrand, Jean-Paul Török. "Claude Chabrol Interviewed," *Movie,* Winter 1970–71. (From *Positif* 115.)
9. Quoted in Robin Wood, Michael Walker. *Claude Chabrol,* p. 64.
10. Ciment et al.
11. Ciment et al.
12. *La Femme infidèle, L'Avant-Scène du Cinéma,* May 1969, p. 27.
13. Nogueira, Zalaffi.
14. *Le Monde,* 1 October 1972.
15. *Village Voice,* 14 November 1974.
16. "Nada," *Sight and Sound,* Spring 1974.

12. ROHMER: Moral Tales: The Art of Courtly Love

1. Rui Nogueira. "Eric Rohmer: Choice and Chance," *Sight and Sound,* Summer 1971.
2. Nogueira.
3. Graham Petrie. "Eric Rohmer: An Interview," *Film Quarterly,* Summer 1971.
4. Petrie.
5. *The Art of Courtly Love,* trans. John J. Parry, ed. Frederick W. Locke, p. 2.
6. Petrie.
7. Fred Barron. "Eric Rohmer: An Interview," *Take One,* January 1974.
8. *Six Contes Moraux,* p. 12.
9. Barron.
10. Nogueira.
11. Petrie.
12. Nogueira.
13. Nogueira.

13. RIVETTE: The Process of Narrative

1. Unifrance Film press release, June 1970.
2. James Monaco. Interview, October 1974. All other quotations of Rivette, unless otherwise attributed, are from this interview.
3. *Naked Masks,* trans. Eric Bentley, p. 231.
4. Unifrance Film press release.
5. "L'Amour fou," *Sight and Sound,* Spring 1969.
6. 16 December 1961.
7. 16 December 1961.
8. Louis Marcorelles. "Interview with Jacques Rivette/Roger Leenhardt," *Sight and Sound,* Autumn 1963.
9. *L'Avant-Scène du Cinéma,* 15 September 1961.
10. *Village Voice,* 22 July 1971.
11. Carlos Clarens, Edgardo Cozarinsky. "Jacques Rivette" (interview), *Sight and Sound,* Autumn 1974.
12. "L'Amour fou," *Sight and Sound.*
13. Clarens, Cozarinsky.

14. James Monaco. Interview, October 1974.
15. Quoted in Yvonne Baby. "Entretien avec Jacques Rivette," *Le Monde,* 18 September 1971.
16. Fred Barron. Interview, October 1974.
17. Jonathan Rosenbaum, Lauren Sedofsky, Gilbert Adair. "Phantom Interviewers over Rivette," *Film Comment,* September–October 1974.

REFERENCES

While the number of full-length studies of New Wave directors is limited, the amount of material (interviews, criticism, history) which has appeared in magazines and journals is now substantial. This reference guide attempts to be comprehensive so far as scripts and book-length studies are concerned, but it is highly selective with regard to magazine articles. Readers are referred to the more extensive bibliographies in the Cinema One Series (Roud, Allen, Ward) and in Collet, Wood and Walker, Braucourt, Crisp, Brown, and Braudy. Various issues of *l'Avant-Scène du Cinéma* include useful bibliographies.

TRUFFAUT

Scripts

"Les Mistons":
L'Avant-Scène du Cinéma 4 (May 1961).

"Histoire d'Eau":
L'Avant-Scène du Cinéma 7 (September 1961).

Les Quatre Cents Coups:
The 400 Blows: A Film by François Truffaut. Ed. and trans. David Denby. New York: Grove Press. 1969. Includes other material.

Les Quatre Cents Coups. François Truffaut and Marcel Moussy. Paris: Gallimard. 1959. Novelization.

In *Les Aventures d'Antoine Doinel.* Paris: Mercure de France. 1970. First treatment and notes only.

In *The Adventures of Antoine Doinel: 4 Autobiographical Screenplays.* Trans. Helen G. Scott. New York: Simon & Schuster. 1971.

Tirez sur le pianiste:

Goodis, David. *Down There.* New York: Fawcett. 1956. Reprinted as *Shoot the Piano Player.* New York: Grove Press. 1963. Novel, not script.

Jules et Jim:

Jules et Jim. Paris: Editions du Seuil. Points/Films. 1971. From *L'Avant-Scène du Cinéma* 16 (June 1962). Includes other material.

Jules and Jim. Trans. Nicholas Fry. London: Lorrimer; New York: Simon Schuster. 1968.

Roché, Henri-Pierre. *Jules et Jim.* Paris: Gallimard. 1953. Novel.

Jules and Jim. Trans. Patrick Evans. New York: Avon; London: Calder and Boyars. 1963. Preface by Truffaut.

"Antoine et Colette" *(L'Amour à vingt ans):*

In *The Adventures of Antoine Doinel* (see above).

La Peau Douce:

L'Avant-Scène du Cinéma 48 (May 1965).

Fahrenheit 451:

L'Avant-Scène du Cinéma 64 (October 1966). Synopsis only.

Baisers volés:

In *The Adventures of Antoine Doinel* (see above).

La Sirène du Mississippi:

Extracts on disc version.

L'Enfant sauvage:

L'Avant-Scène du Cinéma 107 (October 1970).

The Wild Child. Trans. Linda Lewin and Christine Lémery. New York: Washington Square Press. 1973.

Domicile conjugal:

In *The Adventures of Antoine Doinel* (see above).

Les Deux Anglaises et le Continent:

L'Avant-Scène du Cinéma 121 (January 1972).

La Nuit américaine:

Day For Night. Trans. Sam Flores. New York: Grove Press. 1975.

La Nuit américaine et le Journal de Fahrenheit 451. Paris: Seghers. 1974.

Books by Truffaut

Le Cinéma selon Hitchcock. Paris: Robert Laffont. 1966.

Hitchcock. Trans. Helen G. Scott. London: Secker and Warburg; New York: Simon & Schuster. 1967.

Les Films de ma vie. Paris: Flammarion. 1975. Collection of criticism.

La Nuit américaine et le Journal de Fahrenheit 451. Paris: Seghers. 1974.

(Ed.) *Jean Renoir*, by André Bazin. Paris: Editions Champ Libre. 1971.

———. Trans W. W. Halsey II and William H. Simon. New York: Simon & Schuster. 1973. London: W. H. Allen. 1974.

(Ed.) *Le Cinéma de la cruauté*, by André Bazin. Paris: Flammarion. 1975.

(Ed.) *Le Cinéma de l'occupation et de la résistance*, by André Bazin. Paris: Editions 10–18. 1975. With a long introduction by Truffaut.

Books About Truffaut

Allen, Don. *Truffaut*. New York: Viking Press; London: Secker and Warburg. Cinema One 24. 1974.

Braudy, Leo, ed. *Focus on "Shoot the Piano Player."* Englewood Cliffs, N.J.: Prentice-Hall. 1972. London: Prentice-Hall. 1973.

Crisp, C. G. *François Truffaut*. Ed. Ian Cameron. New York: Praeger; London: November Books. 1972.

Fanne, Dominique. *L'Univers de François Truffaut*. Paris: Editions du Cerf. 1972.

Petrie, Graham. *The Cinema of François Truffaut*. New York: A. S. Barnes; London: A Zwemmer. International Film Guide series. 1970.

Major Interviews and Profiles

Anon. "On Film" (interview). *The New Yorker* 36:1 (20 February 1960).

———. "Truffaut." *The New Yorker* 40:37 (31 October 1964).

———. Interview. *The New Yorker*. 46:35 (17 October 1970).

Baby, Yvonne. "A Physical Film About Love: *The Two English Women*" (interview). *Atlas*, February 1971. Reprinted from *Le Monde*.

Bockris, Victor, and Andrew Wylie. "Conversation with François Truffaut." *Oui* 3:9 (September 1974).

Collet, Jean; Michel Delahaye, Jean-André Fièschi, André S. Labarthe, and Bertrand Tavernier. "Entretien avec François Truffaut." *Cahiers du Cinéma* 138 (December 1962). Condensed and trans. in *Film Quarterly* 17:1 (Fall 1963).

Comolli, Jean-Louis, and Jean Narboni. "Entretien avec François Truffaut." *Cahiers du Cinéma* 190 (May 1967).

Cukier, Dan A., and Jo Gryn. "Entretien avec François Truffaut." *Script* 5 (April 1962). Trans. in Braudy.

Dudinsky, Donna. "I Wish . . . François Truffaut" (interview). Trans. Peter Lebensold. *Take One* 4:2 (March 1974).

Flatley, Guy. "So Truffaut Decided To Work His Own Miracle." *New York Times,* Section 2, 27 September 1970.

Gow, Gordon. "Intensification" (interview), *Films and Filming* 18:10, July 1972.

De Gramont, Sanche. "Life Style of Homo Cinematicus—François Truffaut." *New York Times Magazine,* 15 June 1969.

Haskell, Molly. "A Declaration of Love: Truffaut's 'Mermaid.'" *Village Voice,* 16 April 1970.

Jacob, Gilles. "The 400 Blows of François Truffaut." *Sight and Sound* 37:4 (Autumn 1968).

Labro, Philippe. Entretien. *Lui* 9 (September 1964).

Lewis, Marshall, and R. M. Franchi. "Conversations with François Truffaut." *N.Y. Film Bulletin* III:3: 44 (1962). Reprinted in *Interviews with Film Directors,* ed. Andrew Sarris. Indianapolis: Bobbs-Merrill. 1967. London: Secker and Warburg. 1972.

Manceaux, Michèle. Interview. *L'Express,* 23 April 1959. Tr. in *The 400 Blows.*

Marcorelles, Louis. "Interview With Truffaut." *Sight and Sound* 31:1 (Winter 1962). Reprinted from *France Observateur.*

Monaco, James. "Coming of Age: Interview with Jean-Pierre Léaud." *Take One* 5:1 (January 1976).

Parinaud, André. "The Young Cinema Doesn't Exist" (interview). *Arts,* 29 April-5 May 1959. Trans. in *The 400 Blows: A Film by François Truffaut.*

Rayns, Tony. "Interview: François Truffaut." *Cinema Rising* 2 (May 1972).

Samuels, Charles. "Talking with Truffaut," *American Scholar* 40:3 (Summer 1971). Reprinted in *Encountering Directors.* New York: Putnam. 1972.

Truffaut, François. "Journal of *Fahrenheit 451.*" *Cahiers du Cinema in English* 5, 6, 7 (November, December 1966, January 1967). Reprinted from *Cahiers du Cinéma* 175–80 (February–July 1966).

———. "La résistible ascension de Pierre Barbin" (on l'affaire Langlois). *Combat* 7338 (16 February 1968).

———. "Toujours la Cinémathèque." *Combat* 7362 (15 March 1968).

———. "Mein metier." *Filmkritik* 10:4 (April 1966).

———. "Baisers volés" (interview). *Cahiers du Cinéma* 200-201 (April-May 1968).

———. "Is Truffaut the Happiest Man on Earth? Yes." *Esquire* 74:2 (August 1970).

Selected Critical Articles

Armes, Roy. "François Truffaut." In *French Cinema since 1946.* Vol. 2. London: A. Zwemmer; New York: A. S. Barnes. 1970.

Von Bagh, Peter. *"The Bride Wore Black"* (review). *Movie* 16 (Winter 1968–69).

Bluestone, George. "The Fire and the Future." *Film Quarterly* 20:4 (Summer 1967). On *Fahrenheit 451.*

Bordwell, David. "François Truffaut: A Man Can Serve Two Masters." *Film Comment* 7:1 (Spring 1971).

Braudy, Leo. "Hitchcock, Truffaut, and the Irresponsible Audience." *Film Quarterly* 21:4 (Summer 1968).

Canby, Vincent. Review of *Mississippi Mermaid. New York Times,* 11 April 1970.

Crowther, Bosley. Review of *Shoot the Piano Player. New York Times,* 24 July 1962. Reprinted in Braudy.

Dawson, Jan. "Truffaut's Starry Night." *Sight and Sound* 43:1 (Winter 1973–74).

Delahaye, Michel. "Les tourbillons élémentaire" (on *Jules et Jim*). *Cahiers du Cinéma* 129 (March 1962).

Gerlach, John. "Truffaut and Itard: *The Wild Child.*" *Film Heritage* 7:3 (Spring 1972).

Greenspun, Roger. "Elective Affinities: Aspects of *Jules et Jim.*" *Sight and Sound* 32:2 (Spring 1963).

———. "Through the Looking Glass." *Moviegoer* 1 (Winter 1964).

Hess, John. "La Politique des Auteurs" (2 parts). *Jump Cut* 1, 2 (May–June, July–August 1974).

Houston, Penelope. "Uncommitted Artist?" *Sight and Sound* 30:2 (Spring 1961). Reprinted in Braudy.

Jacob, Gilles. *"La Peau Douce"* (review). *Sight and Sound 33:4 (Autumn 1964).*

Jebb, Julian. "Truffaut: The Educated Heart." *Sight and Sound* 41:3 (Summer 1972).

Kael, Pauline. Review of *Stolen Kisses. New Yorker,* 8 March 1969. Reprinted in *I Lost It at the Movies.* Boston: Little Brown. 1965. London: Jonathan Cape. 1966.

Kestner, Joseph. "Truffaut: Tale of Two Brontes?" *The Village Voice,* 14 December 1972. On *Les Deux Anglaises.*

Millar, Gavin. "Hitchcock vs. Truffaut." *Sight and Sound* 38:2 (Spring 1969).

Monaco, James. "Truffaut" (pamph.). Program notes from New School Film Series. New York: New York Zoetrope. 1974.

Oudart, Jean-Pierre, and Serge Daney. *"L'Enfant Sauvage." Cahiers du Cinéma* 222 (July 1970).

Reisz, Karel, and Gavin Millar. "The Technique of *Shoot the Piano Player.*" In *The Technique of Film Editing.* 2d ed. London: Focal Press; New York: Hastings House. 1968. Reprinted in Braudy.

Rhode, Eric. "*Les Quatre Cents Coups*" (review). *Sight and Sound* 29:2 (Spring 1960).

Rivette, Jacques. "Du côté de chez Antoine." *Cahiers du Cinéma* 95 (May 1959).

Shatnoff, Judith. "François Truffaut—The Anarchist Imagination." *Film Quarterly* 16:3 (Spring 1963). Reprinted in Braudy.

Taylor, John Russell. "François Truffaut," in *Cinema Eye, Cinema Ear.* London: Methuen; New York: Hill and Wang. 1964.

Török, Jean-Paul. "Le Point sensible." *Positif* 38 (March 1961).

Truffaut, François. "James Dean." *Arts* 26 (September 1956).

———. "Aznavour donne le 'la.'" *Cinémonde* 1343 (5 May 1960). Reprinted in Braudy.

———. "Questions à l'auteur." *Cinéma 61* 52 (January 1961). Reprinted and trans. in Braudy.

———. "How I Made *The Wild Child.*" Introduction to the English version of the script. New York: Washington Square Press. 1973.

———. "Introduction," *The Adventures of Antoine Doinel.* Trans. Helen G. Scott. New York: Simon & Schuster. 1971.

———. "Why Les Deux Anglaises?" Janus Films press release. Trans. Danielle Gardner.

Wood, Robin. "Chabrol and Truffaut." *Movie* 17 (Winter 1969–70).

GODARD

Scripts

"Charlotte et son Jules":
L'Avant-Scène du Cinéma 5 (June 1961).

"Histoire d'Eau"
L'Avant-Scène du Cinéma 7 (September 1961).

A bout de souffle:
L'Avant-Scène du Cinéma 79 (March 1968). Complete script.
C. Francolin. *A bout de Souffle.* Paris: Seghers. 1960. Novelization.
François Truffaut. Scenario for *A bout de souffle. L'Avant-Scène du Cinéma* 79 (March 1968).
A bout de souffle. Paris: Balland. 1974. Complete text, numerous stills.

Le Petit Soldat:
Cahiers du Cinéma 119, 120 (May, June 1961).
Le Petit Soldat. Trans. Nicholas Garnham. London: Lorrimer; New York: Simon & Schuster. 1967.
Claude Saint Benoit. *Le Petit Soldat.* Paris: Julliard. Novelization.

Une Femme est une femme:

A Woman Is a Woman. Trans. Jan Dawson. In *Godard: Three Films.* London: Lorrimer; New York: Harper and Row. 1975.

Scenario and extracts from disc version in *Godard on Godard* (see below). The ten-inch disc version was never released.

Cahiers du Cinéma in English 12 (December 1967). Scenario.

Cahiers du Cinéma 98 (August 1959). Scenario.

Vivre sa vie:

L'Avant-Scène du Cinéma 19 (October 1962).

Film Culture 26 (Fall 1962). Scenario.

Vivre Sa Vie: Die Geschichte der Nana S. Drehbuch. Cinemathek 9. Hamburg: Marion von Schröder. 1964.

Les Carabiniers:

Cinemathek. Hamburg: Marion von Schröder.

Extracts (in Italian) in *Filmcritica* 150 (October 1964).

L'Avant-Scène du Cinéma 46 (March 1965). Synopsis and photos.

"Le Grand Escroc":

L'Avant-Scène du Cinéma 46 (March 1965).

Le Mépris:

Filmcritica 139–40 (November–December 1963).

Extract in Collet (see below).

Bande à part:

Film (West Germany) 2:2 (February 1965).

Extract in *Filmcritica* 150 (October 1964).

La Femme mariée:

A Married Woman. Trans. Susan Bennett. In *Godard: Three Films.* London: Lorrimer; New York: Harper and Row. 1975.

L'Avant-Scène du Cinéma 46 (March 1965).

The Married Woman. English version based on subtitles by Ursule Molinaro. New York: Berkley Medallion. 1965.

See *Journal d'Une Femme mariée* below.

Eine verheiratete Frau. Cinemathek 15. Hamburg: Marion von Schröder. 1966.

Alphaville:

Eng. trans. Peter Whitehead. London: Lorrimer; New York: Simon & Schuster. 1966.

"Agente Lemmy Caution: Missione Alphaville" in *Filmcritica* 159–60 (August–September 1965.)

Pierrot le fou:

Trans. Peter Whitehead. London: Lorrimer; New York: Simon & Schuster. 1969.

Extracts in *Image et Son* 211 (December 1967).

Masculin-féminin:

Masculine Feminine. Ed. Pierre Billard and Robert Hughes. New York: Grove Press. 1969. Includes supplementary material.

Made in U.S.A.:
English version. Introduction by Michael Kustow. London: Lorrimer. 1967. Includes supplementary material.
Extract in *Image et Son* 211 (December 1967).

2 ou 3 choses que je sais d'elle:
2 or 3 Things I Know About Her. Trans. Marianne Alexander. In *Godard: Three Films.* London: Lorrimer; New York: Harper and Row. 1975.
Paris: Editions du Seuil. Points/Films. 1971. From *L'Avant-Scène du Cinéma* 70 (May 1967). Includes supplementary material.
Scenario and notes in Cardinal (see below).

La Chinoise:
L'Avant-Scène du Cinéma 114 (May 1971).
Filmcritica 182 (October 1967).
Extract in Collet (see below).

"Caméra-oeil" *(Loin du Vietnam):*
Peace News, January 5, 1968.

Le Gai Savoir:
Extracts in *Cahiers du Cinéma* 200–201 (April–May 1968).
Soundtrack transcript. Paris: Union des Ecrivains (no. 2). 1969.

Weekend:
Eng. trans. (with *Wind from the East*). London: Lorrimer; New York: Simon & Schuster. 1972. Includes supplementary material.

Pravda:
Cahiers du Cinéma 240 (July 1972).

Vent d'est:
Eng. trans. (with *Weekend*). London: Lorrimer; New York: Simon & Schuster. 1972. Includes supplementary material.
Cahiers du Cinéma 240 (July 1972).

Luttes en Italie:
Cahiers du Cinéma 238, 239 (May, June 1972).

Tout va bien:
Excerpts in *Cinema Rising* 2 (May 1972).
Excerpts in Vianey. "Deux Petits Soldats" (see below).

Books by Godard

Godard on Godard. Trans. and ed. with commentary by Tom Milne. London: Secker and Warburg; New York: Viking. 1972. Includes the bulk of Godard's criticism and major interviews from 1950 to 1968.

Jean-Luc Godard par Jean-Luc Godard. Ed. and intro. Jean Narboni. Paris: Editions Pierre Belfond: *Collection des Cahiers du Cinéma.* 1968.

With Macha Meril. *Journal d'Une Femme mariée.* Paris: Editions Denoël. 1965.

Books About Godard

Brown, Royal S., ed. *Focus on Godard.* Englewood Cliffs, N.J.: Prentice-Hall. 1972. London: Prentice-Hall. 1973. Includes interviews, reviews, essays, and commentary.

Cameron, Ian, ed. *The Films of Jean-Luc Godard.* London: November Books; New York: Praeger. 1969. Essays by Cozarinsky, Cameron, Guarner, Wood, French, Walker, Bontemps, Hillier, and others.

Cardinal, Marie, and Jean-Luc Godard. *Cet été là—Deux ou Trois Choses que je sais d'elle.* Paris: Julliard. 1967.

Collet, Jean. *Jean-Luc Godard: An Investigation into His Films and Philosophy.* Trans. Ciba Vaughn. New York: Crown. 1970. Includes an essay by Collet, texts and documents, excerpts from screenplays, criticism, and "witnesses."

———. *Jean-Luc Godard.* Paris: Editions Seghers. Collection Cinéma d'aujourd'hui 18. 1963, 1968. Rev. ed. by Collet and Paul Fargier. Paris.1974.

Estève, Michel, ed. *Jean-Luc Godard au-delà du récit.* Paris: Lettres Modernes, Collection Etudes Cinématographiques. 1967. Essays.

Goldmann, Annie. *Cinéma et société moderne.* Paris: Editions Anthropos. 1971. Devoted mainly to "Les Héros godardiens" in his films and those of others.

Gubern, Román. *Godard Polémico.* Barcelona: Tusquets Editor. 1969.

Mancini, Michele. *Godard.* Rome: Trevi Editore. 1969. A cura della revista *Filmcritica.*

Mussman, Toby, ed. *Jean-Luc Godard: A Critical Anthology.* New York: E. P. Dutton. 1968. Essays by Godard, Moullet, Sarris, Milne, Sontag, Collet, Mussman, Kael, Wood, Coutard, and others.

Roud, Richard. *Godard.* London: Secker and Warburg. 1968, 1970; New York: Doubleday (1st ed.). 1968; Bloomington: Indiana University Press (2nd ed.). 1970. Cinema One 1.

Thomsen, Christian Braad. *Jean-Luc Godard: Fra gangstere til rødgardister.* Copenhagen: Rhodos. 1971.

Vianey, Michel. *En attendant Godard.* Paris: Grasset. 1966.

Slide Set

Segal, Abraham, ed. *Jean-Luc Godard: Films 1957–1969.* Paris: L'Avant-Scène du Cinéma. Albums—Diapositives 4. 1970. Includes 120 slides from the films and booklet "Filmographie complète de 1957 à 1969 et légendes des 120 diapositives."

Major Interviews and Profiles

Annaud, Monique. "Jean-Luc Godard: L'Important c'est les producteurs" (interview). *Film Français,* 14 March 1975.

Anon. "Die Kunst ist eine Idee der Kapitalisten." *Film* (West Germany) 7:4 (April 1969). Excerpt in Flash (see below).

———. "Godard in Hollywood," *Take One* 1:10 (June 1968).

Baby, Yvonne, and Martin Even. *"Tout va bien:* Un Grand Film 'décevant,'" *Le Monde,* 27 April 1972. Separate interviews with Gorin and Godard.

Bontemps, Jacques; Jean-Louis Comolli, Michel Delahaye, and Jean Narboni. "Lutter sur deux fronts," *Cahiers du Cinéma* 194 (October 1967). Translated in *Film Quarterly* 22:2 (Winter 1968–69).

Carroll, Kent. "Film and Revolution: Interview With the Dziga-Vertov Group." *Evergreen Review* 14:83 (October 1970). Reprinted in Brown.

Cott, Jonathan. "Jean-Luc Godard." *Rolling Stone* 35 (14 June 1969). Reprinted in Flash (see below).

Cournot, Michel. "Jean-Luc Godard," *Le Nouvel Observateur* 292 (15 June 1970).

Feinstein, Herbert. "An Interview with Jean-Luc Godard." *Film Quarterly* 17:3 (Spring 1964).

Fièschi, Jean-André. "La Difficulté d'être de Jean-Luc Godard," *Cahiers du Cinéma* 137 (November 1962).

Flash, Jack, ed. and trans. "Jean-Luc Godard." *Kinopraxis No. 0.* Berkeley: 2533 Telegraph Avenue. 1970. Includes eight published interviews with or by Godard, as well as a transcript of unedited footage shot for a television program about Godard in the "Cinéma Six" series which was never aired.

Flatley, Guy. "Godard Says Bye-Bye to Bardot and All That." New York *Times,* 17 May 1970.

Gauthier, Guy. "Une Réapparition de Jean-Luc Godard." *Image et Son* 245 (December 1970).

Godard, Jean-Luc. "Ten Questions to Nine Directors." *Sight and Sound* 33:2 (Spring 1964).

———. "Modern Life." *Take One* 1:3 (February 1967). Trans. by Jean Billard from *Le Nouvel Observateur* 100 (12 December 1966).

——— and Michel Cournot. "Quelques évidentes incertitudes." *Revue d'Esthétique* 20:2-3 (April-September 1967). Excerpt in Flash (see above).

———. "Un Prissonier qu'on laisse taper sur sa cassérole." *La Nouvelle Critique* 199 (November 1968). Excerpt in Flash (see above).

Godard, Jean-Luc, on behalf of the Dziga-Vertov Group. "Premiers son Anglais." *Cinéthique* 5 (September-October 1969). Reprinted in Flash (see above).

Godard, Jean-Luc, and Jean-Pierre Gorin, Press release in conjunction with *Tout va bien.* Trans. in *Cinema Rising* 2 (May 1972), with excerpts from a press conference trans. by Tony Rayns.

Goodwin, Michael; Tom Luddy, and Naomi Wise. "The Dziga Vertov Film

Group in America—An Interview with Jean-Luc Godard and Jean-Pierre Gorin." *Take One* 2:10 (March 1971). Reprinted (slightly expanded) in *Double Feature,* by Goodwin and Greil Marcus. New York: Outerbridge and Lazard. 1972.

Goodwin, Michael, and Naomi Wise. "Raymond Chandler, Mao Tse-Tung and *Tout Va Bien:* An Interview with Jean-Pierre Gorin." *Take One* 3:6 (October 1972).

Gorin, Jean-Pierre, and Gérard LeBlanc. "Un Cinéaste comme les autres." *Cinéthique* 1 (January 1969). Extracts in Flash (see above).

Jouffroy, Alain. "Le Cahier de La Chinoise." *Opus International* 2 (July 1967). Includes facsimiles of pages from Godard's notebook.

Kolker, Robert Philip. "Angle and Reality: Godard and Gorin in America." *Sight and Sound* 42:3 (Summer 1973).

Lottman, Herbert R. "Cinéma Vérité: Jean-Luc Godard." *Columbia University Forum,* Spring 1968.

Marcorelles, Louis. "Jean-Luc Godard's Half-Truths." *Film Quarterly* 17:3 (Spring 1964).

Martin, Marcel. "Le Groupe 'Dziga-Vertov,'" *Cinéma 70* 151 (December 1970).

Moullet, Luc. "Jean-Luc Godard," *Cahiers du Cinéma* 106 (April 1960).

Rispoli, Paola. "Cinema Provacazione." *Filmcritica* 194 (January 1969). Reprinted in Flash (see above).

Sarris, Andrew. "Films in Focus: Godard and the Revolution," *The Village Voice,* 30 April 1970.

———, ed. "Jean-Luc Godard." In *Interviews With Film Directors.* Indianapolis: Bobbs-Merrill. 1967. From interview in *Cahiers du Cinéma* 138, trans. Rose Kaplin, and interview by Warren Sonbert; both appeared in *New York Film Bulletin* 46 (Summer 1964).

Svendsen, Juris; Tom Luddy, and David Mairowitz, "Talking Politics with Godard." San Francisco *Express Times,* 14 March 1968. Excerpt in Flash (see above).

Thomsen, Christian Braad. "Filmmaking and History: Jean Pierre Gorin Interview." *Jump Cut* 3 (September-October 1974).

Television Programs About Godard

Episode in *Cinéastes de Notre Temps* series, director: Hubert Knapp; producers: Janine Bazin, André S. Labarthe.

Episode of *Pour Notre Plaisir,* director: Jacques Doniol-Valcroze.

Selected Critical Articles

Apra, Adriano. *"Le Mépris* e *Il Disprezzo."* *Filmcritica* 151–52 (November-December 1964).

Archer, Eugene. "What Makes Us Hate—or Love—Godard?" New York *Times*, 27 October 1968.

Armes, Roy. "Jean-Luc Godard." In *French Cinema since 1946*. Vol. 2. London: A. Zwemmer; New York: A. S. Barnes. 1970.

Bertolucci, Bernardo. "Versus Godard." *Cahiers du Cinéma in English* 10 (May 1967).

Bory, Jean-Louis. "Jean-Luc Godard." In *Dossiers du Cinéma: Cinéastes 1*. Ed. Jean-Louis Bory and Claude Michel Cluny. Paris: Casterman. 1971.

Clouzot, Claire. "Godard and the U.S." *Sight and Sound* 37:3 (Summer 1968).

Coutard, Raoul. "Light of Day." *Sight and Sound* 35:1 (Winter 1965–66). Reprinted in Mussman.

Dadoun, Roger. "Un Cinéma 'sauvage' et 'ingénu,'" *Image et Son* 211 (December 1967). This issue includes several other articles on Godard.

Farber, Manny. "Jean-Luc Godard." In *Negative Space*. New York: Praeger; London: Studio Vista. 1971. Reprinted from *Artforum*, October 1968.

Giannetti, Louis. "Godard's *Masculine-Feminine:* The Cinematic essay." In *Godard and Others: Essays on Film Form*. Rutherford, N.J.: Fairleigh Dickenson; London: Tantivy. 1975.

Goldmann, Annie. "Jean-Luc Godard." *La Nouvelle Revue Française* 165 (September 1966).

Godard, Jean-Luc. "Dziga Vertov Notebook." *Take One* 2:11 (June 1971). Photographs of Godard's notebook for the Palestinian film.

Goodwin, Michael. "Dziga Vertov: An Introduction." *Take One* 2:10 (March 1971). Introduction to two special issues on Godard which include much useful material.

Harcourt, Peter. "Godard." In *Six European Directors*. London: Penguin. 1974.

Henderson, Brian. "Toward a Non-Bourgeois Camera Style." *Film Quarterly* 24:2 (Winter 1970–71).

———. "*Godard on Godard:* Notes for a Reading." *Film Quarterly* 27:4 (Summer 1974).

LeSage, Julia. "*Tout va bien* and *Coup pour coup:* Radical French Cinema in Context." *Cineaste* 5:3 (Summer 1972).

———. "*Wind from the East:* Looking at a Film Politically." *Jump Cut* 4 (November-December 1974).

Luddy, Tom; Ron Green, and Susan Rice. "Dziga Vertov: Three Recent Films." *Take One* 2:11 (June 1971).

MacBean, James Roy. "Politics, Painting and the Language of Signs in Godard's *Made in U.S.A.*" *Film Quarterly* 22:3 (Spring 1969).

———. "Politics and Poetry in Two Recent Films by Godard." *Film Quarterly* 21:4 (Summer 1968).

———. "Godard's *Weekend*, or the Self-Critical Cinema of Spectacle." *Film Quarterly* 22:2 (Winter 1968–69).

———. "*One Plus One*, or the Praxis of History." *Partisan Review*, July 1971.

———. "*See You at Mao:* Godard's Revolutionary *British Sounds.*" *Film Quarterly* 24:2 (Winter 1970–71).

———. "*Vent d'est*, or Godard and Rocha at the Crossroads." *Sight and Sound* 40:2 (Summer 1971). Reprinted in Simon & Schuster script.

———. "Godard and the Dziga Vertov Group: Film and Dialectics." *Film Quarterly* 26:1 (Fall 1972).

Mellen, Joan. "*Wind from the East:* A Review." *Film Comment* 7:3 (Fall 1971).

Merrill, M. "Black Panthers in the New Wave." *Film Culture* 53-4-5 (Spring 1972).

Milne, Tom. "Jean-Luc Godard and *Vivre Sa Vie.*" *Sight and Sound* 32:1 (Winter 1963).

———. "Jean-Luc Godard ou la raison ardente." *Sight and Sound* 34:3 (Summer 1965). Reprinted in *The Married Woman* (see above).

———. Review of *Masculin-féminin. Sight and Sound* 36:1 (Winter 1967).

———. "Jean-Luc Godard." in *International Film Guide 1974*, ed. Peter Cowie. London: Tantivy Press; New York: A. S. Barnes. 1973.

Monaco, James. "Godard." Program notes from New School Film Series. New York: New York Zoetrope. 1974.

———. "Working Films: *Coup pour coup.*" *Take One* 5:1 (January 1976).

Münch, Jacob Friedrich. "Jean-Luc Godard, Hans Lucas und Mich." In *Beobachtungen über das Gefühl des Schönen und Erhabenen in Filmrealität*. Zurich: Doppelgänger Verlag. 1973.

Peary. Gerald, "Jane Fonda on Tour: Answering Letter to Jane." *Take One* 4:4 (July 1974).

Pollak-Lederer, Jacques. "Jean-Luc Godard dans la modernité." *Le Temps Moderne* 262 (March 1968).

Rosenbaum, Jonathan. "Cities and Carwrecks: Godard." *Film Society Review* 4:2 (October 1968).

———. "Theory and Practice: The Criticism of Jean-Luc Godard." *Sight and Sound* 41:3 (Summer 1972).

Roud, Richard. "*Tout va bien.*" *Sight and Sound* 41:3 (Summer 1972).

Sarris, Andrew. "Jean-Luc Versus Saint Jean." *Film Heritage* 3:3 (Spring 1968).

Sharits, Paul J. "Red, Blue, Godard." *Film Quarterly* 19:4 (Summer 1966).

Silverstein, Norman. "Godard and the Revolution." *Films and Filming* 16:9 (June 1970).

Simmons, Steven. "*Tout va bien.*" *Film Comment* 10:3 (May-June 1974).

Simon, John. "Godard and the Godardians: A Study in the New Sensibility." In *Private Screenings.* New York: Macmillan. 1967.

Simsolo, Noël. "La Révolution par le film selon Jean-Luc Godard, ou Comment contester le cinéma de consommation." *Cinéma Pratique* 97 (March 1971).

Sontag, Susan. "Godard." In *Styles of Radical Will.* New York: Farrar, Straus, & Giroux. London: Secker and Warburg. 1969. Essential.

———. Program notes for New Yorker Theatre Godard Festival, 19 October-1 November 1967. Includes quotations from Godard.

———. "Godard's *Vivre sa vie.*" In *Against Interpretation.* New York: Farrar, Straus, and Giroux. 1966. London: Eyre and Spottiswoode. 1967. From *Moviegoer* 2 (Summer-Autumn 1964). Reprinted in Mussman.

Taylor, John Russell. "Jean-Luc Godard." In *Cinema Eye, Cinema Ear.* London: Methuen; New York: Hill and Wang. 1964.

Vianey, Michel. "Deux Petits Soldats." *Le Nouvel Observateur,* 17 April 1972.

Westerbeck, Colin L., Jr. "A Terrible Duty is Born." *Sight and Sound* 40:2 (Spring 1971).

Wood, Robin. "Society and Tradition: An Approach to Jean-Luc Godard." *New Left Review,* September-October 1966. Reprinted in Mussman.

———. "Godard and *Weekend.*" *Movie* 16 (Winter 1968-69).

———. "In Defense of *Wind From the East.*" In *Personal Views: Explorations in Style.* London: Fraser Gallery. 1975. Also in "In Defense of Art," *Film Comment* 11:4 (July–August 1975).

Zimmer, Christian. "Totalisation du Vrac." *Les Temps Modernes* 252 (May 1967).

CHABROL

Scripts

Le Beau Serge:
Marsan, Robert. *Le Beau Serge.* Paris: Seghers. 1959. Novelization.

Les Cousins:
Jehanne, Jean-Charles. *Les Cousins.* Paris: Seghers. 1959. Novelization.

Landru:
Sagan, Françoise, and Claude Chabrol. *Landru.* Paris: Julliard. 1963.

"La Muette" *(Paris vu par . . .):*
L'Avant-Scène du Cinéma 92 (May 1969). Complete.

Les Biches:
L'Avant-Scène du Cinéma 92 (May 1969). Synopsis and photos only.

La Femme infidele:
L'Avant-Scène du Cinéma 92 (May 1969). Complete.

Les Noces rouges:
Chabrol, Claude. *Les Noces rouges.* Paris: Editions Seghers, Collection Filmothèque. 1973. Preface by Jean Curtelin. Complete.

Book by Chabrol

With Eric Rohmer. *Hitchcock.* Paris: Editions Universitaires. 1957.

Stories and Essays by Chabrol

"Musique douce." in *Mystère-Magazine* 109 (1954).

"Le Dernier jour de souffrance." in *Mystère-Magazine* 173 (1956).

Preface to *La Vie exaltante d'Alfred Baugard,* by Jean-Pierre de Lucovich. Paris: Losfeld. 1967. A collection of comic strips.

Preface to *Les Vipères de Paris,* by Jean Curtelin. Paris: La Table Ronde. 1970.

Books About Chabrol

Braucourt, Guy. *Claude Chabrol.* Paris: Editions Seghers, Collection Cinéma d'aujourd'hui 68. 1971.

Wood, Robin, and Michael Walker. *Claude Chabrol.* London: November Books; New York: Praeger. 1970.

Major Interviews and Profiles

Anon. Interview. Unifrance Film press release, May 1973.

Baxter, Brian. "Claude Chabrol." *Film* 54 (Spring 1969).

Braucourt, Guy. "Claude Chabrol: 'Je suis centriste,'" *Nouvelles Littéraires,* 27 August 1970.

———. "La Décade prodigieuse" (interview). *Ecran* 1 (January 1972).

Chabrol, Claude. "Trois entretiens." *Cahiers du Cinéma* 138 (December 1962).

Ciment, Michel; Gérard Legrand, and Jean-Paul Török. "Claude Chabrol Interviewed." *Movie* 18 (Winter 1970–71). From *Positif* 115.

Ebert, Roger. "This Man Must Commit Murder." New York *Times,* 29 November 1970.

Fièschi, Jean-André, and Mark Shivas. "Interview with Claude Chabrol." *Movie* 10 (June 1963).

James, Noah. "An Interview with Claude Chabrol." *Take One* 3:1 (December 1971).

Nogueira, Rui, and Nicoletta Zalaffi. "Conversation with Chabrol," *Sight and Sound* 40:1 (Winter 1970–71).

Rosier, M., and D. Serceau. "Entretien avec Claude Chabrol." *Téléciné* 178 (March 1973).

Shivas, Mark. Interview. *Movie* 10 (June 1963). Reprinted in *Interviews with Film Directors*, ed. Andrew Sarris. Indianapolis: Bobbs-Merrill. 1967. London: Secker and Warburg. 1972.

Selected Critical Articles

Allen, Don. "Chabrol." *Screen* 11:1 (February 1970).

Anon. "Entretien: Claude Chabrol entre Lucie Faure et Dashiell Hammett." *Film Français*, 14 March 1975.

Armes, Roy. "Claude Chabrol." In *French Cinema Since 1946*. Vol. 2. London: A. Zwemmer; New York: A. S. Barnes. 1970.

———. "Claude Chabrol." In *International Film Guide 1970*, ed. Peter Cowie. London: Tantivy Press; New York: A. S. Barnes. 1969.

Braucourt, Guy. "*Les Noces rouges*." *Ecran* 13 (March 1973).

Cameron, Ian. "The Darwinian World of Claude Chabrol." *Movie* 10 (June 1963). Reprinted in *Movie Reader*, ed. Ian Cameron. London: November Books; New York: Praeger. 1972.

Chabrol, Claude. "Evolution du film policier." *Cahiers du Cinéma* 54 (December 1955).

———. "Les Petits sujets." *Cahiers du Cinéma* 100 (October 1959). Reprinted in Peter Graham, ed. *The New Wave*. London: Secker and Warburg; New York: Doubleday. Cinema One series. 1968. Also in *Movie* 1 (June 1962).

Ciment, Michel. "Versailles, petite île" (review of *Juste avant la nuit*). *Positif* 125 (March 1971).

Cornand, A. "*Les Noces rouges*, Chabrol, et la censure." *Image et Son* 279 (December 1973). This is a special issue devoted to Chabrol's work.

Dawson, Jan. "*Ten Days' Wonder*" (review). *Sight and Sound* 41:4 (Autumn 1972).

———. "*Just Before Nightfall*" (review). *Sight and Sound* 42:2 (Spring 1973).

Ebert, J. "Appetite auf Chabrol." *Filmkritik* 16:7 (July 1972).

Giard, Robert. "*This Man Must Die*: Chabrol's *Iliad*." *Film Heritage* 6:3 (Spring 1971).

Haskell, Molly. "The Films of Chabrol: A Priest Among Clowns." *Village Voice*, 12 November 1970.

———. "Psychic Wounds That Scar the Landscape." *Village Voice*, 23 December 1971.

Mancini, Michele, et al. *Filmcritica* 23:224 (April-May 1972). A special issue devoted to Chabrol.

Milne, Tom. "Chabrol's Schizophrenic Spider." *Sight and Sound* 39:2 (Spring 1970).

———. "Songs of Innocence: *La Rupture*." *Sight and Sound* 40:1 (Winter 1970–71).

———. "*Nada*" (review). *Sight and Sound* 43:2 (Spring 1974).

Oudart, Jean-Pierre. "*Que la bête meure*" (review). *Cahiers du Cinéma* 218 (March 1970).

Overbey, David L. "*Les Noces rouges*" (review). *Sight and Sound* 42:4 (Autumn 1973).

Sarris, Andrew. "Fear and Loathing of the Bourgeoisie" (review of *Nada*). *Village Voice,* 14 November 1974.

Siclier, Jacques. "*Docteur Popaul*" (review). *Le Monde,* 1 October 1972.

Taylor, John Russell. "Claude Chabrol" in *Directors and Directions: Cinema for the Seventies.* New York: Hill and Wang. 1975.

Walker, Michael, "Claude Chabrol: into the 'Seventies,'" *Movie* 20 (Summer 1975).

Wolfe, Charles. "Chabrol: The Lyrical Mystery Master." *Village Voice,* 5 September 1974.

Wood, Robin. "Chabrol and Truffaut." *Movie* 17 (Winter 1969–70).

ROHMER

Scripts

"Présentation, ou Charlotte et son steak":
L'Avant-Scène du Cinéma 69 (April 1967).
Scenario in *Cahiers du Cinéma,* May 1952.

"Contes Moraux":
Eric Rohmer. *Six Contes Moraux.* Paris: L'Herne. 1974. Novelization.
———. *Six Moral Tales.* London: Lorrimer. 1976. Novelization.

La Collectionneuse:
L'Avant-Scène du Cinéma 69 (April 1967).

Ma Nuit chez Maud:
L'Avant-Scène du Cinéma 98 (December 1969).

Books by Rohmer

"Gilbert Cordier." *Elizabeth, Les Vacances.*

With Claude Chabrol. *Hitchcock.* Paris: Editions Universitaires. 1957.

Major Interviews and Profiles

Barron, Fred. "Eric Rohmer: An Interview." *Take One* 4:1 (January 1974).

Bonitzer, Pascal; Jean-Louis Comolli, Serge Daney, and Jean Narboni, "Nouvel entretien avec Eric Rohmer." *Cahiers du Cinéma* 219 (April 1970).

Chase, D., and R. Ferdin. "Eric Rohmer Talks About *Chloe in the Afternoon. Inter/View* 27 (November 1972).

Davis, Melton S. "Rohmer's Formula: Boy Talks with Girl, Boy Argues with Girl, Boy Says . . ." *New York Times Magazine*, 21 November 1971.

Ethier, R. "Eric Rohmer parle de ses Contes moraux." *Séquences* 71 (January 1973).

Mellen, Joan. "The Moral Psychology of Rohmer's Tales." *Cinema* (Los Angeles) 7:1 (Fall 1971).

Nogueira, Rui. "Eric Rohmer: Choice and Chance." *Sight and Sound* 40:3 (Summer 1971).

Petrie, Graham. "Eric Rohmer." In *International Film Guide 1972*. Ed. Peter Cowie. London: Tantivy Press; New York: A. S. Barnes. 1971.

———. "Eric Rohmer: An Interview." *Film Quarterly* 24:4 (Summer 1971).

Rohmer, Eric. "L'ancien et le nouveau" (interview), *Cahiers du Cinéma* 172 (November 1965).

Zalaffi, Nicoletta, and Rui Nogueira. "Eric Rohmer." *Film* 51 (Spring 1968).

Selected Critical Articles

Bonitzer, Pascal. "Maud et les phagocytes." *Cahiers du Cinéma* 214 (July-August 1969).

Clarens, Carlos. "Eric Rohmer: l'amour sage." *Sight and Sound* 39:1 (Winter 1969–70).

———. *"Le Genou de Claire"* (review). *Sight and Sound* 40:3 (Summer 1971).

Haskell, Molly. "Eric Rohmer in the Afternoon." *Village Voice*, 12 October 1972.

Hillier, Jim. *"Ma nuit chez Maud." Movie* 18 (Winter 1970–71).

Houston, Penelope. *"L'Amour, l'après-midi"* (review). *Sight and Sound* 42:1 (Winter 1972–73).

Koller, R. "Wenn Man eine Erklärung findet—und man kann das immer—gibt es immer noch eine andere hinter der ersten." *Filmkritik* 16:7 (July 1972).

Rohmer, Eric. "Riscoprire l'America." *Filmcritica* 24:234-5 (May-June 1973). Reprinted from *Cahiers du Cinéma* 54 (December 1955).

———. "Le Gout de la beauté." *Cahiers du Cinéma* 121 (July 1961).

Sourian, Peter. "Eric Rohmer: Starring Blaise Pascal." *Transatlantic Review* 48.

RIVETTE

Scripts

Paris nous appartient:
L'Avant-Scène du Cinéma 7 (September 1961). Photos and short statement by Rivette.

L'Amour fou:
L'Avant-Scène du Cinéma 91 (April 1969). Synopsis and photos.

Céline et Julie vont en bateau:
L'Avant-Scène du Cinéma 157 (April 1975). Synopsis and photos.

Major Interviews and Profiles

Anon. "Jacques Rivette." Unifrance Film press release. June 1970.

Aumont, Jacques; Jean-Louis Comolli, Jean Narboni, and Sylvie Pierre. "Le Temps débordé: entretien avec Jacques Rivette." *Cahiers du Cinéma* 204 (September 1968).

Baby, Yvonne. Interview. *Le Monde,* 2 October 1968.

———. "Entretien avec Jacques Rivette." *Le Monde,* 18 September 1971.

Clarens, Carlos, and Edgardo Cozarinsky. "Jacques Rivette" (interview). *Sight and Sound* 43:4 (Autumn 1974).

Dasgupta, Gautam. "Juliet Berto and Dominique Labourier Interviewed." *Film* 2:24 (March 1975).

Even, Martin. "*Out One:* Voyage au-delà du cinéma," *Le Monde,* 18 September 1971.

———. "Quand le réel court après la fiction, il se passe des choses étranges." *Le Monde,* 19 September 1974.

Houston, Penelope, and Louis Marcorelles. "Two New Directors." *Sight and Sound* 28:1 (Winter 1958–59).

Johnson, William. "Recent Rivette: An Inter-Re-View." *Film Quarterly* 28:2 (Winter 1974–75).

Marcorelles, Louis. "Interview With Jacques Rivette/Roger Leenhardt." *Sight and Sound* 32:4 (Autumn 1963).

Monaco, James. Interview with Jacques Rivette (unpublished), October 1974.

Rosenbaum, Jonathan; Lauren Sedofsky, and Gilbert Adair. "Phantom Interviewers over Rivette." *Film Comment* 10:5 (September-October 1974).

Selected Critical Articles

Armes, Roy. "Jacques Rivette." In *French Cinema since 1946.* Vol. 2. London: A. Zwemmer; New York: A. S. Barnes. 1970.

Haskell, Molly. "One Continuous Impulse Toward Freedom." *Village Voice*, 22 July 1971.

Jeander. *Paris nous appartient* (review). *Libération*, 16 December 1961.

Marcabru, Pierre. *Paris nous appartient* (review). *Combat*, 17 December 1961.

Marcorelles, Louis. *"Paris nous appartient."* *Sight and Sound* 28:1 (Winter 1958–59).

Milne, Tom. *"L'Amour fou."* *Sight and Sound* 38:2 (Spring 1969).

Rivette, Jacques. "Paris nous appartient." *L'Avant-Scène du Cinéma* 7 (15 September 1961).

Rosenbaum, Jonathan. "Work and Play in the House of Fiction." *Sight and Sound* 43:4 (Autumn 1974).

Stein, Elliott. "Suzanne Simonin, Diderot's Nun." *Sight and Sound* 35:3 (Summer 1966).

GENERAL BIBLIOGRAPHY

Books

Armes, Roy. *French Cinema since 1946*. Vol. 2: *The Personal Style*. London: A. Zwemmer; New York: A. S. Barnes. 1970.

Bazin, André. *Qu'est-ce que le cinéma?* 6 vols. Paris: Editions du Cerf. 1958–59.

———. *What Is Cinema?* 2 vols. Selected and trans. by Hugh Gray. Berkeley: University of California Press. 1967, 1971.

Borde, Raymonde; Freddy Buache, and Jean Curtelin. *Nouvelle Vague*. Lyons: Serdoc Premier Plan 9. 1962.

Cahiers du Cinéma 91 (January 1959). A special issue in memory of André Bazin.

Cahiers du Cinéma 138 (December 1962). Special issue entirely devoted to the New Wave.

Le Cinéma français en 1970: situation, perspectives, et plan de redressement. Paris: Centre National de la Cinématographie. 1970.

Clouzot, Claire. *Le Cinéma francais depuis la Nouvelle Vague*. Paris: Fernand Nathan/Alliance Française. 1972.

Collet, Jean. *Le Cinéma en question*. Paris: Editions du Cerf. 1972.

Dictionnaire du nouveau cinéma français. Paris: *Cahiers du Cinéma* 138 (December 1962), 155 (June 1964), 187 (February 1967).

Etats-Généraux du Cinéma. *Le Cinéma s'insurge*. No. 1. Paris: Le Terrain Vague. 1968.

Goldmann, Annie. *Cinéma et société moderne: Godard-Antonioni-Resnais-Robbe-Grillet*. Paris: Editions Anthropos. 1971.

Graham, Peter, ed. *The New Wave.* London: Secker and Warburg; New York: Doubleday Cinema One Series. 1968. A collection of articles: Interview with Truffaut from *Cahiers du Cinéma* 136 (1962); Alexandre Astruc, "La Caméra-Stylo," *Ecran Français* 144 (1948); André Bazin, "The Evolution of Film Language," from *Qu'est-ce que le cinéma?* vol. 1, and "La Politique des auteurs," *Cahiers du Cinéma* 70 (1957); Robert Benayoun, "The King is Naked," *Positif* 46 (1962); Gérard Gozlan, "In Praise of André Bazin," *Positif* 47 (1962); Claude Chabrol, "Little Themes," *Cahiers du Cinéma* 100 (1959); Jean-Luc Godard, "Review of Astruc's *Une Vie,*" *Cahiers du Cinéma* 89 (1958).

Houston, Penelope. *The Contemporary Cinema.* London: Penguin Books. 1963.

Jacob, Gilles. *Le Cinéma moderne.* Lyons: Serdoc. 1964.

Jeancolas, Jean-Pierre. *Le Cinéma français 1969–1974.* Créteil: Maison des Arts et de la Culture de Créteil—Section Cinéma. 1974.

Jeune Cinéma français. Special issues: *Cinéma 64* 88 (1964), *Cinéma 66* 108, *Cinéma 72* 163.

Labarthe, André S. *Essai sur le jeune cinéma français.* Paris: Le Terrain Vague. 1960.

Labro, Philippe, et al. *Ce n'est qu'un début.* Paris: Denoël. 1968.

Martin, Marcel. *Screen Series: France.* London: A. Zwemmer; New York: A. S. Barnes. 1971.

Metz, Christian. *Essais sur la signification au cinéma.* Paris: Editions Klincksieck. 1968. 2nd ed. 1971. Ed. and trans. by Michael Taylor as *Film Language: A Semiotics of the Cinema.* New York and London: Oxford University Press. 1974. *Essais sur la signification au cinéma,* vol. 2. Paris: Klinksieck. 1972.

———. *Propositions méthodologiques pour l'analyse du film.* Bochum, W. Ger.: Unitätsverlag Bochum. 1970.

———. *Language et cinéma.* Paris: Larousse. 1971. Trans. by Donna Jean Umiker-Sebeok as *Language and Cinema.* The Hague: Mouton; New York: Humanities Press. 1974.

Mitry, Jean. *Esthétique et psychologie du cinéma.* Paris: Editions Universitaires. Vol. 1: 1963; vol. 2: 1965.

Rohdie, Sam. ed. "Cinema Semiotics and the Work of Christian Metz." Special double issue of *Screen* 14:1/2 (Spring-Summer 1973).

Sadoul, Georges. *Le Cinéma français (1890–1962).* Paris: Flammarion. 1962.

Siclier, Jacques. *Nouvelle Vague?* Paris: Editions du Cerf. 1961.

Taylor, John Russell. *Cinema Eye, Cinema Ear: Some Key Filmmakers of the Sixties.* London: Methuen; New York: Hill and Wang. 1964.

Articles

Brémonde, Claude, Evelyne Sillerot, Simone Berton. "Les héros des films dits 'de la Nouvelle Vague'." *Communications* I. Paris: Editions du Seuil, 1961.

Burch, Noel. "Qu'est-ce que la Nouvelle Vague?" *Film Quarterly* 13:2 (Winter 1959).

Carlini, F., and M. Marchesini. "L'Altra faccia del cinema: su alcuni 'autori' sopravvissuti al maggio." *Bianco e Nero* 33:7-8 (July-August 1972). A special issue on French cinema since May 1968.

Ciment, Michel. "Une Tendence certaine du cinéma français." *Positif* 144–45 (November-December 1972).

Hartog, Simon. "Etats-Généraux du Cinéma: the Nationalisation of the Cinema." *Cinema Rising* 2 (May 1972).

Henderson, Brian. "The Structure of Bazin's Thought." *Film Quarterly* 25:4 (Summer 1972).

Monaco, James. "The New Wave" (three parts; pamphs.). Program Notes from New School Film Series. New York: New York Zoetrope. 1974.

Morin, Edgar. "Conditions d'apparition de la 'Nouvelle Vague,'" In *Communications I.* Paris: Editions du Seuil. 1961.

Nogueira, Rui, and Nicoletta Zalaffi. "The Seventh Heaven: An Interview with Henri Langlois." *Sight and Sound* 41:4 (Autumn 1972).

Oudart, J.-P. "L'Idéologie moderniste dans quelques films récents (3): Le Horschamps de l'auteur." *Cahiers du Cinéma* 236–37 (March-April 1972).

Oxenhandler, Neal. "The Dialectic of Emotion in New Wave Cinema." *Film Quarterly* 27:3 (Spring 1974).

Pearson, Gabriel, and Eric Rhode. "Cinema of Appearance." *Sight and Sound* 30:4 (Autumn 1961).

Roud, Richard. "The Left Bank." *Sight and Sound* 32:1 (Winter 1962–63).

Siclier, Jacques. "New Wave and French Cinema." *Sight and Sound* 30:3 (Summer 1961).

Truffaut, François. "On the events of May 68," in Philippe Labro et al. *Ce n'est qu'un début.* Paris: Denoël. 1968.

———. "It Was Good to Be Alive" (on André Bazin). in *The 400* Blows, ed. Denby. (see above). Trans. Helen G. Scott, from *Cahiers du Cinéma* 91 (January 1959).

———. "l'Agonie de la nouvelle vague n'est pas pour demain." *Arts* 848 (20–26 December 1961).

STUDIES OF SEMIOLOGY, STRUCTURALISM, AND DIALECTICAL CRITICISM

Barthes, Roland. *Le Degré zéro de l'écriture.* Paris: Editions du Seuil. 1953. Trans. Annette Lavers and Colin Smith as *Writing Degree Zero.* London: Jonathan Cape. 1967. Boston: Beacon Press. 1968.

———. *Eléments de sémiologie.* Paris: Editions du Seuil. 1964. Trans. Annette Lavers and Colin Smith as *Elements of Semiology.* London: Jonathan Cape. 1967. Boston: Beacon Press. 1968. In same volume as *Writing Degree Zero.*

———. *Mythologies.* Paris: Editions du Seuil. 1957. Selected and trans. Annette Lavers. London: Jonathan Cape; New York: Hill and Wang. 1972.

Benjamin, Walter. *Illuminations.* Ed. Hannah Arendt. New York: Schocken; Harcourt Brace and World. 1969. London: Jonathan Cape. 1970.

Communications 23: Psychanalyse et cinéma. Paris: Seuil. 1975. Essays by Metz, Kristeva, Barthes, and others.

Ehrmann, Jacques. ed. *Structuralism.* New York: Doubleday Anchor. 1970.

Jameson, Fredric. *Marxism and Form.* Princeton, N.J.: Princeton University Press. 1971.

Lane, Michael, ed. *Introduction to Structuralism.* New York: Basic Books, Harper Torchbooks. 1970. London: *Structuralism: A Reader.* Jonathan Cape. 1970.

Mehlman, Jeffrey, ed. *French Freud: Structural Studies in Psychoanalysis. Yale French Studies* 48 (1972).

OTHER WORKS REFERRED TO IN TEXT

Althusser, Louis, and Etienne Balibar. *Lire le Capital.* Paris: François Maspero. 1968. Trans. Ben Brewster as *Reading Capital.* London: New Left Books; New York: Pantheon. 1970

Brecht, Bertolt. *Brecht on Theatre.* Trans. John Willett. New York: Hill and Wang, London: Methuen. 1964. Original edition: *Schriften zum Theatre.* Frankfurt am Main: Suhrkamp Verlag. 1964. Willett includes some pieces from other sources.

Cappelanus, Andreas. *The Art of Courtly Love.* Ed. Frederick W. Locke. New York: Frederick Ungar. 1957.

Cocteau, Jean. *Le secret professionnel.* Paris. 1922.

———. *La Difficulté d'être.* Paris. 1947.

Eluard, Paul. *La Capitale de la Douleur.* Paris: Gallimard. 1926.

Fowlie, Wallace, ed. and trans. *Mid-Century French Poets.* New York: Grove Press. 1955. London: Calder and Boyars. 1958.

Mao Tse-Tung. *Quotations from Chairman Mao Tse-Tung.* Peking. 1967.

Pirandello, Luigi. *Naked Masks.* Ed. Eric Bentley. New York: Dutton. 1952.

Ponge, Francis. *Le Parti pris des choses.* Paris: Gallimard. 1926.

Rimbaud, Arthur. *Une Saison en enfer/A Season in Hell.* Trans. Louise Varèse. New York: New Directions. 1945.

Sartre, Jean-Paul. *L'Existentialisme est un humanisme.* Paris: Nagel. 1961.

INDEX

The abbreviation *p* indicates a photograph.

Clorch – wanted to be 7/1/m